Swaziland

the Bradt Travel Guide

Mike Unwin

With a foreword by Richard E Grant

edition
I

www.bradtguides.com

Bradt Travel Guides Ltd, UK
The Globe Pequot Press Inc, USA

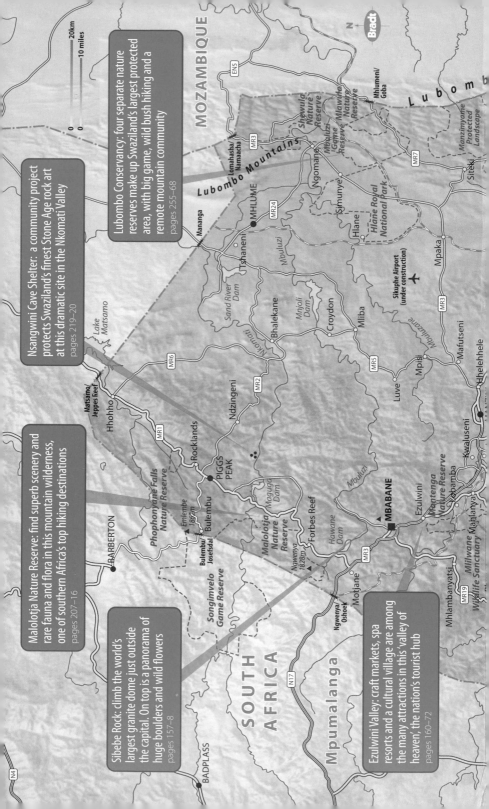

Nsangwini Cave Shelter: a community project protects Swaziland's finest Stone Age rock art at this dramatic site in the Nkomati Valley pages 219–20

Lubombo Conservancy: four separate nature reserves make up Swaziland's largest protected area, with big game, wild bush hiking and a remote mountain community pages 255–68

Malolotja Nature Reserve: find superb scenery and rare fauna and flora in this mountain wilderness, one of southern Africa's top hiking destinations pages 207–16

Sibebe Rock: climb the world's largest granite dome just outside the capital. On top is a panorama of huge boulders and wild flowers pages 157–8

Ezulwini Valley: craft markets, spa resorts and a cultural village are among the many attractions in this 'valley of heaven', the nation's tourist hub pages 160–72

20km
10 miles
0
0

Bradt

N

MOZAMBIQUE

**SOUTH
AFRICA**

Mpumalanga

Lubombo Mountains

Lubombo

Lomahasha/
Namaacha

ENS

MR3

Mhlumeni/
Goba

Mlawula
Nature
Reserve

Shewula
Nature
Reserve

Mbuluzi
Game
Reserve

Manzimnyane
Protected
Landscape

Ngomane

MR7

Mananga

MHLUME

MR24

Simunye

Hlane

Hlane Royal
National Park

Siteki

Tshaneni

Mbuluzi

Mpaka

Sand River
Dam

Bhalekane

Mnjoli
Dam

Croydon

Mliba

Mpaka

Sikuphe Airport
(under construction)

MR3

Nkomati

MR6

Lake
Matsamo

Matsamo/
Jeppes Reef

Hhohho

MR1

Rocklands

Ndzingeni

MR2

MR5

Mlba

Luve

Mpisi

Mbuluzane

Mafutseni

Tshelehlehle

Mbuluzi

PIGGS
PEAK

Emlembe
1862m

Bulembu
Josefsdal

Phophonyane Falls
Nature Reserve

Maguga
Dam

Forbes Reef

MBABANE

Ezulwini

Mantenga
Nature Reserve

Lobamba

Kwaluseni

BARBERTON

Songimvelo
Game Reserve

Malolotja
Nature
Reserve

Ngwenya
1828m

Hawane
Dam

MR3

Motjane

Ngwenya/
Oshoek

N17

Mhlambanyatsi

MR19

Mlilwane
Wildlife Sanctuary

Mahlanya

Sidvokodvo

BADPLAAS

N4

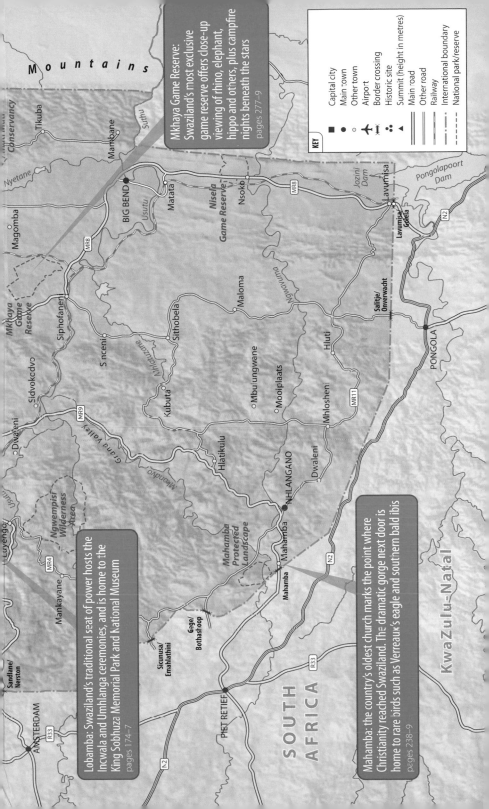

M o u n t a i n s

Conservancy

Tikuba

Mambane

Mkhaya Game Reserve: Swaziland's most exclusive game reserve offers close-up viewing of rhino, elephant, hippo and others, plus campfire nights beneath the stars
pages 277–9

Nyetane

Magomba

Suthu

BIG BEND

Matata

Usutu

MR8

MR8

Nisela Game Reserve

Nsoko

Jozini Dam

Pongolapoort Dam

Lavumisa

Lavumisa/ Golela

N2

Mkhaya Game Reserve

Siphofaneni

Sidvokodvo

Maloma

Ngwavuma

Saltjie/ Onverwacht

S nceni

Sithobela

Mhlatuzane

Dwaleni

MR9

Hluti

PONGOLA

Kubuta

Mbu ungwane

Mooiplaats

MR11

Grand Valley

Hlatikulu

Mhlosheni

Mhondvo

Ngwempisi Wilderness Area

NHLANGANO

Dwaleni

Luyengo

Usuti

MR24

Mahamba Protected Landscape

Mahamba

N2

Mankayane

Mahamba

Gege/ Bothashoop

Lobamba: Swaziland's traditional seat of power hosts the Incwala and Umhlanga ceremonies, and is home to the King Sobhuza Memorial Park and National Museum
pages 174–7

Sicunusa/ Emahlathini

R33

PIET RETIEF

Sandlane/ Nerston

AMSTERDAM

R33

N2

Mahamba: the country's oldest church marks the point where Christianity reached Swaziland. The dramatic gorge next door is home to rare birds such as Verreaux's eagle and southern bald ibis
pages 238–9

S O U T H A F R I C A

R33

KwaZulu-Natal

KEY

Capital city
Main town
Other town
Airport
Border crossing
Historic site
Summit (height in metres)
Main road
Other road
Railway
International boundary
National park/reserve

■ ● ○ ✈ ‡ ∴ ▲

Swaziland
Don't miss...

Traditional culture
Rituals, ceremonies and national festivals help to keep Swaziland's ancient traditions alive
(MU) pages 91–4

Pristine wilderness
Malolotja is Swaziland's premier nature reserve; its attractions include impressive waterfalls and rare wildlife such as the blue swallow and aardwolf
(MU) pages 207–16

Adventure activities

Thrills and spills for adventure lovers in Swaziland include whitewater rafting on the Great Usutu, the country's longest river

(DR) pages 275–7

Handicrafts

Swaziland has a fine carving tradition, both in wood and stone. Figures range from people and animals, like this chameleon, to more abstract creations

(MU) pages 87 & 216

Big game

Mkhaya Game Reserve is one of Africa's finest locations for tracking both black and white rhinos on foot

(MU) pages 277–9

Swaziland in colour

above left Much of Swaziland's population still lives on the land in small rural homesteads, like this one near Hluti (MU) pages 77–8

left The Nsangwini cave shelter, located in the Nkomati Valley near Piggs Peak, protects Swaziland's finest example of San rock art (MU) pages 219–20

below Thousands of girls gather at Ludzidzini every year to dance in the Umhlanga, or 'Reed Dance', Swaziland's most spectacular traditional ceremony (EPA/A) pages 93–4

above left A diviner, or *sangoma*, is traditionally called to communicate with the ancestral spirits on behalf of a community (AZ) page 80–2

above right With royal *ligwalagwala* feathers in her hair and a phone in her hand, this princess embodies the dichotomies of Swaziland today (MU) pages 65–6

below left Lunchtime at an orphan care project in Lobamba. Swaziland's HIV/AIDS crisis has left more than 120,000 orphans and vulnerable children (MU) pages 72–3

below right Markets, such as Manzini Market, are a focal point of life in Swaziland, selling everything from local produce to traditional medicines (AZ) page 198

above   Riders on Mlilwane's Chubeka Trail get to lead their horses among wild game and spend the night in a mountain cave (MU) page 181

left   Abseiling on cliffs beside the Usutu River: one of many adrenalin-fuelled activities that can be enjoyed around Swaziland (AZ) pages 276–7

below   Swaziland's mountainous highveld offers superb hiking, including the ascent of Sibebe Rock, the world's largest granite dome (MU) pages 157–8

AUTHOR

Mike Unwin is a writer of non-fiction books for both adults and children, specialising in travel and natural history and with a particular interest in Africa. Among his other titles for Bradt are *Southern African Wildlife* (2nd edition 2011) and *100 Bizarre Animals* (2010). He also writes regularly for many leading newspapers and magazines, including *The Independent, BBC Wildlife, Travel Africa* and *Wanderlust*, and is editor of *Travel Zambia* magazine. Mike's writing has won him several awards, including the *BBC Wildlife*/Bradt Travel Writer of the Year

2000 and Latin American Travel Association Travel Writer of the Year 2011. He is a regular speaker at travel and wildlife events and occasionally pops up on radio programmes such as Radio 4's *Excess Baggage*. His illustrations and photographs can be found in many publications, including this one.

Mike's involvement in Africa began in Zimbabwe, where he was a secondary school English teacher for two years. Teaching led to educational publishing – and to Swaziland, where he worked for Macmillan from 1993 to 1998, developing textbooks for local schools. Those five years allowed him ample opportunity for a full immersion in Swazi life, from painting murals at the National Museum and playing piano with a local band to volunteering with the Southern African Frog Atlas project, and leading walks and workshops for the Swaziland Bird Club. They also allowed him time to learn a little of the language, explore every nook and cranny of the kingdom and make friends for life. A decade and a half later, he still misses the place and returns whenever opportunity allows.

Mike was born in the UK and studied English at Manchester University. He now lives in Brighton, with his wife and daughter, where he regales all who'll listen – and plenty who won't – with tales of Swaziland.

Introduction

'Where, exactly?'

I've grown used to this question over the years. And by way of an answer I've perfected my back-of-the-envelope sketch map of South Africa, complete with shield-shaped Swaziland thumbnail in the top right-hand corner.

'Oh yes, that place in the mountains,' comes the reply. And patiently I explain that no, Swaziland is the other country; the even smaller one. It's surrounded by South Africa, yes, but lies a little further north and also shares an eastern border with Mozambique. More blank looks – until I mention the king. 'Of course!' they exclaim, as the penny drops. 'The one with all the wives.'

Ignorance is excusable. After all, this tiny country – the smallest continental nation in the southern hemisphere – is all but engulfed by its enormous neighbours. It also lies close to the cluster of former 'homelands' – puppet states created by the South African authorities during the apartheid era – with which it is still often confused. Indeed, it is not unknown for overseas post addressed to Swaziland to end up in Switzerland, unless 'southern Africa' is spelt out on the envelope.

For the record, then, Swaziland is not part of South Africa. Neither is it some fictitious Victorian creation from the pen of H Rider Haggard. It is, in fact, a sovereign nation, proudly independent ever since shrugging off the mantle of British Protectorate in 1968. It is also Africa's only absolute monarchy: a fact that explains the spectacular pageantry and royal extravagance for which it is best known, and which has given it a certain sore-thumb political notoriety in a region that has otherwise – nominally, at least – embraced democracy.

Whatever its status, this peculiar little nation offers treats aplenty for the visitor. Most African travel staples are well represented: big game, traditional culture, picture-book panoramas, wild hiking, adventure sports and exquisite handicrafts. They may not all be on the scale of larger destinations, but come conveniently packaged in a space so small that none is more than a couple of hours' drive from the capital. They also come sprinkled with a beguiling eccentricity that is all Swaziland's own.

Best of all, perhaps, you can still have the place largely to yourself, because Swaziland remains – at least, in the language of international tourism – mainly a 'transit destination'. In other words, most visitors are simply passing through en route between The Kruger Park, Zululand, Maputo and other bigger-hitting attractions over the border. In 2011, tourist board statistics confirmed that the average number of nights per visitor was 1.3. And the fact that this book is the first UK-published guidebook devoted exclusively to Swaziland tells its own story about the country's tourism profile.

At this point I should declare an interest. I lived in Swaziland from 1993 to 1998, working with an educational publisher to help produce textbooks for the nation's schools. Although the quirks of life in the kingdom at times drove me to distraction, those five years were more than enough for me to develop a deep affection for and allegiance to the place that has since seen me return whenever possible and follow its fortunes avidly.

Spend more than a day or two in Swaziland, I soon discovered, and you'll find that all those Africa-in-a-nutshell clichés ring irresistibly true. Take the people: my work led me from the ministerial corridors of power to the most rural communities – sometimes literally from prince to pauper in the course of a morning. And the land: Swaziland may be minuscule on the map but it opens up like the Tardis once you enter, revealing massive, muscular landscapes that belie its bijou dimensions. I was constantly amazed by just how far off the beaten track you could wander in a populous place barely one-third bigger than Yorkshire.

Along the way, I learned enough of the language to discover that, when it comes to making friends and breaking barriers, a little in Swaziland goes a long way. And I discovered – mostly by trial and error – something of what it means to be Swazi: how, for example, well-meaning foreigners like me may come and go but the land is always there; how nothing is decided until everyone has had his or her say; how there is no such thing as an accident; and how not to be surprised if your dinner party guests show up three days late and at two in the morning.

The final parts of this book came together during the general euphoria of the London 2012 Olympics. While I was disappointed not to see a Swazi take the podium, it struck me that the country punches far above its weight in terms of breaking records. It has in Sibebe, for instance, the world's second largest rock; in the mountains of western Malolotja, arguably the world's *oldest* rocks; in Ngwenya, the world's earliest known mine; and in the late King Sobhuza II, the world's longest reigning monarch (and, with 210 children, surely the most prolific). Not bad, I thought, for a country that ranks only number 187 by size.

Unfortunately, Swaziland has other, more unenviable records. During the late 1990s, the country languished at the bottom of the global heap in terms of life expectancy (31.8 years) and HIV infection (50% of adults in their 20s). Recent years have seen improvements, but a generation of orphans and a depleted workforce have not helped the nation's ongoing struggle out of poverty. Neither, argue critics, has Swaziland's undemocratic system of governance, in which the royal elite sometimes seem merely to fiddle while Rome burns.

This book does not pass judgement on Swaziland's politics, however, nor on any other of its anomalies and anachronisms. Few outsiders, I found, can make worthwhile prescriptions in a place that lies so far beyond their own cultural experience. Rather, I have aimed to describe the country, warts and all, in a way that is most helpful to the visitor. Explore for yourself and draw your own conclusions. And, if you can find room in your itinerary for more than just the 1.3 nights, you might enjoy it as much as I did. You might even stay five years.

Part One

GENERAL INFORMATION

Location Southern Africa – in northeastern South Africa against the Mozambique border, south of Tropic of Capricorn

Neighbouring countries South Africa (west, north and south), Mozambique (east)

Size 17,364km² (6,704 square miles)

Climate Temperate/subtropical; temperature and rainfall highest in summer (November–March). Rainfall higher and temperatures lower in western regions.

Status Absolute monarchy

Population 1.1 million (World Bank 2011); growth rate 1.15% (World Bank 2011)

Life expectancy 49 years at birth (2012)

Capital Mbabane; population c80,000

Other main towns Manzini, Matsapha, Nhlangano, Piggs Peak, Big Bend

Economy Principal earners are sugar, forestry and mining; manufacturing (textile and sugar products); services. 75% of population employed in subsistence agriculture; average growth rate since 2001 2.8%; South Africa accounts for 90% of imports and 70% of exports.

GDP US$3.977 billion per annum; US$3,725 per capita per annum (World Bank 2011)

Official languages SiSwati and English (English is language of instruction in schools); minority languages include Zulu, Tsonga and Afrikaans

Religion Christianity (82%), including African Zionist and numerous other evangelical denominations. Also Islam, Baha'i and Hinduism in small numbers.

Currency Lilangeni (SZL), plural emalangeni; parity with South African rand (ZAR)

Exchange rate £1 = 13.87SZL, US$1 = 8.64SZL, €1 = 11.21SZL (October 2012)

National airport/airline Matsapha International Airport (aka Manzini International Airport). No national airline – Royal Swazi International Airways ceased operating in 1999. Airlink Swaziland flies to/from Johannesburg.

International telephone code +268

Time South African Standard Time (UTC/GMT+2)

Electrical voltage 230V (50Hz); sockets take South African 'type M' plugs (three large round pins)

Weights and measures Metric

Flag Narrow horizontal stripes of blue and yellow above and below a broad central band of red, with a horizontal warrior's shield and spears at the centre

National anthem *Nkulunkulu Mnikati wetibusiso temaSwati* ('Oh God, Bestower of the Blessings of the Swazi')

National animals The purple-crested turaco (*ligwalagwala*) is the royal bird; the lion (*ngwenyama*) is symbolic of the king

National sport Football

Public holidays 1 January (New Year's Day); Good Friday; Easter Monday; 19 April (King's Birthday); 25 April (National Flag Day); 1 May (Labour Day); Ascension Day; 22 July (Birthday of late King Sobhuza II); late August/ early September (Umhlanga, reed dance); 6 September (Somhlolo (Independence) Day); late December/early January (Incwala, first fruits ceremony); 25 December (Christmas Day); 26 December (Boxing Day)

1

Background Information

GEOGRAPHY

SIZE AND LOCATION Swaziland is the smallest mainland country in sub-Saharan Africa. The map shows it as a little oblong postage stamp stuck on the top right-hand corner of South Africa. Indeed, Swaziland's big neighbour looms over its borders to the north, south and west, with the southernmost tip of Mozambique – another giant – forming the border to the east.

The total area of this pocket-sized, landlocked kingdom is just 17,364km^2 and it measures, at its broadest, some 175km from north to south and 115km from east to west. This, for the record, makes Swaziland slightly smaller than Wales, that international unit of measurement beloved of lazy UK journalists. Of more local relevance, perhaps, it is also slightly smaller than the Kruger National Park, the South African nature reserve just to the north that attracts most overseas visitors to this corner of southern Africa.

Swaziland used to be much larger. Before the colonial carve-up of the 19th century (see *History*, page 55), the royal kingdom extended loosely from the Crocodile River in the north to the Pongola River in the south and east to Kosi Bay. It even had its own coastline – a memory that remains enshrined in cultural ceremonies today. A few diehard traditionalists still claim that Swazis should have their former lands returned, although given that this would now include Maputo, the Mozambique capital, this would seem a little over-ambitious. The past – literally – remains another country.

THE LIE OF THE LAND Size isn't everything. Swaziland's modest dimensions belie its scenic diversity, from the mountainous west to the dusty east. It owes this variety to its location, straddling southern Africa's eastern escarpment just where the central plateau falls eastwards towards the Indian Ocean. Roughly wedge-shaped in cross section, the country can be divided by elevation into four topographical regions, each with its own distinct climate. A drive of just over one hour can take you from drizzle in the west to drought in the east.

Starting in the west, the 'highveld' (*veld* being Afrikaans for 'field') is a land of hills, waterfalls and great buttresses of ancient rock. The average elevation is 1,200m, with the highest point (Emlembe) at 1,862m. A temperate climate means some rainfall all year round and regular mists in summer. Mbabane, the capital, is located here, as are the regional centres of Piggs Peak in the north and Nhlangano in the south. While timber plantations have replaced much of the natural montane grassland habitat, Swaziland's most impressive nature reserve, Malolotja, protects a good chunk of what remains.

Heading eastwards – and downhill – you soon enter the middleveld. This mid-altitude region of undulating bush and moist savanna lies at an average 700m above sea level. It is home to the bulk of Swaziland's population and Manzini, its only other large town. The parliament at Lobamba and tourist hub of the Ezulwini Valley are here, as is the country's airport and main industrial centre at Matsapha, and the large citrus estates of the Malkerns Valley.

Further east still, you descend into the lowveld. This is hot, dry bush country with an average elevation of 250m but descending as low as 21m in the Usutu River Valley. It seems a world away (though in some places is less than 50km away) from the well-watered highveld, and is Swaziland's hottest, poorest and – to outside eyes – most typically African region. Water is often scarce, although the Usutu and Mbuluzi rivers irrigate the extensive sugar estates. Other than the settlements that service these estates, such as Big Bend and Simunye, there are no major towns. The remaining tracts of wild bush harbour Swaziland's major game reserves.

Along the eastern border, forming a natural barrier between Swaziland and Mozambique, is a line of rugged volcanic hills known as the Lubombos, which rise abruptly from the lowveld to some 600m. This range extends far beyond Swaziland, following the Mozambique border north through the Kruger National Park and south into KwaZulu-Natal. From below, it appears as a single line. In fact, the hills comprise a number of parallel ridges broken by deep gorges where the Usutu, Ngwavuma and Mbuluzi rivers carve through to the Indian Ocean. In many respects, the Lubombo region is an elevated extension of the lowveld, with Siteki, perched on top, its only town of note. However, these wild hills harbour some unusual habitats, with flora and fauna that are found nowhere else in the country.

ADMINISTRATIVE DISTRICTS Swaziland is divided into four administrative districts: Hhohho, Manzini, Shiselweni and Lubombo (see map on page 64). Irritatingly – at least for the purpose of this guidebook – these do not neatly coincide with the four topographical regions. Hhohho district occupies the northwest and includes Mbabane and Piggs Peak; Manzini district – the largest and most populous – runs across the centre-west of the country and includes Manzini, the Ezulwini Valley and the seat of government at Lobamba; Shiselweni district occupies the south, including Nhlangano and Hlatikulu; Lubombo district comprises the lowveld and Lubombo Mountains in the east. Each district is divided into a number of smaller administrative sub-districts, called *tinkhundla,* of which there are 55 in total.

RIVERS AND DAMS Swaziland's location leaves it well served by rivers, which flow east from the highlands towards the Indian Ocean. The largest is the Great Usutu (Lusutfu), which crosses the southern third of the country, via its eponymous kink near the town of Big Bend, before exiting through the Lubombos. Along the way it absorbs several major tributaries, including the Lusushwana (from the north), and the Ngwempisi and Mkhondvo (both from the south). Other major rivers are the Nkomati, which cuts in and out of South Africa through the northwest corner of Swaziland; the Mbuluzi, which rises in the highveld and exits into Mozambique in the northeast; and the Ngwavuma, which flows due east across the south. All feature impressive gorges, both where they descend from the highveld and where they exit through the Lubombos. Many have also been dammed, with the most significant reservoirs being the Maguga Dam on the Nkomati and the Mnjoli Dam on the Mbuluzi. Smaller lowveld rivers flow only with the rains.

GEOLOGY Swaziland is a hotspot for geologists. The country lies on southern Africa's eastern escarpment, where the central African plateau meets the eastern lowlands, and is part of the great fault line that scars the continent from Kenya's Rift Valley to South Africa's Drakensberg. Underlying the mountainous northwest is an ancient sequence of rocks known as the Barberton Supergroup. This contains traces of gneiss and greenstone dating back to the Archaean Eon, some 3.5 billion years ago, which are among the oldest identifiable rocks on earth – indeed, the fossils of the single-celled organisms they contain, dating back 3.3–3.4 billion years, represent some of the planet's oldest life forms. Significant deposits of gold, iron and other minerals have been heavily mined in the past.

Tectonic forces have lifted and folded the rocks of the highveld into the impressive mountains we see today. The oldest, and so most rounded by erosion, are the hills of Malolotja and Bulembu, which extend over the South African border into Mpumalanga. The hills further east, with their exposed outcrops of granite, were formed more recently, when molten volcanic material welled up through the earth's crust and cooled at the surface. Wind and water have eroded their surfaces into impressive boulder formations, known as *kopjes* (pronounced 'koppies') and great naked 'whalebacks'. Nowhere are these formations more impressive than at Sibebe (see *Chapter 3*, page 157), a huge batholith (granite dome) just north of Mbabane that is thought to be the world's largest.

The granite landscape extends into the middleveld, with isolated kopjes also punctuating the lowveld. However, the underlying rock of the lowveld forms part of the Karoo Supergroup, a largely sedimentary rock sequence that underlies much of southern Africa and was laid down 200–300 million years ago, between the Permian and Jurassic periods. The Lubombo Mountains in the east are composed of basalt and rhyolite – igneous rocks that formed when the great Gondwana supercontinent broke apart 180 million years ago, spewing molten material up into the fissures torn in the earth's crust. Erosion over the subsequent millennia has left them raised above the surrounding lowlands as a long ridge.

Glaciation never touched Swaziland. The numerous deep gorges and valleys are the work of rivers carving their way down the escarpment. Like all landscapes, Swaziland's is still a work in progress, with the escarpment continuing to erode westwards into the central plateau.

CLIMATE

Meteorologists describe Swaziland's climate as 'temperate subtropical', but there are significant regional differences. Broadly speaking, the higher you go the cooler and wetter it becomes – so the highveld experiences the heaviest rainfall and lowest temperatures, the lowveld experiences the opposite, and the middleveld strikes a happy medium. Visitors from northern climes may need reminding that this is a southern hemisphere country, so the seasonal pattern is the reverse of what they are used to. Summer lasts from October to April, when conditions are generally

AVERAGE TEMPERATURES

At Mbabane (highveld)	At Big Bend (lowveld)
September–October (spring) 18°C	September–October (spring) 23°C
November–March (summer) 20°C	November–March (summer) 27°C
April–May (autumn) 17°C	April–May (autumn) 23°C
June–August (winter) 13°C	June–August (winter) 20°C

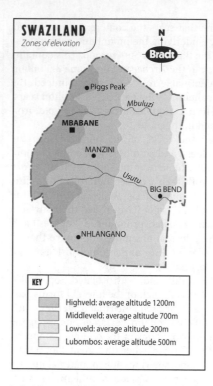

warm and humid, with temperatures sometimes touching 40°C in the lowveld. Winter lasts from May to September, when it is dry in the east and in the west can be decidedly cool at night. (Once every 20 years or so it even snows.) Annual rainfall averages 1,000–1,600mm in the highveld but less than 700mm in the lowveld. These rains do not quite conform to the dry season/rainy season pattern of tropical Africa, however, with the picture muddied both by altitude and latitude. In the highveld, rain may fall in any month – though it often takes the form of mist and drizzle, which may last days at a time.

Swaziland's weather can be spectacular. Summer brings violent electrical storms, usually in the late afternoon, when cataclysmic flashes light up the landscape. Indeed, Swaziland has one of the highest incidences of electrical storms in the world and lightning is a very real danger at this time (see box, *Strike force*, below). Powerful summer rainstorms can transform dirt roads to unmanageable torrents in minutes and turn city streets into rivers, with dirt and debris swept down side roads into the centre of town. In the highveld, rain may suddenly turn to hail, battering cars with marble-sized pellets of ice ('golf ball-sized' is often claimed,

STRIKE FORCE

Lightning in Swaziland certainly does strike twice. The country's estimated ground lightning flash rate of 12 flashes per km² per year is exceptionally high and has serious consequences. One investigation identified 123 confirmed human fatalities from lightning strikes between 2000 and 2007, giving an average annual rate of 15.5 people per million – the highest in the world. These occurred from September to May, usually during the afternoon, with most victims struck while walking, sheltering (inadvisedly) under a tree or trapped inside a thatched hut that was struck and set ablaze. But you don't need statistics: chat to any Swazi and invariably they will know of somebody who has been killed or at least struck. As well as this tragic human toll, lightning kills livestock and plays havoc with the national power supply.

For those safe indoors, Swaziland's summer storms make impressive viewing. They occur mainly in late afternoon, turning the sky black with alarming speed and then breaking with deafening violence. At night the flashes are so intense that the landscape lights up as though for a split-second of daylight. Stay safe by getting indoors or inside a car. Avoid touching taps or metal window frames, and do not make a call on a landline.

but I have yet to see this). Heavy mists descend like a blanket, posing a serious hazard to road users, and hikers heading off into the hills are best advised to wait for a clear day.

FIRE Wild fires are a part of life in Swaziland – and a mixed blessing. As a natural phenomenon, fire is vital to grassland and bushveld habitats. Annual dry-season burns, often started by lightning strikes, race across the parched land, leaving ash and charcoal in their wake. They burn off old growth, return nutrients to the soil and control the encroachment of trees. Most fire burns just above ground level, so grasses, which have their buds at the base of the plant, survive the flames and sprout as soon as the rains fall. Most mature bushveld trees are fire-resistant, since the vital growth layer – the cambium – lies beneath the tough outer trunk.

Swaziland is also subject to many rather less welcome fires during the dry season. Farmers have always burned off old growth to generate fresh grazing – and the visitor may be amazed by the flames that advance up hillsides and race along road verges, and the charred, smoking landscapes they leave behind. Many such fires get out of control, making their way into the outskirts of towns and sometimes sweeping through rural homesteads. Lives are lost, and the impact on the economy can be severe – most notably, in recent years, due to the destruction of forestry plantations. In July 2007, fire destroyed more than 80% of the Mondi plantation in Piggs Peak and, in August 2008, 40% of the Sappi forests around Mhlambayatsi (see *Chapter 6*, page 241), the latter leading in 2010 to the closure of the Usutu pulp mill at Bhunya and the loss of around 600 jobs.

HABITATS

Swaziland's natural environment has felt the inevitable impact of human population growth and development. Indigenous habitat has been replaced by agriculture – notably forestry in the highveld, sugar in the lowveld and small-scale subsistence farming nationwide. On Swazi Nation Land (see page 67), especially, the fauna and flora has suffered from habitat loss and overgrazing. But the country still has many wonderful wild corners where flora and fauna abound, particularly in its numerous nature reserves.

Swaziland's varied habitats support a collective biodiversity that conservationists recognise as globally significant. Eastern Swaziland lies within the Maputaland Centre of Plant Diversity (one of the world's biodiversity hotspots), for instance, while the western region falls within both the Drakensberg Escarpment Endemic Bird Area and the Barberton Centre of Plant Endemism. Some understanding of these habitats can be a big help when it comes to watching wildlife, alerting you to which species you can expect to find, and where, and explaining how and why they co-exist.

GRASSLAND Grasslands carpet western Swaziland, generally occurring at 900m and above, and are the dominant natural habitat of the highveld. Summer rainfall averages over 1,000mm per year up here and numerous streams drain the hills, forming marshy patches known as *vleis* in low-lying areas. In winter, fires scorch the open terrain (see above) and it is this, combined with the harsh winter climate, which accounts for the natural dearth of trees. The grasses comprise mostly short 'sour' species, such as *Themeda triandra, Hyparrhenia hirta, Diheteropogon amplectans* and *Monocymbium ceresiifrome*. Wild flowers flourish among them, including the towering pale-blue *Agapanthus*, the fiery red-hot poker (*Kniphofia*) and the pink candelabra flower (*Brunsvigia radulosa*). Rocky outcrops and steep slopes, where the flames can't reach, provide shelter for trees and shrubs, such as aloes, sugarbushes (*Protea* species) and cabbage trees (*Cussonia* species). Deeper gorges shelter pockets of indigenous forest, where the winter flowers of the bottlebrush (*Greyia* species) add a splash of scarlet to the greenery.

Highveld grasslands – known across Africa as Afromontane grasslands – are very important in conservation terms. Within Swaziland, they are home to species found nowhere else, from fish such as the chubbyhead barb to birds such as Denham's bustard. Some, such as the blue swallow, are international rarities. Sadly, natural grasslands are in a sorry state across southern Africa, and Swaziland is no exception. Livestock has replaced the wild herds of yesteryear, bringing overgrazing and an artificial burning regime that depletes biodiversity, while invasive alien plants like wattle have overwhelmed indigenous vegetation. Nonetheless, there is no better grassland reserve in southern Africa than Malolotja, where you will find blesbok cropping the sward, crag lizards basking on boulders and widowbirds cruising the vleis in a scene that could be centuries old.

SAVANNA (BUSHVELD)
Savanna is the correct ecological name for what many in southern Africa call 'bushveld'. The former term evokes east Africa's vast open grasslands, so the latter – which combines the English 'bush' with the Afrikaans word for field, and thus describes the habitat's roughly equal mix of trees and grass – may be more helpful in a southern African context. Whatever you call it, this terrain carpets much of Swaziland at altitudes of 200–900m. It is rich in animal life, with around twice the number of vertebrates found in grassland. Swaziland's bushveld comes in three main types.

Sourveld
Sour bushveld, or simply 'sourveld', is the dominant middleveld savanna, and occupies an intermediate zone between the western temperate and eastern subtropical regions. It occurs at 400–900m, mostly on east-facing slopes, where there is plentiful rainfall and soils are thin. Vegetation typically comprises a fairly dense growth of trees over a ground cover of tall, 'sour' grass species such as red grass (*Themeda triandra*) and guinea grass (*Panicum maximum*). These grasses get their name from their coarse, unpalatable texture, which means this is not a great habitat for grazing animals. Typical trees include bushwillows (*Combretum* species) and silver cluster-leaf (*Terminalia sericea*). These may form denser forest patches and thickets around rocky outcrops.

Sourveld underlies many of Swaziland's most densely populated regions, including the Manzini, Ezulwini and Malkerns areas. Here, the forces of development, including overgrazing, land clearance and fire, have left it heavily depleted. Disturbance also clears the way for invasive plant species, such as guava (*Psidium guajava*), sicklebush (*Dichrostachys cineria*) and lantana (*Lantana camara*), which can overwhelm native vegetation, forming dense thickets – especially along watercourses – in which biodiversity is impoverished. To appreciate the habitat in its pristine state, visit protected areas such as Phophonyane or Mantenga Falls, or remote regions such as Ngwempisi Gorge.

Lowveld bushveld
This is low-altitude savanna, occurring at 200–400m, where richer soils and lower rainfall support a variety of sweeter grasses and, generally, a thinner tree cover than sourveld. The tree composition changes as you head east, shifting from broad-leaved species such as combretum and terminalia in higher areas to predominantly acacias lower down. Acacias are the archetypical savanna

Savanna and grassland habitats across Swaziland are punctuated by outcrops of rock – known locally as kopjes – sometimes eroded into intriguing shapes and improbable arrangements of standing stones. Each one is a little elevated ecosystem, safe from the ravages of fire and grazing animals, offering niches for specialised plants and animals. *Euphorbia* species, such as the candelabra tree (*Euphorbia cooperi*), protect their fleshy limbs with sharp spines and their milky sap is toxic to most browsers. The large-leafed rock fig (*Ficus abutilifolia*) manages without topsoil by extending sinuous roots over the rock surface and into its crevices. Kopjes provide homes and refuges for many animals, from hyraxes to pythons.

tree, with their tiny compound leaves adapted to reduce heat loss, and wicked paired thorns to restrict the browsing of herbivores. There are many species, of which the widespread umbrella thorn (*Acacia tortillis*) is the best known, with a flat-topped silhouette that has become emblematic of Africa. The knobthorn (*Acacia nigrescens*) is more robust, and has a spiny trunk when young, while the fever tree (*Acacia xanthophloea*) – common near water in the far east – has distinctive powdery yellowish bark and owes its name to the belief of early pioneers that it harboured a fly that was responsible for malaria.

Other notable lowveld trees include the marula (*Sclerocarya birrea*), which often grows in association with the knobthorn and is prized by man and beast alike for its yellow, plum-like fruits (locally harvested to make a seasonal liquor called *buganu*; see *Drink and drinking* on page 85); and the leadwood (*Combretum imberbe*), which grows very slowly and – as the name suggests – has wood so dense that it weighs up to 1,200kg per cubic metre. Beneath these trees grow an equally impressive diversity of grasses. These range from 'sweet' grasses such as guinea grass and red grass, which provide good grazing in low-lying areas, to less palatable thatching grasses such as *Hyperthelia* and *Hyperrhenia* species, which prefer moist environments and the presence of which is usually a good indication of past disturbance. Bush encroachment is also a problem in this habitat: the removal of native plants by overgrazing or land clearance paves the way for invasive species, such as sicklebush, that form impenetrable thickets – especially along watercourses – and ruin the habitat for everything else.

Lowveld bushveld is big-game country. It naturally supports a greater density and variety of large mammals than any other habitat, and these in turn help shape and maintain the landscape. In Swaziland the great herds of yesteryear are largely gone. But in reserves, such as Hlane, Mkhaya and Nisela, you can still see many of the species that once roamed this land in great numbers, including impala, zebra and blue wildebeest. The reintroduction of heavyweights such as rhino and elephant has helped complete the picture but, in the confined spaces of Swaziland's reserves, has introduced other habitat-management problems. Birds – notably raptors – are prolific in both variety and number, and the abundance of life on a smaller scale, from tortoises to dung beetles, is endlessly diverting.

Lubombo bushveld This is a higher-altitude extension of the lowveld savanna, rising to about 800m, but harbours its own distinct plant community. Typical trees are combretums such as bushwillows, while a number of specialised plants – including some endangered cycads and aloes – flourish on the rocky outcrops and

DOMOINA AND THE DISAPPEARING OWL

In late January 1984, Swaziland battened down the hatches as Cyclone Domoina swept in from the Indian Ocean to wreak havoc across the lowveld. This violent tropical storm, which originated to the northeast of Madagascar, made landfall in southern Mozambique on 28 January and then moved slowly south, bringing violent winds and torrential rain to northern KwaZulu-Natal, Mpumalanga and Swaziland until, by 2 February, it had blown itself out. Coastal flooding claimed 214 human lives and countless livestock across the region, and precious wildlife habitats were hit hard, including the St Lucia lake system in KwaZulu-Natal. In Swaziland, rainfall exceeding 700mm swelled the Usutu, Nkomati and Ingwavuma rivers, which burst their banks and destroyed prime riverine forest, including many ancient sycamore fig trees. This proved too much for Pel's fishing owl, a large nocturnal fish-eater – and prize quarry of birders – that depends upon this habitat. It has never bred in Swaziland since.

hillsides. Steep gorges contain pockets of dry forest, while more open grasslands spread across the top of the plateau. The fauna is similar to that of the lowveld, though generally occurring in lower densities, with antelope such as greater kudu and nyala browsing the thickets. The birdlife includes some species not found elsewhere, such as the African broadbill. The Lubombos remain the most unpopulated – and hence undisturbed – part of Swaziland, and in reserves such as Mbuluzi and Mlawula you can see this precious habitat in a largely pristine state.

FOREST True forest – as opposed to woodland – is defined as a dense growth of largely evergreen trees that forms a closed canopy and grows only in areas of high rainfall. Indigenous forest is in short supply in Swaziland – and in southern Africa generally, where it occupies less than 1% of land area. This stems partly from the fact that the climate is not generally suitable, but also reflects centuries of deforestation, both for timber and land. Today Swaziland's indigenous forests remain as scattered patches, tucked into the more inaccessible clefts of the western escarpment and Lubombos, and lining the larger watercourses of the lowveld. There are three distinct types.

Afromontane forest 'Afromontane' is the technical term for highveld indigenous forest – occurring at above 1,000m, generally in gorges or clefts where it has escaped the twin ravages of fire and people. This forest is often shrouded in mist, and inside is dark, dank and dominated by the imposing trunks of evergreens such as ironwood (*Homalium dentatum*). Creepers including the rope thorn (*Dalbergia armata*), with its torture-chamber spines, snake through the tangled branches, which are festooned with mosses, lichens and epiphytes; tree ferns and ancient cycads grow beside streams; and fungi flourish on the forest floor. There are few larger mammals, though you might surprise the odd red duiker. Birdlife concentrates in sunlit glades and forest edges, and you might come across canopy specialists such as the crowned eagle and knysna turaco, or elusive species of the deep forest such as the orange thrush (*Zoothera gurneyi*). Some of the best examples of this forest in Swaziland are in Malolotja; most are off trail and require a steep scramble to reach them.

Riverine forest Riverine or riparian forest forms ribbons of greenery along the larger rivers of the lowveld, where rich alluvial soils and a ready water supply allow trees to flourish. These trees typically have a dense crown and include the Natal mahogany (*Tricheilia emetica*), jackal-berry (*Diospyros mespiliformis*) and sausage tree (*Kigelia africana*), the last of which sports enormous sausage-shaped fruit and attractive blood-red flowers pollinated by fruit bats. The impressive sycamore fig (*Ficus sycomorus*) is the giant of the riverine forest, with a huge buttressed trunk and a rich crop of figs clustered along its branches. Riverine forest supports fruit-eaters such as turacos, bushbabies, fruit bats and monkeys, and cover-hugging browsers such as bushbuck and bush pigs, which hide out in the riverbank thickets. Unfortunately, the larger trees are often felled or dismembered for timber, and the thickets are quickly overwhelmed by invasives such as lantana. Riverine forest is also very vulnerable to flooding, which in severe cases can remove big trees entirely.

Lubombo forest Like montane forest, the forests of the Lubombos tend to be tucked into ravines and other inaccessible locations, but they are generally dryer in character. Conspicuous among the trees are stands of Lebombo ironwood (*Androstachys*), and a number of localised succulents and cycads flourish on the forest floor. Among the wildlife are species absent elsewhere in Swaziland, such as the samango monkey.

WETLANDS AND WATERWAYS Swaziland has various aquatic habitats, both natural and manmade. Each is a distinct ecological landscape, with its own flora and fauna. Up in the hills, fast-flowing streams support specialised fish and amphibians, such as the striped stream frog, plus hunting grounds for shy Cape clawless otters and breeding sites for rare southern bald ibis. The vleis (marshes) associated with these highveld water catchments support many interesting frogs and birds, including rarities such as the striped flufftail.

As these rivers cross the lowveld, they slow down and spread out, offering prime habitat for Nile crocodiles, which may disperse upstream during the rains, and – in the Great Usutu and Mbuluzi – even a small population of hippos. Large dams along these rivers, such as those at Mnjoli and Sand River, support plentiful fish. Natural waterholes in arid areas are created by the flow of rainwater into depressions and then enlarged and consolidated by the actions of large mammals. They may wither to baked mud in the dry season, before bursting into life with the rains to support a community of small creatures, from frogs and terrapins to dragonflies and sandpipers.

Even the smallest water bodies in and around town can offer a lifeline for wildlife. These range from small dams or settling ponds, which attract weaver colonies and egret roosts to their overhanging trees, to irrigation channels and abandoned quarries, which are breeding grounds for frogs during the rainy season, and offer rich pickings for kingfishers, crakes and other waterbirds.

THE HUMAN LANDSCAPE The human footprint is inescapable in Swaziland. The country's first inhabitants, the San, harvested their resources sustainably. With the arrival of the Bantu pastoralists and – especially – the first European pioneers, however, a process of plunder began that changed the country with shocking speed. Within just 150 years or so, pristine tracts of habitat were lost forever to farming and development. Today, bar some remote nooks and crannies in the Lubombos and highveld, there is no true wilderness: rivers are dammed, bush fenced and overgrazed, grasslands drained and forests felled.

Nature is tenacious, however, and even the most desecrated environment has homes for wildlife. Today's sugar estates, for instance, may be a poor substitute for the bushveld they replaced, but cane fields attract rodents, which feed a healthy population of snakes, while citrus orchards draw fruit-eaters such as fruit bats and mousebirds. Forestry plantations offer shelter to raptors such as the black sparrowhawk, while the ripe, nutritious soup of sewage farms and settling ponds is a magnet for ducks and waders. Aardvark, common duiker and greater kudu are among the larger mammals that can subsist on ranch land, the last of these able to leap most fences with ease.

Meanwhile, keep your eyes open for wildlife wherever you are. Tar roads at night after rain attract frogs, which in turn lure snakes. Power lines provide good vantage points for birds such as lilac-breasted rollers and magpie shrikes. In town, watch the skies: Mbabane, for example, can be a good place to spot white-necked ravens and sometimes lanner falcons overhead. Even your hotel offers a safari in miniature: by day tree agamas stake out the patio, sunbirds flit around the flowerbeds and hoopoes probe the lawn; night brings the chirp of an African scops owl, bats dipping over the pool, and geckos ambushing moths under the terrace lights. Who needs lions and elephants?

WILDLIFE

Swaziland's rich variety of habitats gives it a profusion of fauna and flora, with the sheer number of species mind-boggling by most European standards. The country is too small to offer the big-game bonanza of destinations like the Kruger National Park. However, several parks house a good selection, with rhinos being a notable speciality, and this is the perfect place to see smaller creatures that are often overlooked on safari elsewhere. Swazi Nation Land (see page 67) is relatively impoverished, wildlife-wise, with the habitat damaged by overgrazing and larger species persecuted. The greatest concentrations of wildlife are generally on private land or reserves.

MAMMALS Some 132 species of mammal have been recorded in Swaziland: about one-third of sub-Saharan Africa's total. Around 33% of these are bats or rodents. Over the first part of the 20th century, hunting, human population growth and development drove out many larger species. But an ambitious conservation programme starting in the 1960s (see page 52) managed to preserve the last scattered game herds in the lowveld and has since succeeded in boosting their populations and reintroducing many other 'lost' species. Today you can certainly also see 'charismatic megafauna' such as giraffes and elephants, although not in quite the same unconfined space as elsewhere in southern Africa.

Herbivores
African elephant (*Loxodonta africana*) This is the world's largest land animal: a mature bull weighs six tonnes and stands 4m at the shoulder, with the cow about half his weight. The trunk is a mega nose that also serves as a fifth limb, delicate enough to pluck a seedpod and strong enough to tear down the branch. The huge ears provide acute hearing and also cool down the whole animal by circulating its blood supply through a network of capillaries. The tusks are outsized incisors that can dig up roots, split tree trunks or impale an enemy. And the spongy soles of the dinner-plate-sized feet absorb sound so effectively that elephants can move almost silently across the woodland floor.

By the 1890s hunters had slaughtered Swaziland's last lowveld elephant herds. Wandering bulls continued to appear until at least the 1950s, usually crossing over from Mozambique. Then in 1986 elephants were reintroduced in two separate groups to Mkhaya and Hlane. These youngsters, the survivors of Kruger Park culls, have since matured and bred, increasing their numbers in both parks. To control their population, a contraception programme was introduced in 2009. Today, the elephants are confined within fenced areas. You can see them on guided game drives or, at Hlane, on their nightly visits to the Ndlovu Camp waterhole. From the mid-1990s until around 2008 two young elephant bulls also took up residence in Malolotja Nature Reserve, having wandered over from South Africa's Songimvelo Reserve via the Nkomati Valley (see page 207).

Reintroducing elephants to Swaziland has proved a conservation challenge. These animals have more impact on their own landscape than any mammal except man. A mature bull will consume over 150kg a day: grass is torn up, roots dug out and trees ransacked – or often simply pushed over. In unconfined environments, this apparent devastation can be surprisingly beneficial, offering browse for other herbivores and a micro-habitat for smaller animals, while returning nutrients to the soil, both via fallen vegetation and the elephants' droppings. But in Swaziland's relatively small parks the habitat has no chance to recover. Numerous dead knobthorns at Hlane, victims of relentless ring-barking, show just what elephants can do.

Another potential problem lies in the herd composition. Elephant society is matriarchal. The dominant female is a repository of experience, leading the herd to food and water and away from danger, while other females – organised along matrilineal lines – help rear the youngsters. An orphan herd, deprived of this structure, grows up like a bunch of delinquents. In the absence of mature bulls, young males become sexually active earlier and quickly grow aggressive towards other elephants, animals and, potentially, people. Reintroduction programmes in South Africa, for example at Pilanesburg National Park, have encountered serious problems, with young elephants attacking vehicles and killing rhinos. Swaziland's conservation authorities are monitoring the situation closely and acting where necessary.

Rhinoceroses Swaziland is one of the best places in Africa to observe the continent's two rhino species. The **white rhinoceros** (*Ceratotherium simum*) is the world's largest land mammal after the two elephant species: a mature bull can top 2,500kg and his front horn – composed of compressed, hair-like keratin fibres – can exceptionally reach 1.5m. It is certainly not white, however. This misleading name derives from the Afrikaans *weid*, which describes the animal's 'wide' muzzle, adapted for grazing grass. The black rhino, by contrast, is a browser and has a hooked upper lip with which to pluck twigs. The white rhino is also bigger, carries its huge head low to the ground, and has a distinct hump on the neck and fin-like ridge on the spine. It is generally held to be a more even-tempered animal than its irascible relative.

White rhinos represent one of the world's great conservation success stories. They disappeared from Swaziland – and pretty much everywhere else – at the end of the 19th century. But a handful survived in what is now KwaZulu-Natal, and intensive protection has since seen numbers build steadily to 20,000 across southern Africa. Reintroduction to Swaziland began in 1965 and the species became re-established in the lowveld. Heavy poaching during the late 1980s took a further toll, but today there is a good breeding population in both Hlane and Mkhaya, where you can get very close to white rhinos, both by vehicle and – even better – on foot.

13

White rhino

Stepping out into rhino territory allows a fascinating insight into the animals' ecology. These huge beasts spend up to half their time grazing, rotating feeding areas to maintain regular 'lawns'. They drink daily, usually at dusk, and cool off by day in mud wallows. Beside favourite wallows you will usually find a 'rubbing post': a low stump polished to a smooth finish by generations of itchy rhinos seeking to rid themselves of skin parasites. You will also find large (up to waist-deep) middens of grass-filled dung that rhinos deposit at strategic points around their territory. Furrows in a midden show where its creator has scraped his back feet, picking up a signature scent to spread along the trail.

The **black rhinoceros** (*Diceros bicornis*), by comparison with white rhinos, seems a dynamic, streamlined animal. Indeed, this species is surprisingly agile for its

THE 'RHINO WARS'

The 1980s marked a low point for rhinos across Africa. An increase in demand for rhino horn in the lucrative markets of the Far East, where it fetched higher prices per kilo than gold, fuelled a rapid escalation in poaching. Heavily armed gangs, backed by powerful overseas syndicates, slaughtered rhinos in the middle of national parks. Desperate wildlife authorities met force with force, gun battles claiming the lives of both poachers and rangers.

In November 1988 this war reached Swaziland. By the time it ended in December 1992 around 100 rhinos – 80% of the population – had been killed. Hlane lost 39, before those that remained were dehorned for their protection. Mlawula, which was less well protected, lost its entire population. The poachers soon moved on to Mkhaya, where four rhinos were lost in 1992. Meanwhile general crime rose around Swaziland, fuelled by the poaching syndicates, and Petros Ngomane, chief ranger of Big Game Parks, survived two attempts on his life. Big Game Parks (see page 52) approached King Mswati III with a recommendation either to relocate Swaziland's remaining rhinos to South Africa or to fortify the battle against the poachers. The result was the Amended Game Act of 1991, which gave BGP far-reaching new powers. Their rangers now took on the poachers with more authority and better weapons. This culminated in the March 1992 'Big Bend shootout', when a trap was laid for poachers in the car park of a Big Bend hotel. A gunfight erupted in which two poachers were killed and the others captured. The incident divides opinion to this day. However, it effectively put an end to Swaziland's rhino wars.

Ever since then Swaziland has been able to boast the best-protected rhinos in Africa – until 3 June 2011, when poachers killed a female rhino in Hlane. After a second rhino died there on 27 September, rangers tracked down the South African poachers and, during a gun battle, shot three dead. These incidents followed a massive upsurge in poaching in South Africa from 2009, in which hundreds of rhinos have already died – mostly in the Kruger Park. The BGP conservation force saw the problem coming; it remains to be seen whether they can deal with it once again.

bulk, and can top 50km/h at full tilt. It's much smaller than a white rhino, weighing 'only' 900–1,200kg, and is no more black than a white rhino is white. The key ID features are its smaller head – generally held up – with a hooked upper lip, plus a lighter build and distinct saddle to the back.

Black rhino

The black rhino is seriously endangered. As of 2012, only about 4,200 are thought to remain in Africa. This means that the tiny population at Mkhaya, where the species has been reintroduced to Swaziland, is of international significance. By contrast with the white rhino, this animal was common across Africa for much of the 20th century and white hunters slaughtered thousands with impunity. Its accelerated decline since the 1960s – due largely to the eastern market for rhino horn – has been a conservation catastrophe. Today, the majority remain in secure, fenced areas, like Mkhaya.

The good news is that Mkhaya is one of the best places to get a decent look at this shy creature. Black rhinos are much harder to find than white, generally sticking to dense cover, but rangers can lead you directly to where one has most recently been seen. Tracking a black rhino on foot through thick bush is one of Africa's more adrenalin-charged wildlife experiences. This nervy animal has acute smell and hearing but poor eyesight, so is quick to imagine a threat and may opt for a blind charge as the best form of defence. This can occasionally require you to seek refuge behind – or even up – the nearest tree, although the rhino is just as likely to charge off in the other direction.

Black rhinos browse on woody plants, including some – such as euphorbias – that are toxic to other animals. Their prehensile upper lip pulls twigs into the mouth, where the slanted cheek teeth shear them off, and their droppings are full of clippings, all snipped at the same 45° angle. Like white rhinos, black rhino bulls maintain territorial dung middens. Also like their larger cousin, this species gives birth to a single hornless calf after a gestation period of 15 months, the youngster remaining with its mother for two to three years.

Hippopotamus (*Hippopotamus amphibius*) Two small indigenous populations of hippos survive in Swaziland's lowveld: one in the Usutu River, near Big Bend, and the other in the Mbuluzi River, near Simunye. Wanderers from these groups sometimes turn up in other nearby rivers and dams, and the odd hippo has even followed the Nkomati River from South Africa into Malolotja. Visitors, however, can best see hippos in one of the three reserves to which they have been introduced: Mlilwane, Hlane and Mkhaya.

Indigenous or otherwise, there's no mistaking this heavyweight herbivore. Fattest of Africa's giants, a mature bull can top 2,500kg. Its extraordinary shape reflects its amphibious lifestyle. Immersed in water by day, its great bulk provides buoyancy, while tiny eyes, ears and nostrils on top of its head enable it to breathe, see and hear while submerged. Out on land by night, its short, sturdy legs enable it to wander up to 30km in search of grazing, using its toughened lips to crop neat 'hippo lawns'.

A male hippo defends a stretch of river, where he presides over a group of females and young, and drives away rivals. He marks his territory on land and in the water by scattering dung with a rapid flicking of his tail. Rivals settle disputes by ritual displays of size, using 'yawns' to flaunt their impressive teeth – massive incisors and

15

canines that serve solely as weapons. Battles, when they break out, sometimes prove fatal. Females give birth to a single calf after a gestation of eight months. The infant suckles underwater at first, protected by its mother from large crocs and rampaging male hippos.

Hippos have a murderous reputation. Certainly you should always respect their space – especially on land, when they tend to rush in panic for the water, bulldozing anything in their path. You will know you are in hippo country from the distinctive parallel, four-toed tracks leading to the water. Their call – a deep, resonant grunting, culminating in a great whinny and snort – is the classic sound of an African river.

Wild pigs Two species of wild pig occur in Swaziland. The **warthog** (*Phacochoerus africanus*) is much the better known. Reintroduced to Mlilwane in the 1960s, it has since also re-established itself on many lowveld reserves and ranches, and at Malolotja in the highveld. There is no mistaking this popular porker: its enormous head, with bizarre warty protrusions, lavish whiskers and impressive tusks, seems out of proportion to its dainty hindquarters, and its hide is frequently plastered with the mud in which it wallows. Among various warthog idiosyncrasies are grazing on bended fore-knee and trotting along in line with tails held up like radio antennae. Sows live in small groups with their young, while males generally stay apart. Home is a hole – often a disused aardvark burrow that the hogs dig out further using their spade-like muzzle. They enter backwards, enabling them to dash out like a cork from a bottle, tusks at the ready. Females give birth to two or three piglets, each weighing less than 1kg, and will defend them fiercely.

Warthog

The **bushpig** (*Potamochoerus larvatus*) is a secretive forest animal that is fairly widespread, including on Swazi Nation Land, but seldom seen. It lies up in thick cover by day before venturing out at night to feed. Its diet ranges from roots and tubers – grubbed up with a tough snout – to carrion and even small animals, and bushpigs can wreak havoc in cane plantations. Roughly warthog-sized (60–100kg), it sports a thick coat of red-brown hair, whitish mane and tassled ears. Its protruding incisors are much shorter than a warthog's tusks – though formidable weapons, nonetheless. The sow has her litter in a nest of dry grass and the youngsters, like many forest animals, are striped for camouflage.

Giraffe (*Giraffa camelopardalis*) The steep gorges of the Nkomati River appear to mark the southernmost limit of the giraffe's natural range, and it is thought never to have been native to Swaziland – although it did occur just to the north. In recent times, however, giraffes have been introduced to several lowveld reserves, where they flourish in the acacia savanna.

The giraffe is the world's tallest animal: males, slightly larger than females, may tower 5m and reach 1,200kg. This allows them to browse from the crowns of acacias, where they pluck leaves and pods from among the thorns with a long, prehensile tongue, and are well camouflaged against the foliage by their blotched pattern. Drinking is trickier: a giraffe scans long and hard for danger before spreading its front legs and lowering its head awkwardly. An efficient digestive system enables it to extract every drop of moisture from its food, however, and for such a huge animal its droppings are tiny.

Bull giraffes associate with cows only during courtship, when they compete for mating rights by ritual 'necking': two males swing their heads at each other in what appears to be a leisurely manner, but is actually a series of sledgehammer blows to the opponent's flanks. Great height and excellent vision make giraffes the 'eyes of the bush' for many prey animals – although in Swaziland, with no free-roaming lions, they have nothing to fear. A sure way to tell male giraffes from females is by their horns: those of the former are thicker and worn smooth by years of fighting. A female gives birth to a single 100kg calf after a gestation period of 15 months. The youngster can walk within an hour, and must follow its mother as she moves on quickly.

Burchell's zebra (*Equus quagga burchellii*) Zebras were widespread across the lowveld until the 1950s, by which time hunting had reduced them to just a small population in the Hlane area. Those survivors formed the nucleus of a restocking programme that has since re-established zebras in all lowveld reserves, as well as Mlilwane and Malolotja.

Burchell's zebra is the southern African race of the plains zebra. Standing about 1.3m tall and weighing 290–340kg, this stocky animal inhabits wooded and open savanna, where it requires plentiful grazing and easy access to water. Its stripes may serve as camouflage in the long grass, but zebras can look conspicuous against a green backdrop and alternative theories hold that this pattern may have evolved to confuse a predator trying to select a single target from a herd, or even to deter biting insects. Small family units comprise a single stallion plus his mares and foals. The stallion generally brings up the rear but will take the lead in riskier situations, such as when approaching a waterhole. Zebra are highly aggressive, both in disputes between rivals and in self-defence, when even lions take care to avoid their jaw-breaking kicks. Listen for their hiccupping *kwa-ha-ha* call. A female has a single foal, weighing 30–35kg, after a gestation period of 12 months. It sticks close to its mother and can move with the herd within half an hour.

African buffalo (*Syncerus caffer*) Swaziland's indigenous buffalo herds were exterminated decades ago. Subsequent reintroductions failed in both Malolotja and Mlilwane, but a programme at Mkhaya has since fared well and the species is now established there. This animal's supposed ferocity is the stuff of bush legend. In reality, however, there is generally little to fear from what is essentially a big black cow. Bulls weighs up to 800kg, and their formidable curved horns, set in a massive 'boss', may each measure a metre. Females are 25% smaller, with no boss, and calves are reddish-brown.

Buffalo are highly sociable, and elsewhere in Africa form herds of thousands. They prefer wooded savanna with plentiful grass and available water, and usually drink in the early morning or late afternoon, often wading waist-deep into a waterhole. Both males and females within a herd maintain dominance hierarchies based on age. A single calf is born after a gestation period of 11 months. In Swaziland a buffalo's only potential predators are hyenas or large crocodiles. Elsewhere, lions are a significant threat – although it takes several of them to bring down an adult, and it's a risky business. Buffalo betray their presence with trampled 'cowpat' droppings and a lingering earthy scent. If you meet the herd, the animals will often appear curious, approaching to sniff out your identity then thundering off in a dust cloud. In a herd they generally pose no threat. Solitary old males are best avoided, however. These have left the herd and now hang around in mud wallows and thickets nursing grudges.

to bring down birds in flight. Caracals are widespread across southern Africa but much persecuted by farmers. In Swaziland, records exist from Malolotja, Mlilwane and Mkhaya; I once saw a caracal cross the road in South Africa not far from the Ngwenya border. The **African wild cat** (*Felis sylvestris*) is the ancestor of our domestic moggie, first tamed by the Ancient Egyptians over 5,000 years ago. It has a faintly striped coat and rufous ears. This animal has been found dead on the road near the Lavumisa border so may occur in Swaziland.

Dogs (Canidae)
Jackals These medium-sized canines – a little larger than a fox – pair for life, with youngsters staying to help adults raise their next litter. The **black-backed jackal** (*Canis mesomelas*) is the most common of Swaziland's three dog species, and easily identified by the distinctive black and silver-grey saddle across its sandy coat. It preys on anything from insects to young antelope, and often steals carrion from larger predators. Widespread across the lowveld, notably in the northeast, it also ranges into protected areas of the middleveld and highveld. You may spot one on the road after dark or hear its characteristic high, wailing call during the breeding season. The **side-striped jackal** (*Canis adustus*) is less common, restricted largely to the Big Bend and Nsoko area. It is greyer than the black-backed jackal, with a white-tipped tail and pale stripe along each flank. It is also more nocturnal, less vocal and generally keeps to itself, feeding largely on fruit and rodents.

African wild dog (*Lycaon pictus*) This highly nomadic animal has long been extinct in Swaziland as a breeding resident but occasionally turns up out of the blue. The last couple of decades have seen sightings at both Malolotja and Hlane, and in 1992 a pack of four even appeared at Mlilwane, where they tucked into the local impala. Such wanderers probably come from the small breeding population in KwaZulu-Natal. Larger and longer-legged than a jackal, the wild dog is identified by its Mickey Mouse ears, white-tipped tail and coat mottled like a tie-dye rug. Packs hunt by day in open country, using speed and stamina to run down prey such as medium-sized antelope. Each pack centres upon one dominant breeding pair. Litters are unusually large, up to ten or more, and females co-operate in raising the pups. Persecuted for years as 'vermin', this is now one of Africa's rarest mammals and – with fewer than 4,000 individuals remaining – the focus of intense conservation concern.

Hyenas (Hyenidae)
Spotted hyena (*Crocuta crocuta*) Hyenas have always suffered a bad press but are fascinating and impressive creatures. This species is the largest, weighing up to 70kg. Once common in Swaziland, it is now reduced to a small breeding population in the lowveld, with known dens in both Mlawula and Mkhaya. You may glimpse one on the road at night, but are more likely to hear its far-carrying whooping calls or spot the distinctive droppings, which are white with crumbled bone. Any glimpse will reveal the unmistakable loping gait and front-heavy profile, built around a long neck and powerful shoulders to support massive, bone-crunching jaws. This versatile animal is equally adept as hunter and scavenger. Its complex social life is highly matriarchal; females even have false male sex organs, which explains the myth that the species is hermaphrodite. Adults mark their territory with a pungent secretion from the anal gland. A litter of one or two cubs is born in an underground den and not weaned until 12–16 months, by which time they are almost full-grown.

Aardwolf (*Proteles cristatus*) This uncommon, little-known species is the smallest member of the hyena family, weighing just 6–11kg, although its shaggy mane can create a deceptive appearance of size. Malolotja is one of the best places in southern Africa to spot one: your best chance is in the Logwaja/Ngwenya high grasslands on late afternoons during winter, when foraging individuals are often out and about before nightfall. Farmers have long persecuted aardwolves for their alleged lamb killing. In fact, this specialised carnivore lacks the teeth to tackle meat, and feeds almost entirely on termites, licking them up with its tongue. It dens in the old burrows of other animals, notably aardvarks.

Aardwolf

Mongooses (Herpestidae) Among seven species of mongoose recorded in Swaziland most common is the **slender mongoose** (*Galerella sanguinea*), which often frequents built-up areas. This solitary, squirrel-sized predator captures rodents and reptiles, including venomous snakes. It is as slim as its name suggests, with a fawn coat and long, black-tipped tail that it arches high over its back when dashing for cover. The **banded mongoose** (*Mungos mungo*) is chunkier and its greyish-brown coat is marked with distinctive dark bands. This highly sociable animal lives in troops of around 20 that co-operate closely, both in foraging and self-defence. It is restricted to the northern lowveld and protected middleveld areas, such as Phophonyane. The **dwarf mongoose** (*Helogale parvula*) is dark brown and much smaller – at 350g it is hardly rat-sized – but similarly sociable. It inhabits protected areas in the lowveld, finding a home in termite mounds or hollow logs. Troops betray their presence with bird-like chirrups. The **water mongoose** (*Atilax paludinosus*) is a much larger, nocturnal species, weighing up to 4kg. It hunts frogs and crabs at the water's edge, where it can be distinguished from an otter by its shaggier coat and more pointed face. The even bigger, but rarer, **white-tailed mongoose** (*Ichneumia albicauda*) is found in the far eastern lowveld. Also nocturnal, it is an insect-eater that forages with head held low and hindquarters raised, displaying its white plume of tail. The large **Egyptian mongoose** (*Herpestes ichneumon*) and medium-sized **Meller's mongoose** (*Rhynchogale melleruin*) are both solitary species that may occur in Swaziland but have not yielded a confirmed record for decades.

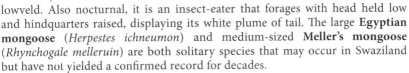
Slender mongoose

Weasels and relatives (Mustelidae) The largest of Swaziland's four members of the weasel family, or mustelids, is the **Cape clawless otter** (*Aonyx capensis*), which occurs in protected riverine areas. This is a typical otter, with the streamlined body, short legs and sturdy tail of an animal built for swimming. It uses dextrous toes to capture crabs, fish and molluscs. Sightings are rare but look out for telltale droppings full of crushed crab shell deposited on prominent riverside rocks. The **honey badger** (*Mellivora capensis*) is a scarce resident of the Lubombos. A stocky animal, with black underparts, a silvery back and powerful forelimbs for digging, it feeds on anything from insects to small mammals. Honey is a particular delicacy, a tough coat protecting the badger against stings as it breaks into bees' nests, and only species in its own unique order, the Tubulidentata. It is sparsely haired and solidly built, weighing some 40–70kg, with short legs, a thick tail, a long snout and rabbit-like ears. In Swaziland, aardvarks are restricted to protected areas and are most numerous in the lowveld. They inhabit open terrain where they subsist on termites, hacking into termitaria with the spade-like nails on their front feet and extracting the quarry with a long, sticky tongue. Flies around a burrow entrance indicate when an aardvark is at home, but vacant burrows may house other animals, from warthogs to porcupines, and in Swaziland offer nest sites for the rare blue swallow.

Ground pangolin (*Manis temmincki*) This bizarre mammal has a covering of sharp, overlapping scales, almost like a reptile. It is, like the unrelated aardvark, a nocturnal animal that uses its long tongue to eat ants. A handful of records exist from northeastern Swaziland but the animal is almost mythically elusive. Adults reach a metre in length and weigh 5–18kg. By day they curl up in burrows or dense cover; at night they forage for termites, moving on their hind legs with long tail extended as a counterbalance. When threatened, pangolins curl into a tight ball, protecting the head and underparts beneath their scales. This species is under threat from the traditional medicine trade, which ascribes various miraculous properties to its scales.

Rock hyrax (*Procavia capensis*) This small furry mammal, known locally as a dassie, looks much like an oversized guinea pig but, bizarrely, shares its ancestry with elephants and sea cows. The largest of four hyrax species in southern Africa, it weighs up to 4.5kg, and its rotund, tail-less body is brownish in colour. Tiny, hoof-like toenails provide traction among the boulders and crevices where it lives. A hyrax colony has a strict pecking order. Each morning the members emerge to bask in the sun before moving off to feed on nearby vegetation, sometimes clambering into low trees to browse. Colonies seldom venture far from base and always post a sentry to sound the alarm. Females produce two to four young after a gestation period of seven to eight months. This is a highveld species in Swaziland. Look out among boulders at Malolotja (notably around the campsite), Mahamba Gorge and Pine Valley. All these sites support the Verreaux's eagle, which preys almost exclusively upon hyraxes and would soon disappear in their absence.

Hares (Lagomorpha) Hares do not use burrows, as rabbits do, but lie up by day in shallow scrapes called forms, and graze by night. Among their numerous survival adaptations are an ability to maximise sustenance by re-ingesting their own droppings (always a useful trick, I find) and to use their huge ears as temperature regulators. They produce up to four litters per year, born in a shallow nest lined with fur. Two species occur in Swaziland: the **scrub hare** (*Lepus saxatilis*) is widespread in open habitats, including on ranches, where it feeds in areas cleared by grazing; the **Natal red hare** (*Pronolagus crassicaudatus*) is stockier, with reddish fur and shorter ears, and is restricted to a few rocky sites in the Lubombos and near Mbabane, where it leaves distinctive latrines of pellets among the rocks.

Rodents (Rodentia) Rodents are the world's most successful group of mammals and characterised by their chisel-like incisor teeth, adapted for gnawing. Eight families, comprising at least 24 different species, occur in Swaziland, but most pass unseen by the average visitor. The **Cape porcupine** (*Hystrix africaeaustralis*) is by far the most easily identified, being 18kg in weight and bristling with quills. Contrary to popular myth these modified hairs cannot be fired at enemies but are loosely embedded in the skin and so easily shed on contact. A threatened porcupine erects its quills, turns its back and rattles its tail as a warning. Predators who try their luck may retreat so badly punctured that crippling injuries can develop. Porcupines occur sparsely across Swaziland and emerge after dark from their multi-chambered burrows to forage along regular trails. Look out for their telltale diggings, scattered quills and clusters of fibrous droppings. Food includes roots, bulbs and bark. Pairs are monogamous, with the male unusually active in helping raise the litter of two to four young. The **greater cane-rat** (*Thryonomys swinderianus*) is a close relative of porcupines. This stocky rodent, weighing up to 5kg, has a short tail and grizzled fur. It feeds on roots and stems, leaving characteristic runways through vegetation, and can damage sugar-cane fields if unchecked by natural predators. Rural people prize this animal as good eating.

True rats and mice belong to the Muridae family, and are hard to spot, let alone identify. Notable species in Swaziland include the **pouched mouse** (*Saccostomus campestris*), a dumpy, hamster-like species with a short tail and capacious cheek pouches; the **striped mouse** (*Rhabdomys pumilio*), a highveld species that is often out during daylight; the **vlei rat** (*Otomys irroratus*), which resembles a mini cane-rat and builds similar runways; and the **multimammate mouse** (*Mastomys natalensis*), which has up to 12 pairs of teats and produces litters of over 12 young after a gestation period of just 23 days. Other small rodents include the **woodland dormouse** (*Graphiurus murinus*), which has a furry tail and may breed inside houses, and the **common mole rat** (*Crytomys hottentotus*), which uses formidable incisors to dig extensive tunnel systems – and infuriate gardeners.

Insectivores (Insectivora) Shrews and other insectivores may resemble mice and other small rodents but actually comprise an ancient order of mammals that feed on insects and other invertebrates. All have tiny eyes, with longer snouts and shorter tails than most mice, and many can be identified only in the hand or laboratory. Shrews live a brief, high-octane life, and feed voraciously to fuel their high metabolism. Of at least ten species in Swaziland, the 20cm **giant musk shrew** (*Crocidura flavescens*), of the high grasslands, is one of the region's largest. The **Hottentot golden mole** (*Amblysomus hottentotus*) also occurs in the highveld – including in gardens – where it uses strong front claws to dig winding burrows just beneath the surface. Like all golden moles it has soft silky fur and no visible ears, eyes or tail. It feeds on insect larvae and earthworms and so, unlike the molerat, is of no concern to gardeners. The eastern **rock elephant-shrew** (*Elephantulus myurus*) is not an insectivore at all, let alone a shrew, and belongs to the ancient order Macroscelididae, endemic to Africa. Elephant-shrews have big, mouse-like eyes and ears, and elongated, twitching snouts, from which they derive their name. This species forages by day around granite kopjes, where it shelters under boulders and dashes out after ants and termites.

Rock elephant-shrew

Bats (Chiroptera) After snakes, bats must be the most misunderstood of all animals, perhaps because their nocturnal habits make them hard to observe and easy to fear. For the record, bats don't become entangled in hair, nor do they suck blood (at least not in Africa). In fact, these remarkable creatures have a range of talents – including the powers of flight and echolocation – that helps explain their proliferation into the second largest order of mammals. Around 900 species occur worldwide, including at least 24 in Swaziland.

Bats fall into two suborders. Fruit bats (Megachiroptera) are larger, with dog-like faces and large eyes. They feed on fruit, buds and flowers and are often blamed for damaging orchards – although they also play a crucial role in pollinating fruit trees and dispersing their seeds. **Wahlberg's epauletted fruit bat** (*Epomorphus wahlbergi*) is widespread in the middleveld and lowveld. The monotonous pinging of territorial males, given as they roost after feeding, is a characteristic night-time sound of riverine forests, orchards and gardens with large fruiting trees.

Insectivorous bats (Microchiroptera) are smaller than fruit bats, and navigate by echolocation: ultrasonic sounds produced in the throat (largely inaudible to the human ear) are bounced off objects and interpreted by the brain to map their surroundings, enabling the bats to catch tiny insects on the wing. Different families are classified by the shape of their tail, ears or facial skin adornments, although it takes an expert to identify most individual species. Free-tailed bats (Molossidae) have a tail tip that projects 'free' from the membrane between the two back legs; the **little free-tailed bat** (*Chaerephon pumila*) occurs everywhere except highveld grasslands and may nest in very large colonies – often around human habitation, where their excited chittering can be heard as sunset approaches. Vesper bats (Vespertilionidae) are the largest group and have a simple mouse-like face; they include the tiny **banana bat** (*Pipistrellus nanus*), which is widespread in the middleveld and lowveld, usually around banana plantations, where it roosts in the rolled ends of banana leaves. Horseshoe bats (Rhinolophidae) are named for the odd structure on their nose, which works like a satellite dish to receive echolocation calls: **Geoffroy's horseshoe bat** (*Rhinolophus clivosus*) is a highveld species that may roost by the thousand in old mine workings.

BIRDS Some 500 species of bird have been recorded in Swaziland. This puts it roughly on a par with France (517) or, for a more local comparison, the Kruger National Park (505); it is a remarkable tally for such a tiny country that, being landlocked, has no sea or coastal birds. It owes this tally to its diversity of habitats, with several very different bird communities occurring side by side. For sheer number of species, the lowveld is the richest region: a keen birder in Hlane or Mlawula can easily top 100 species in a day – especially during summer, with all the migrants in. The highveld has fewer species but is home to many that are hard to find elsewhere. Indeed, Swaziland harbours 52 southern African endemics and is one of the only breeding sites for the blue swallow, one of Africa's rarest breeding birds. And the beauty of birds is that they are not confined to reserves: throughout the country, from road verge to hotel garden, there are plenty to be seen. This account outlines some key groups, and a few more interesting or conspicuous species. Serious birders will need a field guide (see *Further Information*, page 302).

Ducks, geese and other waterbirds Water bodies in Swaziland host various waterfowl species. Most abundant is the **Egyptian goose** (*Alopochen aegyptiaca*), which has a red face and white wing panels and defends its territory fiercely. Others include the **yellow-billed duck** (*Anas undulata*) of highveld wetlands, identified by its bright-yellow bill, and the **white-faced duck** (*Dendrocygna viduata*), which takes to the air in whistling flocks. Swimming birds not to be confused with ducks include the **little grebe** (*Tachybaptus ruficollis*), a dumpy bird that dives frequently, and cormorants, such as the **reed cormorant** (*Phalacrocorus africanus*), which perch on waterside branches with wings held out to dry. The **African finfoot** (*Podica senegalensis*) is a shy riverine species that superficially resembles a duck or cormorant but belongs to an unrelated family. It occurs along the Mbuluzi River in the northeast.

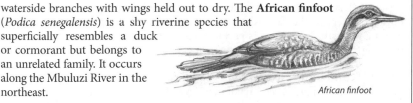

African finfoot

Herons and egrets These long-legged, long-necked, dagger-billed birds generally live near water. The large **grey heron** (*Ardea cinerea*) is common in the lowveld and will be familiar to visitors from Europe. The similar **black-necked heron** (*Ardea melanocephala*) is distinguished by its black head and neck, and often feeds away from water. The **black-crowned night heron** (*Nycticorax nycticorax*) is a smaller species that roosts in colonies among trees overhanging water and is active after dark. Egrets are essentially white herons: the common **cattle egret** (*Bubulcus ibis*) gets its name from feeding on insects around the feet of cattle and other grazing animals. The **great egret** (*Egretta alba*) is larger and more solitary, fishing patiently on dams and lakes in the lowveld.

Storks and ibises Storks look a little like herons, but have heavier bills and fly with their necks extended rather than retracted. The huge, 150cm-tall **marabou stork** (*Leptoptilos crumeniferus*) is one of the world's largest flying birds, and its breeding colony at Hlane National Park is the southernmost in Africa. This scavenger has a featherless head and neck, and often joins vultures at a carcass. The smaller **white stork** (*Ciconia ciconia*) is a summer migrant from Europe – the baby-carrier of legend – and arrives in October in large flocks. Ibises are smaller than storks and probe for food using a distinctive down-curved bill. The **sacred ibis** (*Theskiornis aethiopicus*) is a common sight in wetlands, and nests and roosts in mixed colonies with herons. The rare **southern bald ibis** (*Geronticus calvus*), which has metallic blue-green plumage, a bare head and red bill, is restricted to a few areas of montane grassland, where it breeds on steep cliffs over water. Swaziland's colonies at Malolotja, Mantenga Falls and Mahamba Gorge are of international significance. The **hamerkop** (*Scopus umbretto*) is an odd-looking bird with a clumpy crest that gives its head the hammer shape from which it gets its name. Usually seen near fresh water, it builds a huge domed nest and is feared in local tradition as a harbinger of ill fortune.

Southern bald ibis

Shore birds Among various smaller wading birds poking around exposed shorelines are migrants from northern Europe such as the **wood sandpiper** (*Tringa glareola*), as well as local breeding birds including the exceptionally long-legged **black-winged stilt** (*Himantopus himantopus*) and the diminutive **three-banded plover** (*Charadrius tricollaris*). The **crowned lapwing** (*Vanellus albiceps*) is an upright bird that feeds on open grasslands away from water. It gets its name from the distinctive ring around its crown and is quick to take to the air with a shrill alarm call. The **water thick-knee** (*Burhinus vermiculatus*) is a nocturnal, well-camouflaged species that loafs at the water's edge by day and utters its mournful piping call at sunset. The **African jacana** (*Actophilorsis africanus*) occurs on lowland waters in the east, where it uses its unusually long toes to skip across floating vegetation. This bird is polyandrous, meaning that females have multiple male partners, to which – after laying their eggs – they leave all domestic duties.

Large ground birds
No bird comes bigger than the flightless **ostrich** (*Struthio camelus*), which stands over 2m tall, can top 80kg and gets around on long, strong legs at speeds of up to 60km/h. Ostriches were exterminated in Swaziland during the early 19th century; today's population is descended from domesticated stock introduced from South Africa. You can see them on lowveld reserves and at Mlilwane. **Denham's bustard** (*Neotis denhami*) is much smaller but nonetheless a large, impressive bird. It struts around the highveld grasslands at Malolotja, where males are conspicuous during their spring breeding display, when they puff up their dazzling white under-plumage. The **secretary bird** (*Sagittarius serpentarius*), which resembles a crane, is a large ground-dwelling raptor. It strides on long legs through grassland in search of reptiles, rodents and other prey, despatching victims with powerful blows from its feet. Standing up to 120cm tall, it is pale grey with a hooked bill, drooping crest, long tail and black 'leggings'. This species has declined in the lowveld but may be seen in Malolotja and other highveld areas.

Game birds
Galliformes, better known as 'game birds', are prized around the world for food and sport. They comprise several families of plump, noisy, ground-dwelling birds that use strong legs to scratch for food and only take flight reluctantly. The common **helmeted guineafowl** (*Numida meleagris*) forms fussing flocks of up to 40. It has a grey body, polka-dotted in white, and a naked blue-grey head crowned with a fleshy red 'helmet'. Its less common relative, the **crested guineafowl** (*Guttera pucherani*), frequents riparian thickets in eastern Swaziland and is distinguished by its feathered topknot. Francolins and spurfowl are smaller and browner than guineafowl. **Swainson's spurfowl** (*Francolinus swainsonii*), one of seven species in Swaziland, is widespread. The **red-winged francolin** (*Scleroptila levaillantii*), by contrast, is confined to montane grasslands and best seen at Malolotja.

Eagles and vultures
Swaziland has a rich complement of raptors. Largest are the vultures, distinguished by their naked heads – an adaptation for poking into carcasses. The **white-backed vulture** (*Gyps africanus*) can be seen soaring on its 2.2m wingspan high over the eastern lowveld and Lubombos, where it breeds in protected areas and sometimes flocks to carcasses. Even bigger is the **lappet-faced vulture** (*Aegypius tracheliotus*), a rare breeder at Hlane, which has a 2.8m wingspan and a massive bill adapted to rip open all but the toughest hides. Most eagles are predators rather than scavengers. The easiest to identify of Swaziland's 14 species is the **African fish eagle** (*Haliaeetus vocifer*), with its striking white head and distinctive yodelling cry. Look out for this expert fish-catcher around lakes and dams in the east. Another distinctive eastern species is the **bateleur** (*Terathopius ecaudatus*), which has a short tail, long wings and flies low over

Verreaux's eagle

open country with a rocking glide reminiscent of someone trying to catch their balance – hence its name, which means 'tightrope walker' in French. You may also spy one of Africa's three biggest eagles: the **martial eagle** (*Polemaeutus bellicosus*) has white underparts and soars high over open bush on a wingspan approaching 2.3m; the similar-sized **crowned eagle** (*Stephanoaetus coronatus*) prefers forested habitats, including at Mlilwane and Phophonyane, where it uses massive talons to capture monkeys; **Verreaux's eagle** (*Aquila verreauxii*) has bold white markings on its otherwise jet-black plumage and hunts for hyraxes along cliffs, including at Pine Valley, Mlilwane, Malolotja and Mahamba Gorge.

Smaller raptors Among numerous smaller birds of prey, the **black-shouldered kite** (*Elanus caeruleus*) is a handsome black, white and grey species that hunts by hovering and often perches on power lines. Other species you may encounter include the **jackal buzzard** (*Buteo rufofuscus*), a broad-winged bird with a rufous tail that hunts over highveld grasslands, notably at Malolotja, and the **African goshawk** (*Accipter tachiro*), a dashing predator that pursues small birds in wooded habitats. Falcons have longer, more pointed wings than hawks or buzzards: the **lanner falcon** (*Falco biarmicus*) is the largest species and breeds on cliffs in the highveld.

Jackal buzzard

Pigeons and doves Pigeons feed largely on the ground. Of 11 species in Swaziland, the **Cape turtle dove** (*Streptopelia capicola*) is the most common and announces its presence with a cooing 'work harder, work harder' call. The **red-eyed dove** (*Streptopelia semitorguata*) has a similar black neck ring but is slightly larger, with a striking red eye. The **emerald-spotted dove** (*Turtur chalcospilos*) is a smaller species, whose mournful descending call is said to intone 'My mother is dead, my father is dead, oh woe is me, oh woe, woe, woe…'. The **African green-pigeon** (*Treron calvus*) is unlike other species, feeding on fruits and clambering around lowveld fig trees like a parrot, its bright-green plumage sporting flashes of red and yellow.

Cuckoos and coucals Most cuckoos are brood parasites, laying their eggs in the nests of other birds. The several species found in Swaziland are all inter-African migrants and, being much more often heard than seen, are best identified by their distinctive call. The **red-chested cuckoo** (*Cuculus solitarius*) is among the most common, and its distinctive descending three-note phrase continues relentlessly throughout the summer months. Coucals are larger relatives of cuckoos that make their own nests. **Burchell's coucal** (*Centropus burchelli*) inhabits rank vegetation and marshy areas, often foraging low down in thickets. Its repetitious, bubbling call, like liquid poured from a container, has earned it the nickname 'water bottle bird.'

Parrot, turacos and trogon Swaziland's only parrot is the **brown-headed parrot** (*Poicephalus cryptoxanthus*), found in the far east and a common visitor to bird tables around Simunye. Like all parrots, it feeds in fruiting trees – especially fig trees – and has a fast flight and screeching call. Turacos are also fruit-eaters but belong to an order that is unique to Africa. They have a characteristic long-tailed and crested profile, and typically bound through the tree canopy rather than

33

taking flight. The **purple-crested turaco** (*Gallirex porphyreolophus*) is decked out in rich blue and green, with crimson primary feathers that flash in flight. This is Swaziland's national bird, known in SiSwati as *ligwalagwala*, and those red flight feathers traditionally adorn the hair of royalty. The **Knysna turaco** (*Turaco corythaix*) has similar gorgeous plumage but is far less common, being restricted to pockets of indigenous forest in the far east and far west. The **grey go-away bird** (*Corythhaixoides concolor*) is a plain-coloured member of the group found in the bushveld, where its harsh '*g'waaay*' call is a characteristic sound. The **Narina trogon** (*Apaloderma narina*) is a beautiful forest bird that is unrelated to turacos but also sports vivid green (above) and red (below) plumage. Swaziland is a hotspot for this elusive species, notably at Mkhaya and Phophonyane.

Owls and nightjars

Night in Swaziland brings a select cast of nocturnal birds to the stage. Owls are predators, equipped with sharp bill, wicked talons and hearing so keen that they can capture prey in near darkness. Among the largest of 11 species is the **spotted eagle owl** (*Bubo africanus*), which sports prominent ear tufts and bright-yellow eyes. Much smaller is the starling-sized **African scops owl** (*Otus senegalensis*), which feeds on insects and is camouflaged at its daytime roost by cryptic bark-like markings. Its call – a frog-like *prrrrp* – is characteristic of the lowveld night. Equally distinctive is the quavering whistle of the **fiery-necked nightjar** (*Caprimulgus pectoralis*), which reputedly intones 'Good Lord deliver us'.

African scops owl

Nightjars capture insects in flight and are more closely related to swifts than owls. This year-round resident is the most widespread of five very similar species in Swaziland.

Bee-eaters and rollers

These extremely colourful birds are hole-nesting insect-eaters. Bee-eaters have long tails and curved bills, and catch their prey in repeated aerial sallies from a favourite perch. The **white-fronted bee-eater** (*Merops bullockoides*) is a permanent resident in scattered middleveld locations, notably Mlilwane, where colonies breed in sandbanks. The **European bee-eater** (*Merops apiaster*) is a common summer visitor from Europe, with a dazzling plumage of blue, rufous and gold. Flocks often feed high overhead or perch on telephone lines. Rollers are chunkier than bee-eaters, with sturdier bills and more blue in their plumage, which they flaunt during tumbling aerial courtship displays. The **lilac-breasted roller** (*Coracias caudatus*) often perches atop lowveld thorn bushes, from where it drops onto prey below, revealing its spectacular plumage and long central tail feathers. The larger but shorter-tailed **European roller** (*Coracias garrulus*) arrives in October as a summer visitor, gathering before departure in March.

Hornbills and hoopoes

Hornbills are comical-looking birds that sport a large, unwieldy bill. Many species follow a curious breeding routine in which the female seals herself into the tree cavity nest using a plug of mud and droppings, leaving just a small aperture through which the male feeds her while she waits for the chicks to fledge. The **southern yellow-billed hornbill** (*Tokus leucomelus*) is a common bushveld resident. The larger **trumpeter hornbill** (*Bycanistes bucinator*) has a heavy casque (horny outgrowth) on its bill, and frequents riverine habitats in the lowveld, announcing its presence with a call like a wailing baby. A rare visitor to Swaziland, the turkey-sized **southern ground hornbill** (*Bucorvus leadbeateri*) is a ground-feeding bird with black plumage, a scarlet face and a hatchet for a bill. Small family parties occasionally turn up in protected locations.

Green wood-hoopoe

A hysterical cackling may alert you to a group of **green wood-hoopoes** (*Phoeniculus purpureus*) as they clamber acrobatically among the branches probing for insects with their long, curved red bill. The local name of these glossy black-green birds is *inhleka bafazi*, which means 'laughing women'. Their cousin the **African hoopoe** (*Upupa africana*) also has a curved bill but is otherwise very different, with cinnamon plumage and black-and-white markings that give its floppy wings a moth-like appearance in flight. It raises a jaunty crest whenever it alights, and is often seen probing lawns or delivering its distinctive '*hu hu hu*' call from a high perch.

Kingfishers These compact birds have a short tail and long, heavy bill that they use to chisel out a nest tunnel in earth banks. Some species live beside water where they, indeed, feed on fish – capturing their prey with a plunge dive. Several, however, find food on dry land. Among the former are the tiny, jewel-like **malachite kingfisher** (*Alcedo cristata*), which perches in waterside vegetation and zips over the surface in a fast, direct flight, and the larger **pied kingfisher** (*Ceryle rudis*), which is black and white and hovers above the water before plunging on fish below. Among the latter, the common **brown-hooded kingfisher** (*Halcyon albiventris*) is often seen in towns and gardens, where it swoops down to pluck insects from the lawn. Though less colourful than many kingfishers, it nonetheless flashes bright-blue wings in flight.

Woodpeckers and barbets Woodpeckers have a skull specially adapted to absorb the impact of their hammer blows on tree branches as they chisel out grubs and excavate nest holes. A tapping sound overhead usually gives them away. Seven species occur in Swaziland, of which the **cardinal woodpecker** (*Dendropicos fuscescens*) is the smallest. Most look very similar, with barred upperparts and a red crown, and you'll need patience and good binoculars to tell them apart. The **ground woodpecker** (*Geocolaptes olivaceus*) is quite different, however, both for its plain plumage – with brown upperparts and a pinkish breast – and its habit of foraging for ants on the ground. This species is restricted to the highveld, where small parties forage around rock outcrops. Barbets are chunkier, thicker-billed relatives of woodpeckers. The **crested barbet** (*Trachyphonus vaillantii*) looks slightly scruffy, with a prominent crest, and calls with a long, monotonous trill. The **black-collared barbet** (*Lybius torquatus*) has a vivid red face and a high-speed call, likened to 'one-puddly, two-puddly', that is repeated over and over by the male and female in duet.

Ground woodpecker

Honeyguides These smallish, unremarkable-looking birds are brood parasites – which means that, like cuckoos, they lay their eggs in other birds' nests. Best-known is the **greater honeyguide** (*Indicator indicator*), whose common and scientific names both derive from its unique habit of leading people (and honey badgers; see page 25) to bees' nests, using much frantic twittering and flapping. Once the accomplice has broken in and taken its fill the bird feeds on any wax and larvae left behind. This species is widespread in Swaziland and parasitises hole-nesting birds such as barbets.

Passerines (perching birds) The Passeriformes are by far the largest order of birds, comprising around 6,000 species – some 60% of the world's total. Known loosely as 'perching birds', they differ from other orders in various fine anatomical details. In simple terms, however, most can be described as small birds that sing. Around 45% of Swaziland's bird species are passerines. These fall into around 26 different families.

Swallows and martins (Hirundidae) These aerial birds dart around after insects and often perch on overhead wires. Many species are summer visitors, arriving just before the rains to pair up and construct their mud nests. The **European swallow** (*Hirundo rustica*) is the most common: huge numbers arrive every October, flickering over grasslands and along roads in agile pursuit of airborne prey. The **lesser striped swallow** (*Hirundo abyssinica*) differs from the similar **greater striped swallow** (*Hirundo cucullata*) in its smaller size and bolder markings. Both have a rufous head and streaked underparts, and both nest under eaves. The **blue swallow**

Blue swallow

(*Hirundo atrocaerulea*) is an extremely rare inter-African migrant that breeds in tiny numbers in the highveld, often in old aardvark burrows. This royal-blue bird, with its long tail streamers, has celebrity status among birders. Malolotja in summer is the place to look: try drainage lines near the campsite.

Drongos, crows and orioles The **fork-tailed drongo** (*Dicrurus adsimilis*) is a widespread and lively woodland species with all-black plumage and a forked tail, which hawks its insect prey from a perch but may also pirate food from other birds. Orioles are starling-sized, predominantly yellow birds notable for their liquid call. Most common is the **black-headed oriole** (*Oriolus larvatus*), found in woodland across the country. The **pied crow** (*Corvus albus*) is a large, opportunistic black-and-white bird often seen around towns and settlements. Its even larger relative the **white-necked raven** (*Corvus albicollis*) is black with a white collar and massive, white-tipped bill, and is common in the highveld – including around Mbabane.

Bulbuls and babblers The **common bulbul** (*Pycnonotus tricolor*) is the most widespread of several bulbul species, often frequenting gardens, where its wide variety of calls can be heard late into the evening. The **terrestrial brownbul** (*Phyllastrephus terrestris*) is found in bushveld habitats where small groups forage close to the ground. **Arrow-marked babblers** (*Turdoides jardineii*) are also ground feeders and are aptly named, not only for their white-streaked plumage but also for the excited babbling 'kra kra kra' they make when foraging together. The **eastern nicator** (*Nicator gularis*) skulks in bushveld thickets, and is best located by its loud, jumbled song.

Robins, thrushes and chats Most birds in this group are excellent songsters. The **white-browed robin-chat** (*Cossipha heuglini*) is a handsome, orange-bellied bird with a black head and white eyebrow, commonly seen in gardens. It sings at dusk in a rich crescendo. The **kurrichane thrush** (*Turdus libonyanusis*) is a common but unobtrusive bird that forages on the woodland floor. The **mocking cliff-chat** (*Thamnolaea cinnamomeiventris*) is a striking bird of rocky outcrops, hopping around boulders and flicking its tail upwards upon landing. The **buff-streaked chat** (*Oenanthe bifasciata*) is found around rock outcrops in highveld grasslands, notably Mololotja, the male identified by his black face and orange belly.

Shrikes Some shrikes are known as butcherbirds due to their habit of impaling prey – from insects to small lizards – on a thorn bush or barbed-wire 'larder'. The **common fiscal** (*Lanius collaris*) is a dapper black-and-white bird found everywhere but the lowveld; it often terrorises other garden birds. The **gorgeous bush-shrike** (*Telophorus viridis*) is a more colourful species but skulks deep in bushveld thickets so is more easily heard than seen, the male and female singing in a perfectly synchronised duet. Among relatives of the shrikes

Magpie shrike

are the skulking **black-crowned tchagra** (*Tchagra senegalus*), which has a lilting, whistled song; and the **white-crested helmet-shrike** (*Prionops plumatus*), which flits through the bushveld in small parties – according to folklore, always in sevens. The most easily identified shrike must be the **magpie shrike** (*Corvinella melanoleuca*), of the eastern lowveld, which has a very long black tail and often perches prominently on overhead wires.

Flycatchers These birds dart out from a perch to snap up their insect prey in mid-air. Most striking is the **paradise flycatcher** (*Terpsiphone viridis*), an inter-African migrant, whose breeding males sport long and flowing chestnut tail feathers. The **southern black flycatcher** (*Melaenornis pammelaina*) is a quiet, all-black bird that resembles a subdued fork-tailed drongo (see above), and is often seen in gardens. The **chinspot batis** (*Batis molitor*) is a dapper little bird of acacia savanna whose descending three-note melody sounds like 'Three Blind Mice' in a minor key.

Warblers and relatives Warblers and several similar families of small, insect-eating bird are the 'little brown jobs' beloved of birdwatchers who relish a challenge. Among the more common are the **rattling cisticola** (*Cisticola chinana*), a bushveld resident with a repetitive song; the **willow warbler** (*Phylloscopus trochilus*), a tiny migrant from northern Europe that frequents the woodland canopy in summer; and the **tawny-flanked prinia** (*Prinia subflava*), which hops about in rank vegetation near water with its tail cocked. The warbler-like **Cape white-eye** (*Zosterops virens*) belongs to a separate family of largely fruit-eating birds. It is green with a prominent white eye-ring, and common in wooded highveld habitats, often moving through gardens in small parties.

Starlings and oxpeckers Most starlings have iridescent, blue/green plumage. They include the **Cape glossy starling** (*Lamprotornis litens*), a common bushveld bird that nests in tree holes; and the **red-winged starling** (*Onychognathus morio*), a longer-tailed highveld species with vivid chestnut wings that is found around rocky cliffs and in towns. The **violet-backed starling** (*Cinnyricinclus leucogaster*) is a widespread and more solitary summer visitor, with stunning purple upperparts that contrast with its clean white belly. The **red-billed oxpecker** (*Buphagus erythrorhynchus*) is closely related to starlings but feeds by picking off ticks and other blood-sucking insects from the hides of large animals, including cattle, giraffe and rhinoceros. It occurs at Hlane and Nisela.

Sunbirds These small, colourful birds are like an Old World equivalent of hummingbirds (though unrelated), with their thin, curved bill adapted for probing flowers, and the vivid iridescent plumage of the males. The **scarlet-chested sunbird** (*Chalcomitra senegalensis*) is a bushveld species that suspends its nest from the outer twig of a thorn tree; the black male has a vivid red breast. Look out around gardens and forest edges for the **greater double-collared sunbird** (*Cinnyris afer*), which has a broad red chest band and often feeds on aloes. The male **malachite sunbird** (*Nectarinia famosa*) is a brilliant metallic green with long central tail feathers. It frequents highveld grassland and feeds on proteas – as does **Gurney's sugarbird** (*Promerops gurneyi*), a streaky-brown relative of the sunbirds, found only at Malolotja.

Malachite sunbird

Weavers and relatives These seed-eating birds are named for the intricate suspended nests woven by males to lure a mate – often a thankless task since, if the female rejects his handiwork, the male must start all over again. Each species works to a different design. Males in many species have yellow breeding plumage but at other times are streaky brown, like females. The **Cape weaver** (*Ploceus capensis*) breeds in highveld grassland, colonies usually constructing their nests beside water. The **village weaver** (*Ploceus cucullatus*) is more widespread and the male, as in several species, has a distinct black mask. The **red-billed quelea** (*Quelea quelea*) is a small, sparrow-like bird that may form flocks hundreds of thousands strong. These swarms can be the scourge of cereal farmers, capable of stripping fields bare of grain.

Waxbills and relatives These tiny seed-eating birds tend to feed in small parties, often on the ground, and are best located by their high, sibilant contact calls. The **common waxbill** (*Estrilda astrild*) is one of the dullest – plain brown with a red face – and flutters in small flocks through rank waterside vegetation. More colourful is the **blue waxbill** (*Uraeginthus angolensis*), a common bushveld bird with pastel-blue underparts. Also in this group is the **bronze manikin** (*Spermestes cucullatus*), which flits though gardens and wooded areas in small busy flocks, and the **African firefinch** (*Lagonosticata rubricata*), which has pink-red underparts and keeps to dense, low undergrowth. The **pink-throated twinspot** (*Hypargos margaritatus*) is an exquisite bird with a polka-dot belly that is rare in southern Africa but reasonably common in eastern Swaziland – although easily overlooked as it feeds discreetly on the ground.

Pink-throated twinspot

Widows, whydahs and bishops Widows are seed-eating birds, named for the black plumage of breeding males – usually set off by a prominent marking in red, white or yellow. The **long-tailed widow** (*Euplectes progne*) is found only in the western grasslands, where the male dangles his outrageous tail in a slow flapping display flight. The **red-collared widow** (*Euplectes ardens*) is more widespread, though absent from the eastern bushveld, and has a tail not quite as long. Whydahs are brood parasites, like cuckoos (see page 33), each species having its own waxbill host; unlike cuckoos, however, the fledglings grow up alongside the host's nestlings rather than turfing them out. Like widows, breeding males sport very long tails but for the rest of the year resemble the duller females. The **pin-tailed whydah** (*Vidua macroura*) is an aggressive little bird that often drives other species from the bird table; the **long-tailed paradise whydah** (*Vidua paradisaea*) is a bushveld species that flaunts its tail streamers from treetops and power lines. The **red bishop** (*Euplectes oryx*) is a rotund little bird of marshy habitats, the breeding male puffing out his fluorescent scarlet plumage into a Day-Glo ball.

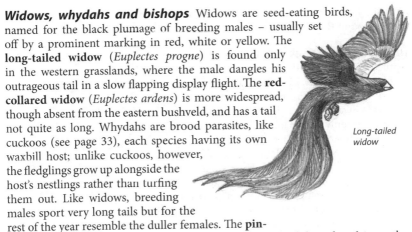

Long-tailed widow

REPTILES AND AMPHIBIANS Reptiles are not top of the average visitor's wish list. If you'd like to become better acquainted with these fascinating animals, however, Swaziland is a good place to start. Some 111 species have been recorded, including one endemic and two near-endemics, and all three main orders are represented: the Crocodylia (crocodiles), the Chelonia (turtles and tortoises) and the Squamata (lizards and snakes). Many species hide away in cracks, foliage or underground, but you're bound to spot a few – especially during summer, when they are more active. The following are among the better known and more conspicuous.

Nile crocodile (*Crocodylus niloticus*) This prehistoric predator is Africa's largest reptile, exceptionally reaching 5m in length and 1,000kg in weight. Its choice of prey changes as it matures, from small fish and amphibians when young to large mammals when fully mature. It launches its attack with a thrust of the powerful tail, dragging its victim underwater to drown in the grip of the strongest jaws known in the animal kingdom. Crocs also steal kills from other animals and happily tuck into carrion. Valved nostrils and a 'gular flap' at the back of the mouth enable them to seal off their airways and so feed underwater. Their slow metabolism means adults can go months without feeding.

Male crocodiles establish territories along a stretch of river. Females excavate a shallow sandbank nest in which they lay about 80 hard-shelled eggs. The temperature inside determines the sex of the hatchlings: below 31.7°C or above 34.5°C and they will be female. The youngsters hatch after three months, whereupon the female digs them out and carries them in her mouth to the shallows, guarding them until they are big enough to survive alone. Breeding sites in Swaziland are restricted to remote gorges in the Lubombos. Nonetheless, crocodiles are widespread in rivers and dams throughout the lowveld, and may travel more widely during the rainy season – even as far west as Maguga Dam on the Nkomati. Despite persecution and a natural wariness of people, these formidable predators claim a handful of human victims every year so it's best to keep back from the water's edge anywhere in the lowveld. The easiest crocs to see are those at Mkhaya and Mlilwane, which have been introduced to the dams.

Turtles and tortoises (Chelonians) What these
reptiles lack in speed they make up for in protective armour. The **leopard tortoise** (*Geochelone pardalis*) is the largest of three species in Swaziland, weighing up to 10kg, and is commonly seen in bushveld habitats during summer. Like all tortoises, it is vegetarian – feeding on plants and wild fruits – though will gnaw bones for their shell-building calcium. Its shell, fused to the skeleton, consists of the carapace on top and plastron below; you can identify males by a depression in the plastron that allows them to balance on the female while mating. Females bury their eggs in a pit. With their head retracted into the impregnable shell, adults are safe from most threats except fire, but various predators will happily snap up hatchlings. **Speke's hinged tortoise** (*Kinixys spekii*) is a smaller bushveld species that can be distinguished by its more flattened shell, with a hinged flap at the rear. The **serrated hinged terrapin** (*Pelusios sinuatus*) is an aquatic relative of tortoises, with a smoother shell. It inhabits bushveld rivers and dams, often sunning itself on logs or sandbars. Its diet includes fish, amphibians, carrion and some plant matter.

Leopard tortoise

Lizards Lizards form the largest group of reptiles in Africa. Like snakes, they have scaly skin that they shed regularly as they grow. Most have a long tail and four limbs; legless species are distinguished from snakes, like all lizards, by their external ear openings, moveable eyelids and the absence of enlarged belly scales. Many lizards can shed and regenerate their tail as a defensive strategy. The following are among the more conspicuous of Swaziland's approximately 44 species.

Monitors (Varanidae) These are Africa's largest lizards, with strong limbs, long claws, a whip-like tail and loose, beaded skin. The colourful patterns of juveniles fade with age. Monitors feed on anything from small animals to carrion, using their flickering forked tongue – like a snake's – to track down prey by scent. They swim well, climb trees and run with a bounding gait. They will also lash out with their tail and bite fiercely in self-defence. Two species occur in Swaziland. The **water monitor** (*Varanus niloticus*) may reach 2.2m, over half of which is tail. It lives near water, and is usually seen foraging at the bank or using its long oar-like tail to swim across the surface, head protruding. This species will steal crocodile eggs from an unattended nest. In spring, the female breaks into a termite mound and lays up to 60 eggs inside. The termites repair the damage, leaving the clutch to incubate in the humid warmth until they hatch with the following spring rains, the hatchlings breaking out through the damp soil. The **rock monitor** (*Varanus albigularis*) is a stockier species, seldom exceeding 1.5m, with a blunter snout and shorter tail. It occurs in rocky bushveld, where it inhabits rock crevices or large tree holes. Females generally dig their own nest hole but may also use a termite mound.

Rock-loving lizards Rock outcrops are hotspots for lizards and several families are specially adapted to this terrain. The **giant plated lizard** (*Gerrhosaurus validus*) is, at 60cm, Swaziland's largest lizard after the monitors, but has a flatter body

and a distinct fold of skin along each flank. When pursued, this shy creature will wedge itself into a crevice by inflating its body. The **Drakensberg crag lizard** (*Pseudocordylus melanotus*) is one of several similar, large-headed species that bask on top of rocks then dash for cover when disturbed. It is common at Malolotja, and easily identified by the male's bold black and orange patterning. The smaller **common flat lizard** (*Platysaurus intermedius*) belongs to the same family. Small colonies inhabit exfoliating granite outcrops in the central and southern bushveld, where they squeeze their flattened body into the narrowest of cracks. Breeding males flaunt a gaudy livery of red, blue, green and orange. The **southern tree agama** (*Acanthocerus atricollis*) is a chunky lizard with a thin tail and big triangular head. It often basks on rocks in the highveld but elsewhere is invariably seen on tree trunks. The male nods his bright-blue head vigorously in display and pursues his rivals in territorial battles. The duller female is well camouflaged against rough bark. Tree agamas are not poisonous – despite popular belief – but, when captured, gape their bright-orange mouth lining and bite fiercely. They feed mostly on ants.

Southern tree agama

Skinks (Scincidae) These small lizards generally have short legs, a long tail and a polished appearance. A few legless species live underground. The **variable skink** (*Trachylepis varia*) is among the most common lizards in Swaziland, at home in suburbia, and is identified by the white stripe along each flank. The more colourful **rainbow skink** (*Trachylepis margaritifer*) dashes around rocky outcrops, especially near rivers. Females and young have a striped body and electric-blue tail, while adult males are olive brown with a golden-yellow tail.

Geckos (Geckonidae) These unusual little lizards have jewel-like, lidless eyes, and miraculously adhesive toes, equipped with pads of hair-covered scales called scansors that allow them to grip surfaces as smooth and vertical as glass. Many species are nocturnal. The **tropical house gecko** (*Hemidactylus mabouia*) is the most widespread in Swaziland, though less common in the highveld. It often feeds around buildings, snapping up insects drawn to electric lights. The **Cape dwarf gecko** (*Lygodactylus capensis*) is a smaller houseguest, found in the east, and feeds by day, picking off ants from their trails. The **giant Swazi flat gecko** (*Pachydactylus bibronii*) is a large (150cm) nocturnal gecko with a diagnostic 'W' marking on the back of its head. Confined to rock outcrops in the northwest, notably around Maguga Dam, this threatened species is Swaziland's only endemic reptile.

Chameleons (Chamaeleonidae) Widely feared in African folklore, these slow-moving lizards are completely harmless. Adaptation to life in the trees has furnished them with various bizarre characteristics: a flattened body adorned with leaf-like flaps and crests; long legs, opposable toes and a prehensile tail for gripping flimsy foliage; conical eyes that focus independently on prey; and a sticky tongue that shoots out twice the body length to capture insects. Last, but not least, the famous colour changing – achieved by the rapid compression of pigment cells called chromatophores – provides versatile camouflage, and also expresses distress or arousal. Chameleons are often seen crossing roads by day (sadly, their trembling-leaf act is of little use against the wheels of a truck), and after dark glow eerily white in torchlight. The **flap-neck chameleon** (*Chamaeleo dilepis*) is the region's largest and best-known species, and is common everywhere but the highveld. It feeds primarily on beetles and grasshoppers but must itself avoid predatory birds and snakes – notably boomslangs.

Flap-neck chameleon

Females dig a small pit in which they lay up to 50 small eggs. The **Swazi dwarf chameleon** (*Bradypodion transvalense*) is smaller and more elongated. It is restricted to the highveld, where you may spot one clinging to a fence or overhead wire.

Snakes (Serpentes)

Snakes, along with lizards, make up the squamates order of reptiles. They differ from most lizards in having no legs, and also lack eyelids and external ears. All are carnivores, and can dislocate their lower jaw in order to swallow prey. Other neat adaptations include a retractable tongue that flicks in and out to 'taste' the air and, in some species, venom with which to subdue prey. Snakes move by pushing their S-shaped coils against bumps in the ground, though heavy species such as the puff adder and python may employ 'rectilinear motion', using their belly scales to push forward in a straight line. The very idea of snakes unsettles many people, but these sensitive reptiles pick up the vibration of your footsteps and generally slither off long before you see them. Only seven of Swaziland's 61 species are potentially dangerous to humans and even these few do their best to avoid us. Snake sightings are rare and usually brief.

Southern African python (*Python natalensis*) This is the region's largest snake, exceptionally reaching 5m – although smaller youngsters are more often seen. It is widespread throughout the lowveld and middleveld but absent from the cool highveld. Whatever its size, you can identify a python by the muscular body, long head and ornate camouflage. It hunts by ambush, seizing prey in sharp teeth and throwing its coils around it. Death comes from asphyxiation, not crushing, and the victim is swallowed immediately, starting with the head. A big meal takes months to digest. Prey ranges from rodents to antelope. Prime habitat is bushveld, often near water – into which pythons may retreat when disturbed – and around rock outcrops. A female lays up to 50 round eggs. Though not venomous, pythons defend themselves vigorously and can inflict nasty wounds with their sharp teeth.

Cobras and mambas (Elapidae) The elapid family contains Africa's most feared snakes. All deserve a healthy respect. Cobras are known for their impressive habit of rearing up and spreading a hood when threatened. They hunt at night for small vertebrates such as mice and birds. The **Mozambique spitting cobra** (*Naja mossambica*) is common in Swaziland and, along with the puff adder, responsible for the most serious snakebites. It can spray its venom up to 3m in defence, which causes excruciating pain if it enters the eyes – though immediate bathing in clean water prevents lasting damage. The **snouted cobra** (*Naja annulifera*) is a larger, stockier snake that

Mozambique spitting cobra

The sight of a snake often provokes hysteria. Swaziland is home to only seven species known to have caused human fatalities, however, all of which do their best to avoid people. Meanwhile, many snakes play an important ecological role in controlling rodents and are thus an ally to the farmer. At least 20 times more people in southern Africa die from lightning strikes than from snakebites, and snakebite victims are invariably rural villagers, not tourists. So don't panic. Rather, take simple precautions, like wearing closed shoes in the bush, watching where you put your hands and feet (don't rummage for firewood after dark) and, of course, not messing with any snake you find. The most common circumstance in which people are bitten is when attempting to kill a snake. In the rare event of a bite, get urgent medical help. Meanwhile lie the victim down, and keep them still and calm. Avoid aspirins. Never apply a tourniquet or cut an incision (see *Snakebite*, page 119).

Remember: snakebite is not the same as envenomation. Most snakes can bite, and the trauma of being bitten – even by a harmless species – may produce phantom poisoning symptoms. Envenomation occurs only when venom enters the bloodstream. Few bites from venomous snakes prove fatal. Often no venom is injected at all – this is known as a 'dry bite'. There are three principal kinds of venom: cytotoxic venom, found in vipers, causes blood vessel and tissue damage; neurotoxic venom, found in mambas, acts on the nervous system to cause paralysis; haemotoxic venom, found in boomslangs, prevents blood from clotting. Antivenom is specific to different snakes so it helps if you can identify the culprit. But never take a risk.

can reach 2.5m and varies in colour from dull yellow to brown. This uncommon bushveld species is highly venomous. The **rinkhals** (*Hemachatus haemachatus*) is a highveld snake, identified by its black-and-white colouration. Not a true cobra, it can nonetheless spread a hood and spit its venom, and may even sham dead in an effort to fool its attacker. The **black mamba** (*Dendroaspis polylepis*) is the longest venomous snake in Africa, averaging 2.5m but exceptionally exceeding 3.5m, and has inspired more fearful folklore than any other. It is not black but grey/brown, with a long, narrow head and prominent eyebrow ridges that give it an angry expression. Mambas can move very fast, usually away from the intruder, but if cornered will rear high and hiss menacingly, exposing their black mouth lining. Their neurotoxic venom can cause death through respiratory failure unless treated immediately with antivenom, but bites are rare. Black mambas are reasonably common in eastern Swaziland and penetrate west along major river valleys. They hole up in a termite mound, hollow log or abandoned building and hunt by day for rodents. Contrary to popular belief – and it being the name of a local football team – the arboreal **green mamba** (*Dendroaspis angusticeps*) is absent from Swaziland.

Typical snakes (Colubridae) The colubrid family of 'typical' snakes comprises over half of southern Africa's species and is well represented in Swaziland. The **mole snake** (*Pseudaspis cana*) is a large constrictor, common in the highveld, that hunts moles and rodents underground. The **brown house snake** (*Lamprophis fuliginosus*) is also a constrictor and does a similarly useful job. This attractive, red-brown species has a python-like head, though seldom reaches more than 70cm long. The **spotted bush snake** (*Philothamnus semivariegatus*) is at home in the trees, where it uses camouflage and agility to hunt prey such as geckos and frogs. With its large eyes this species is often mistaken for a boomslang (see below). The closely related **green water snake** (*Philothamnus hoplogaster*) prefers aquatic habitats, where it hunts for frogs and birds. The larger **olive grass snake** (*Psammophis mossambicus*) is sometimes confused with the black mamba because of its speed, colour and length (up to 1.5m), but is only moderately venomous. The harmless **common egg-eater** (*Dasypeltis scabra*) is remarkable on two counts: first, it can swallow an egg three times the size of its head – working its mouth slowly over the prize until the shell is pierced by the 'gular tooth', a projecting vertebra in the throat, and the contents swallowed; second, its markings mimic those of the venomous night adder, and it can even imitate an adder's hiss by rubbing its coils together.

Boomslang and vine snake Though few colubrids are seriously venomous, there are two significant exceptions. The **boomslang** (*Dispholidus typus*) has one of the most potent venoms of any snake (though it took the death of a top Chicago herpetologist in 1957 to discover this). This common species has large eyes and grows up to 1.3m. Females are brown and males leaf green. It uses excellent vision to capture birds and reptiles in the branches, and often raids weaver nests. Its haemotoxic venom is potentially lethal, but its fangs are set too far back to get much purchase on a human and bites are very rare. The **vine snake** (*Thelotornis capensis*) is also arboreal, back-fanged and possessed of a potent haemotoxic venom. Its pointed head and thin, twig-like body are perfect camouflage among the branches, where it often freezes for concealment.

Puff adder (*Bitis arietans*) Vipers are venomous snakes with a large head and long, hinged fangs that swing forward in striking. The puff adder is the largest and most common species in Swaziland, found right across the country, and is responsible for more serious bites than any other snake in southern Africa. Fat and sluggish, this ground-dweller opts for camouflage over flight and so bites tend to occur when people tread on one by accident. When disturbed, it hisses threateningly – hence the 'puff' in the name. Look out for the flat, triangular head and bold chevron pattern. Large specimens may exceed a metre in length. Puff adders hunt by night for small vertebrates, striking from a hidden position then tracking down their prey by scent as the venom takes effect. Their habit of basking on warm

Puff adder

roads, especially during the rains, can prove their undoing. This species gives birth to live young – usually 30–40, although one litter of 156 in Kenya is the world record for any snake.

Frogs Amphibians differ from reptiles in having smooth, permeable skin, which they must keep moist in order to absorb oxygen, and by starting life in an aquatic larval stage (ie: as a tadpole). They are represented in Swaziland by 44 species of frog. Most hide in damp retreats by day and come out after dark to feed on invertebrates, which they capture with a long sticky tongue. All have big eyes for hunting at night and large tympana (eardrums) for tuning in to courtship calls. Eggs (frogspawn) are usually laid in water, although some species use a moist burrow or nest. Frogs are best located by their voice, and wetlands after dark often resound to a chorus of croaks, barks and whistles as males compete over breeding

territory. The trained ear can identify each species by call: the
bubbling kassina (*Kassina senegalensis*) for instance has
a loud liquid '*quoip*', like a heavy drop of rainwater; the
brown-backed treefrog (*Leptopelis mossambicus*) barks its
spasmodic '*yack-yack*' from a tree; and the **painted reedfrog**
(*Hyperolius marmoratus*) generates a shrill whistling from
reedbeds.

Painted reedfrog

Frogs have many adaptations to suit their differing lifestyles.
Treefrogs use adhesive suckers on their fingers and toes to clamber up any surface –
even glass. The **foam nest treefrog** (*Chiromantis xerampelina*) deposits its eggs on a
branch in a mucus ball, which it whips into a frothy meringue-like 'nest' with its back
legs. Inside, the eggs stay moist and develop into tadpoles, which then plop down
into the water below. The **guttural toad** (*Bufo gutturalis*) is a widespread species
that often waddles around buildings at night, snapping up insects attracted by the
light. The **bushveld rainfrog** (*Breviceps adspersus*) is a short-limbed, rotund little
frog with a face squashed like a tiny Pekinese dog; it remains underground through
the dry season in a cocoon of mucus before re-emerging with the rains to feed and
breed. By contrast, the **common platana** (*Xenopus laevis*) is almost totally aquatic,
with a slimy skin and feeble forelimbs that are useless on land, but large clawed feet
that enable it to propel itself underwater with powerful kicks. Among several rare
highveld species, the **Natal ghost frog** (*Heleophryne natalensis*) is restricted to fast-
flowing streams, where tadpoles cling to rocks using sucker mouths.

FRESHWATER FISHES Some 54 indigenous freshwater fish species are recorded
from Swaziland. This is generally of more interest to the angler than the average
wildlife watcher, as you are unlikely to meet most of them other than on the end
of a hook. Nonetheless, it is further evidence of the rich diversity of Swaziland's
aquatic habitats.

At the tiddlers end of the scale, the **threespot barb** (*Barbus trimaculatus*) is the
most common of several barb species, reaching some 15cm, and is distinguished by
its dorsal spine and three prominent spots on each flank. Much larger, at 40cm or so,
is the **Mozambique tilapia** (*Oreochromis mossambicus*), a chunky species with red-
tinged fins that is found in all major river systems and is an important protein source
for local communities. The **sharptooth catfish** (*Clarias gariepinus*) is the largest of
several catfish species, reaching 1.4m, and feeds on the bottom in still waters, using
tentacle-like barbels around its mouth to detect food in the murk. The **Swaziland
rock catlet** (*Chiloglanis emarginatus*) is a much smaller catfish, just 7cm, which uses
a sucker-like mouth to anchor itself to rocks in rapids. The **longfin eel** (*Anguilla
mossambica*) breeds at sea and migrates back up rivers to mature, although dams
prove a major obstacle to its dispersal upriver. The **tigerfish** (*Hydrocynus vittatus*) is
a large, predatory species with impressive teeth and a serious fan base among sport
anglers. It is found around Big Bend, notably in Sivunga and Van Eck dams, and in
the nearby Usutu River. A number of exotic species, including
rainbow trout (*Oncorhynchus mykiss*) and **largemouth
bass** (*Micropterus salmoides*), have
been introduced to Swaziland to
provide sport for anglers. These
disrupt natural ecosystems and
join numerous other factors –
from dam building to industrial run-
off – that pose a threat to native fish.

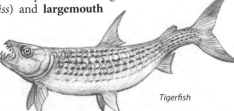
Tigerfish

45

INVERTEBRATES Rhinos and mambas may steal the headlines, but Swaziland's wildlife is actually at its most prolific lower down the scale where, munching through the vegetation, tunnelling into the ground and swarming through the skies, invertebrates form the engine room of the great food pyramid. This account describes just a few of the better-known creepy-crawlies you may encounter.

Lower invertebrates Numerous primitive animals fall into this broad bracket, and you are bound to see a few of the more obvious. Largest of Swaziland's molluscs is the huge **African land snail** (*Achatina fulica*), whose 15cm-long shells litter the bushveld. The **freshwater crab** is a scavenging crustacean that may move around by land during wet conditions. **Millipedes** are vegetarians that belong to the subphylum Myriapoda. They trundle along on a twinkling forest of tiny legs – their local name *lishongololo* means 'steam train' – and roll into a tight ball when disturbed. A millipede's body comprises some 60 segments, with two pairs of legs on each. **Centipedes**, by contrast, have only one pair on each of their 25 body segments, and are nocturnal predators of insects and other small animals. Some large centipedes (Scolopendromorpha) have a very painful bite, so you should heed the warning in their orange colouration. Female centipedes curl around their young to protect them, showing more parental care than many vertebrates.

Spiders and scorpions (Arachnida) Arachnids differ from insects not only in having eight legs but also in their lack of antennae and their two- rather than three-part body. Most spiders possess some kind of venom but none in Swaziland poses a threat to people. Among the more conspicuous are **golden orb-web spiders** (*Nephila* species), which string large cat's-cradle webs of yellow silk between bushveld trees. The big black-and-yellow female usually sits at the centre, waiting for a catch. These webs are so strong that even small birds are sometimes ensnared. **Kite spiders** (*Gasteracantha* species), whose spiny, triangular abdomens look like something from *Star Wars*, also build an orb web, and can be very common in forest habitats. **Baboon spiders** (*Harpactira* species) are large, hairy spiders – like African tarantulas – that lurk down silk-lined tunnels, from where they ambush prey when alerted by its footfalls. **Rain spiders** (*Palystes* species) chase down their prey, and often hunt around houses at night. **Sun spiders** (Solifugae) belong to a different order from spiders and are not venomous. These large, hairy hunters often dash around the campfire after dark, despatching prey such as beetles with an audible crunch of their impressive jaws. **Scorpions** (Scorpiones) keep their venom in the sting on their tail; the fearsome-looking pincers at the front are simply for grabbing and, in some species, digging. All scorpions can deliver

Sun spider

a painful sting but none of Swaziland's 12 or so species is dangerous to humans; in general, those with thin pincers and a thick tail pack a more potent sting than those with the opposite. Scorpions venture out at night from their hiding places in search of prey, which they detect on air currents using tiny sensory body hairs. Mating partners lock pincers in a courtship pirouette, and a female carries her newborn young on her back.

Ticks (Ixodida), like spiders and scorpions, are arachnids. They are also the strongest disincentive to wearing shorts in the bush, especially in long grass. These tiny parasites wait on grass tips and clamber aboard animals that brush past. Once on, they pierce the skin and gorge themselves on the host's blood, swelling up like

The San once trusted their survival to finding and interpreting the clues that animals leave behind. Today, some awareness of these clues will greatly enrich your own wildlife experience. Here are a few to look for.

TRACKS Any animal that touches the ground leaves tracks. The clearest are laid on surfaces that hold an impression, such as firm mud or damp sand. Early morning is the best time to look: the tracks are still fresh, and the low-angled light throws any imprint into sharper relief. Some tracks are unmistakable: a zebra's are horseshoe shaped; an elephant's are round and dinner-plate sized, the hind feet smaller and more oval than the forefeet. Rhinos (both species) have a three-toed cloverleaf shape, while hippos, a similar size, show four toes. Cloven-hoofed ungulates are told apart by size and shape, with a giraffe's huge steam-iron prints spaced far apart by its long stride. Among predators, look for evidence of claws: cats don't show them; dogs and hyenas do. A hyena also has its toes curved and squashed together, as though from a too-tight shoe. Monkeys show five digits, like handprints, with the thumb/big toe clearly visible. Among larger reptiles, a crocodile shows five toes on the forefeet, four toes on the back feet and a heavy tail furrow; monitor lizards show long-clawed tracks either side of a wavy tail dragline; most snakes leave S-shaped ripples, but pythons and puff adders can move caterpillar-fashion, leaving a broad, straight furrow that shows belly scales.

DROPPINGS An elephant's dung is, again, unmistakable: fibrous, football-sized and widely scattered. Rhinos pile up theirs in deep middens: a white rhino's, fine and grassy in texture; a black rhino's full of twigs. Hippo dung is scattered high over vegetation beside trails. A buffalo's falls in loose folded 'pats', like cattle's. Antelope leave neat piles of small pellets; many use communal dung heaps. A giraffe's are similar – surprisingly small, but scattered by the height of their fall. A zebra's are kidney shaped, as are a warthog's, but smaller. Predator 'scats' are cylindrical, often twisted at one end, and smellier than herbivore dung: a hyena's turns chalky white due to its bone content; a civet's are heaped in a midden and contain fur, berries and bits of millipede; an otter's contain crushed crab shell and are deposited on prominent rocks.

OTHER CLUES Good trackers will find numerous other clues that reveal the presence or passing of animals. Holes are often worth investigating – or at least watching. Tree holes may contain nesting birds, such as hornbills or hoopoes, or roosting nocturnal animals such as bushbabies. Holes in the ground, often dug by aardvarks, may harbour warthogs or porcupines (look for signs of occupation, such as porcupine quills), while holes in a termite mound may house mongooses, monitor lizards or even a black mamba. Vegetation can also be a giveaway, from the flattened grass of a reedbuck bedding spot to the shiny 'rubbing post' used by itchy rhinos or warthogs. Look for feeding signs, too: freshly broken branches are the work of elephants, while bushes frayed and nibbled at head height may be kudu and bark stripped around the foot of a tree probably means porcupines. Equally distinctive are an aardvark's excavations in a termite mound, a bush pig's diggings on a forest trail or the small overturned stones left by a troop of baboons.

Background Information   WILDLIFE

peas. Different species choose different hosts: cattle and dog ticks infest domestic livestock, and the minuscule, red 'pepper ticks' that plague hikers are their larvae. Some species transmit diseases (see page 118). The common form of 'tick-bite fever' is not dangerous but unpleasant. Ticks can be discouraged with insecticide spray and removed by carefully pinching them out, taking care not to leave the mouthparts embedded. Oxpeckers (see page 38) have honed this to a fine art and, with up to 20,000 ticks being recorded on a single giraffe, they're seldom short of a meal.

Insects Insects differ from other invertebrates in their three-segmented body (head, thorax and abdomen), three pairs of legs and – in most cases – two pairs of wings. They are the most abundant life form on earth, with at least 80,000 species identified in southern Africa, of which Swaziland has plenty. To many, insects are simply pests, and certainly the likes of head lice, cockroaches and mosquitoes do not always endear themselves to us. However, they are integral to a healthy environment, whether as pollinators (bees, flies, butterflies), waste-disposal agents (dung beetles, termites, blowfly larvae) or providers of such precious natural resources as silk and honey.

Insects fall into 26 different orders, with a bewildering variety of families and lifestyles. Some, such as **dragonflies** (Odonata), are predators, dashing around their wetland territories and capturing other insects in flight. The larvae of **antlions** (Myrmeleontidae) are ambush specialists: they dig a conical pit in loose sand – a common sight in the lowveld – wait for their ant prey to stumble in then seize it in powerful jaws. **Praying mantids** (Mantodea) hunt using stealth and camouflage: they clasp their lethal forelegs together as if in prayer, before snatching out at victims – often around lights, after dark. **Crickets and grasshoppers** (Orthoptera) are vegetarians, not hunters. They have powerful hind legs for leaping, and proclaim their territory with bleats and chirrups, produced by rubbing various body parts rhythmically together. **Stick insects** (Phasmatodea) are also vegetarians, and their bodies exactly mimic a twig or grass stem. Like mantids and grasshoppers, many flash bold markings on their hind wings to confuse an attacker. **Cicadas** (Cicadidae), like all true bugs (Hemiptera), use piercing mouthparts to suck juices from plants. Nymphs may take years to develop underground. Adults live for only a fortnight or so, during which time males attract mates with their ear-splitting zinging call, created by the rapid vibration of their hollow abdomen.

Beetles (Celoeoptera) This is the largest order in the animal kingdom, with over 18,000 species recorded in southern Africa alone. All beetles have biting mouthparts and forewings modified into hardened cases (elytra). **Ground beetles** (Carabidae) are wingless predators that chase down their prey by sight. **Blister beetles** (Meloidae) are day-flying vegetarians that congregate on flowers, and whose bright colours warn that they pack a noxious defensive spray. **Fireflies** (Lampyridae) are beetles (not flies) of the cantheroid group, the adults of which light up their abdomen using bioluminescence to attract a mate. **Dung beetles** (Scarabaeinae) are chunky black or brown beetles that pile into fresh animal droppings and roll away balls of dung, often battling violently in their haste to secure the prize. Inside these 'brood balls' a female lays her eggs. One ball can be 40 times the

Dung beetle

weight of its roller. Some species eschew the rolling and simply lay their eggs right under the mound. Either way, these insects are vital to soil fertility.

Flies and mosquitoes (Diptera) Flies may not be popular but, as with many so-called 'pests', they perform vital ecological services such as waste disposal and pollination. Their mouthparts are adapted to feeding on liquid matter, which they digest outside the body. Among numerous varieties are predators such as **robber flies** (Asilidae), which snatch other insects in flight, nectar-feeders such as **hoverflies** (Syrphidae), which sup from flowers, and carrion-eaters such as **blowflies** (Calliphoridae), which lay their eggs in carcasses so that their larvae can feast on the rotting flesh. Unfortunately some flies spread disease. The most serious in this respect are **mosquitoes** (Culicidae). Although primarily nectar-feeders, females also suck blood from vertebrate hosts and it is females of the *Anopheles* genus – identified by a body angled downward at rest – that are responsible for transmitting malaria, estimated to kill more than a million people in Africa each year. Malaria is caused by a microscopic parasite in the mosquito's saliva. It occurs in eastern Swaziland (see page 112), although recent records are negligible.

Butterflies and moths (Lepidoptera) Gaudy and fond of flowers, butterflies are the hippies of the insect world and enjoy a better press than moths. In fact, there is little distinction between the two. Broadly, butterflies are day-flying insects with thin, clubbed antennae that hold their wings vertically at rest, whereas moths are night-flying insects with feathery antennae that fold their wings down flat. Adults of both uncoil a long proboscis to sup on nectar, sap and fruit juices. Their eggs hatch into voracious caterpillars that develop into pupae, from which new adults emerge. Moth pupae are often encased in a silk cocoon. Among Swaziland's more prominent butterfly species are the **yellow pansy** (*Junonia hierta*), which displays distinctive purple spots when sunning its black-and-orange wings; the **African monarch** (*Danaus chrysippus*), which is toxic to predators, and says so with a bold black, white and orange warning pattern; and the **citrus swallowtail** (*Papilio demodocus*), which flutters around flower borders and whose caterpillars resemble bird droppings. Look out, too, for the **brown-veined white** (*Belenois aurota*), which gathers by the millions in mass migrations that sometimes pass through Swaziland. There are many more species of moth than butterfly. Among the more distinctive are **emperor moths** (Saturnidae), with their broad wings (up to 15cm across), bold eye markings and, in some species, long tails; and the dashing **hawk moths** (Sphingidae) with their solid body and delta-shaped wings.

Termites (Isoptera) These primitive insects are unrelated to ants, with which they are often confused, but are similarly social creatures that have evolved many similarities. Most species form colonies, in which soldiers protect the nest, workers care for young and forage for food, and a single queen lays eggs. All are plant-eaters: some carry micro-organisms in their gut to digest cellulose; others cultivate a fungus (*Termitomyces*) to do this job for them. The mound-building termites belong to the Macrotermitidae family and you can see the enormous monuments of their industry all over Swaziland. Each is a complex multi-chambered structure, with numerous dedicated cells – including the queen's royal cell, in which she produces up to 30,000 eggs a day – and an ingenious air-conditioning system that allows the termites to maintain the 100% humidity and constant temperature of 29–31°C required to produce eggs and young. After rains, the queen produces a reproductive caste of winged males and females – called imagos – which set out in mass 'emergences' to mate, disperse and establish new nests. Although termites damage timber and crops, they also do essential work in draining, enriching and aerating the soil.

Ants (*Formicidae*) Ants belong to a more advanced order (Hymenoptera) than termites, with a larval and pupal stage. Some live in huge underground colonies. Others form smaller colonies inside hollow acacia thorns or build their nests in trees. Each colony contains one queen and many wingless workers, some of which are soldiers responsible for defence. **Driver ants** (Dorylinae) swarm over large areas in a relentless quest for food, devouring any prey unable to escape; **myrmicine ants** (Myrmicinae) produce their own food by 'farming' aphids inside their nests, stimulating them to produce honeydew (excreted plant sap) for their larvae. Threats are repelled with bites, stings or – in **formicine ants** (Formicinae) – a spray of formic acid.

Wasps and bees These day-flying insects are closely related to ants. Female wasps of many species use their modified ovipositor (egg-laying organ) to inflict a powerful sting in self-defence. This lethal weapon is also used by parasitic species, such as **spider-hunting wasps** (Pompilidae), to paralyse prey, which they feed to their carnivorous young. Other wasps, such as **potter wasps** and **paper wasps**,

THE BIGGER PICTURE

Conservation in Swaziland has acquired a broader regional dimension, courtesy of the Lubombo Transfrontier Conservation and Resource Area. The concept of Transfrontier Conservation Areas (TFCAs) in southern Africa arose during the 1990s, and these areas now receive funding and support from the South Africa-based Peace Parks Foundation. The aim is to establish a network of protected ecosystems across international borders, enabling sustainable conservation while also improving life for communities in the region.

The Lubombo TFCA is one of ten in southern Africa. It straddles South Africa's KwaZulu-Natal province, southern Mozambique and Swaziland, and covers a total of 4,195km², extending from the Malolotja/Songimvelo highlands in the northwest to the Indian Ocean in the east and Lake St Lucia Wetlands in the south. Within its orbit is the globally significant Maputaland Centre of Endemism and five Ramsar sites. Among numerous wildlife highlights are Africa's southernmost population of hippos and crocodiles, breeding leatherback turtles, significant numbers of both rhino species, and the last naturally occurring elephant populations of KwaZulu-Natal and southern Mozambique, whose ancient cross-border migration routes may be restored. The area's rich cultural heritage also includes the birthplace of the Zulu and Swazi nations, and ancient archaeological sites.

The project began with the signing of the Lubombo Transfrontier Trilateral Protocol between the three countries at the World Economic Forum Summit on 22 June 2000. South Africa's conservation authorities have since been working with the SNTC and the Mozambique Ministry of Tourism to establish the five separate transfrontier conservation areas that make up the TFCA, of which four extend into Swaziland. These areas are as follows:

LUBOMBO CONSERVANCY–GOBA TFCA (Mozambique/Swaziland): Brings together Swaziland's Lubombo Conservancy (see *Chapter 7*, page 255) with the Goba construct nests for their young, working with mud and wood pulp respectively to create delicate multi-celled apartment structures. **Bees** (Apoidea), unlike most wasps, feed their young on nectar and pollen, helping pollinate plants in the process. Some, such as the hole-drilling **carpenter bees** (Xylocopinae), are solitary. Others, such as the **honeybee** (*Apis mellifera*), are colonial. A honeybee colony, often located in a tree hole, may house thousands of individuals. Female workers collect food and maintain the colony, while males mate with the queen who lays her eggs in the wax cells. Though wild honey is a great delicacy, honeybees can be extremely dangerous when their nest is threatened.

CONSERVATION IN SWAZILAND
Swaziland offers a case study of the challenges and compromises involved in African conservation. Trying to safeguard a shrinking natural environment in the face of ever burgeoning human pressures has been a process of trial and error. All things considered, it's remarkable – and a tribute to those involved – how much of this environment remains.

Conservation history
In the pre-colonial past, the kingdom had a large, free-roaming population of big game. By the turn of the 20th century, hunting had already taken a heavy toll. To protect what remained, the colonial authorities declared two reserves in the lowveld: Hlatikulu (1905) and Lubombo (1907).

section across the border in Mozambique. Protects precious Lubombo ecosystems, with endemic flora, and nurtures Swazi cultural values. Situated on the eastern route between the Kruger National Park and KwaZulu Natal and already offers numerous accommodation options.

SONGIMVELO–MALOLOTJA TFCA (South Africa/Swaziland): Links the Songimvelo Game Reserve in South Africa with the adjacent Malolotja Nature Reserve, Makhonjwa Mountains and Phophonyane Conservancy in Swaziland, to preserve some of the most impressive landscapes and important ecosystems of the eastern Drakensberg escarpment. Includes the Barberton Centre of Endemism.

USUTHU–TEMBE–FUTI TFCA (Swaziland/South Africa/Mozambique): In South Africa, links Tembe Elephant Park and Ndumo Game Reserve. In Mozambique, focuses on the Maputo Special Reserve and the Futi corridor, a swamp system that links the reserve with Tembe. Recently extended to include the Usutu area in Swaziland (see page 297).

NSUBANE–PONGOLA TFCA (South Africa/Swaziland): Centres on the Pongolapoort Dam (Jozini Dam), which straddles Swaziland and South Africa. In South Africa, incorporates the Pongola Nature Reserve and adjoining private game farms and community areas. Swaziland portion currently remains as undeveloped ranch land, following the shelving of the 'Jozini Big Six' project (see box on page 285).

PONTA DO OURO–KOSI BAY TFCA (Mozambique/South Africa): Links two coastal regions either side of the Mozambique/South Africa border, with rich marine, wetland and dune forest ecosystems. Does not involve Swaziland.

However, a 1917 outbreak of the livestock disease *nagana* (sleeping sickness, caused by tsetse flies) led to a misguided programme to eradicate all large grazing animals and by 1922 both reserves had gone. Over the next three decades Swaziland's last herds of game gradually petered out.

Enter Ted Reilly, founder of modern conservation in Swaziland. Born in 1938 on the family farm at Mlilwane (see page 180), he set out to save the nation's wildlife. In 1960 he conducted a nationwide survey and concluded that two areas – Hlane and Malolotja – should be made into reserves. The British authorities were not interested, on the grounds that abundant wildlife watching was already available on South African game reserves just outside Swaziland. King Sobhuza, however, proved more receptive, allowing Reilly to capture game from around the country and transport it to Mlilwane, initially as a kind of secure holding pen. Soon Mlilwane started admitting visitors. In 1966 it was declared Swaziland's first game sanctuary, under the Game Act of 1953, and Reilly was appointed royal advisor on conservation. In 1967, under Sobhuza's instructions, he set out to turn Hlane into a reserve. The ensuing forceful removal of poachers caused such uproar that the king was forced to step in and explain the importance of the project to the nation. With Hlane secured, game was reintroduced from Mlilwane and from elsewhere in southern Africa.

In 1972 Reilly and his wife Liz were among the founders of the **Swaziland National Trust Commission** (SNTC), a government body with responsibility for safeguarding the nation's natural heritage. The SNTC undertook another survey of areas in need of protection, which endorsed the proclamation of Malolotja Nature Reserve in 1977. Mlawula followed in 1980 (on the site of the old Lubombo reserve) then Hawane in 1992 and Mantenga in 1994. The SNTC also took over cultural heritage sites, such as the National Museum and King Sobhuza Memorial Park.

Reilly, meanwhile, had continued to run Mlilwane as a private, self-funding nature reserve. In 1978/79 he also bought Mkhaya (see page 277) – originally to protect Swaziland's last indigenous Nguni cattle but in 1985 declared a game reserve and developed as a refuge for endangered species. By now, however, his relationship with the SNTC had deteriorated – exacerbated by what he perceived as mismanagement of conservation priorities. Things came to a head with the 'rhino wars' of the late 1980s (see box on page 14), when the SNTC proved unable to combat the slaughter of Swaziland's rhinos. Reilly resigned from the SNTC and re-launched his own organisation as **Big Game Parks** (BGP). He also persuaded King Mswati III (who remains like his father before him, a supporter of Reilly) to amend the Game Act, boosting the powers of conservation authorities, with stiffer sentences for poachers and rights for rangers caught in life-threatening circumstances to defend themselves – lethally, if necessary.

The success of a newly empowered Big Game Parks persuaded the king to transfer responsibility for the Game Act from SNTC to the King's Office and then delegate its implementation to BGP. This unusual step – effectively outsourcing law enforcement to a private body – was contentious then and remains so today. But it was a measure of the respect that Reilly's long-standing commitment to Swaziland's conservation had earned him.

Conservation today
Today Swaziland's most important protected areas can be divided largely between those managed by Big Game Parks and those managed by the SNTC, with a number of smaller private reserves and game farms in between. BGP has proved most successful in restoring Swaziland's large mammals, the reintroduction of the likes of rhinos having largely proved too difficult for the SNTC.

But protecting big game is not the only object of conservation, and all agencies – private or otherwise – are engaged in a more fundamental battle: to save the nation's natural habitats. The biggest threat to Swaziland's native fauna and flora today is the loss of these habitats, either by degradation or conversion to other forms of land use. The enemies in this battle are more powerful than any poachers: overgrazing by livestock causes devastating erosion and damage to plant life; non-native plantations replace indigenous plant communities and deplete biodiversity; toxic run-off from agriculture and industry poisons rivers; the sprawl of development eats up habitat; and invasive species – from plants such as chromoleana and lantana to animals such as rainbow trout – overwhelm native species, fatally skewing the ecological balance.

In the face of such threats, Swaziland's reserves are precious indeed. At present Swaziland has 17 protected conservation areas, each described at length in Part Two of this book. Meanwhile, work continues at all levels to protect Swaziland's wider environment for future generations. Nationally, the SNTC works alongside private outfits such as Big Game Parks to manage protected areas and educate the community. Internationally, Swaziland falls within cross-border initiatives, such as the TFCAs (see *The bigger picture*, page 50), which aim to shore up the kingdom's biodiversity in a regional context. And locally, grass-roots, community-based organisations are working to encourage the sustainable use of resources and protect Swaziland's environment from exploitation. Respect for the environment is, after all, rooted in Swazi culture: indigenous plants have long been harvested sustainably for their medicinal properties, for instance, while the annual national hunt (*Butimba*) requires the preservation of wild bush for its wildlife.

The scientists have also been at work: **Swaziland's National Biodiversity Strategy and Action Plan** was launched in April 2001, with a multi-pronged approach to tackling the erosion of Swaziland's biodiversity. And, as a visitor, you are also doing your bit. A high proportion of Swaziland's visitors come to see its wildlife or enjoy its natural beauty. This makes a significant contribution to the economy – not just in fees to reserves but also via all the tourism spin-offs such as employment. It provides a huge incentive for Swazis to protect the natural riches with which the country has been so lavishly blessed.

HISTORY

There have been people in Swaziland for almost long as our species has occupied the planet. It is impossible to make sense of the kingdom's recent history, however, without delving into that of South Africa. Indeed, the 19th-century struggles between Boer, Brit and Zulu – among others – were the crucible in which the nation of Swaziland was forged. And South Africa's bitter racial divisions during the 20th century were the backdrop against which modern Swaziland came to define itself. The following account, therefore, makes no apologies for spending some of its time over the border.

EARY DAYS Some of the earliest known hominid remains, including those of our proto-hominid ancestor *Australopithecus*, have been discovered in South Africa. That such fossils have not been found in Swaziland may simply reflect a lack of the limestone in which they might have been preserved, but a human skull at least 100,000 years old has been found close to the Swazi border in KwaZulu-Natal. This individual was most likely an immediate ancestor of the Khoisan, the indigenous peoples of southern Africa.

Although fossils may be in short supply, there is plenty of other evidence of Swaziland's prehistoric inhabitants. Hand axes and other stone artefacts date back to the Early Stone Age, some 200,000 years ago. Stone spears, arrowheads and other more advanced tools represent the Middle Stone Age, which lasted until around 35,000 years ago. This was when people first started using fire, both for heat and cooking, and took to living in caves. The most impressive evidence of the Middle Stone Age in Swaziland is Ngwenya Mine in Malolotja (see page 203), where haematite ore was mined at least 41,000–43,000 years ago, making this the oldest known mine in the world. This was long before the advent of smelting, and the ore was used for ritual cosmetic purposes and rock art.

More sophisticated tools and rock art dating back to at least 25,000BC are evidence of the Late Stone Age, when the Khoisan people occupied the kingdom. 'Khoisan' lumps together two distinct groups: the Khoi became pastoralists and spread south around the coast; the San – known colloquially as 'bushmen' – pursued a nomadic hunter-gatherer lifestyle in the hills of the interior, and were thus Swaziland's true indigenous inhabitants.

THE FIRST SWAZIS Unfortunately for the San, their Swazi idyll didn't last. Life changed irrevocably with the arrival of the Bantu from the north. These people, who originated in the Niger Delta region and started migrating south and east across Africa some 2,500 years ago, were the ancestors of today's Swazis. They were pastoralists, who grew sorghum and other crops, farmed livestock, lived in settled villages and had developed iron smelting. Around 1,500 years ago the first Bantu crossed the Limpopo and made their way down the east coast of southern Africa. They arrived in small waves rather than a single mass migration. Some groups, now known as the Sotho–Tswana peoples, moved inland. Others, now known as the Nguni peoples, stayed along the coast. This latter group included the Swazis, along with the Zulu, Xhosa and Ndebele.

According to tradition, the Swazi nation has its origins during the 15th century on what is now the Mozambique coast, when the Dlamini clan and its various followers – thought to be descended from the Tembe tribe further north – settled in the Catembe area, near today's city of Maputo. In the 1750s, these settlers, led by their king, Ngwane III, crossed west over or around the Lubombo mountains into what is now southern Swaziland. They were known as the Bantfu BakaNgwane (the people of Ngwane), and they set about conquering the scattered chiefdoms and tribal communities they encountered, incorporating them into the Ngwane kingdom.

By the early 19th century, the Bantu had driven the last of the San from the land, bringing down the curtain on the Late Stone Age. Today a few San still pursue their traditional hunter-gatherer lifestyle in Botswana's Kalahari but all that remains of them in Swaziland is their signature rock art, preserved at sites such as Nsangwini (see page 219).

THE EUROPEANS ARRIVE Meanwhile, the Europeans had been arriving in southern Africa. The earliest were the Portuguese, the first mariners to navigate around the Cape in their voyages to the spice islands of the East. They never showed any inclination to settle the storm-battered Cape, however, instead continuing east around the coast to the more sheltered bays of the Indian Ocean. By the late 19th century the Portuguese had established Portuguese East Africa, now Mozambique, founded largely on slavery.

By the late 16th century the Dutch and the British were following the Portuguese. The Cape became a regular stopover for the Dutch East India Company, which, under Jan van Riebeck, established a permanent settlement from 6 April 1652. Relations with the local Khoi were largely hostile, but more Dutch settlers arrived to farm the area, and these 'free burghers' began expanding into the hinterland. The settler population was swelled by waves of other European immigrants, including the Huguenots fleeing religious persecution, and large numbers of slaves imported from Dutch colonies in Madagascar and Indonesia. Clashes with the local Khoi were settled with increasing brutality, with survivors pressed into labour for the growing colony. This ethnic mix of European, Khoi and imported slaves became the basis of today's 'coloured' population.

By 1806 the British had seized the Cape from the Dutch, inheriting an established colony of some 60,000 white settlers, Khoi and imported slaves. Power rested with a white elite in Cape Town and racial discrimination was already deeply entrenched. Much of the Brits' energy was spent on resolving disputes between the Boers and Xhosa on the colony's eastern frontier. A new wave of immigrants settled the towns of this area, consolidating the British presence, and a pattern soon emerged whereby the urbanised British dominated politics, trade, mining and so on, while the uneducated Boers retreated to their farms.

BRITISH, BOERS AND ZULUS AT WAR Two major events during the first half of the 19th century were to have a significant bearing on the formation and history of Swaziland. The first was the expansion of the Zulu kingdom to the south. Shaka, a charismatic leader and master strategist, organised the scattered Nguni tribes of the KwaZulu-Natal region into a unified, militaristic state. He then embarked on a massive expansion programme known as the Mfecane (crushing), slaughtering or enslaving those he conquered, and causing shock waves far across the region. Shaka was killed in 1828 by his half-brothers, one of whom – Dingane – replaced him as king. This triggered the slow decline of the Zulu nation, but not before it had caused a seismic shift in the relations of peoples across southern Africa – including in Swaziland.

Meanwhile, the Boers had grown increasingly fed up with British rule in the Cape colony, and rejected the British proclamations of equality among races. From 1835, in search of greater independence, they began to set off in groups north into the interior, accompanied by their slaves and Khoi retinue. This upping of sticks was known as the Great Trek and became fundamental to the Boer sense of identity. The nomads, known as *voortrekkers* (pioneers), found deserted lands and scattered peoples – the result of the Mfecane – and met little serious resistance until they reached the Drakensberg Mountains, where King Moshoeshoe I had started to forge the Basotho nation (now Lesotho), and the wooded valleys of Zululand, where the Zulus held sway.

After establishing a republic at Thaba Nchu, near present-day Bloemfontein, some Boers headed north into the Transvaal and others east into Zululand. The eastern party, led by Piet Retief, entered an agreement with Dingane, Shaka's successor – trading land for cattle – but the deal turned sour, and Retief and his followers were all slaughtered. This marked the start of hostilities between Boer and Zulu, and the former had their revenge at the Battle of Blood River in 1838. The Boers, driven by the ideals of the Dutch Reform Church, saw this victory as fulfilling their divine destiny.

The Boers' dreams of a Natal republic were, however, dashed by the arrival of the British in 1843, who annexed the area and founded their new Natal colony at present-day Durban. The British began settling Natal and establishing the sugar-cane plantations that remain integral to the region's economy today. But stiff resistance from the Zulus escalated into the Anglo–Zulu wars. In 1879 the Battle of Isandlwana marked one of the British army's most humiliating colonial defeats, with over 1,400 soldiers falling to the Zulus. It was a turning point: the British redoubled their efforts and used superior firepower to divide and destroy the Zulu nation and establish control over Zululand (now KwaZulu-Natal). The Zulus would not labour for the British, however, and so more than 150,000 'indentured' Indians were imported to work the cane fields in what would become the largest Indian colony outside Asia.

The Boers, meanwhile, pressed on with their search for land and freedom, and established various republics, including the Transvaal and the Free State. But chaos broke out when the discovery of diamonds near Kimberley in 1869 brought an invasion of labourers and prospectors that derailed the Boers' plans. The British stepped in to annex the area, increasing the Boer's long-standing resentment of them. By 1880 this had escalated into the first Anglo–Boer War – seen by Afrikaaners as a war of independence. The Boers quickly won a decisive victory at Majuba, reclaimed the Transvaal, which had been under British control from 1877, and declared their independence as the Zuid-Afrikaansche Republiek (South African Republic).

The British, undeterred, forged ahead with their plan to bring all the southern African colonies and republics into a British-administered federation. In 1886, gold was discovered in the Witwatersrand, precipitating another chaotic deluge of adventurers, founding the city of Johannesburg and pushing the Boers further towards the sidelines. The Boers, still essentially farmers, were losing out on the mineral wealth of their new lands and were not happy about it, precipitating the second Anglo–Boer War in 1899, after the British demanded voting rights for foreign whites on the goldfields. This war lasted longer than the first, but the British were better prepared and, using brutal new tactics such as concentration camps and scorched earth, they prevailed. A peace treaty was signed in 1902, in which the Boers acknowledged British sovereignty and the Brits undertook to reconstruct the areas under their control.

THE EUROPEANS REACH SWAZILAND

Changes were taking place in Swaziland while the British, Boers and Zulus were at each other's throats in South Africa. Ngwane II, the first king, died towards the end of the 18th century and was succeeded by his son Ndvungunye, about whom little is known. Ndvungunye gave way, in turn, to Sobhuza I, Ngwane's grandson, who reigned from 1815–39 and was known as Somhiolo, meaning 'the wonder'. Sobhuza consolidated, conquering many independent chiefdoms and incorporating them into the Ngwane kingdom. Sobhuza also moved the seat of power from the south up into the country's heartland, and fortified the army to defend against the Zulu threat from the south.

Sobhuza died in 1839 and was succeeded by his son, Mswati II. Before his death, however, he reputedly experienced a troubling dream in which people with strange hair, 'like cows' tails', arrived in the kingdom, carrying a book in one hand and a small circular object in the other. The dream warned him that the first of these gifts should be accepted but the second rejected. It also advised that the strangers should not be harmed.

These bizarrely coiffured dream people were, of course, the first Europeans, their book the Bible, and the circular object money. Or so the story goes. And it was in 1844, during Mswati's reign, that the kingdom received its first European visitors: Wesleyan missionaries, who turned up at Mahamba (see page 238). They didn't stay long, fleeing the country after witnessing a massacre in the mission station. But, in a pattern that was to characterise future European dealings with Swaziland, the missionaries were not harmed and it wasn't long before the first Boer settlers turned up. Meanwhile Mswati was building the Swazi kingdom into a significant regional power. During his reign from around 1840 to 1868 he expanded his lands both westward and northward, dealt brutally with any dissent from within, and forged alliances with the British to protect against the Zulus. It was from a corruption of Mswati's name that the Europeans derived the term 'Swazi', and hence the kingdom, formerly called Ngwane, became known as Swaziland.

After Mswati came Mbandzeni, who ruled from 1875 to 1889. By now, with South Africa's gold rush in full swing, fortune seekers were arriving in Swaziland from far and wide. In 1879, gold was discovered in the northwest, swelling the influx of prospectors, who persuaded the king to grant them concessions for minerals, land and trade in return for tribute. Swazis could not grasp the Western concept of land ownership, believing all land belonged by divine right to the king, so were taken aback when the concessionaries started claiming this land as their own rather than simply occupying it as their guests. But the deals had been struck and the newcomers had the military muscle to get what they wanted. Swazis today reflect out ruefully that they should have heeded the warning about money in Sobhuza's dream.

Mbandzeni helped the British settlers in the area by forming an alliance against the baPedi tribes to the north in return for a promise of autonomy, which was signed in a convention in 1881. This promise amounted to little, however, when in 1894 – to protests from the Swazis – the kingdom was placed under the administration of the then South African Republic (Transvaal). That same year King Bhunu came to the throne, taking over the reins from Tibati Nkambule, who had served as regent since the death of Mbandzeni. Bhunu's reign was not a happy one, troubled by internal dissent and animosity with the Boers. By the time he died towards the end of 1899, the British and Boers were at loggerheads.

SWAZILAND DURING THE BOER WAR
The second Boer War broke out with Swaziland effectively in Boer hands and administered from the colonial headquarters at Bremersdorp (now Manzini). In 1899, with war looming, colonists started evacuating the area – many fleeing to Mozambique or Natal. With the white authorities gone, and just diehard settlers remaining, King Bhunu was informed he would be left in charge. Meanwhile the Boer authorities began arming their remaining burghers. A commando unit was formed, and started making raids on British settlers and outposts. Bhunu took advantage of the general confusion to start settling old scores among his own people. Convinced he'd been bewitched, he became increasingly violent and, reputedly, turned to drink. Some of his victims had close ties to the colonial authorities and at one point the Boers had Bhunu up on a murder charge.

When Bhunu died on 10 December 1899 his son, Sobhuza II, was just a few months old and so too young for the throne. His mother Labotsibeni Mdluli stepped into the breach as queen regent. She attempted to stay neutral in the ongoing settler conflict but was worried about the Boers' interference in the royal succession – they had been grooming a rival candidate for the throne, Prince Masumphe, in defiance of Swazi heredity conventions. Labotsibeni thus made contact with the British and agreed to give them her support in return for their protection.

Defeats for the Boers in the sieges of nearby Barberton and Komatipoort meant that Swaziland became increasingly important to them as a conduit for trade and diplomatic contacts with Lourenço Marques (later Maputo) in Mozambique. From December 1900 to February 1901, British forces pursued the Boers into Swaziland and inflicted defeats on them in a number of skirmishes. Labotsibeni rallied her soldiers, helping drive the Boers from the land – even though the Swazis had been officially prohibited from entering the conflict. The situation was chaotic, with renegade bands of mercenaries and military incursions from both sides, and in July 1901 Bremersdorp was burned to the ground. It all finally ended in February 1902 with the defeat of the last Boer unit in Swaziland.

THE PROTECTORATE AND SOBHUZA II Britain acquired Swaziland as the spoils of victory in the Boer War. In 1906 it declared the country a 'protectorate'. The idea behind this slightly nebulous concept was that the state remained an autonomous territory, with full sovereignty under international law, but received protection from a superior power in return for meeting specified obligations. In practice, however, Swaziland remained so subordinate to Britain that it had no independent statehood worth the name and, effectively, differed little from a colony.

The Swazis had an ambivalent attitude towards this British 'protection'. It had been clear, ever since the demise of the Zulu kingdom, that colonialism was an irresistible force. The British, however, seemed a lesser evil than either the Boers or the Portuguese. And these new colonisers, having inherited the kingdom by default, were reasonably hands-off. They did not ship in boatloads of settlers or start dismantling the Swazi traditional hierarchy.

Yet for Swazis, the lack of power and self-determination grated. Although the king had some responsibility for the country's internal affairs, he had no say in external affairs and answered to the colonial office in all matters. Indeed, as the British recognised only one king in their empire (their own), he was not even allowed the official title 'King' and had to settle for 'Paramount Chief'. The highest authority in the protectorate was the resident commissioner, who answered to the British High Commissioner for South Africa.

The next king didn't follow immediately, however. Labotsibeni continued to rule as queen regent and now turned her attention to the vexing issue of land. By the end of the Boer War the British had transferred most land concessions into freehold, thus effectively robbing the Swazis of their birthright. In 1907, in an attempt to end disputes over concessions, the British drew up an agreement that returned one-third of Swaziland's territory to its people, as Swazi Nation Land, and divided what remained between freehold and Crown land. Labotsibeni set about increasing this Swazi portion by buying back land using remittances from Swazi migrant labourers on the South African goldfields.

The queen regent, meanwhile, had been preparing for succession by ensuring that the future king, Sobhuza II, received a Western education alongside his traditional Swazi one. She abdicated in 1921, after 20 years in power, as soon as Sobhuza came of age. Sobhuza was to become Swaziland's most important monarch, leading the country to independence and, after his death, being afforded a near-divine status that seems only to strengthen as disappointment in today's status quo mounts. His legacy is widely acknowledged as being one of tolerance, ensuring that relations with both colonial rulers and neighbouring states always remained reasonably harmonious, whatever the disagreement and conflict in the wider region.

The early years of Sobhuza's reign saw him continuing where Labotsibeni had left off, pressing for a return of more of the land denied to Swazis in the 1907 agreement. By 1944, about half the country had become Swazi Nation Land, and the process continued of buying up farms and turning them over to the king in trust for the nation. Until now, the British had paid little attention to development. After World War II, however, they began looking for ways to make Swaziland more productive and a number of large-scale agricultural projects were launched – two of which, forestry and sugar, remain the country's largest formal employers. The British also provided a basic working infrastructure, with mission schools, clean hospitals and a police force. But, assuming that Swaziland would at some point become part of South Africa, they didn't take things much further.

APARTHEID AND THE WIND OF CHANGE On the global stage, more significant change was afoot. By now, Britain – impoverished by the war – was struggling to finance its colonies and the cracks in the empire were showing. India's independence in 1948 marked a turning point and tremors were soon being felt in Africa. Ghana in 1957 was the first in a series of tumbling colonial dominos across east and west Africa, and by 1960, when Prime Minister Harold Macmillan delivered his famous 'wind of change' speech to the South African parliament (making clear Britain intended to grant independence to many of its colonial territories), it was obvious that southern Africa – including Swaziland – lay directly in the path of this wind.

In South Africa, though, Macmillan's words fell on deaf ears. The authorities there, alarmed by the prospect of black majority rule, were heading in a different direction. When François Malan's National Party won the elections of 1948, it immediately set about formalising the country's already deep racial divisions using the policy of apartheid. Meaning 'separateness', this ideology maintained that it was in the country's interests for South Africa's four principal ethnic groups – defined as white, black, Asian and coloured – to be kept apart. It was enforced via a rash of unpleasant laws, such as the Group Areas Act of 1950, which determined where each racial group was entitled to live. In effect, it meant power and privilege for the white minority, maintained through discrimination and oppression. Increasingly isolated from the rest of the world, which reviled apartheid, in 1961 South Africa declared itself a republic and withdrew from the Commonwealth.

The ugly history of apartheid is well documented elsewhere. Suffice it to say that, after decades of dissent, resistance and international pressure, an untenable system eventually collapsed with the election in 1994 of Nelson Mandela. But it had by then left the region deeply scarred and provided the backdrop against which the independent nation of Swaziland was born.

Elsewhere in southern Africa, as South Africa battened down the hatches, things were moving fast. First came the break-up in 1964 of the Southern African Federation, which saw Northern Rhodesia and Nyasaland assume independence as Zambia and Malawi respectively (with Southern Rhodesia left in limbo by Ian Smith's Unilateral Declaration of Independence until Zimbabwe came into being in 1979). Then came the independence of Britain's three protectorates in the region: Botswana (formerly Bechuanaland) in 1966; Lesotho (formerly Basutoland) in 1967; and finally Swaziland in 1968.

INDEPENDENCE AND THE DEATH OF SOBHUZA Apartheid prompted a volte-face from the British in their approach to Swaziland. No longer happy to see the kingdom become part of South Africa, they began preparing it for independence. In 1952, Sobhuza was granted further powers that gave Swaziland a degree of autonomy unprecedented in a protectorate, and in 1963 the new Swaziland Independence Constitution was drawn up. By now, several political parties were agitating for independence. Among these was the party of the king and his inner council, the Imbokodvo National Movement (INM), which campaigned on a promise to safeguard the traditional Swazi way of life. When elections were held in mid-1964 for the first Legislative Council of Swaziland, the INM won all 24 seats.

The INM pressed for immediate independence. In 1966, a joint committee agreed on a constitutional monarchy for Swaziland, with self-government to follow parliamentary elections in 1967. The elections were duly held and Swaziland became independent on 6 September 1968. At last, 47 years after coming to the throne, King Sobhuza II had led his people to self-determination.

Shortly before independence, the British had at last granted Sobhuza the right to call himself 'King' rather than 'Paramount Chief'. He now began to earn the title, using his new executive powers and immense popularity to rule Swaziland with an authority that no monarch had wielded since Mswati II. Democracy, however, was not part of the plan. When Swaziland's first post-independence elections were held in May 1972, with the INM receiving around 75% of the vote, another party, the Ngwane National Liberatory Congress (NNLC), also received around 20% and thereby gained three seats in parliament. Sobhuza was dismayed. To prevent this from happening again, he repealed the inherited Westminster constitution and established a more traditional version that blended African and European law. When parliament reopened in 1978 the king had assumed all powers of government and the constitutional monarchy had become an absolute monarchy. Political activities and trade unions were banned, seen as alien forces incompatible with the Swazi way of life. In January 1979, a new parliament was convened, chosen partly through elections and partly through direct appointment by the king.

In 1981 Sobhuza celebrated his Diamond Jubilee, marking 60 years since his coronation. When he died the following year, his nominal rule of 82 years and nine months was the longest precisely dated reign of any monarch since antiquity. And, in keeping with royal tradition, Sobhuza had not stinted on wives. He married 70 women, who between 1920 and 1970 gave him 210 children (an average of three per wife) and, reputedly, more than 1,000 grandchildren. Among his sons-in-law was King Goodwill Zwelithini kaBhekuzulu of the Zulu Nation, while a daughter-in-law is Zenani Mandela, daughter of Nelson Mandela. Whole generations of Swazis had known no other ruler but Sobhuza, with his wisdom and benevolence seen as the embodiment of the nation's virtues.

MSWATI III TAKES THE THRONE Sobhuza's death in August 1982 heralded a turbulent time of limbo that has become known as the 'Liqoqo Period'. The Liqoqo was a traditional council of state whose role was to appoint and advise a queen regent until a new king could be appointed. The first regent appointed was Queen Dzeliwe Shongwe but, following bitter palace in-fighting, she was replaced in 1983 by Queen Ntombi Tfwala. The new regent's only child, Prince Makhosetive ('King of Nations') Dlamini, was named heir to the throne and promptly bundled off to Sherborne public school in England in order to prepare him for the role. Meanwhile Ntombi demonstrated her power by dismissing leading figures from the Liqoqo.

The heir apparent had been born at the Raleigh Fitkin Memorial Hospital in Manzini on 19 April 1968, just four months before independence. He grew up at Etjeni, one of Sobhuza's residences, attending Masundwini Primary School and Lozitha Palace School, and becoming the first young cadet to join the Umbutfo Swaziland Defence Force (USDF). Swaziland received a sneak preview of their future king when he was introduced as crown prince to the nation in September 1983. However, they had to wait until 25 April 1986 when, aged 18 years and 6 days, he took to the throne as Mswati III. This made him the world's youngest reigning monarch until the ascension of King Jigme Khesar Mangyel Wangchuck of Bhutan on 14 December 2006.

With Mswati on the throne, the troubles of the previous four years came to an abrupt end. One of the young king's first acts was to abolish the Liqoqo. In

November 1987, a new parliament was elected and a new cabinet appointed. Since then, however, while it has been all change for Swaziland's neighbours – notably the end of civil war in Mozambique in 1992 and the end of apartheid in South Africa in 1994 – the kingdom has remained pretty much as it was during Sobhuza's time.

SWAZILAND TODAY Mswati's reign has, to date, proved something of a disappointment to progressives. Many had hoped that the young king would overhaul what they saw as Swaziland's outmoded political system and take more modernising strides into the 21st century. In fact, he has done little of the kind and Swaziland today remains an absolute monarchy – the only one left in Africa – in which the king rules by decree. Critics argue that this is incompatible with democracy, freedom of speech and civil rights. In 1988 and 1989 an underground political party, the People's United Democratic Movement (PUDEMO), first began calling for reforms. There has since been a trickle of political change, including the restoration of a parliament, dissolved by Sobhuza, and in 2004 the overhaul of the constitution. But not enough to appease the critics.

The 21st century has seen the grumblings gather strength. After the end of apartheid in 1994, which broke the long gaze of international scrutiny on South Africa, Swaziland was left more exposed to criticism from outside. Those agitating for democracy have enjoyed the support of the trade unions in South Africa, who in recent years have called for mass action and encouraged the boycotting of cultural events. Meanwhile international pressure groups such as Amnesty International have described aspects of Swaziland's system of governance as an infringement of human rights.

Mswati's own conduct has not helped the case against him. The king has continued the Swazi custom of polygamy, acquiring 14 wives with whom he has fathered 23 children. This process has troubled human rights groups, who have claimed that some wives were effectively abducted (although the one case that went to the high court was dropped when the girl in question confirmed that she had gone willingly). They argue that the king's behaviour has undermined the battle for women's rights in Swaziland and that, despite his initiatives to encourage chastity in an effort to combat the AIDS pandemic, he has been unable to lead by example. Meanwhile his lifestyle has attracted the attention of the foreign press, where he has been caricatured as a playboy despot. With most Swazis struggling in poverty, exacerbated by global recession, the luxury vehicles, private jets and palace refurbishments have fuelled criticism. Protest marches have become a backdrop to national celebrations.

Criticism of Mswati, however, often does not allow for the fact that many of his actions are governed by Swazi tradition, as regulated by the council of elders. The king does not, for example, have the authority to appoint his heir, and at least two of his wives are not his choice. Meanwhile, although criticism is voiced by an urban, educated minority, the monarchy still retains widespread and loyal support from the rural masses. Supporters argue that it is Swaziland's traditional values, embodied in the monarchy, that have made the country an island of peace and stability amid the violence and turmoil that have often afflicted its neighbours. 'If it ain't broke,' so their argument goes, 'don't fix it.'

Swaziland today finds itself at a crossroads. The pressures both from inside and outside do not look set to go away. The monarchy has become a conspicuous anachronism in a part of the world that has fought bitterly for its democratic rights. And the Arab Spring of 2011, at the other end of the continent, has provided enough of a lesson in people power to put the frighteners on any intransigent

African leader. Change will come to Swaziland. Exactly how and exactly when will depend upon the monarchy's ability to adapt. We can only hope that the nation's long history of pragmatism and diplomacy will help it chart a course that is not too turbulent or traumatic.

GOVERNMENT AND POLITICS

Politics in today's Swaziland is a thorny issue. This book passes no judgement but rather offers a brief description of the somewhat confusing blend of Western structures and Swazi traditions by which the country is governed. Talk to people and read the papers. You will hear many shades of opinion, freely expressed, and can then make up your own mind.

Swaziland calls itself a constitutional monarchy, on the basis that power is nominally shared between the monarch and parliament. However, any legislation passed by parliament only becomes law if passed by the king, and it is the king who appoints the prime minister. To the wider world, then, the king's overarching authority, and the lack of a democratic alternative, means that the monarchy is more absolute than constitutional. Indeed, Swaziland is generally described as being the last absolute monarchy in Africa.

THE MONARCHY The king is Swaziland's head of state. He is known as Ingwenyama, which means lion (in an emblematic sense, as opposed to *bhubesi*, which is lion in a zoological sense). By tradition he rules alongside his mother, who is known as Ndlovukazi or 'Great She Elephant'. She is responsible for the ritual side of governance and does not make public pronouncements. If the queen mother dies, one of the king's wives replaces her.

In former times the queen mother was in control of the military, as well as rain-making and other key functions in the spiritual life of the nation. The idea was that she acted as a check and counterbalance to the king's power. During Sobhuza's long reign, however, her role was downgraded to something more symbolic. Today it is King Mswati III who is firmly in charge, supported by an advisory body of traditional councillors. He holds supreme executive, legislative and judicial powers, is commander-in-chief of the defence forces and enjoys legal immunity.

The monarchy is hereditary, with all kings being from the Dlamini clan. The king's mother, however, must be from an unrelated family, as Dlaminis never intermarry. Although the position of king is hereditary, it is not simply passed to the previous king's eldest son. Instead the Royal Council plays a key role in selecting the new monarch after the death of his father. The exact process is cloaked in secrecy. However, certain conditions are public knowledge: the new king's mother must not be the first or second wife of his father, and he must be her only son. It is

TINKHUNDLA

Swaziland consists of four administrative regions: Hhohho, Manzini, Lubombo and Shiselweni. Following a system devised by Sobhuza in 1978, each is divided into a number of districts called *tinkhundla* (singular: *inkhundla*). These *tinkhundla*, in turn, comprise a number of chiefdoms, or *umphakatsi*. A representative of each *inkhundla* is elected to the House of Assembly in local community elections held every five years. Elections are on a non-party basis, with candidates for each constituency nominated by their local council.

Human rights are addressed in Swaziland's constitution. As opposition to Swaziland's status quo has mounted, however, so critics – including the US State Department and Amnesty International – have raised concerns about various practices used by the authorities, including arbitrary arrest, intimidation, mistreatment of detainees and the prosecution of human-rights defenders. The rights of women are also seen as widely neglected.

Problems have increased, claims Amnesty, since the passing in 2008 of Swaziland's Suppression of Terrorism Act, which it believes threatens freedoms of expression, association and peaceful assembly. Swaziland would not, of course, be the only nation in recent times to use anti-terrorism legislation as a means of suppressing internal dissent. However, this claim comes against a backdrop of wider criticism, with Swaziland's political system itself seen as an infringement of its citizens' rights. Amnesty's 2011 report urges Swaziland to 'take concrete and immediate measures to guarantee the independence and impartiality of the judiciary, and to amend laws that discriminate against women without delay'. A number of amendments to the constitution in these areas have been ratified but not yet implemented.

also thought that the new king must be a minor. The king is not crowned, as such, but takes up his position following various rituals, both secret and public.

The Royal Council is responsible for selecting the king's first two wives, with the first always being from the Matsebula clan and the second from the Motsa clan. Thereafter the king has more freedom, although he is still advised to select from a broad spectrum of Swazi society. This tradition aims to cement his position by uniting sectors of the community in marriage; it means, effectively, that everyone in the country is in some way related to the king.

The monarchy is well housed. There are over 20 royal residences, ranging from traditional beehive huts to opulent palaces complete with Louis XIV-style interiors. The big palace at Lozitha was built for Sobhuza but, preferring a simple life, he never spent a night in it. Mswati commissioned his own, at Nkoyoyo, just outside Mbabane. Each of the king's 14 wives has her own mansion.

PARLIAMENT AND THE PRIME MINISTER The king appoints the prime minister, with the advice of his Royal Council. He also appoints a small number of legislators to parliament, and has the freedom, if required, to appoint unelected representatives of special-interest groups, including women, people of disability or different race, scholars, chiefs and members of the business community. The idea is to ensure an even balance of views.

Swaziland's parliament, the Libandla, is located at Lobamba, the spiritual capital of the nation. It consists of two chambers: the upper chamber or Senate (Indlu ye Timphunga) comprises 30 members, 20 appointed by the king and his advisors and ten elected by the House of Assembly; the lower chamber or House of Assembly comprises 65 seats, 55 occupied by representatives from Swaziland's 55 constituencies, or *tinkhundla*, and ten appointed by the king and his advisors. There is also one woman representative for each of Swaziland's four regions, and the attorney general. Representatives of both houses all serve five-year terms. Parliament is open to visitors, so you may turn up and listen to the House of Assembly debating the affairs of the nation, in both English and siSwati.

THE CONSTITUTION Mswati's father and predecessor, Sobhuza II, produced a new constitution on 13 October 1978, having earlier jettisoned the Westminster one that he inherited from the British. This purported to provide a democratic, participatory form of governance in which power devolved from central government to the wider community. It created a number of administrative districts called *tinkhundla* and a new parliament, to which each district elected a representative. However, these elections were strictly non-party political. Indeed, the new constitution cemented the existing ban on political parties – as legislated for in Sobhuza's 1973 State of Emergency decree – and outlawed large gatherings.

Mounting public dissatisfaction led Mswati in 2001 to set up a constitutional review process, in which a hand-picked committee travelled the country in a widely publicised consultation of the people. A draft of their findings published in 2003 drew criticism from Amnesty International and the Bar Association. The revised draft was released in 2005. It had a few significant tweaks – including guaranteeing freedom of speech, recognising the supremacy of the judiciary and increasing rights for women – but in other respects had changed little. Most significantly it drew upon Sobhuza's 1973 State of Emergency decree to uphold the ban on political parties. Trade unions and strikes also remained outlawed.

FOREIGN RELATIONS You could say that Swaziland has an exemplary record in foreign affairs in that it has never been involved in a war with its neighbours and has managed to retain harmonious relations with other nations across Africa and around the world.

The most important relationship by far is that with South Africa – and it is a complex one. On the one hand, ties are very close: South Africa has been a home for generations of Swazi migrant workers, and many Swazis and South Africans have personal ties that cross the border. On the other hand, there remain grumblings in some quarters – particularly among the ANC and South African trade unions – about historical aspects of Swaziland's role during apartheid. Today, these same trade unions are vocal in their denunciation of Swaziland's political system.

More than a million ethnic Swazis live in South Africa, mostly in the areas of Mpumalanga just west of the Swazi border, which once formed the siSwati-speaking 'Bantustan' of kaNgwane, reincorporated into South Africa after its elections in 1994. The late King Sobhuza once asked South Africa to open negotiations on incorporating these territories into Swaziland but this came to nothing. Today, Swaziland is economically dependent upon its enormous neighbour and seems unlikely to rock the boat.

Relations with Mozambique are also ambiguous but in a rather different way. During and shortly after Mozambique's brutal civil war, which ended in 1992, Swazis enjoyed a sense of superiority over their troubled neighbours. Thousands of Mozambicans lived in refugee camps in the Swazi lowveld (see page 250) and many others entered the kingdom illegally, all of which encouraged a popular view of them as untrustworthy. Crime, especially cattle-rustling, was routinely attributed to Mozambicans, regardless of evidence. At the same time, these enterprising immigrants were much admired for their practical skills and many readily found employment – usually off the payroll – as engineers or mechanics. Since the war ended, things have changed: Mozambique has recovered and developed at a frightening pace. Mozambicans you meet in Swaziland today are as likely to be travelling businessmen as mechanics, and Mozambican seafood is a standard feature on any self-respecting restaurant menu.

Swaziland enjoys good relations with Britain, its former colonial power, although Swazis were understandably put out when Britain closed down its High Commission in 2006 as part of Foreign Office cost-cutting measures. The USA has trumped the Brits in this respect by retaining its embassy and is highly active in development, notably through its Peace Corps volunteer programme. Swaziland's relations with Britain, the USA and the EU have, however, become more strained in recent years as international pressure for political change has mounted.

Among the other embassies or honorary consuls based in Swaziland (all in Mbabane) are those of India and the Republic of China. The latter is significant, as Swaziland is one of the few countries in the world that maintains diplomatic relations with the Republic of China – ie: Taiwan – but not with the People's Republic of China. The kingdom's reward for this loyalty has been abundant aid and investment, notably in the textiles industry.

Swaziland is a member of the United Nations, the Commonwealth, the African Union, the Common Market for Eastern and Southern Africa, and the Southern African Development Community.

THE MONARCHY AND THE PEOPLE The monarchy has a grip on Swaziland's life in a way that is hard for outsiders to grasp. A UK tabloid royal wedding frenzy pales by comparison with the attention that Mswati receives: entire news broadcasts will be devoted to showing his wives sitting glumly at a UN reception. This can be explained by the fact that the king has traditionally been not only the ruler but also the spiritual embodiment of Swaziland: his word is law, his health and prosperity directly related to those of the nation.

One upshot of Swaziland's small size – and Sobhuza's prolific fertility – is that royalty seems to be everywhere. On my first drive through the country in 1993 I stopped to pick up a hitchhiker and was taken aback to learn that he was a prince. How should I address him? Should I kneel, bow or put on a chauffeur's cap? The novelty wore off over time, however, as I discovered that there are princes and princesses doing their thing in all walks of Swazi life. You can generally identify royalty by the crimson *ligwalagwala* feathers worn in the hair (see *Dress*, page 83). Sceptics may tell you, of course, that not everybody who claims royal descent – and the privileges it confers – is the real deal. Nonetheless, there are still few easier places on the planet than Swaziland to meet bona fide royalty.

The long tradition of loyalty to the king explains why Swazis for many years seemed to harbour so little resentment for his wealth and privilege. His success was seen as their success, even if they struggled by on less than two dollars a day. Times have changed, however, and grievances are now more freely expressed. At first, while prime ministers and other high officials were all fair game, Mswati was exempt from popular criticism: at worse, argued his loyal subjects, he was being misled. Today the royal taboo has weakened. Mswati's lavish lifestyle is compared unfavourably with that of Sobhuza who, despite accumulating massive wealth, lived by a code of personal austerity. There is still huge affection for the king but he is, at last, a human being.

ECONOMY AND INFRASTRUCTURE

Swaziland is classified as a lower-middle-income country, with a GDP of just under four billion US dollars and an average gross per capita income of US$3,725 according to 2010 estimates. Nonetheless, some 65% of the population lives in poverty, surviving on less than US$2 per day. This anomaly can be explained by the typically African disparity between two very different levels of economic activity. On the one hand, more than half the population depends upon small-scale subsistence farming, with very low productivity. On the other, the country supports substantial commercial agriculture and industry, much of this in the hands of non-Swazis. The most important source of income is duty from the Southern African Customs Union (SACU), of which Swaziland's share currently comprises about more than 50% of national revenue (see *Duty calls*, above).

ECONOMIC HISTORY Up until the birth of the Havelock asbestos mine in the 1930s (see page 229), Swaziland had been purely a subsistence economy, with most settlers showing little interest in anything other than small-scale mining and farming on their individual concessions. After World War II, however, the British began to develop commercial agriculture, notably forestry in the highveld, citrus in the middleveld, and cattle and sugar in the lowveld.

The 1960s, the decade of Swaziland's independence, was also the decade in which industrial development really took off, with the growth of the Ngwenya iron-ore mine and the servicing of a new overseas export market via the Goba rail link to Lourenço Marques (now Maputo). The asbestos mine at Bulembu had until this point been the country's largest employer and revenue earner, but forestry and sugar were becoming increasingly important. Industrial development brought a new infrastructure, with electricity, communications, roads and water supply – most of it built with South African money.

From the mid-1980s, Swaziland also became an unwitting economic beneficiary of apartheid, when the intensifying worldwide opposition to South Africa's grubby politics, including trade sanctions, led many companies to up sticks and hop over the border. Of course it didn't hurt these conscience-stricken investors, including Coca-Cola, that Swaziland also offered a highly favourable tax regime. Matsapha

DUTY CALLS

Swaziland is one of four countries – the others being Lesotho, Botswana, Namibia and the Republic of South Africa – that make up the Southern African Customs Union (SACU). Under this arrangement, import duties levied at first port of entry within the region are shared among all member countries. Income from SACU, which comes largely from South African trade, is redistributed disproportionately in favour of the smaller member states. This has served Swaziland very well, contributing up to 60% of national revenue. However, this income has fallen sharply in recent years, with imports such as luxury cars affected by global recession. The ensuing emergency bailout packages have left the kingdom heavily indebted to the union.

soon became the country's industrial hub, home to everything from breweries to textiles. A new north–south railway link through Swaziland, which extended from northern Mpumalanga to Richards Bay and Durban in KwaZulu-Natal, offered an alternative outlet for exports when Mozambique's civil war prohibited access to the port of Maputo.

In more recent years Swaziland's growth has dropped behind that of its southern African neighbours. This has much to do with the devastating impact of the HIV/AIDS epidemic on its workforce. Politics also plays a part: many businesses returned to South Africa after 1994, when the end of apartheid made this politically acceptable; and overseas markets with whom Swaziland enjoys preferential trade agreements – including the US and EU – are threatening to revise these should Swaziland not make some political changes of its own. Meanwhile, in a straitened global economy, the Southern African Customs Union can no longer be milked as it once was. South Africa remains by far Swaziland's most important trading partner, accounting for more than 90% of imports and 70% of exports.

As this book goes to press, Swaziland's economic prospects do not look rosy. Growth has continued at an average of 2.8% since 2001 and in 2011 was just 2% – less than half as that of Africa as a whole. With revenue from the southern African Customs Union (see opposite) set to decline and further austerity measures anticipated, including civil service wages cuts, recovery is still some distance away. And with some two-thirds of the population already living on less than US$2 a day, there is only so far that belts can be tightened.

AGRICULTURE There are two very different kinds of farming in Swaziland. Around 60% of the nation's farmland is known as Swazi Nation Land (SNL). This is held in trust for the Swazi people by the king, according to the traditional land tenure system called *kukhonta* in which small farmers can build their homesteads and till their small subsistence plots but cannot own or sell the land. Some 75% of Swazis live and farm in this way. The rest of the nation's farmland is privately owned, largely by multi-nationals and parastatals, and known as Title Deed Land (TDL). Here, large agricultural enterprises turn a tidy profit. SNL agriculture contributes just 22% of crop production, accounting for only 11% of the value of agricultural output and barely 1% of GDP. The TDL sector, though occupying less than 40% of the cultivated land, accounts for more than 81% of the value of all agricultural output and some 8% of GDP.

It is not hard to spot the difference between these two very different farming landscapes as you travel around the kingdom. Swazi Nation Land is typical ramshackle Africa: poor, with scattered homesteads, small mealie plots, ragged children herding skinny cattle and the soil chronically overgrazed. People scrape a subsistence living, growing their crops, grazing their livestock and selling a few surplus vegetables at the market during good times. Maize is the staple, but other crops include sorghum (mainly for brewing traditional beer), pumpkins and beans. The land is ravaged by soil erosion and there is little by way of fertilisers, irrigation and the other essentials of modern farming. Water – or the lack of it – is a constant worry, and in hard times people may depend on emergency food relief.

Title Deed Land (TDL) presents a different picture: large, orderly, fenced fields and plantations; shiny new machinery; irrigation canals and rotating sprinklers; and neat, uniform clusters of workers' accommodation. The average farm on TDL occupies around 800ha – by contrast with less than 3ha on SNL – and over 60% of TDL is irrigated.

Cultivation Forestry is one of the most significant forms of commercial land use, and swathes much of Swaziland's highveld. You can't miss it: huge plantations of pine and eucalyptus – among the world's largest – carpet the hills, their regiments of dark, alien trees creating a very un-African landscape. These forests supply both lumber and wood pulp, and are managed largely by South African companies. In 2010, however, the Usutu Pulp Mill – managed by Sappi – closed down due to a combination of recent devastating forest fires and the wider economic malaise. Its closure hit the local community hard. Critics argue that forestry in Swaziland has done little to help communities develop, while causing significant environmental problems, including pollution and the depletion of biodiversity, and possibly exacerbating drought through its sponge-like effect on the highveld water cycle.

Sugar is cultivated down in the lowveld, where the great, irrigated cane fields look supernaturally lush and green in the dusty shadow of the Lubombos. There are three major estates, each with its own sugar mill – Big Bend in the south, Mhlume and Simunye in the north – plus a number of outlying smaller producers. Swaziland produces about 500,000 tonnes of sugar per year. Milled sugar is exported via Maputo to the EU and North America. But pure sugar has been overtaken in importance by its derivative, soft-drink concentrate, which supplies the Coca-Cola concentrate plant. The sugar estates are Swaziland's leading private sector employer and are a world of their own, complete with neat, American-style corporate housing, top-performing private schools and well-watered playing fields.

ANCESTRAL HERD

Swaziland's cattle are descended from the original Nguni breed indigenous to southern Africa. This breed represented in turn a hybrid of Indian and African cattle, and was introduced to the region by the first Bantu settlers from the north. It is a medium-sized animal – bulls weigh 500–600kg and cows 300–400kg – and characterised by its multi-coloured skin, patterned in various blotchy combinations of black, white and brown. Instead of the shoulder hump of east African cattle, the Nguni has a swinging dewlap between the front legs. The original breed was as tough as the proverbial old boots into which it must sometimes have been made, and over time became supremely well adapted to the southern African environment, developing a high resistance to drought, ticks and disease. Its importance as a resource for the people of the region is reflected in centuries of social ritual and convention, with cattle being used to advertise the wealth of a man or his village, and serving as the standard currency for a bride's dowry, or *lobola*. King Shaka of the Zulus (see page 55) bred his Nguni herds in different colour strains in order to create uniforms that would distinguish his different regiments. (His elite personal guard wore pure-white hides from the royal herd or *inyonikayiphumuli*.) The cattle that you see roaming Swaziland today are not purebred Nguni. Over the years, crossbreeding with new varieties from elsewhere has seen the original breed decline almost to the point of extinction. Mkhaya Game Reserve (see page 277), however, was originally created to protect the last few purebred individuals. Today Nguni cattle graze the reserve's lush savanna alongside zebra, wildebeest and other wild game in a scene that could be centuries old. The success of this scheme has also allowed the recent introduction of a small population to the endangered species zone at Mlilwane Wildlife Sanctuary (see page 177).

Other important crops include citrus fruits – mostly oranges and grapefruits – and pineapples. These are grown largely for the export market, with most Swazi pineapples being processed at Swazican, near Malkerns (see page 188). Bananas, avocados, guavas, mangoes and lychees are grown widely – the abundance of cheap, fresh, tropical fruit is one joy of life in Swaziland – but are less commercially important. Cotton was once an important crop in the lowveld but has declined in recent years, as has tobacco. Maize, the most important crop on Swazi Nation Land, is stored and marketed commercially by the National Maize Corporation (NMC). Other cereal crops, including sorghum and rice, are of negligible economic importance.

Livestock Cattle are ubiquitous in Swaziland – to the extent that they pose a serious road hazard (see box on page 121). Indeed, the estimated grazing density of one cow per 1.6ha is among the highest in Africa. Their importance lies much deeper than as a mere food source: cows have traditionally served as an indicator of wealth, exchanged in such rituals as the paying of *lobola*, or bride price. Their prestige value thus far outstrips their commercial value, and they are a menace on SNL, causing serious soil erosion with their destructive grazing and far exceeding the capacity of the land to support them. Swaziland's distinctive cows, with their skinny frames, long horns and blotchy hides, are descended from the original Nguni stock brought by the first Bantu settlers to the region around 1,000 years ago (see *Ancestral herds,* opposite).

Cattle are also commercially farmed, mostly on large private ranches in the lowveld. Beef is exported to the EU, and Swaziland Meat Industries (SMI) operates an EU-standard abattoir. In recent years the SMI has encouraged local farmers to sell their cattle younger to make the national herd more productive and reduce its environmental impact. A 2001 outbreak of foot and mouth in the Lubombo region was a setback, and drivers travelling the main road to Siteki must sometimes pass through a veterinary cordon. The national dairy herd produces about one-fifth of Swaziland's milk requirements.

Goats, like cattle, have a destructive effect on the natural habitat. More than 90% of Swaziland's goats do their nibbling on Nation Land. Most are slaughtered for home consumption and ceremonial purposes, and so are of little commercial value. A 1986 survey found that 53% of people in Swaziland owned cattle and 32% owned goats, and it is unlikely that much has changed since then. Chickens also cluck and scratch around every homestead, and commercial poultry and egg production is a growing industry. Other livestock farmed commercially in Swaziland includes pigs, with pork processed at Simunye abattoir, and some wild game. Donkeys are an uncommon sight, and horses found only at riding stables.

INDUSTRY The industrial estate at Matsapha is the heart of Swaziland's industry and manufacturing. Here you'll find (if industrial estates are your thing) factories producing agricultural and forestry products, along with garments, textiles, shoes and various light manufactured goods. There is a brewery, abundant warehousing and a large services industry. The materials for many of these industries come from overseas. The Swaziland Industrial Development Company (SIDC) and the Swaziland Investment Promotion Authority (SIPA) have helped bring many of these industries to the country. A number of Taiwanese textiles companies have located here, and these employ several thousand workers, exporting their products primarily to the US. A smaller, separate industrial area is located at Sidwashini, just outside Mbabane.

Swaziland's most important manufactured product by far is soft-drink concentrate, specifically Coca-Cola. In 1987 the US giant relocated its concentrate plant to Swaziland from South Africa – to avoid apartheid sanctions, enjoy the tax breaks and have easy access to abundant cheap Swazi sugar. The plant exports to countries across Africa and elsewhere. Some estimate that 40% of Swaziland's GDP comes from Coca-Cola. In recent years pro-democracy activists have been highly critical of the company, claiming that their investment is propping up what they see as an illegitimate regime. Coca-Cola argue, of course, that they don't do politics.

MINING The lure of mineral wealth was what attracted the first prospectors and settlers to Swaziland in the late 19th century. They did indeed discover gold and diamonds in the hills of the highveld, and you can still find (or tumble down) abandoned mineshafts from those early days. Yields were never high, however, and it was not precious metals or gemstones that were to make fortunes but more utilitarian products such as asbestos, iron and coal.

Bulembu Mine, near Piggs Peak (see page 229), was once one of the world's largest asbestos mines, and its cableway for transporting its products over the hills to Barberton was for a while the largest such structure in the world. Asbestos propped up Swaziland's economy for decades, producing the bulk of its export revenue. Production plummeted at the end of the 1990s, however, as health concerns about asbestos gathered strength worldwide, and the mine closed in 2000. Former workers suffering from asbestos-related lung disease have since pursued legal actions against the British firm that operated the mine for over 60 years. Bulembu town is now transformed into a national community project for housing orphans (see page 228).

There has been a similar decline in other products – to the extent that in recent years the mineral sector has almost reached the point of collapse. High-grade iron ore, once mined at Ngwenya (see page 203), was exhausted by 1978. Mining for diamonds, which all came from a single kimberlite pipe at Dvokolwako, ground to a halt in 1996. Coal was first mined at Mpaka in the lowveld, and then Maloma in the southeast. The Maloma mine closed in July 2001 following a deadly underground methane-gas explosion but has since reopened under an improved safety regime and is now the only operational mine in the country. Production of crushed stone, quarried at three centres, has been stimulated in recent years by major road-building and construction projects such as the Ngwenya–Mbabane highway and the Maguga Dam.

TOURISM Tourism also does its bit for Swaziland's economy. The industry took off during the apartheid era, visitor numbers increasing from 89,000 in 1972 to 257,000 in 1989, by when it was contributing some 3% of GDP. This owed much to Swaziland's legalisation of gambling, which drew South Africans who were deprived of such pursuits back home. Since the end of both apartheid in South Africa and the war in Mozambique in the early 1990s, however, growth in tourism has declined, with the majority of Swaziland's visitors making just one- or two-night stopovers in the kingdom en route to the better-known attractions over the border. The Swaziland Tourist Board (STA) was established in 2003 and now concentrates on promoting the nation's cultural and natural attractions – from game parks to the Incwala. In 2009, Swaziland received around 1.3 million visitors, with tourism contributing nearly 1% of the nation's GDP.

INFRASTRUCTURE Swaziland has, in African terms, a reasonably healthy infrastructure – which is what makes it such a good destination for the independent traveller. This is partly a legacy of British colonialism, but also reflects the kingdom's proximity to South Africa, for whom it offers an important trade conduit and which has thus long had a vested interest in helping maintain and develop efficient transport and communications.

Transport The kingdom's excellent road network comprises more than 3,000km, of which some 30% is paved. Well-maintained tar roads link all major towns, including a four-lane highway (the MR3) that leads from the Ngwenya border to Mbabane and on to Manzini. Western visitors may complain about pot-holes on some routes but by African standards these are nothing. In rural areas tar soon gives way to dirt, but most gravel roads are regularly graded and generally in good enough nick for a normal family car. It is only in the most remote locations that you might need a 4x4 vehicle.

Swaziland's railways are for freight only. The Kadaka–Goba line links up with Mozambique's Maputo line (providing Swaziland with access to the sea). Since 1986 there has also been a direct connection between Mpaka and South Africa, extending north to Mpumalanga and south to Durban and Richards Bay. Matsapha International Airport is located 8km outside Manzini and offers direct flights to Johannesburg – although Swaziland has no international airline, following the 2000 collapse of Royal Swazi National Airways. A new multi-million-dollar airport is currently under construction near Mpaka (see page 248), with the capacity to handle the largest international jets, but the project has suffered considerable delays so don't hold your breath.

Of course the average Swazi doesn't own a car, let alone have the money for a plane ticket. Thus most people use public transport, travelling by bus and minibus (see page 127) to get from A to B and beyond.

Power The Swaziland Electricity Board (SEB) supplies energy to the nation. Hydro-electric schemes at Maguga Dam, Lupohlo Dam and Matsapha generate up to a quarter of the national requirements. The rest is imported from South Africa's main supplier, Eskom – which means, in theory, that South Africa could black-out the country at will. The power supply can be a little shaky, especially during the rainy season and in the highveld, when electrical storms cause regular power cuts. For this reason most offices and workplaces have back-up generators and UPS (Uninterrupted Power Supply) units, which kick in as soon as the lights go out and computers start bleeping. Small villages and homesteads are beyond the reach of the national power grid, and wood remains an important fuel source for much of the rural population – its harvesting taking a heavy toll on the nation's trees.

Education You won't travel far in Swaziland before speed bumps warn that you are approaching a school. Typically, this is a cluster of low, whitewashed brick classrooms with a Swazi flag planted at the centre of a neatly swept playground, and shady mango trees around the edge. Drive along any rural road on a weekday afternoon and you will pass long crocodiles of neatly uniformed, satchel-swinging schoolchildren trudging the long distance home. On any given day during term time, some 25% of Swaziland's population is at school.

Children in Swaziland undergo seven years of primary education, leading to the Swaziland Primary Certificate, and five years of secondary schooling, which culminates in O levels. Education is neither free nor compulsory, and a 2005 amendment to the constitution guaranteeing free basic primary school education has yet to be implemented. By Western standards, fees are nominal – around

Waterford Kamhlaba, which sits on a hillside just west of the main MR3 highway into Mbabane, is a remarkable school. It is one of 13 United World Colleges worldwide, and the only one in Africa. Dubbed Kamhlaba, which means 'all of one world', by the late King Sobhuza II at its opening in 1963, Waterford was southern Africa's first multi-racial school and pursues the inclusive philosophy on which the UWC network was founded. Its past students include the children of Nelson Mandela, Archbishop Desmond Tutu and ANC stalwart Walter Sisulu. Today Waterford offers a high-school education to Forms 1 to 5, followed by two years dedicated to the International Baccalaureate (IB). It has an excellent academic reputation and sends many students to top universities overseas. Attendance doesn't come cheap, but a bursary programme funds students from disadvantaged backgrounds, who are selected on merit. Students come from at least 50 countries worldwide, with at least 80% from Africa. It is central to the Waterford ethos that all students live side by side with others from a wide range of backgrounds and cultures. Community service is at the core of the curriculum, with every student taking part in activities that benefit some of the most disadvantaged communities in Swaziland.

SZL1,200 (US$144) for the year – but this is a heavy burden for many families, who must also fork out for books and uniforms. According to UNICEF statistics for 2009, net primary enrolment stood at around 83% of those eligible, with about 75% of children continuing to Grade Five. There was a sharp drop-off at secondary level, however, where only 25–30% of those eligible attended.

At the time of independence, Swaziland had just four government high schools and seven mission schools – a measure of how much the British had neglected their responsibilities in this sphere. Today, with the pressing need to educate a burgeoning population, there are at least 529 primary schools and some 160 secondary schools. These have either government, mission or private status, the majority run by missions with government grants. Public expenditure on education in 2008 stood at 6.1% of GDP, slightly more than the 5.7% spent in the UK that same year. The Ministry of Education pays, trains and houses teachers, while student fees and community contributions fund maintenance and other costs. The system is stretched, unsurprisingly, but achievements are nonetheless considerable: the national literacy rate for 15–24 year olds in 2008 stood at 92% for men and 95% for women.

Swaziland has seven institutions of higher education, of which the most important are the University of Swaziland (UNISWA), which has campuses at Kwaluseni and Luyengo (Faculty of Agriculture), and the Swaziland College of Technology (SCOT) in Mbabane. UNISWA is a historical offshoot of the joint University of Botswana, Lesotho and Swaziland, which was established in 1965 and subsequently split into its constituent national parts.

Health – and HIV/AIDS Swaziland has a poor record in public health, given that its healthcare infrastructure and services are the envy of many poorer African countries. Key indicator statistics for 2009 (UNICEF) include a mortality rate among under-fives of 73 in 1,000, a neonatal mortality rate of 20 in 1,000 and an average life expectancy at birth of 49. Given that 95–99% of children receive routine immunisation, that Swaziland is not at war or afflicted by serious famine, that 70% of people have access to clean drinking water, and that both cholera and malaria are virtually absent, these figures are alarming.

The reason, simply, is HIV/AIDS. Some 26% of all Swazis aged 15–49 live with this pernicious disease (2011), with an even higher percentage among pregnant women. This is a drop from the late 1990s peak but is still the highest infection rate in the world. It means that some 200,000 people of all ages are HIV-positive. It also means that Swaziland is home to some 100,000 orphans (nearly one-twelfth of the population and roughly equivalent to the number of adults in formal employment), of whom around 70% have lost their parents to HIV/AIDS. Anybody living and making friends in Swaziland will soon find themselves attending funerals.

This is a catastrophe – not only in terms of individual tragedy and hardship, but also for Swaziland's economy and development, with the national labour force having been savagely depleted in recent decades. It is difficult to know just why HIV has the nation in such a stranglehold. Swaziland is not unique in the region: Lesotho, Botswana, South Africa and Zimbabwe all have very high infection rates. Neither is it in complete denial: a small army of health professionals, educators, charities and NGOs have been striving since the early days to inform and educate Swazis, and the media – unlike in many countries – has never withheld the truth from the public. A student at one of the many 'Anti-AIDS' clubs nationwide can probably tell you much more about the disease, its transmission and sexual behaviour in general than can a UK child of equivalent age. Antiretroviral drugs are also widely available.

The fact remains, though, that Swaziland's traditional leaders hold great sway and many remain unconvinced. Condoms are routinely rejected as 'un-Swazi' and, at worst, the disease is depicted as racist Western propaganda. AIDS, claim the naysayers, stands for 'American Idea to Destroy Sex'. Meanwhile, multiple partners are common for Swazi men – not only in a traditional set-up – and women are often powerless to enforce safer sexual behaviour in their relationships. Young people are sexually active at an early age, and there is a low standard of sexual health in rural areas, where many people will first consult an *inyanga* (traditional healer; see page 80) before a modern doctor. Also, AIDS is not an easily demonstrable killer. It is not as though an entire family or village goes down overnight with the same conspicuous symptoms; instead, there is an irregular drip-feed of victims, whose deaths are generally ascribed to their secondary condition – typically pneumonia or TB.

Against this gloomy backdrop, Swaziland continues to offer a health service across all sectors of society. There is a mixture of public, private and private not-for-profit facilities, with most of the last owned by missions and subsidised by the government. In the public and mission sectors there are six hospitals, eight public health units and five health centres, which offer both preventative and curative services. Community care is in the hands of health clinics and outreach clinics – although, as already mentioned, many people in rural areas will still consult an *inyanga* before visiting a modern medical professional. Swaziland trains nurses but has no medical school, so students must go abroad to obtain a medical degree. Qualified medics often leave Swaziland in search of better opportunities in South Africa or elsewhere. This 'brain-drain' saps many sectors of Swazi professional life.

Defence Swaziland's military might comes down to the 3,000-odd soldiers of the Umbutfo Swaziland Defence Force (USDF). They are deployed primarily during domestic protests, with some border and customs duties, and have never been involved in a foreign conflict. Indeed, Swazis have not fought their neighbours since the late 19th century, when they helped the British subdue the Pedi threat from the north. Ever since Sobhuza took to the throne in 1920, they have prided themselves on being the region's diplomats and peacemakers. In 1941, again in response to a British request for help with the war effort, Sobhuza approved the recruitment of around 4,000 Swazi men, who served in North Africa and Italy. Their experience – fighting and dying in a distant land for someone else's cause – helped fuel the post-war independence movement.

The king is commander-in-chief of the USDF and directly oversees the Ministry of Defence. A Defence Council is responsible for advising him on all defence matters. There is no national service. New recruits are tested for HIV, with only applicants who prove negative accepted. The USDF also maintains a small air force, comprising a couple of fixed-wing light aircraft. This serves mainly to transport the king, plus cargo and personnel, and perform occasional search-and-rescue functions. Military expenditure in Swaziland in 2006 amounted to 4.7% of GDP.

PEOPLE

Swaziland has a population of some 1.1 million. By southern African standards that's fairly populous, with about 68 people per square kilometre (compared with 41 for South Africa, 29 for Mozambique and just three for Botswana). However, it still leaves the country substantially less crowded than many in Europe. The UK, for instance, has around 255 per square kilometre.

Where Swaziland's population differs markedly from that of most developed nations is in its age demographic: as of 2009, some 38% of people were aged 14 or younger, with the median age of 20 being half that of the UK's 39.8. Its current growth rate of 1.2% per year and fertility rate of 3.4 children per child-bearing woman are both relatively low by African standards, although the former is partly explained by a high death rate due to the HIV/AIDS epidemic.

People are fairly evenly distributed, with the largest population centres along the Mbabane and Manzini corridor, and – other than in the larger nature reserves and wilder mountains – you are liable to meet people anywhere you go. What's more, most people you meet will be of pretty much the same stock. Ethnic Swazis make up more than 95% of Swaziland's population and are descended from the original Bantu tribes that settled in the 1500s. Their first language is siSwati, though the majority also speaks English. This ethnic homogeneity has been central to Swaziland's peaceful history, the population having never been split along racial or tribal lines.

Other people in Swaziland include a white minority of some 3%, mostly of British or Afrikaaner descent, and often South African provenance. Some have been in the country for generations and consider themselves Swazi through and through. They also include a number who left South Africa during the bad old days to avoid national service or to give their children a non-racial education. There is a small Asian population, a growing Portuguese/Mozambican population, and a mixed-race – or 'coloured' – population, all of which are predominantly urban.

Swaziland's permanent population is swelled by a fair sprinkling of short-term expatriates. These range from overseas professionals on contract to the staff and volunteers of NGOs and development agencies. The expatriate community ballooned out of proportion to the country's needs during the 1980s and early '90s, when many international organisations preferred to make the kingdom their regional headquarters rather than do business with apartheid South Africa. There is also a pan-African diaspora from countries such as Zambia, Ghana and Nigeria, many of them educated professionals who arrived en route to South Africa but found it easier to stay – whether legally or otherwise. It all makes for a surprisingly cosmopolitan mix.

More than one million ethnic Swazis live in South Africa – about as many as in Swaziland. Most are just over the border in the areas that once made up the siSwati-speaking Bantustan (homeland) of KaNgwane, declared 'independent' by the apartheid authorities in 1981. The late King Sobhuza II once petitioned for the return of these lands to the kingdom, and indeed when passing through them today it certainly feels like Swaziland.

If Swazis were obliged to define their own national traits, high on the list would probably be patience and diplomacy. 'Anginasitsa,' the late revered King Sobhuza II is reputed to have said, meaning: 'I have no enemies'. They attribute their peaceful history over the last century to a capacity for talking things over. Indeed, it remains a convention to debate rural community affairs in regular meetings, with everyone entitled to their say. To impatient outsiders, progress may feel glacial and decisions rare. Foreign enterprises in Swaziland have often foundered when people have rushed into decisions, driven by external agendas, without ensuring that all local parties were consulted and protocols observed. Strong objections are seldom expressed directly, so an outsider may give up and leave, still mystified.

LANGUAGE

Swazis speak siSwati, which means 'of the Swazis'. This is an Nguni language the Nguni being one of two ethnic groups that made up the original southern Bantu peoples. The other group is the Sotho, whose present-day languages include Sesotho (in Lesotho) and Setswana (in Botswana). Other Nguni languages include siZulu (in KwaZulu-Natal), siNdebele (northern South Africa and western Zimbabwe) and siXhosa (South Africa's Eastern Cape). Speakers of all these languages can understand one another; some Zulu speakers claim, cheekily, that siSwati sounds like an infantilised form of their own language.

SiSwati – like all Nguni languages – presents challenges for the non-native speaker, including sounds that the European tongue is not conditioned to articulate. These include various 'click' consonants: the 'c' of Incwala is pronounced with a soft click of the tongue behind the top front teeth, as though tutting; the 'x' of Nxumalo is pronounced with a click at the back of the throat, as though geeing up a horse; and the 'q' of Liqoqo is pronounced with a hard click of the tongue against the palate. Also tricky is the use of 'l' after other consonants – such as after 'd' in Dlamini, when it is pronounced with the tongue behind the top teeth, or after an 'h', as in 'Nhlangano', which requires an unvoiced, breathier sound. English has no equivalents, but you can find them in Welsh – for example, the double 'l' at the start of 'Llanelli'.

SiSwati's structure and syntax also have little in common with English, and hinge largely upon prefixes. Thus one lilangeni (the currency) becomes two emalangeni, with 'ema-' being the plural prefix. Similarly, with verbs, ngiyahamba ('I am going') becomes uyahamba ('you are going') and siyahamba ('we are going'), with 'ngi', 'u' and 'si' denoting first person singular, second person singular and first person plural respectively.

Linguists may also note that siSwati, like most African languages, is 'syllable-timed'. This means that every syllable is pronounced clearly, rather than some being swallowed, as in 'stress-timed' languages such as English where meaning relies more upon intonation. This is why African speakers of English often use much clearer diction than native speakers. All siSwati words – as in most Bantu languages – end in a vowel, which is why Swazi English speakers may append phantom vowels to words that end in consonants: 'big' can sound a little like *biggy*; 'good', like *goody*. This trait is more common in rural areas.

But don't panic. Nearly everyone in Swaziland speaks at least some English. Indeed, English is the medium of instruction in schools and it is only among elderly, rural folk that non-siSwati speakers might struggle. And like everywhere on the planet where English is spoken, Swaziland has a few local dialect variations that may puzzle the first-timer. Some are part of a broader South African lexicon (see *South African English*, opposite). Others are uniquely Swazi. When somebody dies, for example, they are described as being 'late' – not as in 'the *late* Mr Dlamini' but as in 'Mr Dlamini is *late*'.

Contemporary siSwati is peppered with English words and phrases. That's because the Swazi lexicon has no words for many modern or imported things, and also because English (or, more accurately, American) culture is an increasingly pervasive force. Thus the Swazi lexicon has been enriched over time by such loan words as *likhemisi* (chemist), *sikhulu* (school), *dokotela* (doctor) and even *likhefi le-inthanethi* (internet café). Say these out loud and you'll see how it works.

In fact, siSwati has two registers: the informal language of everyday discourse; and the formal language, sometimes known as 'deep' siSwati, reserved for formal and ceremonial occasions and sometimes used to greet elders. Deep siSwati is a very poetic idiom, full of colour and metaphor. Had a bad day? Then you might say '*Ngihambe emalibeni ebatsakatsi*': literally, 'I've endured the sorcery of wizards.'

As a visitor to Swaziland, nobody will expect you to have mastered siSwati, deep or otherwise. In fact, many people of European descent who have lived in the country all their lives hardly speak a word. But taking the trouble to learn a few rudimentary greetings goes down very well, however much you mangle the pronunciation, and can be a real ice-breaker (see *Language*, page 299).

A handful of other languages are spoken in Swaziland: Afrikaans by those of South African Dutch descent; Portuguese by Mozambicans; Tsonga by people along the Mozambique border; and siZulu by people along the KwaZulu-Natal border. Conversely there are as many siSwati speakers outside Swaziland as inside,

SOUTH AFRICAN ENGLISH

South African English has adapted many phrases from Afrikaans, Portuguese and Bantu languages. Here are a few that you may encounter in Swaziland.

bakkie	pick-up truck
biltong	dried meat
boerewors	spicy sausage, popular on a *braai*
braai	barbecue
howzit?	'How is it going?'
jol	to have fun; a party
kraal	enclosure for livestock
lekker	nice, great
mealie	corn cob (maize)
naartjie	tangerine or mandarin
pap	traditional maize porridge
peri-peri	chili pepper
robots	traffic lights
takkies	sneakers or training shoes

You may notice what appear to be inconsistencies in people's names. My first boss in Swaziland introduced himself to me as Ndwandwe. So I was a little puzzled when I first heard him addressed as 'Nxumalo' – and even more so when, in the same conversation, he was also greeted as 'Nkhosi'. In fact, Swaziland has a system of praise names, which invoke historical connections between clans – in this case between the Ndwandwe and the Nxumalo – and which may be used to greet or thank somebody. These might also include praise phrases such as *wena wekunene* ('you of the right'). Respect is conferred by the use of 'Nkhosi', which is the praise name of the royal Dlamini clan, to whom all Swazis are connected according to traditional ties. It is perfectly acceptable – indeed, right and proper – to address an older man as 'Nkhosi', whether or not you know his family name.

Spelling can also be puzzling, particularly with respect to proper nouns such as surnames and place names. Is it 'Mndzebele' or 'Mndebele', for instance? 'Usuthu' or 'Lusutfu'? In each case the words refer to exactly the same person, place or thing. The discrepancies can be partially explained by differences between siSwati and siZulu, with the two languages overlapping either side of the border, and by different Swazi regional dialects.

mostly in the former KaNgwane, just over the border. Altogether there are some three million speakers of siSwati.

CULTURE

Swaziland's traditional culture is its biggest tourist attraction, and used to sell everything from postcards to guidebooks (see the front cover of this one). The appeal is self-evident: this tiny kingdom has managed to retain traditions that date back to pre-colonial times and that, despite all the challenges of modernity, remain visibly fundamental to its cultural life. Of course Swaziland is not a living museum. Nonetheless, the fact remains that you can get a better idea of traditional African culture here than pretty much anywhere else in the region, and that what you will see, including spectacular festivals, has not simply been resuscitated for the tourist dollar but is the real deal.

Today there is an increasingly sharp distinction between people living in urban and rural areas. The rise of a middle-class 'Western' lifestyle in the former, transforming everything from marriage to employment, has left many traditional practices on the wane – although their undercurrents still inform society in ways that are not always apparent to the outsider. To get a better idea of traditional Swazi culture you need to visit the rural areas.

THE HOMESTEAD The basic building block of Swazi society is the homestead (*umuti*). Traditionally this comprises a number of huts, each built for a particular purpose. Sleeping huts house family members, while other huts serve for food storage, brewing and other functions. Larger homesteads – according to the status of the headman – might have additional structures such as bachelor quarters and guest accommodation. The area around and between huts is kept free of grass and the sand swept clean – traditionally to guard against snakes and reveal the footprints of any unwelcome intruders.

At the centre of a homestead is a circular cattle kraal (enclosure), the *sibaya*, fenced with solid logs and branches, where the cattle are housed every night. This has symbolic importance as a store of wealth and prestige. Women are traditionally barred from the cattle byre. Opposite it is the great hut, *indlukulu*, occupied by the mother of the headman and used as the family shrine.

The huts in such homesteads would once have been 'beehive' huts. Today most rural homesteads are a mixture of traditional huts and more modern, brick-built dwellings. Either way, you can visit and enter homesteads when exploring rural Swaziland, and will receive a warm welcome providing you show suitable respect and follow correct protocol. If in doubt, travelling with a guide on a cultural tour (see *Tour operators* on page 102) will make things easier. Mantenga Cultural Village (see page 171) is an excellent working reconstruction of a traditional homestead from around the 1850s, where you can discover in detail all the complexities and nuances of traditional Swazi life.

MEN, WOMEN AND MARRIAGE Traditional Swazi society was strongly patriarchal, with the roles of men and women sharply defined. Men were responsible for the cattle – only they were permitted to herd and plough. Women, meanwhile, wove basketware, ground maize and brewed beer. Both sexes tilled the fields, although most of this work fell to women. As children grew up, men would spend time with boys to prepare them for manhood, while women taught girls their domestic responsibilities and prepared them for marriage.

The traditional family unit was a polygamous one – or more accurately, polygynous, in that one man had a number of wives. A homestead would include the headman (*umnumzane*), his wives, unmarried siblings and married sons with their wives and children. Each wife would have her own hut and would be ranked according to her role in the household – older wives might no longer sleep with the headman, for instance, but continue to play an important role in advising the younger child-bearing wives.

Marriage aimed to cement ties between families and thus solidify the clan structure. Once a suitable bride was found and the match approved, the marriage was sealed by payment by the groom's to the bride's family of a bride price called *lobola*. This took the form of cattle. Precise details were negotiated using an intermediary, but a typical rate would be 15 cows for a standard bride and 25 for one of more distinguished birth. Today other forms of livestock, such as goats, or simply cash, may form part of the deal – and payment may come in instalments or involve credit arrangements.

A traditional wedding (*umtsimba*) was held during a weekend in the dry season. The bride and her relatives would arrive at the groom's homestead on the Friday evening. On the Saturday, they would gather in the morning by the nearby river and feast on a goat or cow that had been slaughtered by the groom's family, then in the afternoon they would dance. On the Sunday morning, the bride – accompanied by her female relatives – would stab the ground with a spear in the man's cattle kraal. She would then present gifts to her new husband and his relatives. Later she would be smeared with red ochre to symbolise the couple's bond until death returned them to the soil.

Today, many of these customs still prevail, especially in the rural areas, but things have become more complicated. Polygamous marriage is not recognised in Swazi civil law and the custom is declining as better education leads more women to question their lot. Some have also blamed polygamy for facilitating the spread of HIV/AIDS. It remains hard to challenge this custom, however, when the ultimate role model – the King himself – has 14 wives and counting. Of more practical concern for many men is the rising price of cattle, which means that paying *lobola* for multiple wives is beyond their reach. Meanwhile, a Western-style church service has become the norm for weddings – although the ceremony may well still incorporate many traditional components.

Many Swazi men still have children by multiple women, whether or not these women are officially their wives. But the blurring of boundaries between customary practice and civil law has brought an increase in marital conflicts – and a rise in divorce rates. Women today form an increasing percentage of the urban workforce and NGOs are working hard to advise rural women of their rights. In the rural areas, however, the divisions remain clear: you will not see women herding cattle or men behind a vegetable stall, and boys still tend to be the favoured children – sent to school in preference to their sisters, for instance, when the family can't afford to educate everyone.

CRADLE TO GRAVE Most women in Swaziland have children very young, often before marriage, although having fewer children and having them later is an increasing trend in urban society. Part of the deal with *lobola* was traditionally that the husband also bought rights over the children. If the bride price remained unpaid, the child remained with the mother's family. Today it is not uncommon for children from a youthful pre-marital liaison to be reared by grandparents or the extended family. A future husband may welcome the existence of such children by another man as proof of his wife's fertility – it is not the taboo that you might expect from other cultures – but he may not be prepared to take them on and provide for them.

A newborn baby is welcomed into the world with white 'luck' beads placed around its waist, wrist or ankles. Traditionally, infants were not recognised as people until their third month of life, and could not be touched by men during that time. Mothers carried the child in a sling on their back as most women, traditional or modern, still do today. From the age of three, the child would play with other children in the homestead. But aged around six, girls and boys would be separated in preparation for their respective adult roles. A boy was taught male matters by male members of the family, entering a regiment (*libutfo*) in which he trained with boys of similar age from other clans. A girl, meanwhile, learned domestic responsibilities and social conventions from her mother and female relations. At her first period, she was isolated in a hut for several days. Today, these customs have weakened with mixed primary schooling for all. Nonetheless, you will not travel far in rural Swaziland without meeting young boys herding cattle and young girls carrying water back to the homestead.

Swazis generally live in large extended families. Western visitors to a Swazi home, even a modern one, often struggle to grasp who is related to whom. The head of the household may be looking after children from relatives out of town, while an older niece might be working as a live-in home help. Terms such as *bhuti* (brother), *sisi* (sister), *make* (mother) and *babe* (father) are used loosely, and you will soon discover that the narrow Western notions of a nuclear family are irrelevant. In general – and with the usual caveat about changing times – the elderly are treated with a deference that seems largely to be vanishing in the West. In a Swazi homestead it is grandparents who traditionally teach the young to respect the parents, and also act as an intermediary between parents and children in times of strife. These elders are seen as repositories of wisdom, both spiritual and practical.

Death in Swazi society generally invokes the ancestral spirits. Traditionally, various rites are performed for the deceased, with more elaborate ones reserved for those of higher status. Funerals are lively affairs, with mourning often loud and histrionic. Commoners are buried by their homestead, with a headman traditionally laid to rest at the entrance to his cattle enclosure. Kings and royals are buried in caves in sacred sites such as Mdzimba. The traditional mourning period is longer for a widow than a widower. A widow was once expected to continue her husband's lineage by becoming the wife of her deceased husband's brother, but this tradition is on the way out.

Funerals play a significant social role in Swaziland, providing an opportunity for the extended family to get together. The very public grief on such occasions, with widows and female relatives often falling to the floor, beating their breasts and wailing, while elders loudly exhort the ancestral spirits, can be alarming to the Western visitor more used to stoical reserve and tears discreetly dabbed with a hankie. Yet it becomes clear this is almost a form of celebration to mark the passing of the deceased into the next world. As a result funerals are treated in a similar way to weddings, with relatives flocking to enjoy the bereaved family's hospitality – often staying for days to take advantage of the feasting.

Recent decades have seen a problem with this tradition. The HIV/AIDS crisis has made funerals ever more commonplace. This, coupled with economic hardship and the trend towards increasingly lavish 'celebrations', has put a severe strain on resources. Families who have just lost a breadwinner find themselves obliged to fork out for food, drink and hospitality on top of the ever-rising costs of the funeral itself, and many are driven into debt. A recent steep rise in the number of unclaimed bodies in morgues – a phenomenon once considered so 'un-Swazi' as to be inconceivable – has shocked the nation. In 2002 Mswati issued a general proclamation warning people that to exploit one another's hospitality during hard times was itself un-Swazi.

SPIRITUAL LIFE Swaziland is a highly spiritual nation in which the great majority of people believe in an afterlife of some kind. As with so many things Swazi, however, religion today is caught between two worlds. Some 82% of the population is nominally Christian, yet for many – especially in rural areas – this Christianity is strongly informed by traditional African belief systems.

Traditional beliefs
The pre-Christian Swazi belief system revolves around ancestral spirits (*emadloti*). These are thought to take many forms, sometimes possessing people and influencing their welfare, including their health. They are ranked by clan, like their living descendants.

This traditional spirituality is most strongly evident in the role of the diviners and healers – crudely labelled 'witch doctors' by Westerners – who have long been pivotal to Swazi society. A diviner is known as a *sangoma* (plural *tangoma*) and is a kind of spirit medium, supposedly called to the profession through possession by ancestral spirits. *Tangoma* undergo a lengthy training called *kwetfwasa*. In the traditional homestead a hut was set aside for the *sangoma*. In times of trouble, such as sickness or drought, he or she was petitioned to intercede by communicating with the spirits. This process, called *kubhula*, involved a kind of trance, and would often result in various sacrifices to appease the ancestors. Diviners are often women, with the queen mother accorded the ultimate symbolic responsibility as custodian of rain medicines.

For medical matters, villagers consulted a traditional healer called an *inyanga* (plural *tinyanga*). He or she was a herbalist who tackled illness using natural materials such as roots, bark and leaves. Like *tangoma*, *tinyanga* also used spiritual rituals such as bone throwing (*kushaya ematsambo*) to determine the cause of the sickness. Traditionally, they received first a goat, spear or other items by way of initial payment, followed by a gift of meat during treatment and, if successful, a cow in gratitude for services rendered. Today most charge set fees.

Tangoma enjoy higher status than *tinyanga*, as ancestral spirits are believed to work through them directly. Nonetheless, *tinyanga* remain much respected in society. According to traditional belief, serious diseases emanate from evil spirits and are directed at somebody out of ill will. Today people still differentiate between ailments they regard as 'foreign', such as cholera, for which they are happy to receive orthodox medical treatment, and those they see as 'Swazi'. For the latter, which includes sexually transmitted diseases, children's illnesses, migraines and various forms of mental illness, many will first consult an *inyanga*. This can lead to problems – especially since treatment may involve incisions and thus risks the transmission of HIV/AIDS and other diseases via infected razor blades. Mental illness is also a difficult area, where violent rituals intended to drive out evil spirits may be prescribed for somebody suffering from depression or trauma.

Outsiders find it easy to dismiss traditional healers as representing little more than primitive superstition. However, these figures have been and undoubtedly can still be a positive force in rural society. They were, after all, serving their communities for centuries before Western medicine reached Swaziland. Most have an extensive practical understanding of natural products, which they employ to good effect,

MUTI

The natural ingredients used by traditional healers are known collectively as *muti*. They comprise plant products such as herbs and bark (the word derives from the Zulu *umuthi*, meaning 'tree'), but also mineral products and many animal body parts. These animal products are often employed for symbolic value. For example, the hand of a bushbaby – an animal admired for its strong grip – may be used in rituals aimed at preventing a man's wife from straying, or even a goalkeeper from dropping a ball. Nose around the stalls in Manzini Market (see page 198) and you will find many such products.

The use of *muti* in magic charms is alive and well today. The practice is not confined to rural communities but enters all areas of modern life, including business, sport and politics. A businessman, for example, might employ a *sangoma* to help further his prospects or weaken that of his rivals, which may well entail rituals involving *muti*. This is often the cause of controversy. In 2009, for instance, people were outraged to discover that someone had been digging holes in the football pitch at Somhlolo national stadium in order to insert *muti* underneath, presumably in an effort to influence match results.

At the most extreme and shocking level are *muti* murders, in which people – often children – are killed so that their body parts can be used in ritual. This is very rare and many grisly stories are apocryphal. But it does happen. Indeed, the last person to be executed in Swaziland was restaurant owner Philippa Mdluli, who on 2 July 1983 was hanged after being found guilty of murdering small girls for ritual purposes. As recently as 2011 there were a number of *muti* murders reported in the southern Shiselwini region, in which victims were mutilated for body parts. Such horrific crimes invariably have big money behind them. This practice, which featured in Alexander McCall-Smith's *The No. 1 Ladies' Detective Agency* books, set in Botswana, remains a problem across southern Africa.

and also have the ear of their communities, which enables them to perform an effective counselling role. There are charlatans among them, of course, but that's true of both doctors and faith healers anywhere. Today most are officially registered within traditional healers' organisations and subscribe to accepted codes of conduct, including sterilisation of blades and other practices that promote hygiene.

Christianity and other faiths Today Swaziland is a predominantly Christian country, with some 82% of the population registered as regular churchgoers. Indeed, Westerners who admit to not being churchgoers may meet with incredulity, especially as the very idea of a Church came from overseas. Methodists established the first mission in Swaziland at Mahamba in 1912 (see page 238). In the century since, however, the Christian faith has diversified. As well as Catholics (Swaziland falls within the Diocese of Manzini), Protestants and Anglicans, there are numerous evangelical denominations and sects, including the Seventh-Day Adventists, Jehovah's Witnesses and Church of Jesus Christ of the Latter-Day Saints. Most are funded from overseas, enabling their shiny new churches to mushroom around the country with almost miraculous speed. Revivalist preachers, many from the USA, broadcast through local radio, spouting salvation and damnation to their Swazi brethren.

Swaziland's most popular formal religious denomination, claiming some 40% of all worshippers, is the African Zionist Church. This is the largest religious movement in southern Africa, with some 15–18 million followers (*amaZioni*). Founded by John Alexander Dowie of the Christian Catholic Church in Zion, Illinois, who sent missionaries to South Africa in 1903, it has since evolved through various African incarnations and today offers Swazis a means of combining Christianity with African traditional beliefs and customs. The practices of Zionism include faith healing, water baptism, the wearing of robes – different colours for different sects – and the carrying of staffs. If you see a column of people dressed in white robes with coloured belts, as though heading for a martial arts tournament, they're probably African Zionists.

Other religions in Swaziland make up a very small minority. They include Islam (0.9%), with mosques in Manzini and Mbabane, Bahai'i (0.5%), with a centre on the Malagwane Hill, and Hinduism (0.15%). Religious tensions have never really troubled the kingdom: the revised constitution of 2005 provides for freedom of religion and the school curriculum incorporates a multi-faith approach.

In spiritual terms then – as in so many other respects – Swaziland finds itself caught between the old and the new. When wandering around modern downtown Mbabane, or talking to educated Swazis, it can be hard to believe that traditional spiritual beliefs still hold such sway. Yet many people who seem otherwise 'Westernised' will still place their trust in a traditional healer for many matters and will talk routinely about a person being 'bewitched'. This legacy of traditional African belief may also explain a certain *que sera sera* fatalism (the siSwati phrase is *'kuba njalo nje'*). 'It was his time,' is a sentiment that you will often hear – even to explain the death of somebody in what to most westerners would seem a completely arbitrary accident. Indeed, there can be few places that illustrate more vividly than Swaziland the complex interrelationship of tradition and modernity. A young Swazi today may drive a company car, eat at a Chinese restaurant and communicate via social networking – but at the weekend, she may have to cover her head and go down on bended knee to enter the hut of her rural mother-in-law. Small wonder that people seek spiritual answers to change, and that these answers are themselves often a reflection of the two different worlds.

DRESS Attire is used in traditional Swazi culture to convey numerous messages relating to age, gender and status, and today remains pivotal to such festivals as the Incwala and Umhlanga (see pages 92 and 93).

A man's traditional clothing consists of a sarong-style, knee-length cloth skirt called a *lihiya* (plural *emahiya*), over which he wears an animal-skin apron called a *lijobo* (plural *emajobo*), typically the hide of a hare or small antelope. Strict rules govern how these items can be worn and in what combinations –*lijoba* without *lihiya*, for instance, is unthinkable. A married man wears a cloth wrap around his upper torso, fastened over one shoulder. Grandfathers and elderly men might wear a headband of animal hide.

Girls, traditionally, wore nothing but a string of beads until the age of eight, at which point they would add a short skirt of grass or cloth (*lihiya*), but never a long skirt until the age of 15. A married woman put up her hair in a bun called a beehive, wore a heavy, cow-skin skirt and covered her upper torso with a wrap of cloth or goatskin. This wrap was fastened under the armpits by a newly-wed then raised over one shoulder after the birth of a first child.

On top of these basics came many accessories for ceremonial occasions. Men embellished their outfit with a *ligcebesha* (neckband) and *umgaco* (wrist and ankle ties), and carried weapons such as the *sagibo* (knob-stick), spear and tasselled shield. Girls carried a switch and small ornamental shield, along with traditional headgear, tassels and a beaded loincloth. The colours and combinations of beads revealed social and marital status, or different stages in a courtship. Most important remain the red feathers of the purple-crested turaco, or *ligwalagwala*, which are worn in the hair of royalty.

Today the average Swazi does not wander around in full traditional regalia. Western-style clothes such as T-shirts and jeans are the norm, with women often donning elaborate modern hairstyles. Nonetheless, most people keep traditional attire in their wardrobe for formal or ceremonial occasions, and those of an older generation may mix and match – perhaps *lihiya* and *lijoba* below, with jacket and tie on top. Wraps, skirts and *emahiya* tend these days to be in colourful printed fabrics, typically featuring a portrait of a youthful Mswati and often in Swaziland's national primary colours. Traditional dress is, needless to say, more common in rural areas, and you will often spy a distinguished gent from out of town walking along a crowded shopping street in full warrior garb, complete with knob-stick and leopard-skin loincloth.

FOOD AND DRINK Traditional Swazi food is both regional and seasonal, as you would expect in a country of subsistence farmers. The staple diet is maize, ground

HOT STUFF

Lovers of fiery food should look out for the Eswatini Swazi Kitchen range of spicy preserves (*www.eswatinikitchen.com*). This company was set up in 1991 by a Catholic priest and an Anglican nun to create jobs for local communities and generate funds for Manzini Youth Care, an NGO caring for children affected by HIV/AIDS. It has since grown considerably, won numerous prizes, and exports under the Fair Trade banner to 14 different international destinations, including the US and UK. The products, which include such delights as kumquat atchar, are made entirely from local natural ingredients, with no artificial additives or preservatives.

into a coarse powder known as mealie meal (corn cobs, known locally as mealies, are whiter than the yellow Western varieties). Mealie meal is cooked into a stodgy, starchy dish called *pap*, which may be eaten plain or made into a porridge using fermented sour milk – a dish with many local variations that is called *lipalishi* (a corruption of 'porridge'). It is served with a vegetable sauce known as relish, which generally consists of onions, tomatoes and often various spinach-like leaves. One particularly slimy spinach dish called *ligusha* is seen as so typically Swazi that locals are often highly amused when an outsider claims to have tried and enjoyed it.

Meat is a luxury in rural households, animals generally being slaughtered only for special occasions, and is still generally considered a high-status food across Swaziland. Chicken and goat are both popular, with beef reserved for special occasions. Stews may be spiced with chillies. Most parts of an animal are eaten, with tripe, offal, hooves, trotters and chicken gizzards all very popular. When people do eat meat, they tend to eat a lot of it: it's worth attending a wedding just to marvel at how much charred flesh one person can cram onto a single plate. African Zionists do not eat pork.

Other popular foods include pumpkin, beans and rice, where available. Sweet potatoes are widely cultivated and sorghum is farmed in some areas. Fruits include many tropical varieties in season, such as mango, guava, paw-paw, banana and avocado, which grow freely around most homesteads. The best time for most fruits is the late rainy season, from December to March, when market stalls are heaving with the stuff.

For the ordinary rural Swazi, breakfast usually consists of tea, bread and/or sour-milk mealie porridge. Bread or leftovers are eaten for lunch. A typical dinner will be *pap*, vegetables and – with luck – meat. Traditionally this would be cooked in a three-legged pot over an open fire. Today most rural Swazis supplement their diet at the local store, where tinned fish, corned beef and other preserved foods offer reasonably cheap protein. Here they will also buy bread, potato chips, and a wide variety of sweet cakes that tend to be large and, frankly, tasteless. Market stalls will also often serve hot food such as roasted mealies and paper wraps of boiled groundnuts. A particularly tasty and filling roadside snack is *sinkhwa semmbila*, or mealie bread, which is steamed and wrapped inside the sheath of the corncob.

SOME TRADITIONAL SWAZI FOODS

sishwala	thick porridge normally served with meat or vegetables
incwancwa	sour porridge made of fermented mealie meal
sitfubi	fresh milk cooked and mixed with mealie meal
siphuphe setindlubu	thick porridge made of mashed groundnuts
emasi etinkhobe temmbila	ground mealies mixed with sour milk
emasi emabele	ground sorghum mixed with sour milk
sidvudvu	porridge made from pumpkin mixed with mealie meal
umncweba	dried uncooked meat (biltong)
umkhunsu	cooked and dried meat
siphuphe semabhontjisi	thick porridge made of mashed beans
tinkhobe	boiled whole maize
umbidvo wetintsanga	cooked pumpkin leaves mixed with groundnuts
emahewu	drink made from fermented mealie meal

Drink and drinking Drink for the average rural Swazi tends to mean either water – often from a borehole – or home-brewed mealie beer known as *tjwala* (or, in South Africa, *umcombotsi*). This beer is also sold commercially in cardboard cartons, with various popular brands. Bottled soft drinks are popular, including many exceptionally sickly South African varieties, with their relatively high prices mitigated by a deposit system for empties. A popular local drink is *emasi*, or sour milk, often served with sugar.

During the January–March *marula* season, when the marula tree produces its plum-like fruits, the nation's drinkers have a treat in store. The fruits are gathered from beneath the tree when green and stored until they ripen to a creamy yellow. They are then placed in water and sugar added. The mixture ferments and is distilled into a potent alcoholic drink called *buganu*, or marula beer. *Buganu* is served at township and roadside shebeens that mushroom around the country. Truly dedicated *buganu* drinkers may go AWOL from their place of work for days. A marula festival is held in the lowveld every February and attended by the king and queen mother. Crime levels soar at this time, and you should take special care when driving; I have had to dodge drinkers lying comatose on the verge.

Alcohol divides opinion in Swaziland. As a general rule, people tend to drink either a great deal or nothing at all. There is little middle ground, and the standard Western-style compromise – say, an occasional glass or two of wine at a party – is not the norm. It is perhaps telling that Swazis offering you a drink generally ask whether you 'take' beer or wine, that verb suggesting a choice of lifestyle as much as a choice of drink. Bottle stores are a feature of even the smallest rural community. The connoisseur, meanwhile, will find a good selection of South African wines in towns and hotels. Drinking and driving is, of course, as illegal as anywhere else. But the law is not strictly enforced and among Swazis and expatriates alike there is less of the social taboo that surrounds this lethal practice in the West. Be careful.

BUILDINGS AND ARCHITECTURE

The traditional Swazi dwelling is the beehive hut. This round, dome-like structure is made of coarse thatching grass on a frame of saplings. It has one extremely low door, through which you must bend double to enter – a defensive measure to guard against a quick smash-and-grab by enemies. The circular design aims to guard against evil spirits from lurking in corners. A typical homestead comprised a number of beehive huts built close beside one another, some larger than others according to who or what they were for. The 'great hut' at the centre was reserved for the ancestral spirits.

Beehive huts may seem dark and poky to the outsider, but their design has many advantages, being warm in winter and cool in summer. The floor is raked sand, and a fire is generally kept lit in the middle, with the smoke helping fumigate the hut against insects before exiting through the thatch. The hut – indeed the homestead as a whole – traditionally had no chairs. People sat and slept on grass mats, using carved wooden headrests as pillows. Tourist-friendly beehive huts at resorts such as Hawane, Mlilwane, Nisela and Phophonyane tend to come with bed, linen and a shower. To see the real deal, and learn about its construction and use, visit the Mantenga Cultural Village (see page 171) or try a cultural home-stay tour (see page 128).

Today a more widespread hut is based on the Sotho version, with mud walls and a pointed, thatched roof. This also has a full-size door and often windows, too. However, mud and grass structures of any kind are increasingly giving way to brick dwellings, with glass windows, solid wooden doors and a corrugated iron roof – somewhere, in other words, where you can install a gas stove and fridge, and pipe water to a tap. Roofs are often weighted down with old car tyres in an erroneous belief that this protects them from lightning strikes. Such homes are easier to build and more compatible with modern life, and many fear that the traditional beehive construction skills will soon be lost to history. Whatever the building material, however, and even if the roof now sports a satellite dish and a Toyota is parked outside, the configuration of the buildings within a homestead has changed relatively little.

In town, most Swazis inhabit high-density suburbs known as townships. Here there is better access to amenities such as electricity and piped water than in the rural areas, but much of the accommodation is quite rudimentary by Western standards, and is often poorly served by inadequate street lighting, refuse collection and other services. At the other end of the scale are the more opulent dwellings of the well-to-do: politicians, business people, expatriates and those from the aid/diplomatic community. Wander the plusher suburbs of Mbabane and you will see high walls topped with razor wire and patrolled by uniformed security guards. Behind the walls are manicured lawns, glittering swimming pools and large, low-rise houses with sweeping verandas. Relatively cheap land and relaxed planning laws have allowed some with money and architectural ambitions to create flamboyant dream homes. Take a peek at the larger houses along Pine Valley, just north of Mbabane (see page 158), where some amazing houses have been discreetly – or not so discreetly – smuggled into the boulder-strewn hillsides.

ARTS AND CRAFTS Swaziland has a fine artisanal culture, with many of its products now adorning ethnic craft boutiques around the world. Some are the product of tradition; other crafts have been imported – notably by South Africans, who came over the border during apartheid to find a liberated land of skills and enterprise that was ripe for cottage industry. There are numerous outlets around the country – both formal and informal – where you can admire and purchase this work. Some of it may seem familiar: Swazi candles, mohair blankets and grass mats are now widely available overseas, at overseas prices. But here you can watch its creators in action. And at socially responsible outlets (see page 88) you can meet the women for whom the work provides both income and empowerment in poor rural communities.

Painting The first art in Swaziland was daubed by the indigenous San on the granite walls of cave shelters: images of hunters and animals etched in natural materials, including tree gum, milk, animal fat, urine, egg-white and animal blood. The colours that have endured best are the red, obtained from haematite ore, and the black, made from charcoal. The artists used their fingers, and tools made from sticks, feathers and thin bones, and it is thought that their images were inspired during shamanic trance dances. The most impressive and accessible example is at Nsangwini, near Piggs Peak (see page 219). There are other sites in gorges and mountains around the country, and no doubt more to be discovered. If you stumble across one, treat it with respect: do not touch the images or – as some tourist vandals are wont to do – splash water over it for a clearer photograph.

Today, Swazi artists paint in a variety of media. Typically their works are on board or canvas, and depict colourful scenes of local culture and nature – often in an African naïve style. You can find a wide selection at craft markets and at various galleries (see page 88). Well-known Swazi artists include Jeffrey Mabuza. Recent political protests have been credited with inspiring a boom in local art, with the incorporation of a wider range of contemporary styles among a new generation of young artists, and regular exhibitions. Good galleries include Guava Gallery (Ezulwini; see page 167), Indingilizi (Mbabane; see page 157), House on Fire

(Malandela's; see page 185) and Stik in Mud (Lobamba; ☎ 7651 4466), the last of these a tiny room in a poor neighborhood that shows local pieces by adults and children, often raw and quite challenging.

Batiks Swaziland's Batik industry is based at Baobab Batik (see page 188), which started in 1991. It has outlets at the Malandela's and Swazi Candles complexes (see page 187), where you can choose from among clothing, cushion covers, table linen and the like. You can also watch the artists in action at Under African Skies, their workshop near the back entrance to Mlilwane Game Sanctuary (see page 177).

Candles If you've encountered just one Swazi craft item overseas, the chances are it's a candle. These exquisite items come from the Swazi Candle Factory near Malkerns (see page 187), where you can watch the workers doing their stuff with coloured wax. This is now one of Swaziland's main tourist attractions, and is at the centre of a complex of handicraft outfits.

Carvings and sculpture Swaziland has a fine tradition of carving, both in wood and stone. You'll find various wooden items in craft markets around the country – mostly functional pieces such as bowls and salad servers made from kiaat wood and polished to a fine sheen. A recent trend for carving with chainsaws has spawned some larger, more abstract sculptures, mostly in jacaranda wood. Stone carvers work largely with soapstone, turning their skilled hands to everything from palm-sized ashtrays to larger-than-life human sculptures, the latter demanding more than your average baggage allowance. A variety is available at most tourist outlets, but perhaps the best – and certainly the best bargains – are to be had at roadside stalls such as those near Malolotja (see page 216). For a more modern, irreverent take on Swazi art and sculpture, the House on Fire studio (see page 186) showcases a collection of flamboyantly original work by a resident artists' collective.

Glass-blowing At the Ngwenya Glass factory near the Ngwenya border (see page 201), you can watch glass-blowers creating everything from tableware to animal figurines, all from 100% recycled glass. This award-winning enterprise now exports all over the world, and has a sister workshop in Johannesburg and a boutique in Cape Town.

Grass weaving Most markets and craft stalls display beautifully patterned baskets woven from grass or sisal and coloured with natural dyes. This tradition has spawned two impressive enterprises: Tintsaba near Piggs Peak (see page 227) and Gone Rural at Malandela's (see page 185). Both now produce and export a wide range of products and employ hundreds of local women, making a major contribution to their surrounding communities.

Jewellery Traditional Swazi jewellery is beadwork, used in bracelets, anklets, necklaces and other accessories, with messages conveyed in the patterns and motifs. Today it ranges from ethnic pieces incorporating such natural products as seedpods and feathers, to fine items in gold and silver. The most interesting involve a combination of the two. Good outlets include Guava Gallery, Indingilizi, Tintsaba, Malandela's and Likhweti Craft; see *Arts and crafts outlets*, page 88.

Mohair weaving Mohair weaving came to Swaziland in 1949 with Coral Stephens, who established her workshop in the Piggs Peak area (see page 227).

Teaching traditional skills to local women, she produced a range of fine, hand-woven fabrics – curtains, carpets, blankets and the like – that have since found a worldwide market. Rosecraft, south of Matsapha (see page 243), now creates a similar range of products using traditional techniques. Both enterprises employ many local women.

Arts and crafts outlets Handicraft stalls are everywhere in Swaziland. Those around tourist hubs have the greatest variety but also the highest prices. You'll find more bargains among the dusty stalls of Manzini or Mbabane markets, while rubbing shoulders with the locals. Root around for charming and original items, such as carved wooden Coca-Cola bottles, African birds (hoopoe, sunbird, crested barbet, etc) made from painted jacaranda pods, and all manner of ingenious wire toys – including motorbikes and helicopters. And check the roadside: stone carvers outside Malolotja, for instance, display wonderful creations along the verge. For tourist-friendly shopping, try the following centres:

African Queen (Ezulwini; see page 167) Boutique at the Lugogo Sun Hotel with products from most of Swaziland's handicraft enterprises, plus clothing, jewellery & interesting collectables from around Africa.

Ezulwini Craft Market (Ezulwini; see page 167) Large collection of craft & curio stalls, recently relocated from the Ezulwini roadside. Local products supplemented with regular deliveries from Johannesburg.

Indingilizi Gallery (Mbabane; see page 157) Town gallery with impressive collection of African art & artefacts & an excellent courtyard café.

Lonhlupeko Craft Market (Siteki; see page 254) Community tourism project with handicraft stalls, including carvings, batik & beadwork, embroidery, candles, basketware, glassware & jewellery.

Malandela's complex (Malkerns/Mahlanya; see page 185) Family-owned complex of craft outlets, plus restaurant, performance venue & guesthouse. Includes Gone Rural (grass weaving) & House on Fire (sculpture).

Mantenga Craft Centre and Guava Gallery (Mantenga/Ezulwini; see page 167) Diverse collection of arts & crafts outlets, including rugs,

curios, baskets, mohair & jewellery. Nearby Guava Gallery has a jeweller's & art gallery.

Manzini Market (Manzini; see page 198) Large, lively local market that sells produce, clothes, handicrafts & local herbal medicines from countless stalls. Best on Thu.

Mbabane Market (Manzini; see page 156) Less lively than Manzini Market, but still with plenty of local products & produce for those with time & initiative to explore.

Ngwenya Glass Complex (Ngwenya; see page 201) Cluster of handicraft stalls & shops centred around Ngwenya Glass workshop & showroom. Popular tourist destination, with café & children's play area.

Peak Craft Centre (Piggs Peak; see page 227) Includes Coral Stephens Hand-weaving (mohair), Tintsaba (sisal), Likhweti (jewellery) & other smaller outlets & vendors' stalls. Good café with fine view.

Swazi Candles complex (Malkerns; see page 187) Swazi Candles Factory, plus numerous other craft outlets, including Baobab Batik, Rosecraft (mohair) & other outlets. Popular tourist destination with an excellent café.

SPORT AND RECREATION

Soccer Swaziland's sporting life – like that of many African countries – is dominated by soccer. The dustiest rural homestead sees barefoot children contesting fierce matches using a ball fashioned from rolled-up plastic bags, and most villages have their pitch – often a stony, uneven square complete with a few desultory goats nibbling at the penalty spot.

This passion for the beautiful game is reflected among Swazis in an encyclopaedic knowledge of the English Premier League, locally available via South African television, which can prove a handy conversational ice-breaker. Indeed, English soccer has been popular ever since two teams, Liverpool and Tottenham Hotspur, visited Swaziland during the 1980s (being obliged by the cultural boycott to avoid South Africa) and played exhibition matches at the national stadium. Football fans of a certain age may be amused to know that the former Tottenham striker Steve Archibald remains something of a cult figure. Today, Arsenal, Chelsea and Manchester United are predictably popular, and you will often spot boys wearing replica kits with the names of icons such as Drogba emblazoned across their shoulders.

Sadly, this enthusiasm has never translated into international success – which is hardly surprising given Swaziland's size. The national team, which is known as Sihlangu Semnikati (King's Shield) and plays at Somhlolo Stadium (see page 176), stood at 179 in the 2012 FIFA world rankings, between Afghanistan and the British Virgin Islands. Swaziland have never qualified for the Africa Cup of Nations finals, let alone the World Cup. Their high point to date was probably 8 June 2008, when they notched up a glorious 2–1 home victory in a World Cup qualifier over 2006 finalists Togo.

At a domestic level, Swaziland has two leagues: the MTN Premier League and, below it, the PLS First Division. Among the top clubs in the former are Mbabane Highlanders, Mbabane Swallows, Manzini Wanderers, Royal Leopards and – surely one of the best-named club sides anywhere in the world – Eleven Men in Flight, a team from rural Siteki, who have achieved great things against the big city clubs. A number of Swazi footballers have found success with well-known clubs in South Africa, including Sibusiso Dlamini (Kaizer Chiefs) and Dennis Masina (Supersport United).

Other sports and games Other sports in Swaziland fall under the auspices of the Swaziland National Sports Council, a part of the Ministry of Sports, Culture

SWAZI SCALES THE HEIGHTS

On 26 May 2003, Sibusiso Vilane – an ex-ranger from Malolotja Nature Reserve – became the first black African to reach the summit of Mount Everest. Vilane grew up in Swaziland, where he completed his O-levels at Mater Dolorosa school in Mbabane. His mountaineering exploits were inspired and sponsored by ex-British High Commissioner John Doble, and began in the Drakensberg, moving on to Kilimanjaro and finally the Himalayas. 'The fact that I was able to do it despite coming from a non-climbing background shows the world and every African that we also have what it takes to achieve greatness,' said Vilane. 'It is a message to all those who overlook Africa.' This message was endorsed at the highest level: 'He has shown the heights we can all scale in life if we put our shoulder to the wheel and work at things without flagging,' said the then South African president Thabo Mbeki. 'Sibusiso, you have done us proud!'

In 2005 Vilane climbed Everest a second time, raising US$40,000 for two children's charities, and has since become the first black African member of the elite 'Seven Summits' club, named after those who have scaled the highest peak on all seven continents. In 2008, he was the first black African to walk completely unassisted to the South Pole, travelling 1,113km in 65 days through one of the world's most hostile environments. You can read Vilane's account of his adventures in his book *To the Top from Nowhere*.

and Youth Affairs. If the truth be told, there is not a lot going on. A number of European sports, including rugby, tennis, cricket and golf, are largely the domain of expatriates and visiting South Africans, and make little impact on wider Swazi cultural life. Swaziland competed in the Melbourne Commonwealth Games of March 2006 in swimming, boxing, lawn bowls, weightlifting and athletics, with boxer S'manga Shiba bringing home a bronze medal. Meanwhile Swazi children in rural areas make their own entertainment. Both boys and girls play games with various sorts of balls homemade from twine or rubber. Boys build intricate, adjustable toy cars from discarded scraps of rubber, tin cans and wires, while girls make dolls from corncobs.

Swaziland is a superb location for hiking, horseriding, fishing and other outdoor pursuits, and has an excellent reputation across the region for adventure sports such as caving, whitewater rafting and mountain-biking (see page 134). Again, these activities are not a significant part of Swazi culture and are largely the preserve of visitors.

MUSIC AND DANCE Music and dance are embedded in traditional Swazi culture. Women sing together in the fields; men sing or utter praise poetry as they pay tribute to their chiefs or kings. There are traditional songs for every occasion: weddings, royal rituals, coming-of-age ceremonies and national festivals. Children in school or congregations in church sing with a vigour and an ability to harmonise spontaneously that seems remarkable to many Western observers.

Sibhaca dance is the best known of various dance forms. Traditionally it is for men, although today women also take part. The dance is highly strenuous: teams of dancers step forward in turn to perform barefoot high-kicking and stomping, while their companions behind beat drums, chant and sing. All wear traditional dress, with colourful tassels and embellishments. School *sibhaca* competitions are popular, with boys forming their own teams and performing for special occasions. A typical session can last two or three hours, with different songs and styles performed.

Swaziland has a rather quiet contemporary music scene by comparison with South Africa, partly because the industry is still in its infancy and there are few recording facilities or live venues. Gospel choirs dominate both locally recorded music and homegrown music on local radio. One enterprising DJ, Lindelwa 'DJ Lindz' Mafah, plays local music on her Swazi Rhythm Show, but otherwise the most popular contemporary artists tend to be South Africans.

The exception to this rule is House on Fire (see page 186), an extraordinary venue that has invigorated the local music scene since it opened in 2004. Its annual Bushfire festival, held every May, attracts top acts and artists from all over the region, and audiences of up to 20,000.

A number of musicians of Swazi extraction have made their name elsewhere. Rapper and producer Killa Kambi, now based in Montreal, was born in Mbabane, and has influenced such luminaries as Eminem. Ray Phiri, singer and guitarist with South African band Stimela and a major contributor to Paul Simon's 1986 *Graceland* album, is a siSwati-speaker raised in KaNgwane. Among the current crop, look out for Bholoja, a Swazi singer and songwriter whose own brand of Swazi Soul has been winning awards and gaining him new listeners across the region.

LITERATURE AND DRAMA Although Swaziland has a long tradition of oral literature, no siSwati literature was produced in written form before the 1980s. The only locally based publishing house, Macmillan Swaziland, serves primarily

Swaziland can hardly be said to have a film industry. It did, however, feature as a backdrop for *Wah-Wah*, an autobiographical film by actor Richard E Grant, of *Withnail and I* fame and writer of the foreword of this book. The film dramatises the events of Grant's childhood in Swaziland – in particular the break-up of his parents' marriage – against a backdrop of the country's impending independence. It was the first ever made in Swaziland and was shot over six weeks in 2004, with the Stephens' residence of Boshimela (see page 227) near Piggs Peak doubling as the family home. The surrounding highveld countryside features prominently, and keen-eyed viewers will spot a number of other landmarks – including the Royal Swazi Sun and the Highlands Inn hotels – doubling as key locations. Famous faces in the cast include Miranda Richardson, Julie Walters, Gabriel Byrne and Nicholas Hoult. The term 'Wah-Wah' refers to the description by Grant's American stepmother of the speech of the British colonials among whom she found herself marooned. Grant's subsequent book *The Wah-Wah Diaries: The Making of a Film* is a highly entertaining account of how the movie came together and contains rich descriptions of the landscape and people so fondly remembered from his childhood. Grant remains an impassioned champion of the country of his birth and in 2012 was the patron of the Bushfire festival (see page 186).

to produce school textbooks. However, it has also sponsored a number of local writers and published a selection of siSwati literature, including plays, short stories and poetry.

For conventional drama, the country is short of stages. The Mbabane Theatre Club (see page 157) once served up a good 'am dram' menu of Alan Ayckbourn et al, and boasts the film star Richard E Grant among its alumni, but today it functions only as a bar, with the posters of past glories peeling from its walls. Community drama, however, does not need a theatre. An innovative Swazi drama group called Siphila Nje ('How we survive') has since 1988 been performing its homegrown musical dramas around the country, anywhere from community halls to school playgrounds. These dramas tackle social themes such as women's rights or the HIV/AIDS crisis, and have thus found sponsorship from development agencies such as UNICEF. Siphila Nje (☏ 7603 5977) have won numerous awards and performed throughout the Southern African Development Community (SADC) region. Their founder, Modison Magagula, is also the author of some of the only published siSwati literature, including the novel *Kwesukesukela* ('Once Upon a Time').

FESTIVALS AND CEREMONY Swaziland's traditional culture finds its most spectacular expression in two ritual ceremonies: the Incwala and the Umhlanga. Both are living cultural events that, bar the odd pair of sunglasses and mobile phone, have hardly changed in two centuries. Visitors are tolerated, but neither ceremony makes any concession to tourism; even the precise dates are not published in advance, being dependent on the vagaries of ancestral astrology. If you're lucky enough to be around at the right time, get along to the royal parade grounds at Ludzidzini (see page 177) and catch the action. Even if you can't be on the spot, you won't miss the mood of celebration that sweeps the nation, and will doubtless see wandering bands of warriors or maidens decked out in full regalia as they head to or from the festivities.

Incwala This is Swaziland's most important cultural event. It has a spiritual power that is largely lost on outsiders, and indeed many of its inner workings remain shrouded in secrecy. Although often translated as 'first fruits festival', the tasting of the first of the season's bounty is only one part of this long rite. Essentially this is about cleansing and renewal, and – above all – celebrating kingship. Indeed, when there is no king there is no Incwala.

The main event takes place on the fourth day after the full moon nearest 21 December (the longest day) – so between late December and early January. But the preparations get under way at the previous full moon, in November, when a regiment of men known as *bemanti* ('people of the water') set off in two groups from the queen mother's home. The main group heads to Catembe – the ancestral home of the Dlamini clan, just south of Maputo on the Mozambique coast – where they collect seawater. The smaller group heads north to collect water from rivers. Both return to the royal palace at Ludzidzini by the December new moon, whereupon there are two days of dance, song and sacred ritual known as the 'Little Incwala'.

The main or 'Big Incwala' begins 14 days later. On **day one**, thousands of young unmarried men – supposedly those whose purity remains unsullied by sexual experience – are dispatched to collect the branches of the sickle bush (*Dichrostachys cineria*), known ceremonially as *lusekwane*. They march some 50km to a region near Sidvokodvo, where they cut the branches by the full moon. Then, on **day two**, they march back and drop them at the royal kraal. The elders weave these branches into the poles of the *inhlambelo*, the king's private sanctuary.

Day three is the 'day of the bull'. In the morning the younger boys, those too young to fetch the *lusekwane*, are dispatched to a local site to cut branches of red bushwillow (*Combretum apiculatum*), known as 'black *imbondvo*', which is also added to the *inhlambelo* fence. Then, while the king is inside receiving traditional medicines, a black bull is released. The *lusekwane* boys catch and overpower the beast, and return it to the sanctuary. Here they slaughter it, reputedly with their fists, in an act meant to instill solidarity and bravery. The bull's carcass provides more ritual ingredients for the king.

Day four is the key day of the Incwala. All the key players, including the king, his chiefs and the royal governors (*indunas*), perform in a spectacular pageant inside the cattle kraal, decked out in full war dress. The king first performs a dance that he improvises for the occasion, before disappearing inside his *inhlambelo* to sample certain plants of the first harvest. Then, in response to a collective coaxing from his people outside, he emerges to throw the sacred gourd, *luselwa*, which one of the *lusekwane* boys catches on a black shield. It is now, traditionally, that Swazis can start to enjoy the first fruits of their harvest.

Day five is the day of abstinence. The king sits in seclusion, while the *bemanti* roam the royal grounds, enforcing the special rules of the day. This means, traditionally, no sexual contact, touching water, wearing decorations, sitting on chairs or mats, shaking hands, scratching, singing, dancing or general frivolity. You have been warned.

Day six is the day of the log. The king's regiments march to a forest and return with firewood. The elders then prepare a great fire inside the cattle byre, on which they burn certain ritual objects to signify the end of the old year, including the bones of the bull slaughtered earlier, while there is more song and dance inside the royal kraal. The ancestral spirits are asked to bring rain to show their favour. They usually oblige – this being the height of the rainy season – and the fire is put out. This signals the end of the Incwala, but the king remains in seclusion for a period of contemplation, before returning to public life at the next full moon when the *lusekwane* branches are removed from the *inhlambelo* and burnt.

Every Swazi may take part in the public parts of the Incwala. Spectators are permitted but not actively encouraged and you may not take photographs except by special permit. The best day to attend is day four of the Big Incwala, when the feasting and dancing reach a climax, and you will see thousands of people – including warriors in full battle regalia – thronging the royal parade grounds. The songs, dances and ritual that take place inside the royal kraal remain a matter of utmost secrecy and may not be recorded or written down; in 2011 a man was arrested for selling DVDs of Incwala songs.

Umhlanga The Umhlanga or 'Reed Dance' is Swaziland's best known cultural event, and has a more open feel than the Incwala. In this eight-day ceremony, held in late August or early September, young girls cut reeds, present them to the queen mother (*Indlovukazi*) – ostensibly to repair the windbreak around her royal residence – and then dance in celebration. Only childless, unmarried girls can take part. The idea is to preserve the girls' chastity, provide symbolic labour as a tribute to the queen mother and encourage solidarity by working together.

Today's Umhlanga developed from the ancient *umchwasho* chastity rites, in which girls younger than 18 were not allowed sexual contact with men, their virginal status being marked by the blue and yellow tassels around the neck. Those who transgressed were fined one cow. Between 9 September 2001 and 19 August 2005 Mswati imposed a national period of *umchwasho* in an effort to combat the spread of HIV/AIDS. Unfortunately he broke his own rules by choosing a new teenage bride, so fined himself one cow.

The Umhlanga kicks off when the *induna* – a commoner maiden appointed as captain for her dancing prowess and knowledge of royal protocol – announces the dates over the radio. These dates are chosen using ancestral astrology. On **day one**, the girls gather from all over the kingdom at the queen mother's royal village. They arrive in 'regiments', one from each of the 200 or so chiefdoms and each supervised by up to four male escorts appointed by the chief. They sleep in the huts of relatives in the royal villages or in the classrooms of four nearby schools.

On **day two** the girls are separated into two groups: the older (14–22 years) and the younger (8–13 years). In the afternoon, they march – in their chiefdom groups – to the rivers where the reeds grow. This is a serious hike: the older girls often go to Ntondozi (about 30km away) while the younger girls usually go to Bhamsakhe (about 10km). If they have to walk further, trucks are provided for transport. It is dark by the time they arrive, and they sleep in tents and marquees set up for them. Local homesteads once accommodated them, but sheer numbers these days means this is no longer practical.

On **day three** the girls cut their reeds, usually about to ten to 20, using long knives. Each ties her collection into one bundle – traditionally with plaited grass, although nowadays strips of plastic bag serve just as well. On **day four**, they head back to the queen mother's village, carrying their bundles, and arrive at night. **Day five** is a day of rest, on which the girls can get ready for the festivities about to follow, making final adjustments to hair and costumes.

The festivities kick off on **day six**, when dancing gets under way in the afternoon. Each group drops its reeds outside the queen mother's quarters then moves to the main arena, where the members dance and sing their songs. The dancing continues on **day seven**, when the king is present. Each regiment dances before him in turn, ensuring that no maiden escapes his eye. This is traditionally when the king would select a new wife. It all draws to a close on **day eight**, when cattle are slaughtered for the dancers on the command of the king, and each girl collects her piece of meat and heads home.

It may sound straightforward in theory. In practice, however, little prepares you for the sheer scale of the pageantry, with column upon column of girls advancing like vast ululating centipedes across the parade grounds of Ludzidzini, each dissolving in turn into the pulsating mass of bodies around the royal kraal. Up close, it's an almost overwhelming immersion in noise and colour, as the girls stamp, sing and sway in step, anklets rattling, naked flesh and dazzling costume blurring into a living, chanting kaleidoscope. The warrior escorts, adorned with cow tails and clutching knob-stick and shield, are sternly intent on their duties and seem contemptuous of tourists, but the girls are all smiles. It's Swaziland's biggest holiday and, after days of tramping the hillsides, cutting reeds and camping out, they're determined to party.

Today the Umhlanga is as well attended as ever, despite objections from progressive quarters that it demeans women. Indeed cultural historians marvel at how its ever-increasing popularity in Swaziland defies the apparent decline of traditional culture elsewhere. Either way, it offers the visitor a unique experience. There are no special visitor arrangements – except for a special grandstand to accommodate visiting dignitaries – but simply turn up at Ludzidzini and follow the crowds. Police will direct you where to go and where to park. Officially, permits are required for photography. In practice, and with a little discretion, you should be fine without.

2

Practical Information

WHEN TO VISIT

Choosing when to visit Swaziland comes down to personal priorities. This is not one of those African destinations where the seasons force your hand: most roads are perfectly navigable all year round and the wildlife does not all exit the country at certain times. Tourism numbers peak around the Christmas holidays but the place is never congested.

The warmest months are from October to March, when it may become too hot for some people's comfort in the lowveld but remains bearable in the highveld. Conversely, the coolest are from June to August, when it is chilly at night in the highveld but remains pleasantly mild in the lowveld. In other words, because temperatures vary so widely across the country, you can always go where it is warmer – or cooler – according to taste. The rainy season brings violent electrical storms, generally in the afternoon, and mist often swathes large areas of the highveld. In general, however, Swaziland's weather can never be forecast with the same certainty as a little further north in Africa, where the rainy and dry seasons are more clearly defined.

Similarly, from a wildlife-watcher's perspective, there is not the same peak/off-peak seasonal pattern of many safari destinations. The dry season, when vegetation dies back and water sources dwindle, is best for game-viewing in the lowveld. But Swaziland's parks are small, so the game is never hard to find. The rainy season is best for birds, with everything singing and displaying and, from September to March, all the summer migrants – including such rarities as the blue swallow – joining the residents. The rains also bring out reptiles, frogs and insects, which may or may not be your thing but certainly makes a night in the bush much noisier. Mosquitoes and other biting irritants are more prevalent during the rains but never a serious deterrent. For plant enthusiasts, the highveld floral display peaks in October/November.

Seasonal factors do influence certain activities. Hikers should bear in mind that summer brings sapping midday heat and violent afternoon storms, so it's a good idea to make an early start to the day. Heavy downpours also have an impact on whitewater rafting and caving, leaving some rivers too swollen to tackle. For photographers, however, there is no doubt that the rainy season brings the best light, with lush foregrounds and dramatic skies. Dry-season bushfires produce a dusty haze that is not conducive to landscape photography.

As for price, your biggest consideration comes down to international flights. These are available to Johannesburg daily, year round, from numerous airlines (see page 108), but fares shoot up during the European school holidays – particularly Christmas – when availability is also reduced. Onward flights into Swaziland do not present the same problem – and if they do for any reason then you can always drive (see page 125). Some places in Swaziland raise their rates in peak season but not by a prohibitive margin.

If you are visiting Swaziland on a regional tour, you may also want to consider a few other factors. Game-viewing in the Kruger National Park and KwaZulu-Natal is easiest during the dry season but nonetheless good at all times, with extra birds an additional attraction during the rains. The coast of Zululand and Maputoland becomes too humid for some tastes from November to March. This summer season also brings heavy storms and sometimes flooding to these coastal regions, which tend to peak in February/March.

The final consideration is Swaziland's key events (see page 130). The Incwala, for instance, takes place in late December/early January, the Umhlanga in late August/early September and Bushfire in late May. Unless you are hell-bent on making it to one of these, however, you can plan your trip in the sure knowledge that whenever you decide to come it will not be the wrong time. Wildlife, culture, landscapes and adventure are all on the menu all year round. Just adjust your choice of hat accordingly.

HIGHLIGHTS

The list below is a brief alphabetical selection of 18 good reasons to visit Swaziland, comprising key destinations, events and activities. It is by no means exhaustive: you'll find plenty of other attractions scattered through the guide section of this book and, quite possibly, discover a few of your own that I have overlooked entirely. Either way, if you manage to tick off just half a dozen of the following, you're guaranteed a memorable trip.

EZULWINI VALLEY (see page 160) This is Swaziland's tourist hub. Located between Mbabane and Manzini, and just a ten-minute drive from either, it means 'Valley of heaven' and is flanked on both sides by a ridge of rocky hills. Here you'll find hotels, restaurants, backpacker lodges, handicraft centres, a thermal spa, a golf course, a casino, riding stables and the country's only cinema. Mantenga, at the eastern end, has a craft centre, waterfall and cultural village. The valley is the most convenient base for a longer stay in Swaziland and, if you have just one day, offers a whistle-stop tour of many key attractions.

HLANE ROYAL NATIONAL PARK (see page 259) This former royal hunting ground in the northeastern lowveld is Swaziland's largest protected area and managed by Big Game Parks (see page 52). Explore the self-guided trails in search of white rhino, elephant, giraffe, zebra and a variety of smaller wildlife – or, to see lions, book a guided game drive with a ranger. Ndlovu Camp offers self-catering accommodation with waterhole viewing; Bhubesi Camp in the north is a secluded bush retreat. Guided walks are available and birdlife is excellent, especially raptors.

INCWALA CEREMONY (see page 92) Swaziland's most important cultural festival celebrates kingship and the tasting of the first seasonal fruits. It takes place over six days in late December/early January on a date determined by astrology. Royal regiments march to collect water from the Indian Ocean while boys collect branches to rebuild the royal kraal. The sacred rites take place in royal seclusion, while the public joins in the festivities outside. Impressive.

LOBAMBA (see page 174) Halfway between Mbabane and Manzini, this is Swaziland's traditional seat of power, located near the queen mother's residence at Ludzidzini and home to today's parliament. The refurbished National Museum houses exhibitions on history, culture and natural history, and the nearby King Sobhuza Memorial Park is an interesting tribute to the much revered former monarch.

MAHAMBA MISSION AND GORGE (see page 238) This historic site in the far southwest is the country's oldest church and marks the point where Christianity reached Swaziland. The nearby gorge is impressive, and home to rare birds such as the black eagle and southern bald ibis. A community project offers hiking trails and simple self-catering chalets.

MALANDELA'S AND HOUSE ON FIRE (see pages 185 and 186) This charming family farmstead on the road to Malkerns has expanded into a significant tourist complex, with a bed and breakfast, restaurant, internet café and craft centre. Best of all, it has House on Fire, a unique performing arts venue built around a Shakespearian Globe-style theatre that every May hosts Bushfire, a major festival of southern African music and arts.

MALOLOTJA NATURE RESERVE (see page 207) Swaziland's premier nature reserve is one of the top hiking destinations in southern Africa. A mountainous wilderness in the western highveld, its attractions include impressive waterfalls, a dazzling spring flower display and rare wildlife such as the blue swallow and aardwolf. Driving is limited but an excellent trail network allows for short day walks or week-long hikes. There's also good self-catering accommodation and camping, plus a white-knuckle canopy trail zipline and a prehistoric iron mine – the world's oldest – at Ngwenya on the southern boundary. Unmissable.

MANTENGA FALLS AND CULTURAL VILLAGE (see page 171) Mantenga is at the eastern end of the Ezulwini Valley. The falls are set within a small nature reserve, which is also the location of the Cultural Village – an enthralling living recreation of Swazi traditional life, complete with dance displays. The nearby craft centre sells original curios and handicrafts and has, at Swazi Trails, the country's best tourist information centre.

MKHAYA GAME RESERVE (see page 277) This private nature reserve in the southeast that offers Swaziland's most exclusive safari experience. Various big-game species, including elephant, buffalo, giraffe, white rhino and the rare black rhino, have been reintroduced to their former habitat. Guided game drives offer close-up viewing, and this is one of Africa's best locations for tracking both rhino species on foot. You won't see big cats, but you'll hear hyenas and see plenty of smaller game. The charming chalets at Stone Camp have confiding wildlife, excellent birds, a roaring campfire and a genuine bush ambience.

MLAWULA NATURE RESERVE AND MBULUZI GAME RESERVE (see pages 261 and 264) These contiguous parks in the northeast lowveld share the same habitat but are very different in character. Mlawula is a state-funded reserve that protects a rich variety of fauna and flora and extends to the top of the Lubombo Mountains, from where the Indian Ocean is visible. The self-reliant visitor will find genuine wilderness, good hiking and plentiful wildlife, but larger game is scarce and facilities basic. Mbuluzi is smaller but, under private ownership, better maintained, and supports plentiful giraffe, zebra and antelope, plus hippos and crocs on the Mbuluzi

River. Visitors enjoy scenic trails and gorgeous accommodation in riverside self-catering lodges. Both reserves have superb birdlife.

MLILWANE WILDLIFE SANCTUARY (see page 177) Just off the Ezulwini Valley, this Big Game Parks property is Swaziland's first nature reserve, and its most popular and accessible. The terrain is not as wild as in the lowveld reserves, and the game is mostly introduced, but the main camp offers a friendly ambience and good accommodation, and is a popular spot for day visitors. Activities include hiking, mountain-biking and horseriding. Reilly's Rock, now an exclusive lodge, is the former family home of Ted Reilly, father of Swaziland conservation (see page 180).

NGWENYA GLASS FACTORY AND MINE (see pages 201 and 203) Ngwenya means 'crocodile', referring to a large croc-shaped mountain along Swaziland's western border. The Ngwenya mine, which lies inside Malolotja Nature Reserve, holds the oldest iron-ore workings in the world, dated to 43,000 years ago. The nearby glass factory is an innovative enterprise where you can watch the glass blowers at work, and supports several other handicraft stalls and boutiques.

NSANGWINI CAVE SHELTER (see page 219) This community-run project, located in the Nkomati Valley southeast of Piggs Peak, is Swaziland's finest example of San rock art. A local guide will lead you down the short, steep trail and explain the history and significance of the ancient figures and animals painted on the granite overhang.

PHOPHONYANE FALLS NATURE RESERVE (see page 224) This gem of a reserve just north of Piggs Peak has its lodge and accommodation ingeniously landscaped into the lush, indigenous vegetation. Overlooking the Phophonyane River and Falls, which run through the property, it has a good pool and restaurant, and a well-maintained network of self-guided trails with excellent birdwatching. Discreet and highly original.

SIBEBE ROCK (see page 157) The world's largest granite dome lies just 8km outside Mbabane. Steep trails wind up the bare rock face, leading to a wonderland of cliffs and huge boulders at the top. Superb views, plus wild flowers and rural homesteads. Access is from various points, including a community-run project in Pine Valley. Fabulous, but not one to attempt in a downpour or electrical storm.

SWAZI CANDLES COMPLEX (see page 187) Some 20 minutes from Mbabane or Manzini along the road to Malkerns, this craft centre is something of a one-stop shop for the souvenir hunter. As well as the candle factory, where you can watch the artists at work, there are stalls and boutiques selling basketware, carvings, mohair products, batiks and many other products. Also an excellent café.

UMHLANGA CEREMONY (see page 93) Swaziland's most colourful cultural festival is a sacred celebration of chastity held over eight days in late August/early September at the royal kraal, Ludzidzini. Thousands of girls march to collect reeds, which they present to the queen mother, and then join two days of dancing, singing and pageantry before the king. Spectacular.

WHITEWATER RAFTING ON THE GREAT USUTU (see page 275) Most popular of Swaziland's numerous adventure sports is this adrenalin rush along the country's largest river. Spend a full day or half day in the wild gorges, negotiating rapids, waterfalls and even the odd crocodile. The activity has been developed by Swazi Trails, who have put Swaziland on the map as an adventure destination and offer numerous other ways to scare yourself witless amid the wonders of nature.

SUGGESTED ITINERARIES

If there's one thing that Swaziland would like more of from you, it's your time. Anybody involved in tourism bemoans the fact that many visitors are simply whisked through on transit. The following suggestions start with the premise that you will be spending at least one night in the country, and extend to activities to fill a fortnight or more for those with the time and inclination to marinate themselves more thoroughly in its unique flavours. Needless to say, they are only suggestions; by all means cherry-pick to create an itinerary that works for you. Or do something different entirely. The beauty of Swaziland's size is that you can change direction or revise your plans on a whim (advance bookings notwithstanding). Wherever you are in the kingdom, you're never far from where you want to go.

A few considerations. The best viewing times for most wildlife are dawn and dusk, so safari buffs really need to consider staying overnight in a reserve. (Besides, a night around the campfire is the best part of being out in the bush.) The best hikes take a full day or more, and an early morning start will mean you needn't struggle in the midday heat. Finally, none of the destinations in the following itineraries is more than three hours by road from any other.

CAPITAL CONNECTIONS: 1–3 DAYS Base yourself in or around Mbabane. Explore Pine Valley and climb Sibebe Rock (see page 157). Nip down to the Ezulwini Valley for craft markets, Mantenga Falls and Cultural Village (see page 171). Visit the glass factory and ancient mine at Ngwenya (see page 201).

ROYAL HEARTLAND: 1–3 DAYS Base yourself in Ezulwini Valley (see page 160). Visit craft markets, the spa and Mantenga Falls and Cultural Village. Continue to Lobamba for the National Museum and Sobhuza Memorial Park (see page 175), then Malkerns for Malandela's (see page 185) and the Swazi Candles complex. Visit Mlilwane (see page 177) for a braai, horseriding and a game walk.

RURAL RAMBLINGS: 1–3 DAYS A back-roads circuit. From Mbabane head north to Piggs Peak (see page 220), stopping for views at Malolotja (see page 207) and perhaps lunch at Maguga Dam (see page 218). Head east after Piggs Peak, passing back down into the Nkomati Valley. Continue to Manzini via Mafutseni (see page 248) on a scenic route through some of Swaziland's most rural communities. Continue through Manzini and overnight in Malkerns, taking in the craft centres and perhaps a performance at House on Fire (see page 186). Then return to Mbabane along the Tea Road (see page 170) for another scenic slice of rural life and an excellent view of the sacred Mdzimba Mountains and royal parade grounds below.

HEARTLAND PLUS HIGHLANDS: 2–3 DAYS Spend one night in the Ezulwini Valley or Malkerns (see pages 160 and 188), visiting the craft markets, candle factory, House on Fire, Mantenga Falls and Cultural Village, and National Museum at Lobamba. Or stay at Mlilwane Wildlife Sanctuary (see page 177) and visit these attractions from there. Then head up to Malolotja via Ngwenya (glass factory and mine). Stay at Malolotja or Hawane (see pages 212 and 205), and make a day hike into Malolotja Nature Reserve (see page 213). Optional horseriding at Hawane or canopy trail at Malolotja.

2

SOUTHWESTERN CIRCUIT: 2–3 DAYS Starting from Mbabane, spend a night at Foresters Arms (see page 152) for horseriding, fishing, food and forest trails. Then head south via Mankayane to Nhlangano (see page 236). Visit Mahamba (see page 238) to hike the gorge and visit the historic mission. Overnight in Nhlangano or Mahamba community chalets. Return to Manzini via Sidvokodvo along the scenic Grand Valley (see page 235). Optional visit to Nkonyeni Golf Estate (see page 234) for the restaurant and small game reserve – and golf!

FED AND PAMPERED: 2–3 DAYS A splurge at Swaziland's top hotels and restaurants. Spend one night in the Ezulwini Valley at the Royal Swazi Spa complex (see page 162) or Royal Villas (see page 162). Visit top local restaurants, including the Calabash (see page 165), Malandela's (see page 185) or – for a classy take on traditional Swazi fare – Edladleni (see page 154). Then to Summerfield (see page 191), beyond Malkerns, for opulent surroundings in botanical gardens and an excellent restaurant. Both areas are good bases for sightseeing and handicrafts; from Summerfield it is a short excursion to Rosecraft (see page 243) for mohair weaving and a sculpture trail in the hills.

WET AND WILD: 2–3 DAYS Spend one or two nights at Mkhaya Game Reserve (see page 277), tracking rhinos and elephants in the bush – or, for a cheaper alternative, Hlane (see page 259). Then transfer to Sidvokodvo for a half- or full-day's whitewater rafting on the Great Usutu River (see page 275). Rafting company Swazi Trails can tack other adventure activities onto your itinerary, including caving or quad-biking (see page 169), time permitting. Expect to get dirty and wet.

SADDLE-SORE: 2–4 DAYS For horseriding enthusiasts. Visit Hawane Resort (see page 205) for riding in the highveld or Nyanza Stables (see page 188) for riding in the middleveld. Full-day trails and accommodation available at both. Then move to Mlilwane (see page 177) for one of the two- or three-day trails, riding among wild game and overnighting in a mountain cave or trails camp beside the river. Rides are available for all ability levels. Mountain-biking is also available at Mlilwane and Hawane.

BEST OF THE WEST: 4–5 DAYS A full exploration of Swaziland's scenic western highveld. Starting from Mbabane, head north to Malolotja Nature Reserve (see page 207) and stay in the cabins or campsite. Ideally spend two nights, allowing for one full-day hike plus smaller walks and a canopy trail. Mountain-bikes and horseriding are available at nearby Hawane Resort (see page 205). Continue north to Maguga Dam (see page 218) for a restaurant meal and views of Nkomati Valley. Optional overnighting at Maguga allows for a sundowner cruise on the lake. Continue north to Piggs Peak, stopping to view Nsangwini rock art (see page 219). Spend two nights at Phophonyane Falls (see page 221), enjoying the restaurant, waterfall, pools, trails and abundant birdlife. Phophonyane can arrange optional local excursions, including hiking or mountain-biking. Peak Fine Craft Centre (see page 227) with Coral Stephens's mohair weaving is a short drive away.

HIKING HIGHLIGHTS: 4–6 DAYS The best of Swaziland's hiking, for those who want to stretch their legs on the trail. Start with at least two days at Malolotja (see page 207), including at least one full-day hike – or overnight hike, with your own camping gear – following the Malolotja River down to the Nkomati River. Continue north and west, via Piggs Peak and Tshaneni, to Mlawula Nature Reserve (see page

261). Overnight at Siphiso Campsite and hike a selection of day trails, including up into the Lubombos. Return southwest, via Manzini and Luyengo, to Ngwempisi Gorge (see page 233). Hike day trails from Kopho Lodge. Allow at least two nights for each destination, and take your own food.

BIG GAME BONANZA: 4–6 DAYS A tour of the lowveld's main game reserves, starting in the northeast. Stock up with supplies at Simunye (see page 259) then head to Mlawula and/or Mbuluzi (see pages 261 and 264): the former is wilder; the latter has better accommodation and facilities, and easier-to-see game. Then continue to Hlane (see page 259) for game-viewing around Ndlovu Camp, guided rhino walks and drives into the lion enclosure. Head south to Mkhaya (see page 277) for one or more nights at Stone Camp and excellent black rhino tracking, plus white rhino, elephant and other game. Then south again to Nisela Safaris (see page 284) for giraffe and other wildlife in the shadow of the Lubombos. Allow at least one night to get the best from each park you visit.

BIRDING HIGHLIGHTS: 4–5 DAYS Starting at Malolotja (see page 207), explore the short trails for highveld specials, including blue swallows (summer only), and hike to Malolotja Falls for forest birds and the southern bald ibis breeding colony. Continue to Phophonyane Falls (see page 224) for middleveld and forest specials, including Narina trogon. Head east from Piggs Peak on the northern circuit to spend a night at Mlawula or Mbuluzi (see pages 261 and 264), looking for raptors and local specials, including the African finfoot. Then head up to Mabuda Farm (see page 253) near Siteki for forest birds and Lubombo specials, including twinspots. Return via the Ezulwini Valley where, if time allows, Mlilwane and Mantenga have plentiful birds around the visitor camps, while the hillier sections offer a chance of black and crowned eagles. Birding is best in the rainy season, from October to March.

LINGER IN THE LOWVELD: 7 DAYS PLUS A full immersion in the hottest corner of the country. Spend a few nights between Hlane, Mlawula and Mbuluzi for wildlife, hiking and bush nights around the campfire. Continue to Shewula Mountain Camp (see page 265) for traditional Swazi hospitality, rural village life and the most stunning views in the country – right down to the Indian Ocean. Recharge batteries at Simunye Country Club (see page 259), with swimming pool and an excellent restaurant, then head up to Siteki, where Mabuda Farm (see page 253) offers mountain breezes, homespun hospitality and excellent Lubombo trails.

FULL NORTHERN CIRCUIT: 10 DAYS PLUS Northwest highlights (Malolotja, Maguga, Nsangwini, Piggs Peak, etc) followed by northeast highlights (Hlane, Mlawula, Mbuluzi, Shewula, etc). Return via Malkerns, Lobamba and Ezulwini Valley for a day or two of crafts, culture and other activities.

TOURIST INFORMATION AND SERVICES

Sources of tourist information include:

🛈 **Swaziland Tourist Authority** Headquarters: 6th Fl, Dianubheka Hse, corner of Mdada & Lalufadlana streets, Mbabane; ☎2404 9693/9675. Regional tourist info office at Mbabane: Cooper Centre, Soziza Rd, beside the Engen filling station; ☎2404 2531/2409 0112; ⊕ Mon–Thu 08.00–17.00, Fri 08.00–16.00, Sat 09.00–13.00. Regional tourist info office at Ngwenya border post; ☎2442 4206; ⊕ Mon–Thu 08.00–17.00, Fri 08.00–16.00, Sat 09.00–13.00. Both info offices have free maps, leaflets & guides to what's on. Staff will help plan an itinerary & can make reservations for certain destinations, including community projects (see page 140).

☑ **Swaziland Tourist Office (UK)** ✆0115 9727250; e info@thekingdomofswaziland.com; www.thekingdomofswaziland.com. Official Swaziland tourist office for UK & Europe. Offers impartial advice & information. Provides direct links to lodges, hotels & tour & transport companies. Also sends out information packs by email & post.

☑ **Ezulwini Tourist Office** Mantenga Craft & Lifestyle Centre (see page 167); ✆2416 2180 (office hours), 7602 0261 (after hours); e info@

swazi.travel; www.swazi.travel; ⊕ daily 08.00–17.00. The most comprehensive tourist information centre in Swaziland, run by Swazi Trails, a private tour company. Offers guidebooks, travel tips, maps & local information updated daily. The online booking portal has extensive information on all accommodation, tours & activities, & processes bookings directly. Swazi Trails also has an information desk at the Royal Swazi Spa.

☑ **What's Happening in Swaziland** A useful monthly guide, published in tabloid format, with listings & information on all attractions & events. Available free at tourist information centres & attractions, plus hotels & shopping malls.

In addition, most hotels, guesthouses and backpacker establishments – and some other places – have a selection of tourist information, including maps, leaflets and flyers, and helpful staff to give advice and make bookings. Recommended outlets include Indingilizi Art Gallery Mbabane (see page 157), Hawane Resort (see page 205), Lidwala Backpacker Lodge (see page 164) and Ziggy's Internet Café (see page 187).

Bookings for **Big Game Parks** (Mlilwane, Hlane, Mkhaya) can be made at the Mlilwane Wildlife Sanctuary office (*entrance from Malkerns via the Vickery Seedlings Rd*) or on their website (*www.biggameparks.org*). Information on **Swaziland National Trust Commission** properties (Malolotja, Mantenga, Mlawula) is available at the tourist information offices detailed above and at the National Museum; accommodation information on the **SNTC website** (*www.sntc.org.sz*) is not always up to date. Maps to game parks and nature reserves, including hiking trails, are available at each reserve entrance. Always discuss with staff at reception where you intend to go in case they know of any recent local problems concerning roads or trails.

TOUR OPERATORS

IN THE UNITED KINGDOM

Swaziland specialists The following companies offer tailor-made packages to Swaziland exclusively.

Cox & Kings Travel London; ✆020 7873 5000; www.coxandkings.co.uk. Offers luxury & tailor-made tours.

Rainbow Tours London; ✆020 7226 1004; www.rainbowtours.co.uk. Offers a variety of all-inclusive self-drive Swaziland tours that feature Mkhaya, Ezulwini Valley, Phophonyane Falls & other key destinations.

Sense Africa Bristol; ✆01275 877172; www.senseafrica.co.uk. Specialises in Swaziland. Offers a variety of tours, including photographic safari, family safari & a unique Reed Dance package, with an emphasis on getting off the beaten track & experiencing local community life. Founder Jenny Bowen knows Swaziland very well & can tailor-make individual tours. See advert in colour section.

Regional specialists The following companies specialise in southern Africa and include Swaziland on their itineraries, usually as part of a broader regional trip, often in combination with South Africa and/or Mozambique.

Acacia Adventure Holidays London; 020 7706 4700; www.acacia-africa.com
Addictedtotravel Hants; 020 8144 0965; www.addictedtotravel.com
Africa and Beyond Manchester; 0161 789 8838; www.africa-and-beyond.co.uk
Africabound Adventures Birmingham; 01675 481 700; www.africaboundadventures.com
African Explorations Oxon; 01993 822443; www.africanexplorations.com
African Pride York; 01904 619428; www.african-pride.co.uk
Africa Travel London; 0845 450 1520; www.africatravel.co.uk
Africa Travel Resource Surrey; 01306 880770; www.africatravelresource.com
Audley Travel Oxon; 01993 838500; www.audleytravel.com
Baobab Travel Wolverhampton; 0121 314 6011; www.baobabtravel.com
Close Encounters Africa Nottingham/Suffolk; 0844 415 0155; www.closeencountersafrica.com
Connoisseur Travel West Sussex; 01403 272143; www.edwindoran.com
Definitive Tours Altrincham; 0161 929 5151; www.definitivetours.com
Detour Safaris Devon; 0870 446 6321; www.detoursafaris.co.uk
Edwin Doran Sports Tours Kingston on Thames; 020 8939 5259; www.edwindoran.com

Farside Africa Edinburgh; 0131 315 2464; www.farsideafrica.com
Hands Up Holidays London; 020 7193 1062; www.handsupholidays.com
Imagine Africa London; 020 7622 5114; www.imagineafrica.co.uk
Inspirational Travel Peterborough; 01780 784 380; www.inspirational-travel.com
Kumuka Worldwide London; 0800 068 8855; www.kumuka.com
Lateral Life London; 020 7534 4562; www.laterallife.com
Safari Club Ltd Bucks; 0845 054 5884; www.safari-club.co.uk
Safariplans UK London; 020 7924 5557; e rosie@safariplans.co.uk
Scott Travel Bucks; 01908 506656; www.scott-travel.co.uk
Somak Holidays Middx; 020 8423 3000; www.somak.co.uk
Southern Africa Travel Surrey; 01483 425533; www.southernafricatravel.com
Travel Butlers Surrey; 0845 838 2450; www.travelbutlers.com
Tribes Travel Suffolk; 01728 685971; www.tribes.co.uk (see advert on page 94)
VentureCo Warwick; 01926 411 122; www.ventureco-worldwide.com
Voyages Jules Verne London; 0845 404 3127; www.vjv.com

INTERNATIONAL The following is a brief selection of companies that offer Swaziland as a destination, often as part of a tour to South Africa or broader circuit of the region.

Europe
France
Kwamadiba +33 (0) 170 61 48 22; e infos@kwamadiba.com; www.kwamadiba.com

Germany
Boomerang Reisen +49 (0) 651 966 800; e info@boomerang-reisen.de; www.afrika-reise.com
Elangeni African Adventures +49 (0) 6172 2795 90; e info@elangeni.de; www.elangeni.de

Venter Tours +49 (0) 395 555 3185; e info@ventertours.de; www.ventertours.de

The Netherlands
Out in Africa +31 (0) 10 474 6266; e info@outinafrica.com; www.outinafrica.com
Club @frica +31 (0) 297 349 351; e info@clubafrica.nl; www.clubafrica.nl

North America
Adventures Abroad Canada; (0) 1 800 665 3998; e sales@adventures-abroad.com; www.adventures-abroad.com

ATD-Adventure Travel Desk USA; +1 508 653 4600; e info@african-safari.com; www.african-safari.com

2

Palace Travel USA; ✆+1 215 471 8555; e info@ palacetravel.com; www.palacetravel.com

Planet Wildlife USA; ✆ (0) 91 40 23553265; e travel@planetwildlife.com; www.planetwildlife.com

In South Africa A number of South African tour operators visit Swaziland, often in combination with neighbouring areas of South Africa. They include the following:

Africa A–Z ✆+27 (0)11 462 8857; www. africaa-z.co.za

African Ample Assistance ✆+27 (0)21 790 7148; www.aaatravel.co.za

African Tapestry ✆+27 (0)21 851 7975; www. africantapestry.com

Go2Africa ✆+27 (0)21 481 4900; www. go2africa.com

Idube Elihle Tours ✆+27 (0)11 704 1499 / 083 338 0151; www.idubeelihle.co.za

Intende Travel ✆+27 (0)11 421 1635; www. intendetravel.co.za

Pulse Africa ✆+27 (0)11 325 2290; www. pulseafrica.com

Siyabona Africa ✆+27 (0)21 424 1037; www. siyabona.com

Springbok Atlas ✆+27 (0)21 460 4735; www. springbokatlas.com

Spurwing ✆+27 (0)78 802 7777; www. spurwingtourism.com

XO Africa ✆+27 (0)21 486 2700; www.xoafrica. com

IN SWAZILAND A number of Swazi companies organise tours and activities around Swaziland and beyond. Most can tailor-make tours to your requirements.

All Out Africa Ezulwini; ✆2416 2260; m 7631 6767; e info@alloutafrica.com; www.alloutafrica. com; ⊕ Mon–Fri 08.00–17.00. Founded in 2004 by Swazi conservationist Kim Roques, All Out Africa is based at Lidwala Backpacker Lodge (see page 164), which offers simple accommodation & useful tourist information. It also has bases in Tofo (Mozambique) & Cape Town (South Africa). The company has 2 strands: a volunteering programme offers working holidays on conservation or social welfare projects around Swaziland & elsewhere in the region (see page 141); & an adventure travel programme offers guided tours around Swaziland & beyond, ranging from half-day village or cultural tours of Swaziland to week-long expeditions to watch game in the Kruger Park or snorkel with whale sharks off the Mozambique coast. All are no-frills packages, based on simple accommodation or camping. All Out Africa also runs a non-profit foundation that supports social & environmental projects, including field research, wildlife management & vulnerable children.

Chasing Horizons m 7678 3547; e horizonsbookings@gmail.com; www. chasinghorizons.com. New tour company run by Kieren Vincent of Buhleni Farm Chalets in Ezulwini (see page 164). Takes small groups off

the beaten track into rural Swaziland, including to nature reserves, adventure activities & community projects. Developing tours into Mozambique.

Ekhaya Cultural Tours m 7644 3257; www. ekhayatours.com. This Swazi company (whose name means 'at home') uses trained local guides to offer visitors an insight into traditional Swazi culture. The brainchild of Mandla Masuku & his wife Lucie, it arranges visits to local families, schools & craft markets, & samples Swazi food at a homestead. The company aims to practise responsible tourism & to preserve & protect Swazi culture. Tours include day & overnight visits to the local community. You can also arrange for a private guide in traditional attire to accompany you in your own vehicle. Extended multi-day tours are available, & all tours can be given in French, English & Swahili.

Swazi Trails Mantenga; ✆2416 2180; m 7602 0261; e info@swazi.travel; www.swazitrails. co.sz; ⊕ Mon–Sun 08.00–17.00. Swaziland's premier private tour company & the brainchild of adventure-tourism pioneer Darron Raw, who developed whitewater rafting on the Great Usutu River (see page 275). Now runs general & cultural tours & adventure activities, plus corporate team-building & events, & styles itself as Swaziland's one-stop tourism shop. Adventure activities take in the whole country & include whitewater rafting, tubing, caving, quad-biking, canoeing, abseiling & hiking. Tours last from half a day to a week & include general highlights, cultural village & game-viewing. Among the more innovative is the unstructured 'Taste of Swaziland' cultural tour (see box on page 169), on which a local guide takes visitors into the community, often attending one-off events like weddings. Swazi Trails also facilitates specialist activities from other operators, including horseriding & 4x4 game-viewing, & promotes community tourism via significant contributions to local development projects.

Taman Tour ✆2416 3370; e enquiries@tamantours.com; www.tamantours.com. Taman Tours offers various trips around Swaziland, including cultural, handicrafts & wildlife. These include a 3-day highlight tour in & out of Johannesburg. They will also tailor-make self-drive packages, offer a shuttle service to the airport & elsewhere, & make bookings for Big Game Parks. German & Afrikaans (Dutch) guiding services are available.

Time Travel ✆2404 3873; m 7607 2101; e timetravel@realnet.co.sz. French tour operator Serge Petillon runs this local enterprise that offers rural excursions by 4x4 vehicle in the Ezulwini & Mbabane areas. Guests visit the local community & schools, & enjoy a traditional Swazi hot meal in a scenic outdoor location. Itinerary adjusted to guests' interests & whereabouts.

Woza Nawe Swaziland Cultural Tours ✆2505 8363; m 7604 4102; www.swaziculturaltours.com. Woza Nawe ('come with us') offers visitors an authentic slice of rural Swaziland on 1-day & overnight cultural tours. These are based in the village of kaPhunga, some 55km from Manzini, where owner Mxolisi Mdluli ('Myxos') has settled. Visitors are welcomed into the community & encouraged to muck in with village life, from teaching primary classes to dipping cattle & shelling maize. Accommodation is in traditional Swazi beehive huts on grass mats (mattresses available for softies). Myxos runs a pick-up service from Manzini to kaPhunga; alternatively, you can take the 2hr bus journey, or pick up a guide who will accompany you in your vehicle. Other tours include a cultural tour of Manzini market, a 'museum tour' through the Ezulwini Valley & 'Swazi connection' tours to & from Mozambique & Nelspruit. Woza Nawe aims to boost the self-reliance of the local community through income, education & training, & by providing an outlet for local products.

RED TAPE

IMMIGRATION AND VISAS All international visitors to Swaziland require a passport valid for at least three months after their intended departure date and with several blank pages remaining on arrival. (As a rule of thumb in Africa, it is a good idea to have at least six months to run on your passport.) Your passport will be stamped on your arrival.

A tourist or business traveller may visit Swaziland for up to 30 days. Nationals of the UK, USA, Australia, Canada, South Africa, British Commonwealth countries and EU countries **do not** require a visa. You can apply for a further 30-day extension at the Ministry of Home Affairs. You may find it easier, however, simply to slip over the border to South Africa for a day or two; your 30 days will start again on your return. If staying longer than 60 days, you will need to apply for a Temporary Residence Permit (TRP) at the Ministry of Home Affairs (*Ministry of Home Affairs & Ministry of Justice Bldg, Mhlambanyatsi Rd, Mbabane;* ✆ *2404 2941/5, 2404 5880/1*).

Nationals of other countries must apply in advance for a visa from their Swazi embassy or consulate (see page 107). Visas **cannot** be obtained on arrival at the Swazi border, regardless of advice published in some quarters.

For onward travel to South Africa the same visa situation prevails, with no visa required for UK, USA, Australia and Canada, South Africa, British Commonwealth

2

countries and EU nationals. For Mozambique, however, nationals of all these countries require a visa. You must obtain this in advance from a Mozambique consulate or embassy. The Mozambique Embassy in Swaziland (*Embassy of the People's Republic of Mozambique, Princess Dr, Mbabane;* ☏ *2404 3700*) will process a fast-track 24-hour visa application for a fee of 2085 Mozambique meticai (around US$75); simply arrive at 09.00, complete a form, leave your photo and passport and collect your passport with visa at 14.00.

IMMIGRATION FORMALITIES Entering Swaziland by air is a trouble-free experience. Matsapha International Airport is small and friendly. You will need to complete an immigration form and customs declaration, and that's pretty much it. The immigration form requires you to state where you intend to stay in the country. Just one destination will do.

Arriving by road isn't much harder. Swaziland has 13 road borders (see page 108), two with Mozambique and the rest with South Africa. When arriving you must complete exit formalities on the South Africa or Mozambique side and then drive a short distance before doing the same on the Swaziland side. If travelling in a vehicle not registered in Swaziland, you must complete a customs declaration form at Swazi border posts on entry and departure. A road fund levy of SZL50 is payable at the border for all non-Swazi-registered vehicles. You must carry in the vehicle at all times proof of your customs declaration and payment of the road fund levy. Customs officers may ask to search your car. They are generally quick and courteous.

In general, border crossings are relaxed compared with those in many African countries, and certainly compared with what a Swazi may have to endure when entering the UK or US. You should generally be through within 15–20 minutes, unless you have the misfortune to arrive behind a convoy of tour buses. Friday evening is busiest, with Swazis returning from work in South Africa and South Africans arriving for a weekend. At smaller border posts you may find yourself the only visitor. The Mozambique borders take a little longer.

It is a good idea to make copies of all your key travel documents before departure, including passport (with any visas), return plane tickets, driving licence, hire car details and travel insurance – including emergency number – and to keep these somewhere separate from the originals. Also note serial numbers for any valuable goods such as camera or laptop.

POLICE Police in Swaziland are generally helpful and welcoming. You may encounter the occasional security check on the road, which you should treat with patience and courtesy. Speed traps are now increasingly common. This can only be a good thing in a country with such a high traffic accident rate (see box on page 121), and if you are caught then you should learn your lesson, obey the speed limits and congratulate the police on doing a good job. The penalty for offenders is an on-the-spot fine – light by Western standards – and there is no question of alternative financial arrangements (ie: bribes) that might be negotiated in such situations in some other parts of the world. If you are the victim of crime or an accident, you should report it to the police immediately.

The taking or smuggling of drugs is illegal, even though the use of marijuana – known locally as *dagga* – is common in local culture. Foreign nationals have been imprisoned on drug offences and punishments can be severe.

Police & emergency services ☏ 999

EMBASSIES, HIGH COMMISSIONS AND CONSULATES Four countries have an embassy or high commission in Swaziland. Several others have consular offices.

Embassies and high commissions

❺ Embassy of the Republic of China (Taiwan) Makhoskhosi St, Mbabane; PO Box 56, Mbabane H100; ☎2404 2379/4740; e rocembassy@ africaonline.co.sz
❺ Embassy of the United States of America 7th Fl, Central Bank Bdg, Mahlokohla St, Mbabane; PO Box 199, Mbabane H100; ☎2404 6441; e usembswd@realnet.co.sz or usembassymbabane@state.gov

❺ Mozambique High Commission Highlands View, Princess Dr, Mbabane; PO Box 1212, Mbabane H100; ☎2404 3700/1296; e moz.high@swazi.net
❺ South African High Commission 2nd Fl, The New Mall, Mbabane; PO Box 2507, Mbabane H100; ☎2404 46514; e sahc@africaonline.co.sz

Consular offices

❺ Cyprus PO Box 1019, Mbabane H100; ☎2404 2650; e cyprusconsulate@realnet.co.sz
❺ Denmark, Norway & Sweden PO Box 815, Mbabane H100; ☎2404 3547; e citrus@realnet.co.sz
❺ Germany PO Box 1507, Mbabane H100; ☎2404 3174
❺ Indonesia PO Box 196, Mbabane H100; ☎2404 4076; e unionsuppliers@swazi.net
❺ Italy PO Box 31, Eveni, Mbabane; ☎2404 4371; e dorsimmg@realnet.co.sz

❺ Portugal Portuguese Club, PO Box 855, Mbabane; ☎2404 6780; e lopes@posix.co.sz
❺ Seychelles PO Box 3404, Manzini M²00; ☎2505 8454/9388; e nm786naz@gmail.com
❺ UK PO Box A 41, Eveni, Mbabane; ☎2551 6247; e honbritcon@realnet.co.sz. Consular enquiries can also be directed to the British High Commission in Pretoria, South Africa; ☎+27 (12) 421 7500; http://ukinsouthafrica.fco.gov.uk/en.

Swaziland abroad Swaziland has diplomatic representation in the following countries:

Embassies & high commissions
❺ Belgium Brussels; ☎+32 2 347 4771/5725; e brussels@swaziembassy.be
❺ Ethiopia Addis Ababa; ☎+251 11 626 2125; e swazinbi@telecom.net.et
❺ Kuwait Kuwait City; ☎+965 2 531 3306; e swazikuwait@gmail.com
❺ Malaysia Kuala Lumpur; ☎+60 3 2163 2511; e swdkl_2@streamyx.com
❺ Mozambique Maputo; ☎+258 21 491 601
❺ Qatar Doha; ☎+974 44 933 145; e swaziqa@ gmail.com
❺ South Africa Pretoria; ☎+27 12 344 1910/17/25; e info@swazihighcom.co.za
❺ Taiwan Taipei; ☎+886 2 2872 5934; e swazitpi@ms41.hinet.net
❺ United Arab Emirates Abu Dhabi; ☎+971 2 66 69 637; e swazuae@eim.ae
❺ UK London; ☎+44 (0)20 7630 6611; e enquiries@swaziland.org.uk
❺ USA Washington; ☎+1 202 234 5002; e info@ swazilandembassyus.com

Consulates & consulates general
❺ Austria Vienna; ☎+43 1 319 11 38; e herbert. vohryzka@chello.at
❺ Denmark Copenhagen; ☎+45 39 64 24 00; e fjj@haux.dk
❺ Germany Berlin; ☎+49 30 28 09 62 50; e www.swasiland.de
❺ Italy Rome; ☎+352 26 20 43 62; e ibspartners@ibspartners.lu
❺ Luxembourg Luxembourg Ville; ☎+352 26 20 43 62; e ibspartners@ibspartners.lu
❺ Malta Valletta; ☎+356 21 371 032; e swaziland@onvol.net
❺ Mauritius Port Louis; ☎+230 697 8950; e avi2610@netscape.net
❺ Norway Oslo; ☎+47 22 49 10 27; e maltings@online.no
❺ South Africa Johannesburg; ☎+27 11 403 7472/2036
❺ Switzerland Zurich; ☎+41 44 211 52 03; e swazmission-geneva@dsinets.ch

Practical Information RED TAPE 2

BY AIR As of 2012, the only way to reach Swaziland by air is from Johannesburg to Matsapha (aka Manzini) International Airport on Airlink, the sole carrier that flies this route. The much larger Sikuphe International Airport (see page 248), which is planned to replace Matsapha Airport, is currently under construction but has suffered significant delays since work began in 2003.

To Johannesburg Most major international airlines fly to O R Tambo International Airport (formerly Johannesburg International Airport). These include the following:

From the UK British Airways (*www.britishairways.com*), South African Airways (*www.flysaa.com*) and Virgin Atlantic (*www.virgin-atlantic.com*) all operate two or three daily non-stop flights from London to Johannesburg. Other airlines, including Kenya Airways (*www.kenya-airways.com*) and Ethiopian Airlines (*www.flyethiopian.com*), also fly this route but with a stop in Africa, Europe or the Middle East. Non-direct flights are often cheaper. Shop around, and bear in mind that direct flights are at a premium around the Christmas holidays.

From Europe Lufthansa (*www.lufthansa.com*) and South African Airlines fly direct to Johannesburg from Munich and Frankfurt, and United Airlines from Frankfurt. Air France (*www.airfrance.co.uk*) flies from Paris CDG and Iberia (*www.iberia.com*) from Madrid.

From the USA and elsewhere You can fly direct to Johannesburg from New York on South African Airways, from Atlanta on Delta Airlines (*www.delta.com*) and from Washington DC (via Dakar, Senegal) on South African Airways. From Australia, fly direct from Sydney, Melbourne and Perth on Qantas (*www.qantas.com*), South African Airways and Virgin (*www.virginaustralia.com*). Numerous other options are routed through Europe and other stopover destinations.

From Johannesburg to Swaziland The domestic flight from Johannesburg to Matsapha (aka Manzini) International Airport takes around 45 minutes. The airport is located in Matsapha, 8km from Manzini and 25km from Mbabane. Swaziland Airlink is currently the only airline to fly this route (⟨ *2404 1979/88, (traffic Matsapha Airport) 2518 6115; www.flyswaziland.com*). This joint venture between the Swazi government and South Africa Airlink took over operations from Royal Swazi National Airways Corporation (RSNAC), the previous national carrier, which ceased trading in 1999. Flights depart two or three times per day and cost from US$175 one-way and US$350 return. An airport tax of SZL50 (around US$6) is payable when departing from Matsapha Airport.

BY ROAD Driving into Swaziland couldn't be easier, provided you have checked the opening hours of whichever border you are heading for (see page 110). Note that border posts have different names on either side: the main border on the road from Johannesburg, for instance, is known as Oshoek in South Africa and Ngwenya in Swaziland. Drivers approaching Swaziland – especially first-timers in Africa – should take extra care on the final stretch before the border, as it passes through the old KaNgwane 'homeland' (see page 77), where orderly farmland gives way abruptly to ramshackle settlements with pot-holes, pedestrians and wandering livestock.

DISTANCES BY ROAD (QUICKEST MAIN ROUTE)

WITHIN REGION (KM)

	Durb	JHB	Map	Mba	Nels	PR
Durban		568	584	531	711	418
Jo'burg	568		540	371	340	315
Maputo	584	540		224	182	374
Mbabane	531	371	224		171	236
Nelspruit	711	340	182	171		258
Piet Retief	418	315	374	236	258	

WITHIN SWAZILAND (KM)

	BB	Lavu	Manz	Mbab	Nhlan	PP
Big Bend		65	83	116	153	178
Lavumisa	65		143	175	91	238
Manzini	83	143		37	95	100
Mbabane	116	175	37		127	65
Nhlangano	153	91	95	127		155
Piggs Peak	178	238	100	65	155	

From Johannesburg The standard route is around 350km from the airport or city centre to the main Oshoek/Ngwenya border and takes around four hours. Most major car hire companies have a desk at Jo'burg airport (though you will get the cheapest deals by booking online in advance).

Jo'burg (O R Tambo) airport lies east of the city, so you are effectively already on the road to Swaziland. Take the R21 south, signed to Boksburg, then head east on the N12, signed to Witbank. This coal-mining town was officially renamed Emalahleni in 2006 but some road signs still refer to Witbank. The N12 (which becomes the N4 at Witbank/Emalahleni) is the main highway to Maputo and the southern Kruger Park, and takes you halfway to Swaziland. Look out for the old mine dumps as you pass through Jo'burg's outer suburbs.

At Witbank/Emalahleni, 130km east of Jo'burg, the N12 crosses the Olifants River and merges with the N4 from Pretoria. Some 10km later you reach Middleburg Plaza, where you must pay a road toll. Just 1km later is a major service station (Shell UltraCity), which is your first convenient opportunity to refuel and take a break. Its curio shop can prove useful for last-minute gifts on your return journey. If you miss this, you'll find a Total service station after Middleburg and before your next turning.

After Middleburg, turn right off the N4 onto the R33, signed to Carolina. The next stretch is lined in summer with flowering cosmos and is good for birdlife: I have seen secretary bird, long-crested eagle and, among other waterfowl in the roadside pans, large seasonal flocks of flamingos. In summer this route often experiences terrific electrical storms. After passing through the sleepy little dorp (small town) of Carolina – which has shops and filling stations – turn right on the R33, signed to Amsterdam 100km, then left at the next T-junction onto the N17, from where you are signed to Oshoek (62km). You are now on a straight road to Swaziland, and after passing through large forestry plantations the mountains of Malolotja swing into view on the left. The last 10km or so feels more African, as the road passes through the former KaNgwane. Be careful of stray cows here, especially should you be travelling after dark – which is best avoided. The border is open 07.00–22.00. You are now just 20 minutes from Mbabane on the MR3 highway.

Bulembu/Josefdal	08.00–16.00	Mananga	08.00–18.00
Gege/Bothashoop	08.00–16.00	Matsamo/Jeppes Reef	08.00–20.00
Lavumisa/Golela	07.00–22.00	Mhlumeni/Goba (Moz)	24hrs
Lomahasha/		Ngwenya/Oshoek	07.00–22.00
Namaacha (Moz)	07.00–20.00	Salitje/Onverwacht	08.00–18.00
Lundzi/Waverley	07.00–16.00	Sandlane/Nerston	08.00–18.00
Mahamba	07.00–22.00	Sicunusa/ Emahlathini	08.00–18.00

From the north Visitors arriving from the Kruger Park or Mpumalanga direction can choose between three borders – each of which may also be reached from Johannesburg by continuing along the N4, although this would take much longer than the standard Ngwenya route (see page 108).

The Jeppes Reef/Matsamo border (⏰ *08.00–20.00*) lies around 40km due south of the Kruger Park's Malelane Gate on the R570. A pleasant drive takes you through wild hills and extensive fruit orchards. Beware of cattle and pedestrians in the final stretch. From Matsamo, it is a 30-minute drive south to Piggs Peak on the MR1 and another 45 minutes to Mbabane.

Southwest of Matsamo is the Josefsdal/Bulembu border (⏰ *08.00–16.00*), which sits in the mountains at the top of a hairpin climb from Barberton, with spectacular views of Songimvelo Nature Reserve and the old Havelock mine cable car. The road is fully tarred on the South African side but, after passing though Bulembu, degenerates on the Swazi side into a rutted dirt track. This is driveable in a normal vehicle but tricky after rains, and it may take you nearly an hour to cover the 18km to Piggs Peak. The border itself is tiny and closes early. This route is an adventure in itself, but not for those in a hurry.

East of Matsamo is the Mananga border (⏰ *08.00–18.00*), 75km south of Komatipoort along the R571. This is a convenient route to Swaziland after exiting the Kruger Park Crocodile Bridge gate or leaving Mozambique via the Lebombo border post. It also gets you quickly to the Lubombo Conservancy (see page 255). A sign on the left directs you to the Samora Machel monument, commemorating the spot where in 1986 the Mozambique president died in a plane crash (see box on page 271).

From the south and west Visitors from KwaZulu-Natal can enter Swaziland via the Golela/Lavumisa border (⏰ *07.00–22.00*). Simply follow the N2, the main Durban highway, towards Swaziland and, after crossing the Pongola River, make a right turn for the last 11km to the border. Look out for game, such as reedbuck, as you pass through the Pongola Nature Reserve. Lavumisa is 400km from Durban. From the border it is 60km to Big Bend and 150km to Mbabane.

The N2 continues west around Swaziland's southern border past several more border posts. From Pongola, a right turn takes you to Onverwacht/Salitje (⏰ *08.00–18.00*). Some 90km further west is Piet Retief, a larger town, from where you reach the Mahamba border on the R543 (⏰ *07.00–22.00*). Mahamba is 10km from Nhlangano and 150km from Mbabane. Two minor borders closer to Piet Retief are Bothashoop/Gege (⏰ *08.00–16.00*) and Emahlathini/Sicunusa (⏰ *08.00–18.00*), both of which are closer to Mbabane, via Mankayane.

From Piet Retief the R33 skirts north around Swaziland to Amsterdam, from where it is 18km on the R65 to the Nerston/Sandlane border (⏰ *08.00–18.00*). This is one hour from Mbabane, and passes via the Foresters Arms hotel in

Mhlambanyatsi (page 152). Between this border and the main one at Oshoek/Ngwenya (see page 201), there is also the small Waverley/Lundzi border (⊕ *07.00–16.00*), which includes a stretch of dirt road on the Swazi side.

From Mozambique Swaziland has two road borders with Mozambique, both in the far northeastern Lubombo Mountains: the Lomahasha/Namaacha border (⊕ *07.00–22.00*) is at the end of the MR3, some 30km north of Simunye; it is on the EN5, the main road to Maputo. The Mhlumeni/Goba border (⊕ *24hrs*) is 30km north of Siteki; a minor road leads from here to join the EN5. If travelling from Mbabane, Manzini or Big Bend, Mhlumeni is the quicker option. Either way, it is no more than 80km to Mozambique's capital. Mozambique border crossings can be more time-consuming than South African ones and you will need to pay for a certificate of motor insurance. Make sure you have your Mozambique visa.

BY BUS Swazi company Siyeswatini Transmagnific (❅ *2404 9977;* m *7605 9977;* e *info@goswaziland.co.sz; www.goswaziland.co.sz*) runs a luxury minibus service between Mbabane and Johannesburg, stopping at Witbank, OR International Airport and Sandton. It departs every morning at 08.00, reaching Sandton at 12.45 (return departs Sandton 13.00, arriving Mbabane 17.45). A new twice-daily service both ways is scheduled for introduction by the end of 2012. Fares are from SZL500 one-way and SZL950 return. You will find Transmagnific at the Engen garage opposite Mbabane Plaza, next to Imperial Car Rental. Flight Connector (❅ +268 7626 9498/268 7713 0948; e *flightconnector@swazi.net*) is a new service offering daily transfers between Swaziland and O R Tambo in comfortable mini-buses. Arranges direct drop-off and pick up at the Bushfire festival.

HEALTH   *with Dr Felicity Nicholson*

First-timers to Africa often worry about tropical diseases, venomous snakes and other hazards popularly associated with the 'dark continent'. In fact, Swaziland is generally a safe and healthy place in which to travel. Much of the country lies at high enough altitudes to enjoy a temperate climate and none of it is tropical (Swaziland lies south of the Tropic of Capricorn), so many ailments associated with tropical Africa are either rare or absent entirely. Those that do occur are generally confined to the lowveld. A much greater risk than any disease to the average traveller is road accidents, which can be minimised by a few sensible precautions (see page 121).

BEFORE YOU GO
Immunisations Visit your doctor or a specialist travel clinic (see page 113) to discuss your requirements, if possible at least eight weeks before you plan to travel. Check your immunisation status: it is wise to be up to date on tetanus, polio and diphtheria (now given as an all-in-one vaccine, Revaxis, that lasts for ten years) and hepatitis A. Immunisations against rabies may also be recommended for some travellers. Proof of vaccination against yellow fever is needed if you are coming from a yellow-fever endemic area, though a yellow-fever vaccine is not needed for Swaziland alone. Immunisation against cholera is no longer required for Swaziland.

Hepatitis A vaccine (Havrix Monodose or Avaxim) comprises two injections given about a year apart. The course may be available on the NHS. It protects for 25 years and can be administered close to the time of departure. Hepatitis B vaccination should be considered for longer trips (two months or more) or for those working with children or in situations where contact with blood is likely. Three injections are needed for the best protection; for those aged 16 or over, they can be given over a three-week period if time is short. Longer schedules give more sustained protection and have to be used for those under 16. Hepatitis A vaccine can also be given as a combination with hepatitis B as 'Twinrix', though two doses are needed at least seven days apart to be effective for the hepatitis A component, and three doses are needed for the hepatitis B. Again this schedule applies to those over 16.

The newer, injectable typhoid vaccines (eg: Typhim Vi) last for three years and are about 85% effective. Oral capsules (Vivotif) may also be available for those aged six and over. Vaccinations for rabies are recommended for travellers visiting more remote areas, especially if working with animals (see *Rabies*, page 119).

Experts differ over whether a BCG vaccination against tuberculosis (TB) is useful in adults: discuss this with your travel clinic. In addition to these various vaccinations, you must give proper consideration to protection against malaria (see *Malaria*, below).

Malaria

Prevention Malaria is a potentially fatal disease caused by a blood parasite transmitted by the *Anopheles* mosquito. Along with road accidents, it poses the single biggest serious health threat to travellers across much of sub-Saharan Africa. In Swaziland malaria is rare, occurring only in the eastern lowveld and Lubombo regions, with very few cases in recent years. Indeed, you may well read – or hear from locals – that the disease has been eradicated entirely. To be on the safe side, however, it is recommended you take suitable precautions including taking malaria tablets. Pregnant women should be cautious about travelling to malarial parts of Swaziland as they are twice as likely to be bitten by a malarial mosquito than non-pregnant women. Children are also more vulnerable to malaria. Bear in mind that while the main tourist destinations of Mbabane and the Ezulwini Valley are not malarial, any trip to the lowveld means a potential risk. If travelling onward to the Kruger Park or Mozambique, this risk increases.

There is not yet a practical travel vaccine against malaria but there is a range of anti-malarial drugs. Each has its pros and cons, many of which relate to an individual's circumstances or medical history. Seek current advice from your doctor on which anti-malarials are best for you. This will usually be one of the following.

Mefloquine (Lariam) causes unpleasant side effects for some people, so it is best to start 2½ weeks (three doses) before departure to check that it suits you. Stop immediately and consult a doctor if it seems to cause problems.

Malarone (proguanil and atovaquone) is as effective as mefloquine, with fewer side effects, and need only be continued for one week after returning. However, it is expensive and is thus often reserved for shorter trips. A paediatric form is available. Malarone is not yet licensed in pregnancy.

Doxycycline is an antibiotic that, like Malarone, can be started one day before arrival (100mg daily). Unlike mefloquine, it is suitable for most travellers with epilepsy, although certain anti-epileptic medication may make it less effective. It is unsuitable for pregnant women or for children under 12 years old.

Chloroquine and proguanil, once widely prescribed, are no longer considered effective enough for most African countries. They may be considered as a last resort if nothing else is deemed suitable, however, and are available at local pharmacists. The decision to use chloroquine and proguanil should only be made by a trained medical professional.

Tablets should be taken with or after the evening meal, washed down with plenty of fluid and, with the exception of Malarone, continued for four weeks after leaving.

It is important to be aware, however, that no anti-malarial drug is 100% protective, although those on prophylactics who are unlucky enough to catch malaria are less likely to get rapidly into serious trouble. Whatever your medication, therefore, you should also take steps to avoid mosquito bites (see *Avoiding bites and stings*, page 117). Homoeopathic prophylactics are not suitable for malaria and bona fide homoeopaths do not advocate it. It takes at least 18 months residing in a holoendemic area for someone to get any immunity to malaria so travellers to Africa will not acquire any effective resistance to malaria. The best way is to prevent mosquito bites in the first place and to take a suitable prophylactic agent

Travel clinics and health information A full list of current travel clinic websites worldwide is available on www.istm.org. For other journey preparation information, consult www.nathnac.org/ds/map_world.aspx. Information about various medications may be found on www.netdoctor.co.uk/travel.

LONG-HAUL FLIGHTS, CLOTS AND DVT

RISKS OF DVT Any prolonged immobility, including travel by land or air, can result in deep-vein thrombosis (DVT) with the risk of embolus to the lungs. Factors that can increase the risk include:

- Having a previous clot or a close relative with a history
- Being over the age of 40, with increased risk in the over-80s
- Recent major operation or varicose-veins surgery
- Cancer
- Stroke
- Heart disease
- Obesity
- Pregnancy
- Hormone therapy
- Being a heavy smoker
- Severe varicose veins
- Being tall (over 1.8m) or short (under 1.5m)

A deep-vein thrombosis causes painful swelling and redness of the calf or sometimes the thigh. It is only dangerous if a clot travels to the lungs (pulmonary embolus). Symptoms of a pulmonary embolus (PE), which commonly start three to ten days after a long flight, include chest pain, shortness of breath, and sometimes coughing up small amounts of blood. Anyone who thinks that they might have a DVT needs to see a doctor immediately.

PREVENTION OF DVT
- Keep mobile before and during the flight; move around every couple of hours
- Drink plenty of fluids during the flight
- Avoid taking sleeping pills and excessive tea, coffee and alcohol
- Consider wearing flight socks or support stockings (see *www.legshealth.com*)

If you think you are at increased risk of a clot, ask your doctor whether it is safe to travel.

Personal first-aid kit A minimal kit contains:

- A good drying antiseptic, eg: iodine or potassium permanganate
- Small dressings (plasters/Band-Aids)
- Suncream
- Insect repellent; anti-malarial tablets; impregnated bed-net or permethrin spray
- Aspirin or paracetamol
- Antifungal cream (eg: Canesten)
- Ciprofloxacin or norfloxacin, for severe diarrhoea
- Tinidazole for giardia or amoebic dysentery
- Antibiotic eye drops, for sore, 'gritty', stuck-together eyes (conjunctivitis)
- A pair of fine tweezers (to remove insect stings, thorns, splinters, etc)
- Alcohol-based hand rub or bar of soap in plastic box
- Condoms or femidoms

Medical facilities in Swaziland Swaziland has a reasonably extensive healthcare infrastructure, and with hospitals and clinics in all major towns you are seldom more than a couple of hours from medical help. Government hospitals, however, are under great pressure – largely as a result of the HIV/AIDS epidemic – which means that facilities and standards of care are not up to those expected by most overseas visitors. A more reliable (but expensive) alternative is private clinics, such as the Mbabane Clinic and the MediSun Clinic in Ezulwini. Make sure that you have adequate and up-to-date medical insurance.

All the main towns and shopping malls have pharmacists, and general practitioners and dentists are readily available. Visioncare Optometrists have branches at Mbabane (The Mall), Manzini (The Hub) and Piggs Peak.

Hospitals
In case of severe trauma
✚ **Mbabane Clinic** Mbabane (private); ✎ 2404 2423
✚ **Raleigh Fitkin Hospital** Manzini; ✎ 2505 2211

Other
✚ **Manzini Clinic** ✎ 2505 7301
✚ **Mbabane Government Hospital** ✎ 2404 2111

✚ **MediSun Clinic** Ezulwini; ✎ 2416 2800
✚ **Mkhaya Clinic** Manzini; ✎ 2505 5339
✚ **Nhlangano Health Care Centre** ✎ 2207 8421
✚ **Piggs Peak Government Hospital** ✎ 2437 1111
✚ **Siteki Good Shepherd Hospital** ✎ 2343 4133

Emergency evacuations These can be arranged through Trauma Link Swaziland, ✎ 7606 0911.

Water Contaminated water can carry disease. All main towns in Swaziland have safe drinking water. If staying in rural communities, where water may come from less reliable sources, it is best to ensure your drinking water is boiled. Alternatively, water should be passed through a good bacteriological filter, or purified with iodine or the less-effective chlorine tablets (eg: Puritabs). Bottled water is widely available in towns and filling stations.

ON THE GROUND
Common medical problems
Travellers' diarrhoea Swaziland is not a high-risk destination for travellers' diarrhoea. Nonetheless, the newer you are to exotic travel, the more likely you

TREATING TRAVELLERS' DIARRHOEA

It is dehydration that makes you feel awful during a bout of diarrhoea and the most important part of treatment is drinking lots of clear fluids. Sachets of oral rehydration salts give the perfect biochemical mix to replace all the lost fluids. Or try Coke or orange squash with a three-finger pinch of salt added to each glass (if you are salt-depleted you won't taste the salt). Otherwise make a solution of a four-finger scoop of sugar with a three-finger pinch of salt in a 500 ml glass. Or add eight level teaspoons of sugar (18g) and one level teaspoon of salt (3g) to one litre (five cups) of safe water. Drink two large glasses after every bowel action, and around three litres a day if you are not eating. These solutions are still absorbed well if you are vomiting, but you will need to take sips at a time. If you feel like eating, take a bland, high-carbohydrate diet. Heavy, greasy foods will probably give you cramps. If the diarrhoea is bad, or you are passing blood or slime, or you have a fever, you will probably need antibiotics in addition to fluid replacement. You should seek medical help at the first opportunity.

are to suffer. By taking precautions against travellers' diarrhoea you will also avoid typhoid, paratyphoid, cholera, hepatitis, dysentery, worms, etc. Travellers' diarrhoea and other faecal-oral diseases come from getting other peoples' faeces in your mouth. This most often happens from cooks not washing their hands after using the toilet, but you will be safe if your food has been properly cooked and arrives piping hot. Either way, the most important prevention strategy is to wash your hands before eating anything. A good maxim for safe eating is: PEEL IT, BOIL IT, COOK IT OR FORGET IT. This means that hot foods, and fruit you have washed and peeled yourself, should be safe, but raw foods, cold cooked foods, salads, fruit salads that have been prepared by others, ice cream and ice are all risky – as is food kept lukewarm in hotel buffets. That said, plenty of travellers enjoy fruit and vegetables, so do keep a sense of perspective: food served in a fairly decent hotel in a large town is likely to be safe. If you are struck, see box above for treatment.

Eye problems Bacterial conjunctivitis (pink eye) is a common infection in Africa; people who wear contact lenses are most susceptible to this irritating problem. The eyes feel sore and gritty, and they will often be stuck together in the mornings. They will need treatment with antibiotic drops or ointment. Lesser eye irritation should settle with bathing in salt water and keeping the eyes shaded. If an insect flies into your eye, extract it with great care, ensuring you do not crush or damage it otherwise you may get a nastily inflamed eye from toxins secreted by the creature.

Protection from the sun The southern African sun can be fierce, even when conditions appear overcast. Sun exposure ages the skin and, more seriously, increases the risk of skin cancer. Use sunscreen (at least SPF15), wear a hat and keep out of the sun during the middle of the day. If you must expose yourself, build up gradually from 20 minutes per day. Be especially careful of sun reflected off water, and wear a T-shirt and use waterproof suncream when swimming. Cover up with long, loose clothes. The glare and the dust can be hard on the eyes too, so bring UV-protecting sunglasses.

Prickly heat A fine pimply rash on the trunk is likely to be heat rash; cool showers, dabbing dry, and using talc will help. Treat the problem by slowing down to a relaxed schedule, wearing only loose, baggy, 100%-cotton clothes and sleeping naked under a fan; if it's bad you may need to check into an air-conditioned hotel room for a while.

Skin infections Any insect bite or nick in the skin gives an opportunity for bacteria to foil the body's usually excellent defences, so it is essential to clean and cover even the slightest wound. Pepper ticks (see page 48) are practically invisible and cause a red bite, which may become excruciatingly itchy. This could become infected if not left alone. Creams are not as effective as a good drying antiseptic such as dilute iodine, potassium permanganate (a few crystals in half a cup of water), or crystal (or gentian) violet. One of these should be available in most towns. If the wound starts to throb, becomes red or oozes, and especially if you develop a fever, antibiotics will probably be needed: flucloxacillin (250mg four times a day) or cloxacillin (500mg four times a day). For those allergic to penicillin, erythromycin (500mg twice a day) for five days should help. See a doctor if the symptoms do not start to improve within 48 hours.

An itchy rash in the groin or flaking between the toes is likely to be a fungal infection. To guard against this, wear 100%-cotton socks and underwear and shower frequently. Fungal infections need treatment with an antifungal cream such as Canesten (clotrimazole); if this is not available try Whitfield's ointment (compound benzoic acid ointment) or crystal violet (although this will turn you purple!).

Malaria: diagnosis and treatment Even those who take their tablets meticulously (see page 112) and do their best to avoid mosquito bites may contract a strain of malaria that is resistant to prophylactic drugs. Untreated malaria is likely to be fatal, but all strains respond well to prompt treatment. Because of this, your immediate priority upon displaying possible malaria symptoms – including a rapid rise in temperature (over 38°C), and any combination of a headache, flu-like aches and pains, a general sense of disorientation, and possibly even nausea and diarrhoea – is to establish whether you have malaria, ideally by visiting a clinic.

Diagnosing malaria is not easy, which is why you should consult a doctor: there are other dangerous causes of fever, including typhoid or paratyphoid, which also require immediate treatment. Tickbite fever (see page 118) can also produce malaria-like symptoms. Even if you test negative, it is wise to stay within reach of a laboratory until the symptoms clear up, and to test again after a day or two if they don't. Travellers staying in remote rural communities in the lowveld and Lubombo regions would also be wise to carry a course of treatment to cure malaria and a rapid test kit. With malaria, it is normal enough to go from feeling healthy to having a high fever in the space of a few hours (and it is possible to die from falciparum malaria within 24 hours of the first symptoms). In such circumstances, assume that you have malaria and act accordingly – whatever risks are attached to taking an unnecessary cure are outweighed by the dangers of untreated malaria. Malarone or Coarthemeter are the current treatments of choice. Discuss your trip with a specialist either in Swaziland or before you leave.

Bilharzia or schistosomiasis *With thanks to Dr Vaughan Southgate of the Natural History Museum, London, and Dr Dick Stockley, The Surgery, Kampala*
Bilharzia or schistosomiasis is an unpleasant disease that commonly afflicts the rural poor of the tropics. It occurs in still and slow-flowing water, the most risky areas

Insect bites in Swaziland are most prevalent during the rainy season (October–April). As the sun is going down, don long clothes and apply repellent on any exposed flesh. Pack a DEET-based insect repellent (roll-ons or stick are easiest for travelling). You can also carry either a permethrin-impregnated bed-net or a permethrin spray so that you can 'treat' bed-nets in hotels and lodges. The latter makes even very tatty nets protective and prevents mosquitoes from biting through the impregnated net when you roll against it. Otherwise retire to an air-conditioned room, burn mosquito coils (which are cheap and widely available) or sleep under a fan. Coils and fans reduce rather than eliminate bites. Travel clinics usually sell a good range of nets, treatment kits and repellents. Mosquitoes and many other insects are attracted to light. If you are camping, never leave a lighted lamp near the opening of your tent or you will have a swarm of biters waiting to join you when you retire. In hotel rooms, be aware that the longer your light is on, the greater the number of insects that will be sharing your accommodation.

During the day it is wise to wear long, loose (preferably 100%-cotton) clothes as a protection against other bites, especially when pushing through long grass and scrub, which is when you are most at risk from ticks (see page 118). A few species of spider, scorpion and centipede can deliver a painful but not lethal bite (or, in a scorpion's case, sting). Take care when lifting up rocks or logs, packing away tents and groundsheets, and putting on shoes that have been left outdoors. Often overlooked among Africa's more tropical insect bites and stings is the humble honeybee. Wild bees can be extremely aggressive when disturbed. Give a wide berth to any bees' nest you come across (usually betrayed by telltale buzzing from a hole in a tree trunk).

being where infected people use water and wash clothes, etc. The disease – caused by a parasite – is carried by the larvae (cercariae) of certain species of snail. It penetrates your skin when you wade or bathe in infested water, reproduces in your liver and becomes established in your internal organs. Symptoms include fever, cough, abdominal pain, and a fleeting, itching rash called 'safari itch'. The absence of early symptoms does not necessarily mean there is no infection. Later symptoms can be more severe but the general symptoms settle down fairly quickly and eventually you are just tired. 'Tired all the time' is one of the most common symptoms among expats in Africa, and bilharzia is one of the most common culprits. The disease is difficult to diagnose but can be tested at specialist travel clinics and is easy to treat. Ideally, tests need to be done at least six weeks after likely exposure and will determine whether you need treatment. In reality, there are few circumstances in Swaziland in which the average tourist might encounter the disease – no cases are recorded from the section of the Usutu River along which whitewater rafting trips are conducted (see page 275) – but it's as well to be aware of the possibility.

Avoiding bilharzia
• Avoid bathing or paddling near places where people use the water a great deal, especially reedy shores or where there is lots of waterweed.
• If bathing, paddling or wading in fresh water that you think may carry a bilharzia risk, try to get out within ten minutes.
• Dry off thoroughly with a towel; rub vigorously.

- If your bathing water comes from a risky source try to ensure that the water is taken from the lake in the early morning and stored snail-free, otherwise it should be filtered or Dettol or Cresol added.
- Bathing early in the morning is safer than in the second half of the day.
- Cover yourself with DEET insect repellent before swimming: it may offer some protection.

Tickbite fever (*With additional advice from Dr Jonathan Pons, Good Shepherd Hospital, Siteki*)
Tickbite fever is a common problem for travellers in Swaziland, especially among those who go hiking in long grass or thick bush. Ticks are tiny parasitic members of the arachnid class (like spiders and scorpions; see page 46), which feed on the blood of warm-blooded animals, including humans. The disease is known by various different names around the world. It is caused by a bacterium of the *Rickettsia* genus (in Swaziland either *R conorii* or *R africae*), which is carried by the tick and transmitted through their saliva when they bite a human.

The incubation period is five to seven days. Typical symptoms include fever, headache and a rash. There is often an eschar at the site of the tick bite; this is a small ulcer (2–5mm in diameter) with a black centre, and can be difficult to find. It usually appears along with the fever. Lymph nodes near the eschar may be enlarged. A rash is sometimes present, typically starting on the limbs, spreading to the trunk and even the entire body. Conditions that may be confused with tickbite fever include meningitis, malaria, measles and German measles. Antibodies to the bacteria can be detected in the blood but the tests may only become positive after a couple of weeks, so while they may help to confirm a diagnosis they are of less help early on in the infection. African tickbite fever is usually mild – serious complications are very rare – and victims may get better on their own without treatment. Recovery can take up to two weeks, however. It is thus always best to go to a doctor. Treatment with an antibiotic can shorten the symptoms and reduce the chance of a serious side effect. Doxycycline is the preferred agent. Alternatives include chloramphenicol and ciprofloxacin.

The easiest way to prevent tickbite fever is to avoid being bitten. Ticks are most commonly acquired from walking in long grass, especially in the rainy season, so wear insect repellents and long trousers and sleeves. Check yourself carefully in the shower after a day's hike: ticks often settle in warm, sheltered areas, such as armpit and groin. Ideally, it is best to get a travelling companion to help. If travelling with small children, remember to check their heads, particularly behind the ears. Remove any ticks you find as soon as possible, as leaving them on the body increases the chance of infection. It is best to use the special tick tweezers that can be bought in good travel shops. Failing that, you can use your fingernails: grasp the tick as close to your body as possible and pull steadily and firmly away at right angles to your skin. The tick will come away complete as long as you do not jerk or twist. If possible douse the wound with alcohol (any spirit will do) or iodine. Irritants (eg: Olbas oil) or lit cigarettes are to be discouraged since they can cause the ticks to regurgitate and therefore increase the risk of disease. Spreading redness around the bite and/or fever and/or aching joints after a tick bite imply that you have an infection that requires antibiotic treatment, so seek advice.

Other diseases
HIV/AIDS The risks of sexually transmitted infection are as high in Swaziland as anywhere in the world (see page 72), whether you sleep with fellow travellers or

locals. If you must have sex, use condoms or femidoms, which help reduce the risk of transmission. If you notice any genital ulcers or discharge, get treatment promptly since these increase the risk of acquiring HIV. If you do have unprotected sex, visit a clinic as soon as possible; this should be within 24 hours, or no later than 72 hours, for post-exposure prophylaxis.

Animals

Rabies Rabies can be carried by all mammals, including village dogs and 'tame' monkeys around rest camps, and is passed to humans through a bite, scratch or lick of an open wound. If you come into contact with an animal in this way, you must assume it is rabid and seek medical help as soon as possible. Meanwhile scrub the wound with soap under a running tap or while pouring clean water from a jug, then pour on a strong iodine or alcohol solution of gin, whisky or rum. This helps stop the rabies virus entering the body and will guard against wound infections, including tetanus.

Pre-exposure vaccinations for rabies are ideally advised for everyone, but they are particularly important if you intend to have contact with animals and/or are likely to be more than 24 hours away from medical help. Ideally three doses should be taken over a minimum of 21 days, in order to change the post-exposure treatment, though even taking one or two doses may occasionally be better than none at all. Contrary to popular belief, these vaccinations are relatively painless.

If you are bitten, scratched or licked over an open wound by a sick animal, then post-exposure prophylaxis should be given as soon as possible, though it is never too late to seek help, as the incubation period for rabies can be very long. Those who have not been immunised before the exposure will need a product called Rabies Immunoglobulin (RIG) and a full course of rabies vaccinations (four–five doses). RIG however is expensive (around US$800) and may be hard to come by. If you have had three pre-exposure doses of vaccine it is no longer needed – another reason why pre-exposure vaccination is encouraged. And remember that, if you do contract rabies, mortality is 100% and death from rabies is probably one of the worst ways to go.

Snakebite Of Swaziland's 61 snake species (see page 42), only seven are potentially dangerous to humans. Venomous or otherwise, however, snakes do their best to avoid people and very rarely attack unless provoked. Bites in travellers are extremely unusual. You can minimise the risk by wearing closed shoes and long trousers when in the bush. Avoid gathering firewood after dark, especially reaching into woodpiles, and if you do come across a snake leave it alone: snakes only bite humans in self-defence and a high proportion of bites are sustained when people attempt to kill snakes. Remember that many species are more active at night – including the puff adder and Mozambique spitting cobra, which are responsible for most serious snakebites in Swaziland.

If bitten by a venomous snake you may have received only a 'dry bite', ie: one in which no venom was injected. Keeping this in mind may help you to stay calm. Many so-called first-aid techniques do more harm than good: cutting into the wound is harmful; tourniquets are dangerous; suction and electrical inactivation devices do not work. The only treatment is antivenom. In case of a bite that you fear may have been from a venomous snake:

- Try to keep calm – there is a good chance that no venom has been dispensed.
- Prevent movement of the bitten limb by applying a splint.
- Keep the bitten limb BELOW heart height to slow the spread of any venom.

- If you have a crêpe bandage, wrap it around the whole limb (eg: all the way from the toes to the thigh), as tight as you would for a sprained ankle or a muscle pull.
- Evacuate to a hospital with antivenom. Different species of snake require different antivenoms and not all are always available.

And remember:

- NEVER give aspirin; you may take paracetamol, which is safe.
- NEVER cut or suck the wound.
- DO NOT apply ice packs.
- DO NOT apply potassium permanganate.

Try to identify the snake that delivered the bite. If it can be killed or captured – but only without risk, because of the danger of being bitten again – take it to show the doctor. Never attempt to kill or capture a black mamba, and beware that even a snake's decapitated head can deliver a venomous bite.

Spitting cobras Two snake species found in Swaziland – the Mozambique spitting cobra and the rinkhals (see page 42) – will both spit diluted venom over a range of up to 3m. If this spray enters the eye it will cause great pain and, left untreated, can do permanent damage. If this happens, reassure the victim and wash out the eyes as soon as possible with clean water. Then seek medical help. Spitting is a defensive measure and both snakes will usually – though not always – rear up and spread a hood before doing so. If molested further, both can also deliver a serious bite.

Other dangerous wildlife Swaziland has little by way of lethal wildlife. Large, potentially dangerous mammals, including elephant, rhino, lion and buffalo, occur only in enclosed conservation areas so you will encounter them only with a ranger, who will tell you what to do should they get uppity. Hippos occasionally stray onto farmland along the Mbuluzi and Usutu rivers and should be given a wide berth in the unlikely event you encounter one. Smaller, habituated animals around camps generally pose more of a risk. Don't take liberties around warthogs, especially females with young, and beware vervet monkeys, which can be aggressive in their pursuit of a free lunch. Crocodiles (see page 39) are a more serious danger. These predatory reptiles take a small but regular toll of human victims in Swaziland, usually fishermen or children snatched from rivers and dams in the lowveld. Treat crocs with respect by keeping back from the water's edge.

SAFETY AND SECURITY

Swaziland is, by-and-large, a safe country in which to travel. It does not have South Africa's alarming crime rate, and tourists are seldom targeted. Equally, it does not have South Africa's history of racial tension, which means that visitors are unlikely to encounter any antagonism on that basis. Indeed, hospitality is a cornerstone of Swazi culture and the average visitor's experience is overwhelmingly a friendly and relaxed one. The most serious hazards for the independent traveller are on the roads (see opposite).

That said, some South African crime does sometimes creep over the border. This includes occasional 'car-jacking' – the hijacking of drivers, often at gunpoint, for the theft of their car. Armed robberies of wealthier urban residences are not uncommon, and inevitably street crime such as pick-pocketing occurs in busy parts of town. Manzini has a worse reputation in this respect than Mbabane.

In general, the basic guidelines for safe travel are the same in Swaziland as anywhere else. Be alert, avoid obviously compromising situations, and don't play the tourist too conspicuously. It's common sense, really. The UK Foreign Office, which errs on the side of caution, offers the following specific advice:

• Avoid travelling into or out of Swaziland by road after dark, as carjacking has occurred on major routes from South Africa and Mozambique.
• Avoid walking in downtown Mbabane and Manzini after dark.

ROAD SAFETY

Driving in Swaziland is largely a great pleasure: decent roads extend across most of the country, destinations are well signed, and traffic is generally light. Unfortunately, it is also dangerous. The country has earned a poor reputation across the region for its high accident rate. Indeed, the Malagwane Hill (see page 159) once reputedly appeared in the *Guinness Book of Records* as the most dangerous stretch of road in the world, although I have yet to find the edition that confirms this.

Accidents are not generally due to the quality of the roads, most of which are either good or at least driveable. Rather, they reflect a combination of local circumstances, many of which will be new to the first-time driver in Africa. These include the following:

OTHER DRIVERS Driving is often not up to Western standards, with reckless overtaking, failing to signal and stopping in dangerous places all common hazards. Illegal drink-driving is widespread.

OTHER VEHICLES Many vehicles are not roadworthy: faulty lights or brakes, worn tyres or unsecured loads are all commonplace. Broken-down vehicles are often abandoned on blind bends or at other dangerous places.

LIVESTOCK Most roads are unfenced, so cattle, goats and stray dogs wander everywhere. Cattle are a major cause of accidents, especially at night, and are known locally as 'Swazi robots' (robot being the local term for traffic light).

THE WEATHER Highveld mists can reduce visibility to a few metres, often very suddenly and locally. Violent rainy season storms can overwhelm both the road camber and your windscreen wipers, turning gravel roads into a slippery nightmare in minutes.

There are simple ways to reduce the risks. The most important is to avoid driving at night, when the hazards posed by wandering livestock, dodgy vehicles and bad driving increase exponentially. Always keep well within the speed limits (120km/h on motorways and 80km/h on other unrestricted roads). Be especially careful on gravel roads. Always wear a seatbelt (many locals don't), and never accept a lift from anybody who has been drinking. In general, remain alert and drive cautiously. Swaziland is a small place and there is never any hurry. With more time, you can enjoy the landscape.

- Be wary of picnicking in remote areas unless in a large group.
- Keep valuables in a safe place and avoid carrying large amounts of money or wearing conspicuous jewellery.
- Drivers who break down or need to change a tyre should be wary of anyone who offers them help. Do not stop to assist apparently distressed motorists, as this is a technique sometimes used by hijackers. Instead, report the incident to the police.
- Always park in well-lit areas of town.
- Keep car doors locked and valuables such as mobile phones, cameras and handbags out of sight.

The Foreign Office also advises against giving strangers a ride. Offering a lift, however, is part of life in rural Swaziland and can be an interesting opportunity to meet local people. Common sense and experience will enable you to judge when it is safe to do so: a single driver picking up a group of young men after dark on the edge of town is asking for trouble; a car full of tourists picking up an elderly woman with a heavy load in a rural area is a nice gesture. If in any doubt, of course, don't do it.

International terrorism has not yet reared its ugly head in Swaziland, although the Foreign Office urges you to exercise the same vigilance as you would anywhere else in the world. Recent years have seen an increasing number of political demonstrations. You are best advised to avoid these, especially if the police regard them as unauthorised and so decide to disperse them forcefully.

WOMEN TRAVELLERS

Women travellers are unlikely to encounter any problems when travelling around Swaziland – at least, none that is not already familiar from back home – and sexual harassment is less prevalent than in many Western countries. Traditional Swazi culture is strongly patriarchal, but Swazis are used to female visitors travelling independently. In rural areas, it is best to dress with due sensitivity to local culture by not baring too much flesh. Wearing a wrap or sarong over shorts or a short skirt is a good idea – you are unlikely to encounter overt disapproval for failing to do so but it shows respect. In urban and tourist areas people are more cosmopolitan. Be aware, though, that single women in bars may attract unwelcome attention, especially given the local history of prostitution. Don't be put out by questions about your marital status: locals are often curious about single women – especially if unmarried or without children, which is unusual in Swaziland. This is simply a matter of cultural difference. Women should not accept lifts from strangers or walk around town alone after dark. Women's sanitary products are widely available.

TRAVELLING WITH CHILDREN

Swaziland is a great place to take your kids, and local children will enjoy any opportunity to interact with your own. In traditional society, children are expected to be respectful of their elders – which, in rural communities, may extend to not addressing them directly or making eye contact. Again, it is accepted that visitors do things differently, but I for one found no harm in encouraging my own young daughter to respect local culture. There are countless exciting things for kids to do. A few, such as whitewater rafting and guided bush walks, have a lower age limit, typically of 12 years, although exceptions can often be made on request. Half-price discounts for children are the norm with many operators. Children are more vulnerable to some health risks, so ensure that you take all medical precautions.

GAY/LESBIAN TRAVELLERS

Male homosexuality in Swaziland, as in many African countries, remains a strong social taboo. There are, of course, gay Swazis, but there is no 'out' gay culture in the country and thus no gay clubs or meeting places for travellers. By way of illustration, in 2011 the Minister of Justice and Constitutional Affairs, Magwagwa Gamedze, dismissed a recommendation by a United Nations working group on human rights that Swaziland enact a law to protect gay members of society. 'It was difficult for government to formulate a policy on homosexuals or enact a law to recognise them,' said Gamedze. 'Their numbers do not permit us to start processing a policy.'

Very little information is available on same-sex couples in Swaziland. The Gays and Lesbians Association of Swaziland (GALESWA), formed in the 1990s, has only one known member. The constitution does not safeguard the rights of gay people, and 'sodomy' laws dating from the early 20th century that outlaw consensual homosexual acts between adults are still on the books. Human rights groups have criticised Swaziland for its anti-gay legislation.

DISABLED TRAVELLERS

Swaziland lags far behind South Africa in promoting travel for people with disabilities, and visitors will not find the same range of facilities that they might expect in developed countries. In town, for instance, you should not expect level-entry public buildings and curb cuts, while few hotels offer adapted rooms and no disability-specialist operators currently run dedicated trips to Swaziland. That said, with advance notice many hotels and tour operators can meet the needs of disabled travellers and will ensure that accommodation, facilities and itineraries are chosen and/or adapted accordingly. Disabled travellers will find friendly and enthusiastic help wherever they go, though they should remember that helpers may not be trained so will need clear instructions. The Mountain Inn in Mbabane (see page 152) comes recommended by the accessible travel resource www.disabledtravelers.com, while the Ngwenya Glass Complex (see page 201) is wheelchair accessible. You can find general information and advice about disabled travel in Africa at Gordon Rattray's excellent website: www.able-travel.com. Also try *Access Africa: Safaris for people with Limited Mobility* (Bradt Travel Guides).

WHAT TO TAKE

The following items should cover you for most trips to Swaziland.

CLOTHING
- summer clothes (T-shirts/shorts etc)
- sarong/wrap (for women, to cover up in rural areas)
- lightweight longs (long-sleeved cotton shirt, breathable hiking trousers, etc – for lowveld evenings)
- fleece/pullover (for highveld evenings)
- lightweight raincoat/cagoule (for the rainy season)
- walking footwear (sturdy trainers, if no room for hiking boots)
- sandals (best with closed toes)

- swimwear
- smart/casual evening wear (for hotels/restaurants etc; no need for jacket, tie or anything formal)
- jeans or riding breeches (for horseriding, mountain-biking)
- hat (with a brim)
- money belt

GENERAL
- sunglasses
- first-aid kit (see page 114)
- binoculars (especially for birdwatchers)
- sunscreen
- torch (a head torch allows you to use binoculars if watching wildlife after dark)
- camera (with lens suitable for wildlife; see page 139)
- spare batteries and memory cards
- plug adaptor
- credit cards
- local currency in small denominations (South African rand is fine)
- mobile/cell phone (ideally with local SIM card, see page 137)
- anti-malarials (see page 112)
- day pack
- water bottle

DOCUMENTS/LITERATURE
- passport (with visa, if required; see page 105)
- driving licence
- travel insurance details, including emergency number
- photocopies of all important documents
- travel guide (this one, of course)
- field guide(s) (see page 302)

Toiletries and most medical supplies are readily available locally, so you can reduce your packing by buying these on arrival.

MONEY, BANKING AND BUDGETING

Swaziland's currency is the lilangeni (plural: emalangeni). One lilangeni is divided into 100 cents. Lilangeni notes come in 10, 20, 50, 100 and 200 denominations. The lilangeni (SZL) has parity with the South African rand (ZAR). Exchange rates at October 2012 were as follows:

£1 = 13.87SZL
US$1 = 8.64SZL
€1 = 11.21SZL

Rand notes are accepted in Swaziland and are often dispensed at ATMs. South African coins, especially smaller denominations, are less widely accepted. Emalangeni are *not* accepted in South Africa, so use all yours up before you leave. The one lilangeni coin is very similar in size and weight to a UK one pound coin and for a while, I'm told, it was possible to use emalangeni for pound coins in UK slot machines (although strictly against the law, of course). Apparently this is no longer the case, so don't go embarrassing yourself on a station platform after you get home.

The main banks represented in Swaziland are Nedbank, First National Bank, Standard Bank and Swazi Bank. You will find branches in all main towns. Most have ATMs where you can withdraw cash, but you cannot use international credit or debit cards at Swazi Bank. There are also ATMs at some large petrol stations and a few major hotels and casinos, including the Royal Swazi Sun. Weekday bank hours are usually 08.30–14.30. Some banks are also open 08.00–13.00 on Saturdays. There is no international bureau de change in Swaziland but you can change currency at most banks.

BUDGETING Swaziland is very reasonably priced and, at the time of writing, offers a holiday – once you have paid to get there – that is in most respects cheaper than its equivalent in Europe or America by a factor of some 20–30%. Crucially, its parks and reserves do not pursue the 'low impact, high revenue' policy that raises fees in many safari destinations beyond the reach of a lot of independent travellers. Those on a tight budget could manage on US$40 per day by camping, self-catering and taking local transport. A modest mid-range budget, including hotels, restaurants and most activities, could work out at US$100–150 per day. You can enjoy a three-course meal with wine in a decent mid-range restaurant for US$20. Top hotels and lodges are more expensive, and you should allow more for specialised activities (eg: US$100 for a half-day's whitewater rafting, including lunch and transfers). Economy car hire is available from US$180 per week, with fuel costing roughly SZL10.5 per litre (unleaded) as of September 2012.

GETTING AROUND

Most Swazis get around the country by taking a bus or kombi (see page 127) or by walking – often a very long way. Visitors (at least those staying for no more than a couple of weeks) may find it easier to drive.

SELF-DRIVE Traffic in Swaziland drives on the left, as in the UK and the rest of southern Africa. Drivers will need a UK driving licence or an international licence in English. Good, tarred roads link main towns, tourist centres and most borders. The MR3 highway from Ngwenya border to Mbabane and on to Manzini is a good dual-carriageway for most of its length, and well lit at night. Away from towns and main routes you will generally encounter gravel roads ('gravel' meaning dirt, rather than the kind of small pebbles that line an English suburban driveway). These are indicated on most maps. Most are in reasonable repair and regularly graded. Drive slowly (not above 60km/h), and beware the dust clouds left by other vehicles. For remote tracks in rural areas or some nature reserves, you may need a 4x4 vehicle – or at least one with high clearance. Gravel roads can become treacherous during the rains, with deep ruts and loose surfaces. Beware low-level bridges at this time, when the road may disappear underwater. In general, if heading off the beaten track – especially during the rains – take local advice.

It can't be overstated that Swaziland has a very high rate of traffic accidents (see page 121), whether on tar or gravel. So always drive with care and vigilance, wear your seatbelt (which is a legal requirement) and avoid driving at night if at all possible.

Filling stations Swaziland has petrol stations at all main towns, most borders and some key road junctions. A pump attendant is often on hand to fill your

2

vehicle, and may also check your oil and water and give your windscreen a clean; a modest tip is always welcome, though never demanded. Larger filling stations will have a shop with basic supplies, and a garage where they will repair a puncture and fix other minor mechanical problems. The main commercial fuel suppliers in Swaziland are Caltex, Engen, Galp and Total. Large filling stations in cities operate a 24-hour service; smaller stations are generally open 07.00–18.00.

Spares and repairs Nowhere in Swaziland are you more than an hour or two from a garage, so drivers need not worry about travelling without the full complement of tools and spare parts – or the mechanical expertise with which to make use of them. Punctures are common, however, especially on dirt roads, so make sure you have a spare tyre and know how to change it. Check that your hire car comes equipped with spare tyre, jack and wheel brace (and, if necessary, a key for locking wheel nuts). Your most useful tool in the event of a breakdown may be a mobile phone. Always have the emergency number of your car hire company available.

Four-way stops Drivers from overseas may never have encountered a four-way stop before arriving in Swaziland. This arrangement often serves in place of traffic lights or roundabouts at junctions throughout the region (indeed, Swaziland has very few roundabouts – locally called 'circles'). A road sign gives you ample warning you are approaching a four-way stop. The basic rule is that *everybody* stops at the line in their lane and vehicles then proceed in the order in which they arrived – ie: if you arrived second then you let the vehicle that arrived before you proceed first. If two vehicles arrive at exactly the same time, the one to the right has priority. To the uninitiated it may sound like a recipe for chaos but in fact these junctions work very well. Three-way stops, of which Swaziland has a few, work on the same principle.

Vehicle hire The best car rental deals for overseas visitors are invariably to be found by booking in advance on the internet. The following companies are based in Swaziland and can offer local rental deals.

🚗 **Affordable Car Hire** Swazi Plaza, Mbabane; ☎ 2404 9136
🚗 **Avis** Matsapha Airport; ☎ 2518 6222

🚗 **Europcar** Engen Garage, Mbabane; ☎ 2404 0459; & Matsapha Airport; ☎ 2518 4393; e thandi. bhembe@europcar.co.za

Typical local rates start from US$280 (SZL2,400) for seven days for a five-door family car. Cheaper deals are available in South Africa. If driving from South Africa, you will find most major international car hire companies at O R Tambo International Airport in Johannesburg. Vehicle rental is also available at Piet Retief, Mpumalanga Airport (Nelspruit), Richards Bay and Skukuza in the Kruger Park. Make clear when hiring a car in South Africa that you intend to drive to Swaziland. (This is unlikely to affect your premium significantly.) If continuing to Mozambique, your options are more limited and premiums may be higher. Try Drive South Africa (*www.drivesouthafrica.co.za/car-hire*) for cross-border rentals. Expect to pay an extra charge if you want to drop off your vehicle at a different point from where you collected it.

PUBLIC TRANSPORT Some tourism and travel authorities services advise against using public transport in Swaziland, as they do for many African countries. Their concern is that vehicles are often poorly maintained and overloaded, and this represents an unnecessary risk for visitors, who usually have alternatives. They have a point. Certainly local buses are often very crowded and can be unreliable. Nonetheless, this is how most Swazis travel, and it offers the visitor a chance to get a little deeper under the skin of Swazi life. It's your call.

Bus Swaziland is well served by its extensive bus network, which connects every main town. There are no government-owned buses but plenty of private operators vying for the main routes. Mbabane and Manzini both have large bus ranks and all other towns have smaller ones. Departures are frequent and follow a fixed timetable, although this is not usually on public display. If in doubt, ask a local. You buy your ticket as you get on board. Seats are padded and journeys reasonably fast, although you should not expect the same standards of comfort, safety and punctuality as you would on equivalent transport in Europe or other more developed nations. Typical fares include SZL13 for Mbabane–Manzini and SZL25 for Mbabane–Piggs Peak.

Kombi taxi Minibus taxis, locally known as kombis, carry up to 14 people and ply most of the same routes as buses but at a higher speed and for a slightly steeper fare (eg: SZL15 for Mbabane–Manzini). There are no set departure times: a kombi leaves when it is full and then races to its next destination – often at hair-raising speed – to pick up another full load of passengers as soon as possible. Each kombi is licenced to travel only between certain destinations and may not deviate from its route. These destinations are painted on the front and rear of the vehicle. To pick up a kombi, either go to a designated stop – usually beside the town bus rank or at a roadside shelter (ask any local) – or flag one down along the route. To do the latter, simply put out your hand and waggle it as though bouncing a ball. If the kombi has space it will pick you up.

HITCHHIKING Hitchhiking is not recommended in Swaziland, particularly for solo travellers, for the same reasons that it is not generally recommended anywhere – ie: you might draw the short straw and hitch a dodgy ride. Nonetheless, many budget travellers choose to get around in this way, and with regular traffic on most roads they don't usually have to wait too long. You can expect to pay a small fee towards the cost of the ride; it's a good idea to establish how much before you get in.

ACCOMMODATION

Swaziland has accommodation to suit all budgets, from campsites to swanky hotels. Details of individual establishments are listed in the *Where to stay* section of each chapter in *Part Two*, grouped under 'upmarket', 'mid-range' and 'budget'. These listings cover most well-known and recommended places but are not fully comprehensive. Additional places are marked on the maps and listed on the Bradt website (*www.bradtguides.com/guidebook-updates*). Swaziland is a small place, and local recommendations can be invaluable.

HOTELS AND RESORTS At the top end of the hotel spectrum are upmarket resorts such as the Royal Swazi Sun (see page 162), where you will find – at a price – everything you'd expect from such an establishment anywhere in the world. This will include good dining, extensive grounds, a range of sport and leisure facilities, and a comprehensive programme of local activities. Several of Swaziland's top hotels are attached to casinos. A little further down the spectrum come smaller, family-run hotels such as Foresters Arms (see page 152), which may not quite have all the frills but often offer more by way of originality and local flavour. Main towns have decent mid-range hotels, which tend to be more functional than fancy. In the lowest price bracket are the cheaper roadside hotels, or motels, which offer little more than a bed for the night. Most will have a bar, which often doubles as a lively local watering hole.

CAMPS AND LODGES 'Lodge' generally refers to accommodation of a hotel standard set in or around a park or nature reserve, with activities and meals generally on-site. Rooms are in cottages, chalets, safari tents (essentially chalets under canvas) and even traditional beehive huts with a tourist-friendly makeover. Rates may include activities. Most offer a choice of a restaurant or self-catering, with facilities for the latter including fully equipped kitchen and outdoor braai area. Camps and lodges are marked with a faded accommodation symbol (⌂) in the listings.

GUESTHOUSES AND B&BS Guesthouses are generally smaller than hotels, with accommodation all under one roof. Many offer excellent hospitality, with home cooking and a friendly welcome. Bed and breakfast is the standard arrangement, with dinner available on request and self-catering usually an option. Rural guesthouses have larger gardens and may offer outdoor pursuits on the property. Many guesthouses, especially those in the lowveld, offer long-stay deals.

BACKPACKER HOSTELS Swaziland has several backpackers' hostels, mostly in the Ezulwini Valley/Malkerns area. These offer simple, cheap accommodation in large tents, hostels or dormitories, with communal bathrooms, living areas and cooking facilities. They are largely the domain of independent travellers or volunteers who are not overly concerned about luxury or privacy, and double as meeting places for travellers, with local information and a lively grapevine. Many offer activities and excursions, and organise entertainment nights.

STAYING IN THE COMMUNITY A number of rural communities offer accommodation to tourists. The easiest way to organise this is through a specialist tour company (see page 102). You should not expect all the comforts of a hotel or guesthouse, but rather to experience a more authentic slice of Swazi life. Some provision is usually made for guests, with mattresses instead of grass mats and more privacy than a local family would expect. If you are happy to rough it for a night or two this offers a unique opportunity to meet local people. You'll have the opportunity to join in domestic chores, eat traditional food, and share tales around the fire.

Accommodation is also available in several rural community projects. These were set up with donor funding but are now run by the community, bringing revenue and employment to impoverished areas. All are located in remote areas of impressive scenery. Facilities vary from adequate to neglected. Sadly, poor maintenance has seen some fall into disrepair. Those that are in operation, however, offer a memorable experience for the enterprising visitor looking for something different. Some, such as Shewula Mountain Camp (see page 265), allow an opportunity to interact with local people; in doing so, you will be contributing to the well-being of the local community and promoting the benefits of tourism. As well as Shewula, these projects include Mahamba Gorge (see page 238) and Ngwempisi Community Project (see page 241). Bookings can be made through STA and Swazi Trails (see page 104).

CAMPING Camping is available in several parks and reserves, including Hlane, Malolotja, Mbuluzi, Mlawula, Mlilwane and Nisela, and is also an option at some lodges and hotels. Most campsites have clean ablution blocks with warm showers, taps and braai stands. Many also have power outlets. All Out Africa (see page 104) rents out dome tents and mattresses. Stick to designated campsites rather than camping rough around the country, which is not encouraged – and in any case is not permitted without the say-so of the local chief. Lovers of truly wild camping can backpack through Malolotja and camp in designated clearings beside the rivers and trails (see page 212). This is a real wilderness experience, with no facilities other than the clearing itself.

FOOD AND DRINK

There is no shortage of choice in Swaziland when it comes to filling your belly. Standard Western fare is widely available, courtesy of numerous South African supermarket chains, and served at all hotels and guesthouses. Many large hotels offer themed and international menus. Buffets are common and, for those who like their home comforts with cholesterol, the Full English Breakfast is ubiquitous.

EATING OUT Swaziland's top restaurants have renowned chefs, imaginative dishes and excellent service. Among the most popular are the Calabash (see page 165), Foresters Arms (see page 152), Ramblas (see page 154) and Malandela's (see page 185). A cosmopolitan span of restaurants is available in Mbabane, Manzini and the Gables shopping centre, including Thai, Chinese, Italian and Spanish, plus a growing number of trendy little bistros and sandwich bars. A local speciality is Portuguese/Mozambican fare, with numerous restaurants serving excellent seafood fresh from the Indian Ocean, including the famous LM prawns ('LM' being Lourenço Marques, the old colonial name for Maputo).

In town, US-style fast-food joints offer burgers, pizzas, fried chicken and the rest. Among the mostly South African chains are some familiar Western names, including the ubiquitous Kentucky Fried Chicken, although Swaziland is one of the few countries as yet uncolonised by McDonald's ('Hooray!' or 'Boo!' according to taste). For a cheaper meal out or a bite on the hoof, locals tend to visit any of the many street cafés and snack bars that serve hot meals of the stew/curry with rice/pap variety. A popular variation, inherited from South Africa, is 'bunny chow', which consists of a hollow half-loaf filled with hot stew: highly tempting, but with possible spillage disasters for the unwary. Also popular is the 'dagwood', a triple-decker toasted sandwich or burger. Like any responsible travel guide, this one must – of course – warn against the health risks of eating street food. Were it less responsible, though, it would recommend the pap with chicken gizzards, and especially the Swazi oxtail, as absolutely delicious.

To eat traditional Swazi food you really need to stay with a Swazi family, visit a homestead or attend a local event or celebration (such as a wedding). A few lodges and backpacker hostels hold regular Swazi food nights. For a classy take on traditional Swazi cuisine, with authentic ingredients and recipes, don't miss Edladleni, just outside Mbabane (see page 154).

The cost of eating out is reasonable by overseas standards, although prohibitive for Swaziland's rural majority. At mid-range restaurants, which include most hotels, you can expect to pay around US$10–15 for a main course, with a steak typically around US$12. The priciest dishes tend to be fresh fish and seafood, with a seafood platter for two typically around US$30. Cheaper options, such as burgers, will set you back around US$6, with toasted sandwiches (which come, like other 'light meals', with chips and salad) generally the cheapest option at US$2–3. Starters and desserts are generally around US$3–5. The individual restaurant listings in *Part Two* assume this basic price range. Where a particular establishment is significantly cheaper or more expensive, this is indicated in its description. A discretionary tip of around 10% is the norm – although failure to observe this practice, like many imported conventions, does not always trouble locals. Typical restaurant opening hours are 12.00–15.00 and 18.00–22.30; any significant variations are flagged in the individual listings.

BRAAIS Braai – for the newcomer to southern Africa – is essentially the Afrikaans term for barbecue and short for *braaivleis* ('grilled meat'). The ritual of slapping flesh on a charcoal grill has a powerful grip on local culture, white and black alike. As with barbecues anywhere, you'll generally find the men setting the world to rights with beer in one hand and tongs in the other, while the women beaver around in the wings, buttering rolls and preparing salads. Cooking and eating al fresco is a big part of African culture generally and Swaziland is no different. Most self-catering accommodation – including campsites – comes complete with metal grills for braais and often a pile of chopped wood to make a good blaze. Favourite meats include *boerwors* (a long roll of spicy sausage) and steak. Veggies might prefer to keep their distance – although it's worth remembering that mealies, par-boiled slightly first, do very well on a braai.

DRINK Most alcoholic drinks are available in Swaziland, including many wines from South Africa. All towns have a bottle store of some kind, often beside a hotel, and hotel bars tend to attract local drinkers. Beer is mostly lager, with the local Sibebe, brewed by Swaziland Brewers in Matsapha, competing with South African stalwarts such as Lion and Castle. Home-brewed mealie beer, known as *tjwala* (or, in South Africa, *umcombotsi*), is sold in cartons. And if you're going local, you might want to try *buganu* – a home-brewed liquor made from fermented marula fruits, which appears seasonally in February/March and prompts some epic local boozing (see page 85).

Non-drinkers will find a range of soft drinks in stores and filling stations, including some exceptionally tooth-rotting local varieties. In rural stores the relatively high price of soft drinks is mitigated by a deposit system – ie: return your empties and get a discount on the next. Supermarkets sell a good selection of delicious South African fruit juices. A popular local drink is a kind of sour milk called *emasi*, often sweetened with sugar. Tap water is fine to drink across Swaziland, unless you are told otherwise

PUBLIC HOLIDAYS, FESTIVALS AND EVENTS

Swaziland's public holidays are all listed in *Swaziland at a glance* (see page 2). Other dates for your diary include the following.

MARULA FESTIVAL (late February/early March) The marula season begins each year in mid-February and is celebrated with an annual festival known locally as 'Emaganwini'. The largest celebration is held at the royal residence of Ebuhleni, where the royal family joins in the song and dance. Another is held at Hlane village, the family home of the queen mother.

BUSHFIRE (May) Bushfire (*www.bushfire.co.sz*) is an annual performing arts festival held over a long May weekend at House on Fire, Malandela's (see page 185). It is one of the biggest and best of its kind in southern Africa, with everything from live music and theatre to film, workshops and a global food fair – in short, just what you'd expect from Swaziland's answer to Glastonbury.

IMVELO (June) Imvelo is an annual mountain-biking competition held every June at Mlilwane Wildlife Sanctuary (*www.biggameparks.org/imvelo*), sponsored by Nedbank Swaziland and Big Game Parks. It comprises a series of races over different distances, the longest being 64km, and is followed by a party for all cyclists.

SIBEBE SURVIVOR (late July) Sibebe Survivor (*www.sibebe.co.sz*) is an annual charity event, sponsored by the Rotary Club of Mbabane/Mbuluzi, which challenges participants to make their way – by walking or running – up and down Sibebe Rock, the world's largest granite dome (see page 157). Participants must register in advance.

SWAZILAND INTERNATIONAL TRADE FAIR (late August/early September) This annual exhibition is held over ten days at the Mavuso Trade and Exhibition Centre in Manzini (see page 193), and receives support from the king and government. It attracts over 35,000 exhibitors from different private and public sector institutions, as well as foreign companies and governments.

KING'S CUP GOLF EXTRAVAGANZA (September) This annual golf tournament is held at the Royal Swazi Golf Club, one of only two 18-hole courses in the country. A product of King Mswati's 2004 Job Creation Summit, it attracts business people from South Africa and around the region, and tends to pack out the hotels in Ezulwini.

SIMUNYE COUNTRY FAIR (October) This three-day weekend of family fun is held every year at Simunye Country Club (see page 266) and attracts thousands of visitors from around Swaziland and beyond. There are games, rides, children's entertainers, beer tents, goat races and circus acts. A line-up of bands take the stage and manager Thea Litschka-Koen (see page 267) even gives a snake-handling demonstration.

SHOPPING

All large towns have supermarkets, which are pretty much like supermarkets anywhere, with most of the food and other goods you would expect to find overseas. Both Mbabane (Mbabane Plaza and Mall) and Manzini (Bhunu Mall) boast large South African-style malls, complete with furniture stores, clothing boutiques, pharmacies, electrical retailers, stationery and book suppliers – in short, pretty much everything you need – plus the obligatory car parks, escalators, piped music and coffee shops. The Gables shopping centre in Ezulwini (see page 166) is similarly endowed and also has a multi-screen cinema. There are smaller shopping complexes at Big Bend, Matsapha, Nhlangano, Piggs Peak, Simunye and Siteki.

Many outlets at the malls are South African chains. Local independent shops on the surrounding streets are generally less well stocked but often more interesting. Not surprisingly, your retail opportunities decline the further you travel into the rural areas. Nonetheless, most towns and rural centres have a small supermarket, plus usually a 'butchery' (the local term for a butcher's), bottle store and pharmacy. Even the smallest settlement will have a general store, selling staples such as bread, soap, batteries, matches and tinned food, and most road junctions are marked by a cluster of roadside vendors' stalls, selling fruit and vegetables, and often hot take-aways. Larger filling stations also have shops, often with a refrigerated section and charcoal for your braai. All towns have vegetable markets, with the most impressive being at Mahlanya (see page 185). Fresh fruit is seasonal, with the greatest glut being during early summer, when market stalls groan with enormous mangoes, avocados and pineapples.

Even in this consumer wonderland, however, you may not find exactly what you need for your electrical goods – the correct phone charger or camera battery, for example – so make sure you bring these with you. Also bring any specific drugs prescribed by your doctor: the pharmacies are well supplied and helpful but you may require a brand that they don't stock. For toiletries, cosmetics and sanitary products, you should find everything you need.

When it comes to consumer tourism, you're spoilt for choice. Swaziland is simply heaving with gift shops, craft markets and curio stalls (see page 88).

ARTS AND ENTERTAINMENT

Swaziland is not a hotbed of the performing arts – at least, not in a contemporary sense. Certainly, you can watch *sibhaca* dancing and other traditional music and dance forms performed at tourist destinations and on ceremonial occasions. But there are very few venues where you might catch an evening performance of live music, dance or theatre.

Very few, that is, apart from House on Fire (*www.house-on-fire.com*). This inspiring venue (see page 186) opened in 2002 and has since revolutionised the performing arts scene in Swaziland. It not only provides an outlet for local artists but also attracts major names from South Africa and elsewhere. Its Bushfire festival (see page 186), held every May, is one of the biggest such events in the region. And at other times there is a regularly changing line-up of performers, from bands and singers to DJs and performance poets.

Otherwise, a handful of venues – notably the larger hotels in the Ezulwini Valley – have the facilities to host a live show from time to time. These vary from South African bands and local gospel choirs to the occasional touring cultural exchange act or artist invited by the likes of the British Council or Alliance Française, which could be anything from a Welsh brass band to a Canadian stand-up comic. Sadly the Mbabane Theatre Club (see page 157) no longer stages its annual productions. However, a number of community theatre groups – notably Siphila Nje (see page 91) – take drama around the country, often tackling issues of social concern and usually in siSwati.

Regular art exhibitions, often showcasing the work of visiting artists, are held at the Guava Gallery and other art galleries (see page 167). Among numerous community initiatives in the Mbabane and Ezulwini areas – often organised by enterprising expatriates – are everything from ceramics workshops to Portuguese conversation classes. The Natural History Society of Swaziland (℄ *2404 3518;* e *phil@naturalhistorysociety.org.sz*) organises regular events with guest speakers, usually on a topic of local interest.

To find out about performances, exhibitions, workshops and events of any kind, keep an eye on *What's Happening in Swaziland*, a free monthly newsletter with comprehensive listings available from all tourist outlets. And check the noticeboards outside the supermarkets in Mbabane Mall and The Gables. You could also subscribe to the online *Swazi Diary* (e *zdean-smith@africaonline.co.sz*), an informal and useful listings service.

GOING OUT

To a certain generation of white South Africans, Swaziland is still perhaps best known for its nightlife. For decades, the kingdom's liberal laws allowed all manner of dubious recreational diversions to flourish, luring weekenders from across the border like furtive moths to a slightly disreputable flame. In buttoned-down Dutch Reform Church South Africa there were no certainly casinos, strip clubs or blue movies – or, at least, not legal ones. Swaziland had all this in spades. Indeed, 'Valley of Heaven' had a decidedly saucy ring for many visitors to Ezulwini, where the If Not, Why Not Go-Go Bar, attached to the Happy Valley Hotel (see page 163), was notorious across the region.

Times have changed and Swaziland is no longer the honey pot of the '70s and '80s. This partly reflects market forces: the liberalisation of the new South Africa has meant that all this questionable fun is freely available back home and has thus stemmed the weekend flow over the border. It also reflects today's hospitality industry wising up to what is now expected of a respectable, family-friendly tourist destination. Hotels no longer have anything sleazy on their premises – at least, nothing that they advertise. Besides, in the country with the world's highest rate of HIV/AIDS, the question 'If not, why not?' is now easily answered. All that remain of those decadent times are the casinos. Today you can enjoy (or regret) a flutter at the Royal Swazi, Happy Valley, Piggs Peak and Nhlangano hotels. All are reputable gaming establishments that don't intrude on the wider life of these hotels.

For a chance to **strut your stuff**, House on Fire (see page 186) hosts local and visiting DJs, as does the Happy Valley (see above), and Pub and Grill at the Gables shopping centre in Ezulwini (see page 166). Otherwise, check local listings for any music or cabaret events being hosted at hotels near where you are staying. Mbabane and Manzini both have a number of lively nightspots (see the relevant sections in *Part Two*). Some such establishments are definitely not for the unwary tourist; take local advice before venturing downtown, and go with locals who know the scene and can steer you away from any dodgier dives.

To **catch a movie**, go to the Gables (see above), where the five-screen Movie Zone shows the latest blockbusters at three screenings daily. This has taken over from the now-defunct Cinelux in Mbabane as Swaziland's only cinema. The latter, which featured in *Wah-Wah* (see page 91), was once run by a pair of theatrical elderly sisters who, reputedly, would allow you free entrance if you either claimed or bore a striking resemblance to Elizabeth Taylor (although this never worked for me). Some hotels, including the Royal Swazi Sun and Piggs Peak, have private cinemas.

Most other options for a fun evening out in Swaziland revolve around **food and drink**. Numerous establishments hold regular themed functions, such as the popular Friday curry nights at Malandela's (see page 185). If there is a major sporting event going on, such as either the rugby or football World Cup, any big-screen sports bars will be packed with a lively, mixed crowd.

SPORT AND ACTIVITIES

There is no shortage of ways to keep fit and active in Swaziland. With enough time on your hands you could try to work through the following alphabetical list. Details are included under their relevant regional areas in *Part Two*.

ABSEILING Swazi Trails (see page 104) arranges abseiling and rock climbing along the Great Usutu River.

ADVENTURE SPORTS (GENERAL) Swazi Trails (see page 104) started out as Swaziland's only whitewater-rafting operator but now also offers numerous other adrenalin sports and is largely responsible for putting Swaziland on the map in this respect. Check their office and website for the latest.

BIKES Road racing and mountain-biking are both popular, and events include the annual Imvelo race in Mlilwane (see page 131). There are also popular mountain-biking trails at Foresters Arms, Hawane, Hlane, Malolotja, Mbuluzi and Shewula. Bikes are available for hire at some but not all places.

BIRDING Swaziland is home to around 500 species of bird, including a number of regional endemics (see *Birds*, page 30). Each habitat has its own special attractions. Nature reserves offer the best birding, with Hlane, Mahamba, Malolotja, Mbuluzi, Mlawula, Phophonyane and Nisela all outstanding. The Swaziland Tourism Authority publishes an excellent *Birding in Swaziland* brochure, available free at tourist offices.

BOATING Powerboats, yachts, dinghies and canoes may be used on various dams around Swaziland, including Hawane Dam, Maguga Dam, Sand River Dam and Van Eck Dam, although several are only for club members and guests. Houseboats can be hired on Maguga Dam and Sand River Dam.

BOWLS There are bowling lawns at the Royal Swazi Sun and Piggs Peak hotels (see pages 162 and 222), plus some private clubs on the sugar estates.

CAVING Swazi Trails offers adventure caving in the Ezulwini area (see page 169), subject to weather conditions.

FISHING Available at numerous dams and rivers around the country. The Usutu Forest Fly Fishing Club (☏ 2404 3118) manages several well-stocked trout dams within the Usutu Forest. Other top spots include Hawane Dam and Maguga Dam in the Highveld; Mbuluzi and Maluwula reserves in the lowveld; and Sand River, Simunye and Van Eck Dam on the sugar estates. Most rivers and dams contain native species, with tiger fish found in Van Eck Dam and the lower Usutu. Fishing on the sugar estates is generally for club members and guests. Many hotels organise fishing activities. There are several annual competitions. Licences can usually be obtained locally and gear rented or borrowed from clubs or hotels; check in advance.

GOLF Swaziland is a popular destination for golfing holidays and has two championship-standard 18-hole courses: the Royal Swazi Spa Golf Club (☏ *2416*

5000) and the Nkonyeni Golf Estate (✆ *2550 3934*). There are also nine-hole courses at Big Bend Golf Club (✆ *2363 6288*); Mananga Golf Club (✆ *2323 2404*); Manzini Golf Club (✆ *2505 2254*); Mbabane Golf Club (✆ *2404 6531*); Simunye Country Club (✆ *2313 4792*); Nhlangano Golf Club (✆ *2207 8887*) and Usutu Forests Golf Club (✆ *2467 4021*). Most are for private members and hotel guests.

HEALTH AND FITNESS Most large hotels and private clubs have health and fitness centres, complete with gym and sauna; many also offer massages, aerobics, yoga and various beauty treatments. Also try the Cuddle Puddle at the Swazi Spa Health and Beauty Studio (see page 168).

HIKING Swaziland's many superb hiking destinations include Bulembu, Mahamba, Malolotja, Mlawula, Ngwempisi and Sibebe. Well-marked trails offer hikes lasting from a couple of hours to several days. Those with initiative and a good map or GPS can simply head off into countryside. Weather conditions are unpredictable, especially in the Highveld during summer, so always set out well prepared.

HORSERIDING Several stables are located in the lowveld and middleveld, including Chubeka Trails (Mlilwane; see page 181), Hoofbeat Safaris (Ezulwini Valley; see page 161), Foresters Arms Hotel (Mhlambanyatsi; see page 152), Hawane Resort (Mbabane; see page 205) and Nyanza Stables (Malkerns; see page 188). Most stables come with good facilities and experienced instructors, and cater to all levels.

OFF-ROAD DRIVING There are several unofficial 4x4 routes around Swaziland for off-road enthusiasts; the Swaziland 4x4 Club (✆ *2416 1189*) holds regular meetings. All off-road driving must follow standard environmental guidelines.

QUAD-BIKING Swazi Trails runs two quad-bike trails in the Ezulwini Valley area (see page 169). Other destinations that offer quad-biking include Hawane Resort (see page 205) and Nkonyeni Golf Estate (see page 234). This activity is not generally available for children.

RUNNING Local running clubs, including the Hash Harriers and Swazi Slojos, hold regular runs and events. Check local listings.

SQUASH The Royal Swazi Spa Resort and Piggs Peak Hotel both have squash courts. Squash courts are available to members and guests at the Malkerns, Mananga, Manzini, Mbabane, Usutu Forest and Simunye country clubs.

SWIMMING Most hotels and private clubs, and many guesthouses, have swimming pools for guests. The Cuddle Puddle at the Swaziland Health Spa (page 168) also has a large pool. Swimming in lowveld dams is a bad idea as these may have bilharzia (see page 116) and possibly crocodiles. Fast-flowing rivers in the highveld are safer – but take care, especially when rivers rise during the rains.

TENNIS Hotels with tennis courts include the Royal Swazi Spa Resort, Foresters Arms Hotel, Nhlangano Hotel and Piggs Peak Hotel. Most private clubs have tennis courts that non-members may use for a fee.

TUBING All Out Africa offers one- and two-day tubing trips on the Ngwempisi River (see page 243).

WHITEWATER RAFTING Swazi Trails runs a variety of popular rafting trips on the Usutu River near Sidvokodvo (see page 234). These operate all year, although trips may be modified when the river is in peak flow.

ZIPLINING Malolotja Canopy Tours offers a 12-platform ziplining tour in Malolotja Nature Reserve (see page 207). There are also plans to develop ziplining on Nkonyeni Golf Estate (see page 234).

MEDIA

The media has a limited reach in Swaziland, with even the price of a daily paper – let alone access to the internet – beyond the means of many Swazis. Nonetheless, the news is devoured avidly, with most newspapers passing through many hands. Print media is dominated by two daily **newspapers**, both based in Mbabane and widely available. The *Swazi Observer* (*www.observer.org.sz*) is a state-owned publication that tends to toe the line. The *Times of Swaziland* (*www.times.co.sz*) is an independent publication that dates back to 1897 and is generally more questioning. Each also publishes a weekend edition: the *Weekend Observer* and *Swazi News*, respectively. A monthly independent news magazine, *The Nation*, has a more challenging voice but is not widely read.

Broadcasting services are state-owned. **Radio** comprises Radio Swaziland, which broadcasts in both English and SiSwati, and various commercial stations, many of them predominantly religious. BBC World Service and Voice of America can both be received. The **Swaziland Television Authority** (STA) has just one local channel, Swazi TV, with programming in both English and SiSwati, including local news and a mixed bag of international shows. (UK viewers might be intrigued to see random episodes of *The Bill* popping up from time to time.) Otherwise local viewers turn to South African Television (SABC), especially for its soap operas, and an increasing number subscribe to DSTV (Digital Satellite Television) for its plethora of international channels. DSTV is available at most hotels.

By African standards, Swaziland's press has a reasonable history of freedom. During my time in the kingdom during the 1990s the reporting of political dissent

STOP THE PRESS!

Swaziland's newspapers have produced some highly entertaining stories over the years – never more so than in 1995, when a headline in the *Times of Swaziland* proclaimed 'Swazi ship missing'. Baffled readers, unaware that their tiny landlocked kingdom was in possession of any kind of ship, were treated to the full explanation offered to parliament by Transport Minister Ephraim Magagula. 'The situation is absolutely under control,' reported Magagula. 'We believe it is in a sea somewhere. We sent a team of men to look for it but there was a problem with drink and they failed to find it, and so, technically, yes, we've lost it a bit. But I categorically reject all suggestions of incompetence on the part of this government. The Swazimar is a big ship painted in the sort of nice bright colours you can see at night. Mark my words, it will turn up.' If parliament does not prove entertaining enough then you can always try the court reports. 'Accused claims to be every character in bible' (*Swazi Observer*) and 'Pissed-off prisoner pees before court' (*Times of Swaziland*) are among two of the more memorable headlines in recent times.

and voicing of anti-establishment views was accepted in a way that would have been unthinkable in, say, Zimbabwe. Recent times, however, have seen more heavy-handed government attempts at censorship – targeting, in particular, anything critical of the monarchy. This, along with some recent incidents involving the alleged harassment of journalists and editors, has drawn widespread criticism. The mood of distrust has extended towards foreign media, with life sometimes made difficult for international journalists. The amendments to Swaziland's constitution in 2005 (see page 64) purported to guarantee 'freedom of expression'. Nonetheless, US-based NGO Freedom House, which monitors press freedom worldwide, concludes that the media in Swaziland is 'not free' and that it is 'marked by a high level of both official and self-censorship on political and royal matters'.

The **internet** is, of course, an infinitely broader source of information and opinion, and far less easily tamed. At present, access to this resource is largely restricted to the privileged – mostly urban – minority. (In 2008, just 5% of Swazis had an internet connection.) Sites such as Swazi Media Commentary (*swazimedia. blogspot.co.uk*) offer an alternative and often highly critical view of local affairs. The government has in recent times shown a desire to restrict the use of social media such as Facebook from propagating what it sees as divisive messages.

COMMUNICATIONS

TELEPHONE AND INTERNET   Communications in Swaziland are reasonably good. The state-owned Swaziland Posts and Telecommunications Corporation (SPTC) has an almost complete monopoly on telecommunications and is a partner in South Africa's MTN (*www.swazimtn.sz*), the country's sole mobile network. An extensive landline network covers most of the country. However, more than 90% of telephones in the kingdom are mobiles (locally known as 'cell phones') and some 90% of the population lives within range of a mobile network.

Visitors from overseas may find their mobile network provider is unavailable in Swaziland. The cheapest solution is to buy a local SIM card for your phone. Starter packs, including SIM card and start-up airtime, are available at the Ngwenya border, Matsapha Airport and other points of entry. Thereafter you can purchase airtime vouchers from any of the ubiquitous MTN vendors who roam Swaziland in their bright-yellow bibs. Be warned that local SIM cards may not work in smart phones such as Blackberry and iPhone. Contact your supplier for advice before leaving home.

Although most Swazis have access to mobile phones, few have computers. Young people use their phones to communicate via SMS messages (texting) or through social media such as Facebook or Mxit, Africa's biggest social networking site. Internet services are widely available but are expensive and can be slow, with only a handful of Internet Service Providers (ISPs). You will find internet cafés in the main towns, with Real Image Internet Cafés at the New Mall, Mbabane and the Bhunu Mall, Manzini, and Ziggy's Internet Café at Malandela's. Most, but not all, hotels offer Wi-Fi; check in advance.

POST AND COURIERS   If resorting to snail mail, you will find post offices in all towns (⊕ *Mon–Fri 08.00–13.00 & 14.00–17.00, Sat 08.00–11.00*). Local post is reliable but post sent overseas will take anything from two weeks to much longer. A quicker and more reliable – though more expensive – alternative is to use a courier service. DHL International Swaziland (*www.dhl.co.sz*) has offices in Manzini (m *7604 7648;* ⊕ *Mon–Fri 08.00–17.30*), Matsapha (m *2518 5375;* ⊕ *Mon–Fri 08.00–17.30, Sat*

08.30–12.00) and Mbabane (📞 2404 5829; 🕐 Mon–Fri 08.00–17.30; Sat 08.30–12.00). You could also try UPS in Matsapha (📞2518 6368; e pdlamini@ups-scs.com).

CULTURAL ETIQUETTE AND GREETINGS

Swazis are sticklers for politeness and respect. A lack of either is considered 'unSwazi', which is a grave charge indeed. Displeasure at your rudeness may not be expressed – that same tradition of respect means that Swazis tend to be undemonstrative around strangers – but you can rest assured that your behaviour has been noted and that it will not have helped your cause.

Traditionally, respect was expressed though formal conventions, such as the singing of praise names and, for women, the covering of heads and lowering of eyes. Such courtesies were especially important in the presence of elders. Today these conventions are weakening as rural tradition is steadily eroded by urban culture. Nonetheless, it remains important that you address somebody correctly. A few siSwati words will go a long way, but even if your SiSwati fails you, make sure that you greet somebody politely, and allow them to greet you in return, before embarking on whatever it is you want to say – even if you're simply asking for directions or negotiating a price. If you pass somebody while out and about in the rural areas, do greet them. Traditional greetings are lengthy affairs, with enquiries not only about your health but the condition of your cattle, the likelihood of rains and so on, before you get down to business. You won't be expected to know all that, but a throwaway 'Hi' is not good enough. Be especially polite when approaching somebody for a photograph; snapping away without permission or even a greeting tends to make people very cross. And quite right too.

Conversely, you may find it rude – or at least puzzling – that people often avoid eye contact during conversation. This is simply an extension of that same convention of respect. Women, traditionally, are not expected to be too forward when engaging with men, nor children with their elders. Similarly, questions may not be asked or answered directly. Circumlocution is a virtue in Swaziland: people talk things over until everybody has had their say.

In general, Swazis will cut visitors some slack when it comes to other conventions. Traditionally, for instance, you should not use your left hand to pass something, greet somebody or eat food, but few will mind when outsiders get this wrong. Similarly, there are few strict dress conventions that visitors are expected to observe. Women are not generally encouraged to expose too much flesh, especially above the knee, but nobody will take offence at you wearing shorts around a hotel or nature reserve. Use your common sense and assess the context: dressing appropriately is more important, for example, on formal occasions or when entering a Swazi home.

PHOTOGRAPHY

Any trip to Africa brings out the budding photographer, and Swaziland is especially photogenic. Sadly, good pictures are not guaranteed – even with today's excellent gear – and you don't want to find yourself flicking through a load of dud images after the trip of a lifetime. Anybody serious about their snapping should look properly into equipment and techniques. Unless you are such a photographer, though, don't allow your camera to dominate the trip. Untimely equipment crises can ruin a magic moment, while lugging round an awkward pile of gear can prove more trouble than it's worth. Accept that you may miss a few shots and bank some decent memories instead.

The following tips are aimed at the digital photographer. If you're still using film, then you are either too expert or too headstrong to need any advice here.

EQUIPMENT

Camera Make sure you know how yours works. If you buy a new camera then practise before your trip; you don't want to be struggling with mysterious dials and displays at a critical moment. And bring your instruction booklet with you. A digital SLR camera allows greater versatility – including a choice of lenses – than a compact, but is, of course, more of an investment.

Lenses To photograph wildlife effectively you will need a lens with a long focal length – at least 200mm – and ideally one with an image stabiliser. This also helps for photographing people from a distance (see opposite). Zoom lenses are more versatile, though prime lenses (ie: at a fixed focal length) are thought by professionals to be superior. Optical zoom (ie: on the lens) gives sharper results than digital zoom (on the camera body). A wide-angle lens (eg: 28mm) allows panoramic shots, while a macro lens gets you in close to detail. A macro filter is a cheap and effective alternative to a macro lens.

Flash Flash can deaden photos by casting stark, unnatural shadows. If possible, use a flashgun to direct the light away from the subject and thus illuminate it more subtly with 'fill-in' flash. This can also be good during daylight, eg: for wildlife in the shadows or for people with a dark complexion. Experiment with the ISO setting on your camera: by raising this (eg: to 1,000 or higher), you can dramatically lighten your subject – although the image will become more 'noisy' as a result.

Power and storage Use high-storage memory cards (ideally at least 4GB). Take plenty of spares and keep them in different places. Charge up your battery overnight whenever you get the chance as there are some places where this may not be possible. Keep a spare battery, too. If travelling with a laptop, or another portable storage device, download your pictures whenever you get the chance. Never stint on taking pictures but make it an end-of-day ritual to scroll through your day's snaps and delete all the obvious rubbish; this helps you keep on top of things.

Other equipment A tripod is de rigueur for serious wildlife photographers but a hassle to lug around; a small beanbag makes a handy alternative (you can improvise with a packet of rice). A polarising filter brings colour to bleached skies. A sensor-cleaning kit is a life-saver if you have a lens-changing dust disaster.

Protect your gear Always use lens caps; change lenses in sheltered places; use lens cleaning tissue, not spit or paraffin; bring a handy, portable camera bag that holds everything at once.

TAKING BETTER PHOTOGRAPHS

Light Light conditions determine your photographic options: it's harder to use a long lens and fast shutter speed in poor light, while a midday glare may overexpose the subject. An ideal time to take photographs is early morning or late afternoon, when rich colours and long shadows add depth. If your aim is simply to take a clear, well-lit portrait, make sure that the image is not lost against its background. A lilac-breasted roller against the sky will appear silhouetted, but a little background greenery will reveal all its glorious colours.

Composition Think about all the components of the image you are trying to capture, not just its central subject. It helps to frame the image carefully in your viewfinder – even though you can crop it on the computer later. You can often tell a more interesting story by capturing context: try panning out to shrink your subject, or moving it off-centre. Shoot the same subject from different angles and distances. Get down low and shoot upwards. Elements of the background – a curve of hillside, diagonal branch or reflected cloud – can all balance and enhance the image. At the same time they can ruin it in a way that you don't notice at the time: or the telegraph pole that protrudes behind the child's head; beware the white truck entering the pristine wilderness stage left.

Wildlife Good wildlife photographs often owe as much to field skills as to the camera. Anticipate photo opportunities by observing how animals use their habitat. A vehicle can be a movable hide so find a good spot, such as a waterhole, get in position, with the light behind you, and be patient. Don't be afraid of the shutter: in a brief moment of action you may not have time to compose the perfect image but one winner is worth 20 duds. Don't always aim to get as close as possible; watch how the animal behaves – it may move into a better position if you allow it to relax. Avoid sudden movements. If you want to get closer, move when the animal looks away and freeze when it looks up. For smaller animals up close, stay still and allow them to accept you as part of the environment. And when photographing anything on the ground, get down as low as possible to create the impression of entering the subject's world. Always try to capture that vital glint of light in your subject's eye – unless you are purposefully photographing silhouettes. Or backsides.

People Photographing people – at least, people who you don't know personally – is tricky. First, consider how much you would enjoy having a stranger follow you around, thrust a camera in your face then wander off without so much as a greeting. One way to avoid intrusive situations is to use a long lens. This means the subject is not self-conscious and the shallow depth-of-field frames the portrait against a defocused background. A clandestine strategy requires discretion, however, so be prepared to explain yourself if your ruse is rumbled and/or part with a little money.

To photograph more openly, ask first. Some people will be delighted; others will refuse; a few will ask for money – which is fair enough. Payment could take the form of, for example, buying a curio or some fruit from their stall. Always offer to show people their image on the back of your camera – people in rural areas may have seen very few, if any, pictures of themselves. If you agree to send somebody a picture, always make good on your promise: you'll be setting a good precedent. The problem with striking a deal for a photograph is, of course, that you end up with a stilted, posed shot of your grinning subject. But once the ice is broken, you can follow the 'formal' shots with a few more informal ones that better suit your needs.

Restrictions It is prohibited to photograph the royal palace, the royal family, uniformed police, army personnel, army vehicles or aircraft and bank buildings. Visitors wishing to photograph traditional ceremonies should first contact the Government Information Service (✆ *2404 2761*).

TRAVELLING POSITIVELY

Swaziland struggles beneath its burden of poverty. The HIV/AIDS epidemic has wrought havoc, with orphans and vulnerable children now accounting for an estimated 15% of the population. Numerous non-governmental organisations (NGOs), from international bodies to local grass-roots charities, are today working to help the most vulnerable in society. The watchwords for many are empowerment and sustainability – in other words, helping people to help themselves rather than simply providing handouts. This creates opportunities for volunteers, and there are many ways in which to become actively involved during your trip to Swaziland – or, after returning, to give something back. The organisations in the list below are among those that would welcome your money or – even better – your time and skills.

AFRICA COOPERATIVE ACTION TRUST (ACAT) (✆ 2404 4738; e *secretary@acat.org. sz; www.acat.org.sz*) Mbabane-based Christian development charity that supports grass-roots business enterprises for disadvantaged communities.

ALL OUT AFRICA (✆ 2416 2260; e *info@alloutafrica.com; www.alloutafrica.com*) Award-winning local company that runs responsible tours for travellers and also operates a non-profit foundation offering volunteer work in social welfare and conservation projects. Based at Lidwala Backpackers Lodge, Ezulwini (see page 164), it caters largely to gap-year and career-break travellers looking for an inspirational working holiday. The All Out Africa Foundation has a unit for field research, a wildlife fund that manages projects for threatened wildlife, and a children's fund that manages projects for vulnerable children. Conservation projects include monitoring breeding vultures and endangered flora; social welfare projects (mostly in the Ezulwini area) including teaching, orphan care, home building and sports development.

BULEMBU MINISTRIES (*www.bulembu.org*) Innovative Christian project that has rebuilt the abandoned mining community of Bulembu (see page 230) as a care centre for orphans and disadvantaged children. Housing, education and round-the-clock care are provided, and small-scale enterprises (eg: bee-keeping, dairy farming) are developed to boost self-reliance in the local community. Offers volunteering programme and child-sponsorship scheme.

CHESHIRE HOMES (m *7518 6334*; e *info@cheshire.org.sz; www.cheshire.org.sz*) Swaziland's only rehabilitation centre for people with physical and/or learning disabilities. Located in Matsapha, it provides a 20-bed residential unit; wheelchairs, crutches and other equipment; an outpatient clinic, with physiotherapy and occupational therapy services (including Swaziland's only children's therapy clinic); and community outreach services.

EMAFINI CHRISTIAN CONFERENCE CENTRE (✆ 2404 4128/3640; e *info@emafini. co.sz; www.emafini.co.sz*) Mbabane-based Christian charity that works with street children. Places vulnerable children with families.

GUBA (m *7621 3230*; e *info@gubaswaziland.org; www.gubaswaziland.org*) Local NGO that aims to help develop impoverished communities by providing skills in sustainable farming. Projects, including short courses in permaculture and other sustainable land-use and energy techniques, are based on a farm near Mahlanya. Welcomes all donations and anyone with skills to share.

KAMBHOKE SCHOOL AND ORPHANAGE (m *7661 7839*; e *hsmamba@yahoo. com*) Primary school in southern Swaziland set up by retired businessman and ex-government minister Sipho Mamba. Provides free education and accommodation for more then 50 orphaned and vulnerable children. Twinned with a school in Wales.

MOYA COMMUNITY TRUST (m *7528 2043;* e *moya@swazi.net; www.moya.co.sz*) Local charity based in Malkerns that aims to encourage communities in good health practices and life skills, including HIV/AIDS awareness, as well as assisting in the care of parentless children and providing support and safety for those in need. Runs a pre-school for parentless children and free healthcare clinics on Tuesdays and Thursdays. Would welcome your donations, time and skills.

PEACE CORPS (*www.peacecorps.gov*) US government agency that arranges two-year placements in developing countries for US student volunteers. More than 1,480 Peace Corps Volunteers have served in Swaziland since the programme was established in 1969. All are trained and work in SiSwati. Contributions to the Peace Corps Swaziland Country Fund support projects such as water, sanitation and agricultural development, and youth programmes.

POSITIVE WOMEN (*http://positivewomen.org*) A UK international development charity formed in 2005 that works to improve the lives of women and children affected by HIV/AIDS. Develops and manages a number of projects through its partner NGO Swaziland for Positive Living (SWAPOL), based in Manzini. Key areas are education, income generation and creating healthier communities. Has sent over 500 HIV/AIDS orphans to primary school and established a number of income-generation projects led by women in rural communities.

SKILLSHARE INTERNATIONAL (*www.skillshare.org*) International volunteering and development organisation that works with communities in Africa and Asia to reduce poverty, injustice and inequality, and to further economic and social development. Recruits volunteers to share and develop skills and ideas. Projects in Swaziland include working with young people at the High School for the Deaf to empower them with life skills.

SOS CHILDREN'S VILLAGES, SWAZILAND (*www.sos-childrensvillages.org*) SOS is the world's largest charity for orphan and abandoned children, and is supported by sponsors and donors worldwide. In Swaziland it has three large orphanages, each home to over 100 children, who are well cared for by house mothers and can attend school there or nearby. SOS also runs community outreach programmes that provide food, shelter and education for hundreds of children in grandparent-headed or child-headed homes.

SWAZAID (↘ *01978 861821 (UK);* e *trustees@swazaid.org.uk*) UK-based charity that raises support for the people of Swaziland in their struggle with HIV/AIDS, with a current focus on the welfare and education of orphans. Grants aid to Swazi projects, provides skilled UK volunteers, and promotes links between communities in Swaziland and the UK.

SWAZILAND ANIMAL WELFARE SOCIETY (SAWS) ↘ *2404 3446;* e *aws@realnet. co.sz*) Mbabane-based charity that cares for neglected, abused or abandoned animals.

SWAZILAND CHARITABLE TRUST (*www.swazilandcharitabletrust.org*) English registered charity with long tradition of promoting development in Swaziland.

www.stuffyourrucksack.com is a website set up by TV's Kate Humble which enables travellers to give direct help to small charities, schools or other organisations in the country they are visiting. Maybe a local school needs books, a map or pencils, or an orphanage needs children's clothes or toys – all things that can easily be 'stuffed in a rucksack' before departure. The charities get exactly what they need and travellers have the chance to meet local people and see how and where their gifts will be used.

The website describes organisations that need your help and lists the items they most need. Check what's needed in Swaziland, contact the organisation to say you're coming and bring not only the much-needed goods but an extra dimension to your travels and the knowledge that in a small way you have made a difference.

Projects, which are closely monitored and seen through to completion, include grants to schools and charities, an orphan support scheme, and the twinning of a British secondary school with a Swazi one. Also acts as a conduit for other charities. All donations increase the assistance available.

SWAZI VOLUNTEERS (*http://swazivolunteers.com*) Local volunteer scheme aimed primarily at travellers and backpackers who want to experience and contribute to community life. Run by Mxolisi Mdluli of Woza Nawe (see page 105), the projects are based at primary schools, pre-schools and hospitals, and volunteers live at either the backpackers' lodge outside Manzini or in the rural village of kaPhunga. Volunteering packages include activities and excursions.

WATERFORD KAMHLABA (2422 0128; *www.waterford.co.sz*) This private school outside Mbabane (see box on page 72) has a very active community service programme for students and can often find a role for volunteers.

YOUNG HEROES (e *feedback@youngheroes.org.sz*; *www.youngheroes.org.sz*) Local charity that raises funds for vulnerable and orphaned children in the community via a sponsorship programme. Children remain in their homestead, where a caretaker – eg: a grandmother or eldest child – receives monthly financial support to nourish and clothe them. Sponsored families are listed on the website, where sponsors can communicate with them. The idea is to create as direct a link as possible between the sponsor and the family, and minimise administration in between.

Practical Information TRAVELLING POSITIVELY

2

Bradt Travel Guides

Claim 20% discount on your next Bradt book when you order from www.bradtguides.com quoting the code BRADT20

Africa

Access Africa: Safaris for People with Limited Mobility	£16.99
Africa Overland	£16.99
Algeria	£15.99
Angola	£18.99
Botswana	£16.99
Burkina Faso	£17.99
Cameroon	£15.99
Cape Verde	£15.99
Congo	£16.99
Eritrea	£15.99
Ethiopia	£17.99
Ethiopia Highlights	£15.99
Ghana	£15.99
Kenya Highlights	£15.99
Madagascar	£16.99
Madagascar Highlights	£15.99
Malawi	£15.99
Mali	£14.99
Mauritius, Rodrigues & Réunion	£16.99
Mozambique	£15.99
Namibia	£15.99
Nigeria	£17.99
North Africa: Roman Coast	£15.99
Rwanda	£16.99
São Tomé & Príncipe	£14.99
Seychelles	£16.99
Sierra Leone	£16.99
Somaliland	£15.99
South Africa Highlights	£15.99
Sudan	£16.99
Swaziland	£15.99
Tanzania	£17.99
Tanzania, Northern	£14.99
Uganda	£16.99
Zambia	£18.99
Zanzibar	£14.99
Zimbabwe	£15.99

The Americas and the Caribbean

Alaska	£15.99
Amazon Highlights	£15.99
Argentina	£16.99
Bahia	£14.99
Cayman Islands	£14.99
Chile Highlights	£15.99
Colombia	£17.99
Dominica	£15.99
Grenada, Carriacou & Petite Martinique	£15.99
Guyana	£15.99
Haiti	£16.99
Nova Scotia	£14.99
Panama	£14.99
Paraguay	£15.99
Peru Highlights	£15.99
Turks & Caicos Islands	£14.99
Uruguay	£15.99
USA by Rail	£15.99
Venezuela	£16.99
Yukon	£14.99

British Isles

Britain from the Rails	£14.99
Bus-Pass Britain	£15.99
Eccentric Britain	£15.99
Eccentric Cambridge	£9.99
Eccentric London	£14.99
Eccentric Oxford	£9.99
Sacred Britain	£16.99
Slow: Cornwall	£14.99
Slow: Cotswolds	£14.99
Slow: Devon & Exmoor	£14.99
Slow: Dorset	£14.99
Slow: Norfolk & Suffolk	£14.99
Slow: North Yorkshire	£14.99
Slow: Northumberland	£14.99
Slow: Sussex & South Downs National Park	£14.99

Europe

Abruzzo	£16.99
Albania	£16.99
Armenia	£15.99
Azores	£14.99
Baltic Cities	£14.99
Belarus	£15.99
Bosnia & Herzegovina	£15.99
Bratislava	£9.99
Budapest	£9.99
Croatia	£15.99
Cross-Channel France: Nord-Pas de Calais	£13.99
Cyprus see North Cyprus	
Dresden	£7.99
Estonia	£14.99
Faroe Islands	£15.99
Flanders	£15.99
Georgia	£15.99
Greece: The Peloponnese	£14.99
Hungary	£15.99
Iceland	£15.99
Istria	£13.99
Kosovo	£15.99
Lapland	£15.99
Lille	£9.99
Lithuania	£14.99
Luxembourg	£14.99
Macedonia	£16.99
Malta & Gozo	£12.99
Montenegro	£14.99
North Cyprus	£13.99
Serbia	£15.99
Slovakia	£14.99
Slovenia	£13.99
Spitsbergen	£16.99
Switzerland Without a Car	£14.99
Transylvania	£15.99
Ukraine	£15.99

Middle East, Asia and Australasia

Bangladesh	£17.99
Borneo	£17.99
Eastern Turkey	£16.99
Iran	£15.99
Iraq: Then & Now	£15.99
Israel	£15.99
Jordan	£16.99
Kazakhstan	£16.99
Kyrgyzstan	£16.99
Lake Baikal	£15.99
Lebanon	£15.99
Maldives	£15.99
Mongolia	£16.99
North Korea	£14.99
Oman	£15.99
Palestine	£15.99
Shangri-La: A Travel Guide to the Himalayan Dream	£14.99
Sri Lanka	£15.99
Syria	£15.99
Taiwan	£16.99
Tibet	£17.99
Yemen	£14.99

Wildlife

Antarctica: A Guide to the Wildlife	£15.99
Arctic: A Guide to Coastal Wildlife	£16.99
Australian Wildlife	£14.99
Central & Eastern European Wildlife	£15.99
Chinese Wildlife	£16.99
East African Wildlife	£19.99
Galápagos Wildlife	£16.99
Madagascar Wildlife	£16.99
New Zealand Wildlife	£14.99
North Atlantic Wildlife	£16.99
Pantanal Wildlife	£16.99
Peruvian Wildlife	£15.99
Southern African Wildlife	£19.99
Sri Lankan Wildlife	£15.99

Pictorials and other guides

100 Alien Invaders	£16.99
100 Animals to See Before They Die	£16.99
100 Bizarre Animals	£16.99
Eccentric Australia	£12.99
Northern Lights	£6.99
Swimming with Dolphins, Tracking Gorillas	£15.99
The Northwest Passage	£14.99
Tips on Tipping	£6.99
Total Solar Eclipse 2012 & 2013	£6.99
Wildlife & Conservation Volunteering: The Complete Guide	£13.99

Travel literature

A Glimpse of Eternal Snows	£11.99
A Tourist in the Arab Spring	£9.99
Connemara Mollie	£9.99
Fakirs, Feluccas and Femmes Fatales	£9.99
Madagascar: The Eighth Continent	£11.99
The Marsh Lions	£9.99
The Two-Year Mountain	£9.99
The Urban Circus	£9.99
Up the Creek	£9.99

Part Two

THE GUIDE

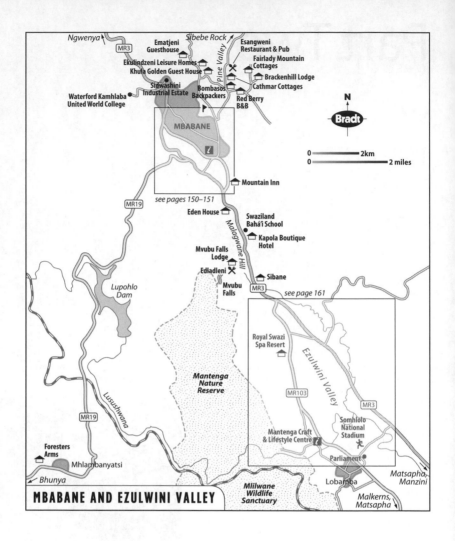

N

0 — 2km
0 — 2 miles

Ngwenya
MR3
Emjatjeni Guesthouse
Sibebe Rock
Pine Valley
Esangweni Restaurant & Pub
Ekulindzeni Leisure Homes
Fairlady Mountain Cottages
Khula Golden Guest House
Brackenhill Lodge
Cathmar Cottages
Sidwashini Industrial Estate
Bombasos Backpackers
Waterford Kamhlaba United World College
Red Berry B&B

MBABANE

Mountain Inn

MR19

see pages 150–151

Eden House

Malagwane Hill

Swaziland Bahá'í School
Kapola Boutique Hotel

Mvubu Falls Lodge
Edladleni
Sibane
Mvubu Falls
MR3
see page 161

Lupohlo Dam

Royal Swazi Spa Resort

Ezulwini Valley

Mantenga Nature Reserve

MR103

MR3

Lusushwana

Somhlolo National Stadium

MR19

Mantenga Craft & Lifestyle Centre

Foresters Arms

Parliament

Lobamba

Matsapha, Manzini

Bhunya

Mhlambanyatsi

Mlilwane Wildlife Sanctuary

Malkerns, Matsapha

MBABANE AND EZULWINI VALLEY

3

Mbabane and the Ezulwini Valley

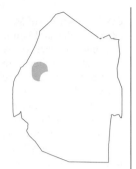

Few people visit Swaziland without passing through Mbabane, its capital city, and the Ezulwini Valley that lies immediately downhill and to the east. Thus, the area covered in this chapter – which falls within Hhohho province – is home to more places to stay and eat than any other.

Mbabane itself has few major attractions, although there are some good ones just outside. Indeed, perched on the edge of the escarpment, just a short drive from the South Africa border at Ngwenya, the city feels rather like the threshold of Swaziland: a gateway to greater riches beyond. Tourism begins in earnest, however, once you leave town and descend to the resorts and cultural attractions of the Ezulwini Valley. Meaning 'heavenly place', this valley has long been Swaziland's playground. And with Ezulwini and Mbabane no more than ten minutes apart by road it is perfectly possible to move between the two on a whim. Many residents of Mbabane nip down to Ezulwini for a night out while residents of Ezulwini, conversely, nip up to Mbabane to do their shopping.

The contrast between the capital and its playground is exaggerated by altitude. Mbabane sits nearly 500m above Ezulwini, so the city enjoys a temperate, highveld climate while the valley has a warmer, middleveld one. Indeed, it can be cool and misty in the former while, just 10km away, it is warm and dry in the latter. The corridor between the two is the Malagwane Hill, down which Swaziland's main highway – the MR3 –makes a dramatic sweeping descent.

MBABANE

'Spend no more than one night in Mbabane.' So said the only Swaziland guidebook I could find when, in 1993, I first set foot in the city that was to be my home for the next five years. And although I subsequently discovered that this advice did the place a disservice – there's plenty to do and see once you know where to look – I could understand the writer's negativity. Mbabane is not a place of great beauty or metropolitan charm. You would not choose Swaziland's capital for a stag weekend or city break.

Mbabane – pronounced *Um-Ba-Ba-Neh* – sits at an average 1,243m, ringed by the craggy Dlangeni Hills. This makes for an impressive setting. However, the city itself is rather messy, having lost any sense of a downtown since its focal point drifted away from the old colonial Gwamile Street quarter towards the adjacent Swazi Mall and Plaza areas, which have mushroomed in recent times. The mess is exacerbated by a number of monstrous, half-built structures that loom over town like a permanent construction site – big-money projects that were abandoned when the money dried up and business partners fell out. Residential areas creep up the lower slopes of the hills around town. These include, to the southeast, the high-density township of Msunduza and, to the north, rather better-heeled districts such as Tembelihle and Fonteyn.

Mbabane's lack of excitement – Manzini, Swaziland's only other large town, is certainly livelier – may be explained by its having always been more of an administrative than a cultural centre. The British had their colonial headquarters here, and today the city is home to government departments, embassies and international organisations. With a population of 80,000, it is also slightly smaller than Manzini. But when it comes to shopping, a bed for the night and a bite to eat, Mbabane certainly offers a greater choice to the visitor.

Should you defy that old guidebook and end up staying more than just the one night, as I did, you will also have ample opportunity to visit Sibebe Rock. This huge granite batholith, the largest in the world, lies just a few kilometres north of Mbabane down the picturesque Pine Valley and offers some serious hikes and spectacular scenery on the very edge of town.

HISTORY Mbabane has officially been a city only since King Mswati conferred that status upon it in 1992. But its history can be traced back to the 1750s, when Chief Mbabane Kunene settled in an area now known as the northern suburb of Dalriach. The chief had been sent by King Mbandzeni to look after his cattle kraals, and it is not known whether the meaning of Mbabane, which translates as 'small, bitter plant', refers to the local flora or is a reflection of the chief's feelings about his king's autocratic behaviour.

The modern town (and later city) developed during the colonial era. The first structure was a small trading store built in 1887 by Bombardier Micky Wells. This paved the way for an influx of more white settlers, including one Allister Miller from Barberton (born Alexander Mitchell Miller in 1864 on a boat to Singapore), who settled in the same Dalriach area in 1888. Miller soon established himself as a man of influence. Politician, cartographer, journalist and founder (in 1897) of the *Times of Swaziland*, he also secured various agricultural concessions around the country – not always making him popular with the locals. Gwamile Street, Mbabane's main street, was named Allister Miller Street until in 1999 the government embarked on a programme of Swazifying street names, and some people still use that name today.

The British chose Mbabane as their colonial capital in 1903, after the end of the Anglo–Boer War (see page 57). The Boer capital had previously been downhill in Bremersdorp (now Manzini), but the British preferred the cooler climate of Mbabane. Besides, the Boers had burned Bremersdorp to the ground before they cleared out. Archive pictures of Mbabane's early days show a cluster of colonial buildings topped by corrugated iron roofs. At that time, heading east down into the Ezulwini Valley and beyond was a serious undertaking, with rutted dirt roads down rocky hillsides and swollen rivers to ford on horseback.

Notable dates for the colonial authorities included, in 1906, the first post office; in 1907, the arrival of the first British commissioner; and, in 1920, the arrival of electricity (at the commissioner's residence). A grand Cape Dutch building, now on Gwamile Street opposite the City Inn, housed the colonial secretariat from 1939 until independence in 1968. (Today it houses the deputy prime minister's office and, unfortunately, was damaged in 1998 by a protester's bomb.) The British amused themselves with various recreational pursuits and amenities, including a golf course, tennis courts, cricket pitch and theatre club. Life centred on the Mbabane Club on Gwamile Street, which today remains very much a going concern. By 1957, Mbabane had overtaken Hlatikulu as the district with the most European inhabitants.

Mbabane began to grow after independence. The Swazi Plaza, with its shops, businesses and restaurants, was built during the 1970s and has kept expanding ever since. The Swazi Mall appeared in 1989, followed a few years later by the New Mall. This area, which also has the busy bus rank, soon became the focus of the town's activity. High-rise buildings mushroomed around town, including the Central Bank building, Mona Flats and Dlanubheka House. The industrial estate of Sidwashini sprang up to the northwest, offering local businesses an alternative location to Matsapha, down the hill. Today the city continues to expand, although a ring of steep hills imposes a natural limit to its ambitions.

GETTING THERE AND AROUND Mbabane is reached on the MR3, a modern dual carriageway that is the main east–west artery across Swaziland, extending east from the South Africa border at Ngwenya to Manzini and beyond. The city lies 23km from Ngwenya and 37km from Manzini, from where it is a drive of roughly 30 minutes. Local buses and kombi taxis run a regular service between Ngwenya, Mbabane and Manzini: some travel directly along the MR3; others take the MR103, which diverts to the south via Lobamba and the Ezulwini Valley (see pages 174 and 160).

The MR3 skirts Mbabane to the southwest. Arriving from Ngwenya, you have a choice of four main turn-offs to the city centre: the first of these (junction 10) follows Somhlolo Street into town; the second (junction 11) follows Sozisa Road and passes the Cooper Centre (tourist information), before a left turn at traffic lights down Dr Sishayi Street towards the Swazi Mall and Plaza; the third (junction 13) takes you to the same traffic lights along the MR19, the last stretch of the Mhlambanyatsi Road (see page 159); and the last (junction 14), which is at the southern limit of town overlooking the Malagwane Hill, takes you back in along the Mshengu Road, via the turn-off to the Highlands View residential suburb. This last road is the one to take if you are heading directly for the Mountain Inn hotel (see page 152) and would prefer to avoid town.

TOURIST INFORMATION Mbabane's tourist information office (✆ 2404 2531/2409 0112; ☉ Mon–Thu 08.00–17.00, Fri 08.00–16.00, Sat 09.00–13.00) is at the Cooper Centre on Soziza Road, just beside the Engen filling station. Here you will find free maps, leaflets and guides to what's on. Staff will help plan an itinerary and can make some reservations. You can also visit the headquarters of the Swaziland Tourist Authority (6th Floor, Dianubheka House, corner of Mdada & Lalufadlana streets; ✆ 2404 9693/9675).

A selection of brochures and other tourist information is available at various tourist outlets in town, including the Mountain Inn hotel (see page 152) and Indingilizi Gallery (see page 157). It is also worth having a peek at the noticeboards at the Swazi Mall and Swazi Plaza to see what's on locally. Pick up a free copy of *What's On in Swaziland* here, at the tourist information office or wherever you find it, for comprehensive listings.

WHERE TO STAY
Upmarket
🏠 **Kapola Boutique Hotel** (8 rooms, sleeps 24) ✆ 2404 0906; e kapola_eden@swazi. net. Located on Malagwane Hill just below Baha'i centre & reached from the downhill (southbound) lane of the MR3. Accommodation in 8 large, comfortable bedrooms (twins & dbls), individually furnished & decorated, with en-suite bathrooms. Each room has DSTV, Wi-Fi, AC & tea/coffee. Dining room offers à la carte menu for lunch, dinner & b/fast. Also: bar, secure parking, braai area & babysitting service. Activities arranged locally. Rates include B&B. $$$–$$$$

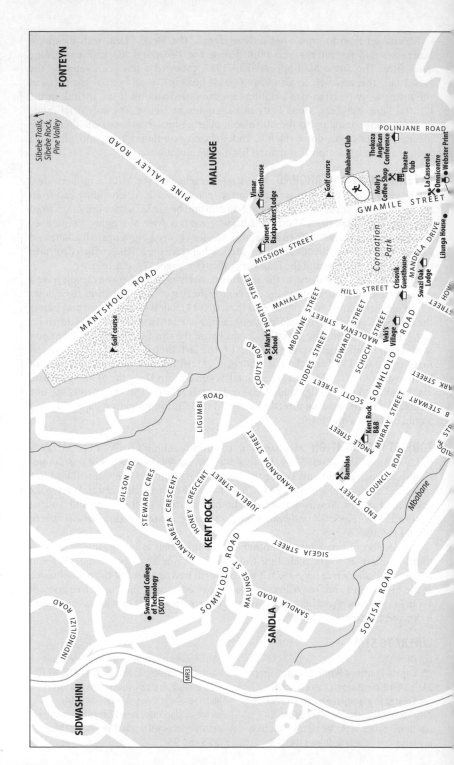

FONTEYN

Sibebe Trails,
Sibebe Rock,
Pine Valley

PINE VALLEY ROAD

MALUNGE

POLINJANE ROAD

Vinar
Guesthouse

Sunset
Backpackers Lodge

Golf course

Mbabane Club

Thokoza
Anglican
Conference

Theatre
Club

Molly's
Coffee Shop

La Casserole

Omnicentre

Webster Print

MISSION STREET

GWAMILE STREET

MANTSHOLO ROAD

Golf course

Coronation
Park

HILL STREET

Crisovik
Guesthouse

Swazi Oak
Lodge

MANDELA DRIVE

Lilunga House

MAHALA

SCOUTS ROAD

St Mark's NORTH STREET
School

MBOVANE STREET

MADLENYA STREET

FIDDES STREET

EDWARD STREET

SCHOCH STREET

Veki's
Village

SOMHLOLO ROAD

B STEWART STREET

HOW

STREET

ARK STREET

ROAD

LIGUMBI ROAD

SCOTT STREET

MURRAY STREET

COUNCIL ROAD

MANDANDA STREET

JUBELA STREET

ANGLE STREET

END STREET

Kent Rock
B&B

Ramblas

Mbabane

GILSON RD

STEWARD CRES

HLANGABEZA CRESCENT

HONEY CRESCENT

KENT ROCK

SIGEJA STREET

SOZISA ROAD

INDINGILIZI ROAD

SOMHLOLO ROAD

MALUNGE ST

SANDLA ROAD

SANDLA

Swaziland College
of Technology
(SCOT)

SIDWASHINI

MR3

150

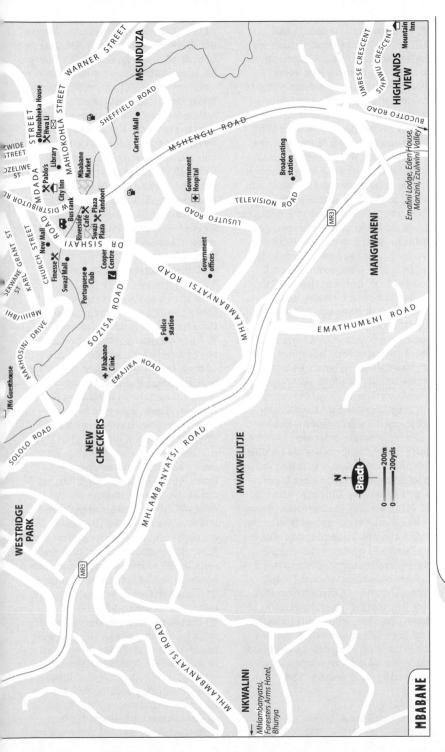

MBABANE

WARNER STREET

MSUNDUZA

SHEFFIELD ROAD

MAHLOKOHLA STREET

MSHENGU ROAD

UMBESE CRESCENT

SIHAWU CRESCENT

HIGHLANDS VIEW

Mountain Inn

BUCTOFO ROAD

STREET

Dlanubheka House
Hwa Li

ZWIDE STREET

DZELIWE ST

MDADA STREET

Carter's Mall

Library

Pablo's

City Inn

Mbabane Market

W DISTRIBUTOR RD

Government Hospital

LUSUTFO ROAD

TELEVISION ROAD

Broadcasting station

MR3

MANGWANENI

Emafini Lodge, Eden House, Manzini, Ezulwini Valley

SEKWANE GRANT ST

KARL STREET

MBULUNI

MAKHOSINI DRIVE

DR SISHAYI ROAD

CHURCH STREET

New Mall

Finesse

Swazi Mall

Bus rank

Riverside Café

Swazi Plaza

Swazi Plaza Tandoori

Portuguese Club

Cooper Centre

SOZISA ROAD

MHLAMBANYATSI ROAD

Government offices

EMATHUMENI ROAD

JN6 Guesthouse

Police station

Mbabane Clinic

EMAJIKA ROAD

SOLOLO ROAD

NEW CHECKERS

MHLAMBANYATSI ROAD

MVAKWELITJE

WESTRIDGE PARK

MR3

N

Bradt

0   200m
0   200yds

NKWALINI

MHLAMBANYATSI ROAD

Mhlambanyatsi, Foresters Arms Hotel, Bhunya

MBABANE

3

🏠 **Foresters Arms** (34 rooms) 📞 2467 4177/4377; e info@forestersarms.co.za; www. forestersarms.co.za. Popular & historic hotel located at Mhlambanyatsi, 25km south of Mbabane on MR19. Accommodation in 34 sgl & dbl rooms arranged around semicircular terrace overlooking lawns & swimming pool in extensive gardens. All rooms have A/C, DSTV, free Wi-Fi & large, comfortable beds. Morning tea/coffee brought to rooms. Very good restaurant, with original menu, local produce & excellent service. Hotel imaginatively decorated throughout, with historic prints, antique furniture & samples of Swazi geology. Other facilities include comfortable lounge with log fire; international newspapers, terrace bar, sauna & fitness centre, DVD library & online birdwatching database, & conference hall for up to 40. Among numerous sports & activities around the property (see page 159) are mountain-biking, horseriding, walking trails, birdwatching, fly fishing & golf at Usutu Forest Golf Club. Altogether, the tranquil setting, rustic charm, sense of history, great service & fine food make this one of the very best hotels in Swaziland. **$$$**

🏠 **Mountain Inn** (52 rooms, 176 beds) 📞 2404 2781/2773; e info@mountaininn.sz; www.mountaininn.sz. Located 4km south of the city in Highlands View Estate overlooking the Malagwane Hill, with easy access to Ezulwini Valley. Accommodation in 52 rooms: sgls, dbls, trpls & family suites. Rooms arranged in 3 blocks linked by covered walkways: North Wing, Pool Side & South Wing, the last of these with fine views across Ezulwini Valley. All rooms en-suite, with AC, DSTV & free Wi-Fi. Friar Tuck restaurant is one of Mbabane's better eating places. Other facilities include a lively bar (downstairs), large swimming pool, conference facilities (for 120) & secure parking. Local excursions & activities arranged, including birdwatching, mountain-biking, fly fishing & horseriding, & local events often held here (including talks by the Natural History Society). Walls hung with original paintings by local artists. Grounds good for birds (including – when I last visited – long-crested eagle). Friendly, comfortable & popular, with excellent service, good food & a superb view. **$$–$$$**

Mid-range

🏠 **Brackenhill Lodge** (8 rooms, sleeps 16) 📞 2404 2887/2551 4095; m 7602 0650;

e brackenhill@realnet.co.sz; www.brackenhillswazi. com. Rural B&B in hills 4.5km north of Mbabane city centre on 150ha estate (on Mountain Dr, off Fonteyn Rd). Accommodation in 8 en-suite rooms, each with private veranda, TV, tea/coffee, fridge, fans & heaters. English or continental breakfast. Dinner available on request, with vegetarians catered for. Water from farm spring; eggs & fresh vegetables from farm. Facilities include tennis courts, gym with sauna, swimming pool, trampoline, Wi-Fi. Hiking trails lead from property to cave paintings, with indigenous forest & excellent birdlife (black & crowned eagles both nest on property). Owners Leon & Frances Takis have been in Swaziland since the 1960s & stamped their character on the enterprise. A homely & tranquil vibe in a scenic setting. **$$**

🏠 **Cathmar Cottages** (8 units, sleeps 14) 📞 2404 3387; m 7608 6229; e cathmar@ visitswazi.com; www.visitswazi.com/cathmar. Self-catering cottages 2km north of Mbabane. Choice of cottages & guestrooms, all with TV, Wi-Fi & private entrance. Attractive grounds with swimming pool & fine views. Birdwatching & other activities arranged on request. Home-cooked breakfasts ordered in advance. Airport shuttle available. Owners also run **Shield Guest House** (10 rooms, 20 beds), which offers B&B & self-catering lodge 5mins from city centre. **$$**

🏠 **City Inn** (24 rooms, sleeps 75) 📞 2404 2406; e cityinn@realnet.co.sz; www.cityinnswaziland. com. The only hotel in Mbabane city centre, located on Gwamile St within 150m of Plaza, bus rank & banks. Large en-suite rooms, with tea/ coffee, Wi-Fi & DSTV. B/fast & other meals served in Pablo's restaurant next-door (also popular with non-guests); lunches available in Caribbean Coffee Room, off reception; conference facilities & meeting rooms. Recently refurbished & upgraded, this hotel is owned by the Ward family (see Mountain Inn) & offers comfortable accommodation at the heart of town, with secure parking. **$$**

🏠 **Eden House** (15 rooms, sleeps 42) contact details as per Kapola (see page 149). Small B&B located c5km south of Mbabane city centre just off Malagwane Hill, signed off northbound lane of MR3. 15 rooms, each with en-suite bathroom, balcony, DSTV, ceiling fans & free Wi-Fi. Also 3 self-catering units (1 sleeps 6; 2 sleep 4) with en-suite bathroom & fully equipped kitchen. Facilities include secure parking, pool, restaurant, bar, shuttle service, conference centre & children's playground. Pleasant retreat, in lush gardens (though within earshot of the main road), with laid-back vibe & some quirky touches, including Adam & Eve reliefs on the gateposts & old barn converted into chapel, where weddings are held. Under same management as Kapola Boutique Hotel (see page 149). Farmhouse breakfast included in rates; dinner optional. **$$**

🏠 **Ematjeni Guesthouse** (5 rooms, sleeps 14) ☎2404 3110; m e ematjeni@swazi.net; www. ematjeni.com. B&B guesthouse in impressive hillside setting 10mins north from town centre. 2 bedrooms & 3 executive rooms, each with en-suite bathroom & balcony with view. Secure parking, fireplace & communal bar. Overlooks Umbuluzi Gorge across Pine Valley to Sibebe Rock. Hikes lead directly from property. Receives excellent reviews for service, food & setting. **$$**

🏠 **JN6 Guesthouse** (5 rooms, 8 beds) ☎2404 8809; m 7680 5353; e jn6guesthouse@swazi. net; www.jn6guesthouse.com. Suburban B&B guesthouse 1km west of city centre catering mostly to business travellers. Clean & comfortable, with Wi-Fi & DSTV. Executive room comes with jacuzzi. Dinner available on request. **$$**

🏠 **Kent Rock B&B** (3 rooms) ☎2404 4826; m 7611 7505; e kentrock@swazi.net; www. kentrockaccommodation.co.sz. Small guesthouse 1km from town centre (Somhlolo Rd). 3 en-suite rooms, each with bar, fridge & tea/coffee. Also: swimming pool, Wi-Fi & DSTV, gardens & terrace. 2min walk from Ramblas restaurant (see page 154) & Serendipity wellness centre. Attached to Kent Rock veterinary clinic. Popular with business travellers. Long-stay discounts available. **$$**

🏠 **Mvubu Falls Lodge** (10 rooms, sleeps 20) ☎2404 4655; m 7627 6757; e versa@realnet. co.sz; www.mvubufalls.com. B&B in rural riverside location just off Malagwane Hill, 6km south of town, with access from northbound lane of MR3. 10 spacious rooms (8 dbls & 2 twins), each with en-suite bathroom, AC, heater & DSTV. Secure parking. B/fast & à la carte dinner served in bush-bar restaurant. Natural rock swimming pool in attractive gardens with fine view. Hiking trails to nearby Mvubu Falls; 5min walk from Edladleni restaurant (see page 154). Wheelchair friendly.

Belgian owners Greta & Marc speak several languages. **$$**

🏠 **Veki's Village** (8 cottages, sleeps 30) ☎2404 8485; m 7603 6396; e veni@mweb.co.sz; www. visitswazi.com/vekis. Self-catering cottages 4.5km from city centre. All cottages with fully equipped kitchen, lounge with fireplace & en-suite bedroom. Facilities include DSTV, internet access, swimming pool & car ports. Attractive garden with fine views, birdlife & indigenous plants. **$$**

Budget

🏠 **Bombasos Backpackers** (5 rooms, 2 dorms, 19 beds) ☎2404 5465; m 7681 9191; e bombasosbackpackers@gmail.com; www. bombasos.co.za. Dorms, private rooms & camping. Originally a home for US Peace Corps volunteers, this is now one of Swaziland's livelier & more imaginative backpackers lodges. Facilities include swimming pool, games room & Wi-Fi. Located 2km north of town at top of Pine Valley, with great views. Close to public transport. **$–$$**

🏠 **Swazi Oak Lodge** (26 rooms, 50 beds) ☎2404 6234; m 7665 2806; e info@ swazioaklodge.com; www.swzioaklodge.com. B&B guesthouse on Somhlolo St, 5min walk from town centre. All rooms en-suite & with DSTV. Facilities include WI-FI. Safe parking & airport transfers available. **$–$$**

🏠 **Fairlady Mountain Cottages** (16 rooms, 28 beds) ☎2608 7613; e falrlady4u@gmail.com. B&B & self-catering north of town centre. Facilities include DSTV & internet. Attractive gardens. Traditional & other meals served on request. **$**

🏠 **Sunset Backpackers Lodge** (9 rooms, 64 beds) m 7675 2828; e sunsetbackpackerslodge@ realnet.co.sz. Located just west of Gwamile Street 10min walk from town centre. A traditional backpackers lodge, with dorms on the top level of a thatched building. **$**

🏠 **Thokoza Anglican Conference** (44 rooms, 93 beds) m 7404 6681; e thokoza@africaonline. co.sz. Christian B&B on edge of town (Pholinjani Rd, nr St Francis High School). Twin & self-catering rooms, some en suite, others share bathrooms, all with TV. Meals served in dining room; internet, TV lounge & chapel. Secure parking. Conference centre seats up to 120. Welcomes people of all faiths. **$**

WHERE TO EAT There is no shortage of places in and around Mbabane to grab a bite, varying from excellent restaurants with original menus to a plethora of local cafés and fast-food joints – the latter including international chains such as KFC, Wimpy, Spur and King Pie.

Recommended

✗ **Edladleni** Malagwane Hill (beside Mvubu Falls Lodge); ☎2404 5743; m 7618 4103; e edladleni@100webspace.net. Highly rated restaurant in scenic location that is one of a kind in Swaziland. Serves traditional Swazi dishes, prepared with authentic local ingredients & techniques, including good vegetarian options. Reasonably priced, with main dishes at SZL75. Buffets arranged for larger parties. Charismatic owner Dolores Goddefroy ('Lola') is passionately committed to local cuisine, especially reviving the use of indigenous crops. Her cookbook of traditional recipes is for sale, & her menus feature interesting cultural information on all dishes. Member of International Slow Food Movement.

✗ **Foresters Arms** (see page 159) Excellent restaurant in popular out-of town hotel, with high-quality food at reasonable prices. Highly imaginative 7-course set menu, with homemade breads & ice creams, farm-fresh vegetables & unusual salads. Lavish Sun stir-fry/BBQ buffet is excellent value. Good selection of South African wines & speciality coffees. Charming old colonial dining room, with outstanding service.

✗ **Friar Tuck Mountain Inn** Good restaurant in popular hotel. Meals served in vaulted cellar with views over mountains. Friendly, intimate ambience & high-quality, good-value food. Broad menu includes excellent seafood, Swazi goat stew & impressive dessert trolley.

✗ **La Casserole** Omnicentre Complex, Gwamile St; ☎2405 0778. Good-quality, good-value restaurant close to town centre. Specialises in German & international cuisine, including pizzas, with broad vegetarian selection. Good wine list & popular bar. Light meals & take-aways available.

✗ **Ramblas** Siphefu St; ☎2405 0452; m 7602 0987. Classy, fairly expensive restaurant 15min walk from Mbabane centre. Popular with international clientele (embassies, NGOs, etc). Owners from Barcelona. Wide-ranging menu features excellent seafood, fish & pizzas, with home-baked bread & 10 types of coffee. Specials board changes every 2/3 days. Attached to Serendipity health & beauty studio.

Other options include:

✗ **Esangweni Restaurant and Pub** Pine Valley; ☎2551 4436. Lively out-of-town venue that attracts young crowd. Simple Swazi meals, with braai nights, DJs, music & functions.

✗ **Finesse** Popular French-owned coffee shop & restaurant between Swazi Mall & New Mall with menu that features original meat & seafood options.

✗ **Hwa Li** Dlan'ubeka Hse, Madada St. Mbabane's best Chinese restaurant, located on ground floor of office block, with comprehensive, good-value menu.

✗ **Indingilizi Gallery & Restaurant** (see page 157) Small café on outdoor terrace behind gallery, with original, good-value menu. Open office hours only.

✗ **Mediterranean** Gwamile St; ☎2404 3212. Cheap & popular restaurant at centre of town that

specialises in curries. Lively atmosphere around sports TV bar.

✗ **Molly's Coffee Shop and Flame Grills** Gwamile/Dzeliwe St. Restaurant & bar inside old Mbabane Theatre Club. Popular lunchtime hangout.

✗ **Plaza Tandoori** Swazi Plaza; ☎2404 7599. Friendly Indian restaurant with curries, grills, burgers & take-aways. Attentive service.

✗ **Pablo's** Gwamile St (beside City Inn); ☎2404 2406. City-centre restaurant attached to City Inn (see page). Popular chicken & pizzas. Inexpensive.

✗ **Portofino** Swazi Mall; ⏰ office hours only. Coffee shop in middle of Mall, with ice cream & cakes.

✗ **Riverside Café** Swazi Plaza; ☎2404 9547. Convenient location. Mozambican & Portuguese specials. Open office hours only.

NIGHTLIFE AND ENTERTAINMENT Mbabane's more popular nightspots include Portugalia, World Café, Swazi Lounge, Jazz Friends and Esangweni Restaurant

(Pine Valley). At these and others you can find local music and DJs. Check the local listings (see page 303) to find out what's on and where. Tourists entering downtown clubs after dark should keep their wallets and wits about them.

SHOPPING AND OTHER PRACTICALITIES Mbabane has most resources and facilities you'll need for stocking up before you head out of town.

Shopping Shopping is loosely divided between the 'old town' area, of Gwamile Street and around, and the more modern cluster of the Swazi Mall, New Mall and Swazi Plaza, off Dr Sishayi Road to the southwest. The latter has secure parking and convenient, if rather generic, one-stop shopping. The former involves more walking around but has greater character.

Swazi Mall, New Mall and Swazi Plaza The Swazi Mall has a large car park with a barrier control. Its focal point is Pick 'N' Pay (⊕ *Mon–Fri 07.30–19.00; Sat–Sun 08.15–18.00*), complete with delicatessen, hot-food counter and all the usual wonders of a big supermarket. Check the notice board beside the trolley racks for local information (especially if you are trying to house a kitten). Other useful outlets include the Green Cross pharmacy, Harveys Travel Agents, Real Image internet café and African Fantasy – the last of these a gift shop with lively T-shirts, cards and other products from local designer Aleta Armstrong (see Guava Gallery, page 167). Portofino (see opposite), a café at the centre, is a good place to recover. A small bridge at the north side leads over the Mbabane River – just a stream at this point – to the New Mall, which has yet more shops, plus the Finesse coffee shop and restaurant (see opposite).

Across Dr Sishayi Road from the Mall is the Swazi Plaza, which has a multi-storey car park at the south side. This is larger and slightly more chaotic than the Mall, with numerous clothing and furniture stores, plus a bookshop and newsagents. It also has some good caterics, including the Riverside Café and Plaza Tandoori (see opposite). The post office (⊕ *Mon–Fri 08.00–16.00, Sat 08.00–12.00*) is at the top of the escalator above a large Jet clothing store.

Gwamile Street Formerly Allister Miller Street, this is the closest thing Mbabane has to a high street and is the original road around which the town grew. It has numerous small local stores, including shoe repairs, cafés and the popular Ritz Saverite supermarket. Halfway along, past City Inn (see page 152), a turning down Mdada Street leads to the back of the bus rank, with market stalls, cafés, bars and street vendors. At the north end, across a five-way junction (with Somhlolo Road and Western Distributor Road), is another parade of shops, where the Omnicentre (a small arcade) houses La Casserole restaurant (see opposite) and Omnifoto, the best photographic supplier in town. The road continues north out of town, past the Mbabane Club (see page 157) on the right and Coronation Park on the left.

Dzeliwe Street This quiet street runs parallel with Gwamile Street just to the east. Here you will find Webster Print, Swaziland's best specialist independent bookshop and stationery supplier. Owner Pieter De Waal is also a local publisher and an authority on the Swaziland natural history scene. Opposite is Indingilizi Gallery (see page 157), with an excellent art collection and good café. Watch out when strolling along Dzeliwe Street in avocado season, when some trees drop their impressive fruit on the pavement.

Sheffield Road Industrial Estate This small industrial state just beside the main road south out of town has – among its warehouses and offices – various garages, mechanics and other useful suppliers. Of particular interest to the independent traveller is Carter's Mall (↘ *2404 3092*), a hardware and electrical store that also offers camping supplies and all sorts of other stuff – from gas stoves to spotlights – that you didn't even know you needed.

Mbabane Market There are fruit, vegetable and other informal market stalls all over town, particularly around and behind the bus rank. The official Mbabane Market, however, is housed in a rather unprepossessing concrete structure just in front of the central bank. It is not as busy or exciting as Manzini Market (see page 198) but is nonetheless worth exploring. There are plenty of bargains among the stalls of curios, clothing and handicrafts, and browsing tends to be hassle free. The food section is impressive for its variety, and the hot take-away stalls serve the full spectrum of local dishes at very reasonable prices.

Services
Banks All Swaziland's banks have one or more branches in Mbabane and all with ATMs. You will find an FNB at Swazi Mall, and a Standard Bank and Nedbank at Swazi Plaza, among others.

Bus rank Mbabane bus rank lies between Dr Sishayi Street and Western Distributor Road, opposite the New Mall. There are regular bus routes and kombis to all destinations, but no reliable timetables. If in doubt, ask.

Filling stations Mbabane has several filling stations. Major ones, open 24 hours, include Galp Fourways filling station (corner of Sozisa and Manzini roads) MBA/ Gardens filling station (corner of bypass and Main Distributor Road) and Mbabane Motors (corner of Sheffield Road).

Health and hospitals Mbabane Government Hospital (*Hospital Hill, Lusutfu Rd*) is at the south end of town. It is under-resourced and overburdened. Travellers in an emergency would do better to visit the private Mbabane Clinic (*St Michael's Rd*; ↘ *2404 7016/7*), which also has a dentist (↘ *2404 2423*). There is a Salvation Army clinic in Msunduza.

Library The public library is on Mahlokohla Street, at the south end of Gwamile Street.

Parks Coronation Park is on Gwamile Street opposite the Mbabane Club. There is a swimming pool and tennis courts. It is not a place to wander after dark.

Police station (↘ *2404 2221*) The police station is off Sozisa Road, opposite the Cooper Centre.

Post office The main post office is on Mahlokohla Street, below Dlanubeka House. It has a large car park.

Sports and fitness The Mbabane Club (*Gwamile St*) has a swimming pool, tennis and squash courts and a nine-hole golf course. These facilities are for members and guests, so befriend a member if you want to use them. Serendipity health and beauty studio (℩ *2405 0452*) is on Siphefu Street, ten minutes from town, beside the Ramblas restaurant (see page 154).

WHAT TO SEE AND DO
In town
Indingilizi Art & Craft Gallery (℩ *2404 6275/6213;* e *indingi@realnet.co.sz; www.swaziplace.com/indinglizi*) This small gallery tucked away on Dzeliwe Street is a treasure trove of African art, with an idiosyncratic collection that features everything from contemporary Swazi canvases to antique west African carvings. The owner, Dori Angus-Verhoog, founded the gallery in 1982 to showcase the work of banned South African Struggle artists – including Mazimba and Bongiwe Dhlomo. The gallery also sells art supplies and has a good selection of local tourist information. Best of all is the excellent terrace café out back. In general, a great place to drop by for a chat and a coffee – whether or not you plan to fork out on the artworks.

Theatre Club This historic colonial institution at the north end of Dzeliwe Street is today looking a little sorry for itself. Once at the heart of the British expatriate cultural scene, and continuing to flourish for a while in the new Swaziland, its stage has not seen any real action for a number of years. Actor Richard E Grant trod the boards here as a youngster and the club features in his autobiographical film *Wah-Wah* (see page 91), for which he coaxed many old friends from the local am-dram community out of retirement to help behind the scenes – and even, in some cases, on screen. Today, sadly, this is little more than a drinking den, with a crowd of regulars propping up the bar that once hosted many a glittering first-night party. It's worth popping in if you're passing: the faded theatrical décor and peeling posters of past glories – *Twelfth Night, Deathtrap* – are still there, and the place has a certain end-of-an-era allure. If that fails to grab you, you can always order a pizza at Molly's coffee shop next door.

Out of town
Sibebe and Pine Valley Sibebe Rock, just north of Mbabane, is one of southern Africa's most impressive geological features. This immense three-billion-year-old volcanic slab, which rises to a height of 1,488m and covers some 16,500ha, is the world's largest granite dome. Only Australia's Uluru pips it to the title of 'world's largest rock'. Uluru is actually an eroded sandstone inselberg – in other words, formed of layers of sediment. Sibebe, by contrast, is a batholith: it welled up through the earth's crust in one great molten bubble before cooling to form a massif of sheer granite. More of a proper rock, I like to think

It is hard to appreciate the scale of Sibebe from below. That's partly because there is no single spot from which the whole rock is visible; and partly, also, because large areas of it are vegetated, with patches of grassy hillside and forested clefts – like toupees on a balding pate – that break up the bare rock into what appear to be discontinuous outcrops. The best way to see it is, of course, to climb it. There are many routes up and over, some starting from private properties on its lower slopes. Unless you are in the company of locals, however, you are best off following the official route via Sibebe Hiking Trails (℩ *2416 2180; www.swazitrails.co.sz*; see below for how to get there), a community project that manages the rock. From here, you can follow a well-marked and manageable path to the top – either alone or with a guide. The going is steep in places, but it's a hike, not a climb, and will take you about an hour to get up.

On top, you will find a wonderland of huge sculpted boulders and gleaming slopes of exfoliating granite. Trails radiate in all directions, leading to caves, waterfalls and hidden pockets of indigenous forest. There is even a large meadow where – amazingly – a small population of wild horses roams the lush grazing. The flora is impressive, with orchids and other wild flowers carpeting the grasslands from October to December, and wild bananas (*Strelitzia nicolai*) fluttering their tattered, flag-like leaves in the forested clefts. You might also spot highveld birds, such as jackal buzzard, buff-streaked chat, ground woodpecker and – if you're lucky – even a Verreaux's eagle or blue swallow. But remember that this is Swazi Nation Land, not a nature reserve. You will also meet wandering cattle and their herdboys, and on the eastern slopes you'll spy the small homesteads of those who live up here.

A word of warning: Sibebe can be dangerous, and serious accidents have happened. The granite slopes are very tempting to the compulsive clamberer – and, with their natural traction, climbing is easier than it might appear – but they are very steep in places, and it is easy to go too far and find yourself in trouble. After rains, the rock glistens silver with countless streams running down its bare face – a magical sight from afar, but slippery and dangerous when you're up there. It is also a very exposed place to be caught in a lightning storm, which is a regular occurrence on afternoons during the rainy season. Always allow enough time for your hike (at least three hours, ideally), keep off the bare rock faces if it is or has just been raining, and consider calling off your trip if you see storm clouds gathering. Also make sure you take plenty of water and suncream: it gets hot on the exposed slopes.

Sibebe Hiking Trails lies a short drive north of Mbabane along Pine Valley. Head out of town on Gwamile Street, which turns into Pine Valley Road, and follow the signs. The road descends steeply from the well-heeled northeast suburbs of Mbabane (whose residents enjoy impressive views) and continues along Pine Valley for 10km, skirting the steep flanks of Sibebe. This valley is an attractive feature in its own right, with rolling farmland to the west, the rock to the east and a stream gurgling down the centre. It is home to an interesting community, including some of Mbabane's more colourful expatriate characters, many of whom have built gorgeous – and in a few cases bizarre – homes among the jaw-dropping scenery. In places the great slab of rock is so close to the verge that you have to crane up to see the looming massif above. At the end of the valley you will reach Sibebe Trails on the right (opposite Mbuluzi School on the left). Here there is a parking area and visitor reception, where you pay your entrance fee (SZL25) and pick up your guide – if you want one. There is a small café, selling drinks and snacks, although this was not open when I last visited.

Swazi Trails (see page 104) also offers a half-day Sibebe climb that follows a route straight up the steepest part of the rock face. And every July sees Sibebe Survivor (*www.sibebe.co.sz*), a fund-raising event organised by Mbabane/Mbuluzi Rotary Club, in which several hundred people walk, scramble or even run to the top.

Rural routes beyond Pine Valley
The tar road through Pine Valley becomes gravel shortly after the Sibebe Trails reception (see above). After another 2.5km it crosses the Mbuluzi River and immediately forks. The left fork leads north to join the Maguga Dam road (see page 218), offering a rural, back-road alternative to the MR1 as a route to Piggs Peak. The right fork bends east until it eventually joins the MR5, from where you can return south to Manzini via Mafutseni (see page 248). If you are tempted to explore in either of these directions, set out with a full tank and, unless you are in a 4x4 vehicle, avoid wandering off down any side roads – especially during or shortly after rains. It is easy to get lost or stuck. Or both.

Foresters Arms and Mhlambanyatsi The Foresters Arms (see page 152) is a popular out-of-town retreat, located in Mhlambanyatsi, 25km south of Mbabane on the MR19 to Bhunya. You needn't be a guest to enjoy this place: the hotel and its surroundings offer a pleasant family day out, especially on a Sunday, when its celebrated buffet is a regular fixture for many Mbabane residents.

The hotel is well signposted from the MR3 highway around Mbabane. Leave the bypass on the MR19 Mhlambanyatsi Road south. After some 7km you will pass Lupohlo Dam, where local legend has it that a seven-headed monster lurks beneath the waters (although confirmed sightings are thin on the ground). Continue into the dense plantations of the Usutu Forest, where the road bends west. The hotel is well signed off this stretch, at the end of an attractive oak-lined avenue that has a European, pastoral feel.

Foresters Arms was built as a bar/lounge in 1955/56 to serve a farming community, and the hotel has since grown around it organically. Owner Ruth Buck, who has been there since the mid-1980s, has imbued the place with a very particular charm, and she and her staff are enormously attentive to their guests. Today the hotel is deservedly popular for its excellent cuisine, with home-baking, fresh farm produce and a menu full of surprises. Equally seductive are the cosy interiors, complete with log fires, deep armchairs and piles of Sunday papers. A range of country pursuits in the surrounding forests and estate include mountain-biking, horseriding and hiking trails to a local waterfall (a map is available in reception). There is also fly fishing at well-stocked dams in the Usutu Forest and excellent birdwatching in and around the grounds (I saw paradise flycatcher, little sparrowhawk, swee waxbill and olive woodpecker on my last visit). Sporting types can enjoy tennis, squash and golf at the nine-hole Usutu Forest Golf Club next door (arranged through the hotel), or dabble in the more sedate pleasures of croquet and boules on the hotel lawns. The lush grounds are an inviting haven amid the dark forestry plantations, and the whole place has a relaxed, family-friendly feel, with a sepia-tinted sense of days gone by. There is nowhere else in Swaziland quite like it.

Malagwane Hill The Malagwane Hill is the steep eastward descent from Mbabane to the Ezulwini Valley, over 400m below. It was once notorious as an accident blackspot, with drivers often coming to grief on its combination of hairpin bends, frequent mists, broken-down logging trucks and wandering cattle. Today the road has been upgraded to 5km of spanking new highway. Nonetheless, if you're driving you'd be well advised to keep your eyes on the road and take no more than the briefest glances at the panoramic view – including Ezulwini Valley and the twin peaks of Sheba's Breasts – that unfolds as you leave the city behind.

The hill is more of a conduit than an attraction in itself. However, it offers a selection of out-of-town accommodation, including Eden House, Kapola Boutique Hotel and Mvubu Falls Lodge (see page 153). The last of these, near the bottom of the hill, is close to the excellent Edladleni restaurant (see page 154). It is also a starting point for the 3.5km trail to the Mvubu Falls, where a series of rock pools and small cascades along the Mvubu River makes a pleasant picnic spot. On the left of the hill, also towards the bottom, is the Swaziland Baha'i School, founded in 1990. The Baha'i faith, which arose in 19th-century Persia and emphasises the spiritual unity of humankind, has always been welcomed in Swaziland and its converts include daughters of the late King Sohbhuza II. When driving down the Malagwane Hill you are unable to make a right turn (or, conversely, a left turn when driving uphill). But a turning point halfway down – where the road divides around a central island – allows you to turn back and retrace your route in the opposite lane.

Ezulwini means 'place of heaven', and the valley that bears this name certainly has its share of hedonistic delights. This is where tourism in Swaziland began, and today its attractions include hotels, restaurants, hot springs, casinos, craft markets, art galleries, riding stables, a nature reserve, a golf course and a cultural village. Most visitors pass this way, and those who spend just one night in the kingdom will probably spend it here.

The valley has no convenient road signs to demarcate where it begins and ends. It is generally understood to extend from the bottom of the Malagwane Hill southeast along the MR103 as far as the Lusushwana River, where the latter crosses the road just west of Lobamba, and is bordered by the Luphohlo/Lugogo Mountains to the west and the Mdzimba Mountains to the east. Some extend this definition to encompass Lobamba, Mlilwane and indeed the entire length of the MR103 as far as Matsapha. But these areas lie beyond the embrace of the two lines of hills and outside the administrative boundary of the Ezulwini area. They constitute attractions in their own right and are described in *Chapter 4: The Heartland*.

The MR103 was formerly the main road from Mbabane to Manzini. Thus for decades Ezulwini's key attractions lined up along the country's busiest thoroughfare. The upgrading of the MR3 in the late 1990s, however, created a new highway to the east, which halved the journey time between the two cities and diverted the flow of through traffic. The valley road quickly became a quieter tributary, used more by locals and visitors than truck drivers and commuters. This was good news for tourists, who can now explore it in a more leisurely fashion.

The development of the Ezulwini Valley goes hand in hand with the growth of tourism in Swaziland. The latter was very slow to start: as late as 1949 there were just four hotels in the entire country. But things began to take off when in 1963 the government passed the Casino Act in an attempt to boost visitor numbers. The Southern Sun group soon arrived and in 1965 opened the Royal Swazi Spa Hotel, complete with southern Africa's first casino. This was sited beside some natural hot springs known as the Cuddle Puddle, which Mbabane residents had long been visiting for late-night frolics. Next came the Ezulwini Holiday Inn, which opened immediately opposite the Royal Swazi in 1974. By the time these two international chains merged in 1983, Ezulwini had become Swaziland's Golden Mile, with a proliferation of hotels, casinos, restaurants and other tourist honeypots.

In the early days, the valley had a distinctly sleazy dimension, luring visitors from South Africa not only with golf and casinos but also strip joints, adult movies and the promise of inter-racial 'liaisons' that were unavailable – and unimaginable – back home. With the liberalisation of South Africa in the early '90s, however, Swaziland began to clean up tourism, placing more emphasis on its natural and cultural assets. Today the many tourist attractions that have sprung up around the original Royal Swazi Spa and Cuddle Puddle – still going strong – are of a more family-friendly variety.

To some, the bright lights of Ezulwini may all sound a bit much. But although it may be busy by Swazi standards, this is hardly Vegas. The buildings and development are still dwarfed by their picturesque mountain backdrop, while tropical vegetation runs riot, dirt roads wind off in all directions and rural Swaziland is just a 15-minute drive away.

GETTING THERE AND AROUND The Ezulwini Valley is a ten-minute drive from Mbabane or a 20-minute drive from Manzini. From the former, simply head south

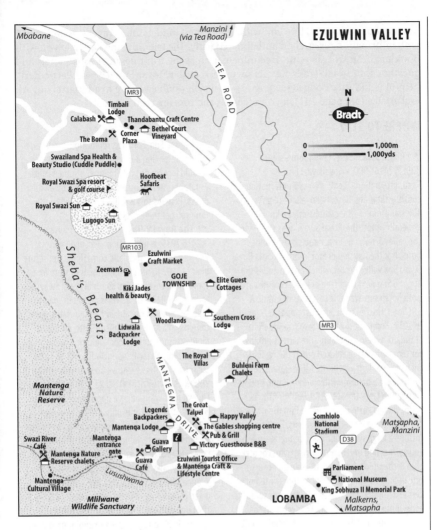

on the MR3 and, at the bottom of the Malagwane Hill, take the first right turn onto the MR103. You can't miss the turning: not only is it signed to the Ezulwini Valley but also to the numerous hotels, restaurants and other attractions that await you. If you were snoozing, however (never advisable on the Malagwane), you will meet two more turnings after a further 3km and 8km, which lead down to the middle and the eastern end of the valley respectively. From Manzini you arrive along the MR3 from the east so can also use any of these junctions. Alternatively you can turn onto the MR103 in Matsapha and then take a more leisurely drive to Ezulwini via Mahlanya and Lobamba (see page 189). Numerous buses and kombis ply this route from both directions and most hotels offer a shuttle service to Matsapha Airport.

TOURIST INFORMATION Ezulwini Tourist Office ((2416 2180; m 7602 0261; www.swazi.travel; Mon–Sun 08.00–17.00) is the best of its kind in Swaziland, with the most comprehensive and up-to-date information. It is located at the Mantenga Craft and Lifestyle Centre (see page 167) and run by Swazi Trails, a private tour company. Here you will find listings, guidebooks, travel tips and maps, with information researched and updated daily. The friendly staff can help you with bookings. You will also find free information at the front desks of most hotels and guesthouses (Swazi Trails has its own desk at the Royal Swazi Spa). Particularly helpful is Lidwala Lodge (see page 164), which doubles as the headquarters of All Out Africa (see page 141), a volunteering and touring company.

WHERE TO STAY
Upmarket

🏠 **Royal Swazi Sun** (149 rooms, sleeps 328) ✆2416 5000; e royalswazi.hotel@ sz.suninternational.com; www.suninternational. com/Destinations/Resorts/RoyalSwaziSpaValley. This handsome 5-star establishment, known generally as just the 'Royal Swazi', was the 1st in the valley & remains Swaziland's most famous hotel. It is the flagship of Sun International's Royal Swazi Spa Valley Resort, which also includes the Lugogo Sun next door (see below). Facilities at both hotels are available to guests of either. A 3rd hotel, the Ezulwini Sun, just opposite, closed in 2012. Rooms at the Royal Swazi range from standard twin to royal suite (the latter perhaps for those who've just lucked out at the casino). All have excellent amenities. More expensive rooms have a balcony with a view. Dining options comprise a large terrace restaurant for buffets & 2 smaller à la carte restaurants. Light meals are served at the pool bar, one of 4 bars. Facilities include a large swimming pool, tennis & squash courts, bowling green, health spa, gym, country club & championship-level 18-hole golf course, one of only two in Swaziland. A large conference centre accommodates up to 600 delegates & hosts everything from international conventions to stage productions & fashion shows. Braais & other outdoor functions are held at a large boma in the grounds. The casino is Swaziland's largest. Other facilities include a Standard Bank (⊕ *Mon, Wed, Fri*), with an ATM & cashier, the Living in Africa gift & curio shop, the Katunka ladies' clothing boutique & extensive car parking. Live entertainment is held every Fri & Sat night. The whole establishment is most impressive: grand interiors, with a sweeping staircase in the lobby setting the opulent tone; lush grounds, with a beautifully landscaped golf course set beneath a scenic slab of hillside. It is set back from the main road down a long tree-lined avenue, free from the bustle of the valley but within easy reach of all attractions & just a short stroll – or 5min free shuttle ride – from its sister

the Lugogo Sun. For all its reputation, however, the hotel was looking a little frayed when I last visited & could have done with improving some facilities – notably internet access – especially given its prices. Perhaps this will have happened by the time you get there. **$$$$$**

🏠 **The Royal Villas** (14 villas, 57 rooms) ✆2416 7035; e reservations@royalvillas.co.sz; www.royalvillas.swaziland.com. Upmarket resort built in 2002 to host visiting heads of state for a conference. Located 3km south of Royal Swazi Sun to east of MR103. Large villas are set in spacious grounds beneath the Mdzimba Mountains, each comprising a king suite, queen suite, standard room & standard twin room. Rooms are enormous & come with all facilities, including Wi-Fi. The Sultan Suite offers exclusive accommodation for VIPs (& the filthy rich) at SZL22,500/night. The Lihawu restaurant offers a good range of African & international cuisine, plus a cellar with over 1,000 wines. Other facilities include the Mdzimba conference & entertainment area, a swimming pool & terrace pool bar, & the Ensangweni bar & lounge. Swanky but expensive; the regular layout, dominated by roads & driveways, seems more gated community than exclusive resort. **$$$$$**

🏠 **Lugogo Sun** (202 rooms, sleeps 404) ✆2416 5000; e lugogo.sun@sz.suninternational. com; www.suninternational.com/Destinations/ Resorts/RoyalSwaziSpaValley. Sister hotel to the Royal Swazi & linked via the resort grounds, with its entrance road located 200m further down the MR103. Not as grand or historic as its sister, but cheaper & with more rooms (often caters for coach parties & large groups), & offers access to all facilities at the Royal Swazi. Comprises 199 twin rooms & 3 mini-suites. All twin rooms have 2 dbl beds with en-suite bathroom. Some rooms are interlinked. Dining is at the iLanga restaurant, where a large buffet seats 220. Light meals are also served at the Pool Bar & Sportsman Bar (the latter dominated by a TV screen showing the latest matches, with Pub Night every Wed). Popular swimming pool features a graduated 'beach' design, making it ideal for children & keeping it warmer than most pools in winters. A children's area, Kamp Kwena (used by both hotels), features a playground, mini-golf & children's entertainer. Other facilities include the African Queen gift shop (see page 167) on the pool deck, which sells local Swazi handicrafts plus fashion accessories, jewellery & gifts. $$$$–$$$$$

Mid-range

⌂ **Happy Valley Hotel** (sleeps 65 rooms, sleeps 168) ✆2416 1061/1199/1898; e reservations@ happyvalleyhotel.com; www.happyvalleyhotel. com. Modern, comfortable hotel, attached to popular casino, located opposite The Gables (see page 166). Portuguese owners & Mediterranean décor, including original murals. Accommodation in 26 pool rooms overlooking pool area, 35 garden rooms, each with private terrace & parking bay, & 4 private suites. All rooms have en-suite bathroom, DSTV, room service & Wi-Fi. Good food served at Palmeira buffet restaurant (b/fast, lunch, dinner) & Bella Vista à la carte restaurant (Portuguese & Mozambican specials). Separate pizzeria & 24hr Tuscana coffee shop popular with visitors. Snack meals served on pool terrace. Also: ATM, gift shop, pool bar & conference venue. Local activities booked at reception. Once more of a roadhouse, notorious for its 'If Not, Why Not' nightclub, this hotel reopened in 2009 after extensive renovation & is now a much classier establishment. It does not have the lush grounds or spacious feel of some Ezulwini hotels but the 24hr casino & pizzeria ensures a busy vibe. $$$–$$$$$

⌂ **Bethel Court Vineyard Hotel** (47 rooms, sleeps 69) ✆2416 1977; e bethelcourt@realnet. co.sz; www.swazibethelcourt.com. Recently refurbished hotel along the start of the Tea Road, with self-catering apts & B&B rooms, plus Vineyard restaurant. Rooms comprise 21 dbls, each with balcony & en-suite bathroom. Self-catering section comprises 15 1- and 2-bedroom apartments, each with lounge & kitchen. Facilities include DSTV. Caters for weddings & functions. $$$

⌂ **Sibane Hotel** (30 rooms) ✆2416 1670/2873; e reservation@sibaneemtinihotel.com; www. sibaneemtinihotel.com. Newish hotel located on the north side of the MR103 at the foot of the Malagwane Hill, shortly before the Tea Road. Chalets comprise sgls, dbls & king suites, all with

DSTV, A/C & Wi-Fi. Restaurant offers buffet & à la carte menus. Also 3 bars, health spa, gym, conference centre & nursery tea gardens with views of valley. $$$

⌂ **Timbali Lodge** (28 rooms, sleeps 78) ✆2416 1156; e timbali@realnet.co.sz; www.timbalilodge. co.sz. Reasonable hotel, located 1.5km along the MR103 (signed to right at mini-roundabout, along with Calabash restaurant) & attached to Boma restaurant. Choice of self-catering & B&B accommodation in 18 executive suites (with spa baths), 5 luxury suites & 5 self-catering family units with kitchen. All rooms have en-suite bathroom, DSTV, minibar, AC, tea/coffee & free Wi-Fi. Also, a large pool, 2 lounges, an 'executive' bar & a conference centre for up to 40. Dining at the popular Boma restaurant next door (see page 165). Local activities arranged at reception. Formerly a caravan park, Timbali Lodge was founded by the late Pat Forsyth Thompson & his wife, Joy, in 1968. Former prisoner-of-war Forsyth Thompson was a significant figure in Swaziland, undertaking various assignments for King Sobhuza II & instrumental in the establishment of Malolotja Nature Reserve & the Swaziland National Trust. $$–$$$

⌂ **Mantenga Lodge** (38 rooms, sleeps 82) ✆2416 1049; e reservations@mantengalodge. com; www.mantengalodge.com. Good-value, owner-run lodge in Mantenga Estate (see page 171). Offers B&B in 38 rooms, with a choice of rustic wooden chalets, standard rooms, luxury business rooms & cheaper poolside rooms. All rooms have en-suite bathroom, AC, TV, Wi-Fi & tea/coffee. À la carte restaurant is set on raised wooden deck with fine view; buffets arranged for larger groups. Also: swimming pool, lush gardens & bar with DSTV. The appeal of this lodge is in its lush natural gardens, with abundant birdlife, & the views across Mantenga Nature Reserve to the panoramic Nyonyane Mountain beyond. The Mantenga Craft & Lifestyle Centre (see page 167) is a 2min walk away. $$

⌂ **Mantenga Nature Reserve** (26 chalets, 70 beds) ✆2416 1151/78; e mnr@africaonline. co.sz. SNTC lodge, upgraded in 2010, located inside reserve beside cultural village (see page 171). B&B in 26 wood-and-thatch en-suite chalets for 1, 2 & 3 people. Each has fridge, tea/coffee, kettle, shower, large dbl bed, cowhide rugs & plentiful sturdy wooden furniture. All chalets nestle into the bush, with private balconies: those on the lower level overlook the river; those on the upper level the falls. The restaurant lies a short walk away & serves a basic buffet b/fast, lunch & dinner, with a TV in the breakfast room. A tranquil spot, offering the most back-to-nature accommodation in Ezulwini, with lush vegetation, wildlife all around, fine views & the sounds of drumming & cattle from the village. Facilities are a little ramshackle & the vervet monkeys, whilst charming, can be a menace. Activities revolve around the cultural village, waterfall & nature reserve. Listen out after dark for bushbabies & other nocturnal wildlife. **$$**

⌂ **Buhleni Farm Chalets** (9 chalets, sleeps 36) ☏ 2416 3505/8; m 7602 4712; e info@ buhlenifarm.co.sz; www.buhlenifarm.co.sz. Self-catering accommodation tucked among forests & orchards of 21ha farm to east of MR103, opposite The Gables. 9 self-catering wooden chalets for 4, each with 2 bedrooms; extra mattresses & cots available on request. Chalets set apart for privacy. Each has living room, b/fast nook, braai area & veranda. New campsite set in shaded paddock has ablutions, tables, chairs, washing & braai facilities. Communal cooking & entertainment area under development. Trails lead around the property, where there are horses & donkeys, & wildlife including vervet monkeys, mongooses & birds. The place has a laid-back, natural charm. Kieren Vincent, son of the owners, runs Chasing Horizons (see page 104) & can advise on local activities. **$–$$**

Budget
⌂ **Southern Cross Lodge** (7 rooms, 11 beds) m 7622 7920; e scl.bookings@gmail.com; www.freewebs.com/enlacruzdelsur. Upmarket backpackers/budget guesthouse in Goje township, east of MR103 (turn-off at Woodlands restaurant). Accommodation in private rooms, dorms & separate 2-room self-catering cottage. Shared bathrooms, shared lounge with fire place, garden with pool & braai facilities. Home-cooked meals available. Friendly Spanish owner, Jesus Goni, helps organise activities & has maps & other tourist info. Secure parking; 1km walk from nearest (Mangozeni) bus stop. **$–$$**

⌂ **Lidwala Lodge** (sleeps 45) ☏ 2415 0901; m 7690 5865; e info@lidwala.co.sz; www.lidwala. co.sz. Excellent backpacker lodge & home of All Out Africa (see page 141), located halfway between Royal Swazi & The Gables shopping centre on west side of MR103. Rustic accommodation includes camping, private tents (4-bed x 3; twin bed x 1), dorms (6-bed x 2; 4-bed x 1) & private rooms with en-suite bathrooms. Communal kitchens & living areas. Natural grounds set on lower slopes of forested hillside, with huge boulders, native trees & stream. Eco-friendly measures on site include waste recycling, solar power & organic vegetable garden. Reception offers a wealth of information for budget travellers & friendly, well-informed staff. Facilities include swimming pool, jacuzzi, jungle gym, trampoline, pool table & computers (with internet). Hiking trail immediately behind the lodge leads up Sheba's Breasts (1.5hrs), with superb views across Ezulwini. Numerous activities & excursions can be organised through All Out Africa. A warm, friendly retreat with a busy vibe – especially on Swazi food night (Wed). Voted 'Best Hostel in Swaziland' in 2009 by Hostels Worldwide, it is the brainchild of Kim Roques, co-founder of All Out Africa, who lives with his family on the property. Kim's wife, Robin, runs a holistic lifestyle & wellness centre (www.wholesum-living.biz) next door. **$–$$**

⌂ **Legends Backpackers** (sleeps 65) ☏ 2416 1870; e legends@realnet.co.sz; www.swazi.travel. Backpacker hostel run by Swazi Trails (see page 104), located next to Mantenga Craft & Lifestyle Centre & 5min walk from The Gables. Comprises dbl rooms (each with 1 dbl bed & either a bunk or 2 twin beds), dormitory rooms (each sleeping 6–14) & shady campsite in the garden. Shared toilets & bathrooms, fully equipped self-catering kitchen, secured parking, braai area, chill-out lounge with DSTV, safe storage for valuables, a bookswap, free tea/coffee, a free hostel laptop & free Wi-Fi. Sustainable practices include waste recycling, composting of organic waste & solar power. Well-organised, conveniently placed hostel, with relaxed atmosphere. **$**

WHERE TO EAT The Ezulwini Valley is home to some of Swaziland's best eating places. If your budget does not run to fine dining, there is no shortage of cafés, take-aways and fast-food chains at which to satisfy your appetite.

✘ **The Boma Restaurant** Timbali Lodge (see page 163); ☏2416 1156; ⊕ daily 11.00–23.00. Popular, African-themed restaurant in upper Ezulwini Valley. Atmospheric interior, with tables arranged beneath a huge circular thatched boma. Claims to have the country's only authentic wood-burning pizza oven, & is – unsurprisingly – best known for its excellent pizza menu. Service slow but prices reasonable.

✘ **Calabash Restaurant** ☏2416 1187; m 7690 4585; e calabash@Swazi.net; www. restaurant-calabash.com. Most locals will tell you that this Swiss/German restaurant, established in 1976, is Swaziland's finest. Behind its modest façade is a plush, traditional interior with an excellent German-influenced menu. Favourites include the celebrated grilled eisbein (SZL143), while ostrich fillet (SZL195) & paella valenciana (SZL240) were among the specials on my last visit. The décor is defiantly Swiss, with framed alpine paintings, & the atmosphere one of European refinement. Pricey, but worth it.

✘ **The Great Taipei** The Gables (see page 166); ☏2416 2300. Good Chinese restaurant that serves a comprehensive selection of dishes in generous portions at reasonable prices (set menu for 2: SZL205). Peking duck can be ordered with 24hrs notice.

✘ **Guava Café** Guava Gallery (see page 167); ☏2416 1343. Friendly, fully licensed restaurant attached to art gallery. Serves homemade meals, snacks, bread & cakes on wooden deck overlooking fine view of Nyonyane Mountain. Claims to offer the 'best toasted sandwiches & salads in Swaziland'. Owned by Finnish family, so Finlandia Curry must surely be worth a try.

✘ **Happy Valley Hotel** (see page 163) Bella Vista à la carte restaurant offers predominantly Portuguese/Mozambican menu (eg: seafood specials & baby chicken), but caters to all tastes, including halal & vegetarian. Mid-range prices. Good wine list. Other dining options in the hotel include the Tuscan Coffee Shop (speciality coffees & cake; ⊕ 24hrs); the Pizzeria (take-aways; ⊕ 24hrs) & the Palmeira Buffet Restaurant.

✘ **Pub and Grill** The Gables (see page 166); ☏2416 1637; e thepubezulwini@gmail.com. Lively, popular eating establishment that attracts a young crowd to its sports bar & regular DJ & party nights. Wide selection of reasonably priced main courses includes good steaks & pub food platters. B/fasts highly recommended. Good service & atmosphere. Dining inside & out. Wi-Fi available.

✘ **Royal Swazi Sun** (see page 162). Swaziland's flagship hotel offers several good dining options, all of them expensive. These include the Terrace restaurant, which serves lavish buffets (b/fast SZL145; lunch SZL165; dinner SZL190), & the more intimate Planters Restaurant & Bar, which serves an à la carte, Asian-themed menu (seafood platter SZL315). The Casino Bar (⊕ daily 15.00–close) has innovative cocktails. Light meals are available at the pool bar on the terrace.

✘ **Royal Villas** (see page 162) The 130-seater Lihawu Restaurant at this upmarket hotel is open to the public 7 days a week. The classy, high-priced menu offers African 'fusion' cuisine from across the continent, with good service in discreet surroundings, & is supported by an impressive selection of some 1,000 wines from the Sivuno wine cellar. Sun BBQ on the pool terrace are popular with families.

✘ **Swazi River Café** Mantenga Nature Reserve (see page 171). Serves straightforward buffets for b/fast, lunch & dinner (eg: lunch buffet at SZL100 includes chicken, beef, rice, pap, potatoes, veg, salad, dessert – ice cream, cake & fruit salad). Pleasant, natural setting on large wooden deck in the bush. Beware thieving vervet monkeys.

✘ **Woodlands** ☏2416 3466/2084. Country-style restaurant & pub located halfway along valley on east side. Good local & international menu, including steaks, curries & seafood, at reasonable prices. 'On The Run' B/fast (SZL57) is huge. Terrace overlooks shaded garden with big trees, though conference centre next door somewhat obscures the view. Limited accommodation available.

NIGHTLIFE AND ENTERTAINMENT The Ezulwini Valley is no longer the pulsating night spot of yesteryear. However, the casinos at the Royal Swazi Sun and Happy Valley hotel are still going strong, and both claim to offer all the very latest in table games (blackjack, roulette and poker), slot machines and other means of squandering your inheritance.

The valley's closest reliable venue for music, dance and live performance is House on Fire at Malandela's (see page 186), a 10–15-minute drive east. Otherwise, nocturnal entertainment centres largely upon the hotels. The two Royal Swazi Spa resorts both stage regular live performances, from cabaret nights to fashion shows, as does the Happy Valley Hotel. Wednesday pub night at the Lugogo Sun's Sportsman Bar is a lively evening out, while the Pub and Grill (see page 165) at The Gables is now reputedly the hottest place in the valley, hosting local DJs and party nights. Check local listings (*eg: www.swazimagic.com*) to find out what's on during your visit.

The Gables is also home to Movie Zone (\ *2416 3552;* e *mzthegables@gmail. com; www.thegables.co.sz/cinemas*), Swaziland's only cinema, which opened in December 2010. This multiplex has four screens, which offer three or four daily screenings, with programmes changing weekly. Wednesday nights are half-price. Don't expect art house.

SHOPPING
Basics
The Gables shopping centre This large shopping complex lies at the southern end of the valley, immediately opposite the Happy Valley Hotel. You can't miss its incongruous concrete arches sprouting from the enormous car park beneath the imposing backdrop of Nyonyane Mountain. A relatively recent addition to the Ezulwini scene (it opened in 2002), this retail hub now allows Ezulwini residents and visitors to get their shopping done without having to slog up the hill to Mbabane.

The centrepiece is a huge Pick 'N' Pay supermarket (\ *2416 3425*), which stays open until 19.00 and includes a bakery, hot food kiosk, large braai section and good news-stand with both local and international papers and magazines. There are also shops for fashion, gifts, gardening, kitchen equipment, mothers and babies, mobile phones, and health and beauty, plus the Ezulwini Pharmacy (\ *2416 3500/1*), hairdressers, travel agents and a computer centre. Other services include branches of all Swaziland's banks, an internet café and a filling station. There are numerous places to eat and drink (see *Where to eat*, page 164), and Swaziland's only cinema, the multi-screen Movie Zone (see page 133). Look out, too, for the useful large-scale map of Ezulwini Valley.

TO HAGGLE OR NOT TO HAGGLE?

Pullela is the siSwati word for discount and most market stallholders in Swaziland will be expecting you to ask for one. But don't go overboard. Some travellers treat haggling as an article of creed – as though beating down a desperate market trader to a fraction of the original asking price somehow rubber-stamps their traveller's credibility. But prices in Swaziland are seldom grotesquely inflated. There is no hidden formula whereby each item is priced at, say, twice its value and your challenge is thus to halve it. Consider what you are prepared to pay. And remember that whatever you buy, you will certainly be getting it far cheaper here than from some ethnic boutique back home. Generally, it is more reasonable to ask for bulk discounts – ie: a reduced cost when buying several items simultaneously. To get an objective idea of what something may be worth, look out for similar items in shops, where prices are fixed.

Other shops and services The Corner Plaza has recently opened on the MR103 by the Tea Road turn-off. This small shopping complex has a SuperSpar supermarket and a pharmacy, among other smaller stores and take-aways. Zeeman's petrol station Galp on the MR103 opposite Ezulwini Craft Market (see below) is open 24 hours. There is a post office by the Calabash restaurant.

Gifts and handicrafts The Ezulwini Valley has – unsurprisingly – a good choice of outlets at which to find that quintessential Swazi gift for the folks back home.

Ezulwini Craft Market This is Swaziland's largest tourist market. Located at the turn-off into Goje township, 800m south of the Lugogo Sun hotel, it comprises some 126 different stalls, whose stallholders once displayed their wares along the MR103 until the market upped sticks in April 2010 and moved off the main road. The new arrangement, with good parking, works much better for the visitor. Give yourself time to browse and compare items from one stall to another. There is seldom a hard sell: most stallholders are happy to sit back and let you decide. Goods include wooden carvings, plates, beadwork, jewellery, textiles, candlesticks, carved walking sticks and traditional garments (including animal skin *emajoba* and *emhiya*; see page 83). Many are fashioned on familiar templates, but look harder and you'll find plenty of variations. Prices are reasonable and usually open to negotiation.

Mantenga Craft and Lifestyle Centre (✆ 2416 1136; ⊕ daily 08.00–17.00) This peaceful, shaded complex, located just before Mantenga Lodge on the road to Mantenga Falls, comprises around a dozen different craft outlets, many of which produce on site the wares they sell. Peek around the back and you can sometimes watch the artists in action. Familiar Swazi brands, including African Fantasy and Rosecraft Weaving, are represented here. Other outlets include the Khaya Craft Market, with woven sisal baskets, Benguni Craft, with an eclectic selection of local curios, including ingenious toys of wire and recycled tin cans; Shiba Rugs, with cotton rugs and furnishings; and Hawu! Pots, with original ceramics. Rainbow Angel gallery has some quirky sculptures, while the Little Silver Shop (✆ 2418 2692) houses a silversmith who will make repairs to gold and silver. Next door there are clean toilets and the offices of Swazi Trails (see page 104), the country's top tourist information office and tour operator.

Guava Gallery (✆ 2416 1343; e afj@realnet.co.sz; www.guavagallery.com) This friendly establishment, with its distinctive painted roof, lies just below the Mantenga Craft Centre. The family-run gallery was built by John and Tuire Thatcher in 1999: John a Canadian geologist; Tuire an artist and designer from Finland. On the same premises you will find Yebo Art Gallery, founded in 2011, where you can also browse (and buy) local artwork, and a jewellery studio where traditional items – featuring beadwork and giraffe hair – are manufactured on site. The delightful Guava Café next door (see page 165) offers home baking with a fine view of the mountains.

Thandabantu Craft Centre This small cluster of stalls sits alongside the main road just south of the turn-off to Timbali Lodge and the Calabash restaurant (see page 165). It comprises a small craft market, selling curios and paintings, plus some fruit and vegetable stalls, and one or two hot take-aways.

African Queen (✆ 2415 8142; e hilda@livinginAfrica.com) This upmarket gift and curio shop sits beside the pool in the grounds of the Lugogo Sun (see page

3

162) and is a favourite with tour groups staying at the Royal Swazi resorts. As well as local crafts, including pottery and jewellery, it stocks a good selection of books, including natural history guides. Affiliated to Living in Africa (✆ 2416 1726) at the Royal Swazi Sun next door.

HEALTH, SPORTS AND LIFESTYLE The Ezulwini Valley offers many ways to work off some energy – or simply to give your travel-weary body a bit of a break.

Cuddle Puddle (✆ 2416 1164) The Swazi Spa Health and Beauty Studio is just 500m north of the Royal Swazi Spa resort, to the west of the MR103. Better known by its time-honoured nickname 'Cuddle Puddle', this natural thermal spring – the magnesium-rich waters of which remain at a constant 42°C – was luring bathers and pleasure-seekers downhill from Mbabane long before there was a single hotel in the Ezulwini Valley. Indeed, its popularity explains why in 1965 Southern Sun chose to build the Royal Swazi where they did. What those first frisky bathers got up to after dark explains the nickname – and probably also the signs, still there today, stipulating that 'bathing suits must be worn'.

The hot springs are channelled into a large swimming pool that steams away gently beneath overhanging trees. Beside it stands a collection of white concrete domes, styled to resemble Swazi beehive huts, in which the health and beauty studio is housed, complete with gym and sauna. Since the 1980s this has been in the hands of German masseur and fitness instructor Horst Sayler, who doubles as fitness consultant for Swaziland's Olympics teams. Today various treatments are available, from massages to oxygen multi-step therapy, all conducted to suitably ambient Eastern music. Monthly membership is available – if you happen to be in Swaziland for a month. Otherwise there is an entry fee (SZL30 for adults) for use of the pool only. Locals get around this by bathing outside the fence in a natural pool formed by the Cuddle Puddle's warm overflow.

Other health and beauty centres Located next to Woodlands restaurant, **Kiki Jades** (✆ 7650 2055; e ciara.bissett@gmail.com; ⊕ Tue–Fri 09.00–17.00, Sat 09.00–15.00) offers a long list of massages and beauty treatments, with prior booking recommended. You could also try Camelot Spa at the Royal Swazi Sun (see page 162).

Golf and swimming The 18-hole, championship-standard golf course at the Royal Swazi Sun is reckoned to be one of the most impressive in southern Africa and is one of the jewels in Swaziland's tourism crown. The sweeping par 72 course, opened in 1966, is laid out along the lower slopes of the rugged hills that flank the valley, and there are numerous bunkers, thickets and gullies to keep the golfer on his or her toes. Green and fairways are always pristine. There is a putting green beside the clubhouse, and among the memorabilia and trophies inside is a photograph of celebrated Swazi golfer Joe Dlamini, along with his no 1 wood. A full round costs around SZL180 for non-members.

Most hotels in Ezulwini have swimming pools. The larger ones, including the Royal Swazi and Royal Villas, also have tennis courts. Other sports available include squash, bowling and snooker.

Horseriding
Hoofbeat Safaris (✆ 2416 6580; info@oofbeatsafaris.com; www.suninternational. com) This riding centre operates out of Ezulwini Stables beside the now defunct Ezulwini Sun Hotel. Trails of different distances and durations lead across the

valley and into the hills (60-minute trail SZL180). Riders of all ages and levels of experience are welcomed. Bookings through Lugogo Sun and Royal Swazi Sun (see page 162).

Quad-biking Located in Ezulwini Vally, **Swazi Trails** (*www.swazitrails.co.sz*) offers one-hour and two-hour quad-bike trails (*1 hour trail from SZL790*). The 7km circuit, known as Devil's Cauldron, lies behind the Royal Swazi hotel on the site of an old tin mine. Now reforested, its abandoned gulleys – or dongas – make a perfect playground for ATVs (all-terrain vehicles) and it has been described as one of the most interesting quad trails in southern Africa. The 250cc Suzuki 'Ozard' bikes used are suitable for both beginners and the more experienced. The lower age limit is 16 and a maximum of eight bikes are accommodated at one time. Pick-up and drop-off are from the Swazi Trails office in Mantenga (see page 104).

Adventure caving Those who want to get beneath the surface of Swaziland – literally – could try this innovative activity run by Swazi Trails (*www.swazitrails. co.sz/adventure-caving*). Launched in 1999, it explores a unique cave system formed by the Kophola River that flows underground between Msunduza and Kophola Mountains, just off the Malagwane Hill. Would-be speleologists don headlamps and battery packs to squeeze through subterranean passages on an 800m course some 90m below ground. This is the only major granite cave system known in southern Africa, and comprises a series of water-eroded chambers with names such as Key Hole, French Connection and (for Harry Potter fans) Platform Nine and Three-Quarters. Progress is slow and strenuous – expect belly crawls, body jams and fluttering bats – but no experience is necessary. Participants must be reasonably fit, aged 8–65, and able to fit through narrow passageways. Swazi Trails provides the gear (including overall, helmets and lamps), and trained guides conduct a thorough safety briefing before leading you through the two-hour course. Strong boots are recommended but running shoes with decent traction will do. Trips

---

A TASTE OF SWAZILAND

'Yebo Nkosi!' Our guide Sandile calls out the traditional praise greeting from the rickety homestead gate. A skinny dog twitches in the shade. Eventually an elderly woman appears and, eyes lowered respectfully, we clap our hands in greeting and enter the dusty compound. A girl in school uniform brings us water as we hand over our gifts: soap, bread and tinned fish. Formalities over, Make (Mrs) Matsebula sits us down and proceeds – at some length – to bemoan the bride price for her grandson's forthcoming nuptials.

This innovative 'Taste of Swaziland' tour (*www.swazitrails.co.sz*) has taken us off the Ezulwini tourist trail for an authentic, warts-and-all glimpse of Swazi life. Earlier we wandered Lobamba market, sipping warm, fermented sour *emaheyu* from a tin cup while the regulars at the mud-walled shebeen next door – grown garrulous on potent *buganu* home-brew – exhorted us to join them. And we mucked in with local parents to dig a pit latrine at Esitjeni Primary School, piling up shovel-loads of red soil beneath the picture-book backdrop of Nyonyane. Now there is no agenda: we meander along dusty back roads, stopping at anything interesting, with Sandile to make introductions and provide explanations. It seems an ideal way to find out how the other half live. Indeed, how the other 90% live.

include transport and refreshments, cost SZL1,300 per person, and run morning and evening from the Swazi Trails office in Mantenga (registration 30 minutes before departure in order to fit clothing and gear). A 15-minute drive followed by a 30-minute walk takes you to the site. The post-caving massage and hot springs sauna is optional, but recommended. Trips do not run after heavy rainstorms, when the underground rivers become too dangerous.

WHAT TO SEE AND DO

Ezulwini Tourist Office (Swazi Trails) Stuck for ideas? You could do worse than pop into the tourist office at Mantenga Craft and Lifestyle Centre (see page 167), run by Swazi Trails (\ *2416 2180;* m *7602 0832;* e *info@swazitrails.co.sz; www. swazitrails.co.sz*). Here you will find all the maps and information you might need and, if you don't have your own transport, can arrange excursions further afield. Swazi Trails activities focus on adventure sports such as caving (see page 169) and whitewater rafting (see page 275), but also cultural excursions, such as the Taste of Swaziland tour (see page 169). The office is open seven days a week. If it can be done, they'll know how, when and where.

The Tea Road This rural back route into the hills northeast of Ezulwini makes an interesting morning (or afternoon) excursion. The road gets its name from a failed attempt to establish tea plantations here during the 1960s, the plants proving unable to survive the fierce highveld frosts. Today it offers a scenic meander into the Mdzimba Mountains, with panoramic views back across Ezulwini and Lobamba, and can be extended into a circuit via Manzini.

The road starts at a turn-off from the MR103, opposite the Calabash turning and just before the Thandabantu Craft Centre. After 1.5km it crosses over the MR3 and then continues to a fork, among some houses, where it becomes gravel and you turn left. From this point, the route winds steeply into the hills and you soon find yourself among a landscape of huge boulders and scattered homesteads, with a patchwork of mealie fields wherever level ground permits. The long dramatic escarpment of the Mdzimba Mountains extends to your right (the southeast). This is sacred ground, off-limits to the public, and hides secret burial caves for royalty among its rugged boulderscape. Sentry families guard the caves by royal appointment.

On top, the escarpment flattens out onto a plateau, where you will see a trig beacon perched on a prominent dome. From here you can look back down the way you came and see the entire Ezulwini Valley laid out before you. To the south is Lobamba (see page 174), with its national stadium and royal parade grounds. Behind Ezulwini are the twin peaks of Sheba's Breasts, which are said to have inspired the setting for Rider Haggard's classic 1885 novel *King Solomon's Mines* – the author having spent some time in the area.

Continue and you will see on the left the terraces and a few abandoned structures that are all that remain of the ill-fated tea enterprise. You will pass a right turn to an army base (again, off-limits) and a left turn that follows a rural back route into Mbabane, via Msunduza. To complete the circuit – a total journey of some 62km – continue to bear right and, if in doubt, stop and ask. You will eventually return to the MR3 via Kwaluseni (see *Chapter 4,* page 192) or Manzini. Alternatively, simply retrace your steps to Ezulwini. The road is gravel for almost its entire length but has a decent surface and is navigable in a normal car. Take care after rain, especially on steeper stretches. And don't forget to bring binoculars, for the view.

Mantenga Nature Reserve (*www.sntc.org.sz/reserves/mantenga*) This small reserve is a five-minute drive from the heart of Ezulwini. Follow Mantenga Drive off the MR103, take the turning to Mantenga Lodge and continue left past the lodge for another 1.5km to the entrance. The reserve is an SNTC property (see page 52), purchased in sections between 1979 and 1994. It comprises a mix of highveld and middleveld habitat, with a thick tangle of native vegetation along the river, but also large stands of gum trees that occupy nearly a third of its area. The prime attraction is Mantenga Falls, Swaziland's largest waterfall by volume, which tumbles over a rock shelf in the Lushushwana ('Little Usutu') River. This river continues via a series of pools and mini cascades along the reserve's southern boundary, where it forms the dividing line with Mlilwane.

Visitors can explore the reserve's marked trails, one of which leads to the falls, where there is a small picnic site. A surprising variety of small to medium-sized mammals has been recorded, including baboon, rock hyrax, porcupine, bushpig, serval, nyala, klipspinger, red duiker, common duiker and even greater kudu. The mammals you are most likely to see, however, are vervet monkeys, since a habituated troop hangs out around the lodge. Birdlife includes middleveld species such as black-collared barbet, red-capped robin-chat and red-chested cuckoo. Pride of place goes to the rare southern bald ibis, which often roost on the cliffs above the falls and have established a small breeding colony – one of only three in Swaziland.

For many visitors the reserve's main attraction is Mantenga Cultural Village (see below). The entry gates are open for day visitors from 08.00 to 17.00, with the Swazi River Café (see page 165) serving light meals and a lunch buffet. For overnight guests, a lodge comprising 26 chalets (see page 163) offers bed and breakfast accommodation just upstream from the village.

Mantenga Cultural Village Mantenga Cultural Village lies 1km inside the park entrance, just before the lodge and restaurant. It comprises a replica Swazi village of the mid 19th century, constructed using authentic materials and techniques. While such reconstructed villages elsewhere – for instance, in KwaZulu-Natal – are often over-commercialised tourist traps discredited by cultural historians, this one has won plaudits for its accuracy. It certainly looks impressive, with its thatched beehives and imposing boma of tall branches against the looming backdrop of Nyonyane Mountain.

On payment of the SZL100 entrance fee, you are free to wander around the village at your leisure. But for a true insight into its construction and underlying culture – both past and present – you should take one of the excellent guided tours, which depart at 09.00, 12.00, 14.00 and 16.00. Your guide will explain the construction of the huts: how the best earth is gathered from anthills and mixed with cow dung; and how the tightly woven saplings of the walls are designed to thwart the spears of enemies. He or she will also explain the huts' configuration: how each had a specific role, such as a shelter for cooking, brewing or sleeping, indicated by the plaited grass motifs woven into its walls; and how the women's huts were positioned around the outside as a form of insurance, as women were generally not attacked. You will enter the *indlugudlu*, or ancestor's hut, where elders communed with the spirits and children were safe from a beating; the hut of the *sangoma*, whose herbs are planted outside; and the sacred cattle kraal, from which women were traditionally barred. Inside a sleeping hut you will probably puzzle at the back-breakingly low doorway, smoky interior and hard wooden 'pillows', until the purpose of each – guarding against sudden enemy intrusion, fumigating the hut from biting insects, and leaving ears open for danger, respectively – are explained. Among the huts you will meet village women preparing food, plaiting grass and making traditional beadwork, which you can buy.

At a small showground behind the village a dance troop performs traditional *sibhaca* routines twice daily (11.15 and 15.15). It's a lively show, with the cast ranging from primary school youngsters to young men and women. *Sibhaca* comprises vigorous high-kicking, pulsating drumming and some rousing singing, with individuals stepping forward in turn to do their stuff. Your guide will explain the stories that are being enacted – and, if you really enjoy it, you can buy a CD. After a couple of hours wandering around the village and watching the dancing, the cold drinks at the Swazi River Café are a godsend.

4

The Heartland

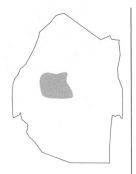

The area covered within this chapter falls within Manzini Province – and indeed it includes Manzini, Swaziland's second largest city. This region is effectively the eastern half of Swaziland's central corridor, the western half of which is described in *Chapter 3*. I have termed it Swaziland's 'heartland' not only because it lies at the country's geographical centre, and is the hub of its industry and agriculture, but also because it is the historic seat of the monarchy, and the stage setting for the traditional ceremonies that still constitute the nation's beating heart are enacted.

The region sits firmly in the middleveld. It is lower and warmer than temperate Mbabane but higher and cooler than the subtropical lowveld, which falls away immediately to the east. Little is left of the dense 'sourveld' savanna that once carpeted the land, the natural habitat having long since been replaced by agriculture and development. Indeed this is one of the most populous parts of Swaziland. In Matsapha it has the nation's main industrial estate, and its fertile soils make it the nation's breadbasket – producing not only the bulk of its market produce but also extensive fields of pineapples and other commercial crops. It also has the nation's only university, its only airport and its only music festival – one of the biggest in southern Africa.

Not that all this development makes the region unattractive. Like everywhere else in Swaziland, its horizons are ringed with hills, with the sacred Mdzimba Mountains forming an imposing escarpment along its northern flank. And the open country between has a pleasant, pastoral sense of space. Swaziland's first and best-known nature reserve, Mlilwane, is also here. Though not as wild as Malolotja or the lowveld, its picturesque terrain embraces the impressive 'Executioner's Rock' of Nyonyane and is home to plentiful wildlife.

If you're heading from Mbabane, Swaziland's heartland starts where the Ezulwini Valley ends, continuing east along the MR103 after it crosses the Lusushwana River. First up is Lobamba, home of parliament, the national stadium and museum (see page 174), and the royal kraals at Ludzidzini, where the Umhlanga and Incwala (see page 91) take place. Next, passing Mlilwane to the south, the road reaches the market hub of Mahlanya, from where a diversion south along the MR27 leads into the Malkerns Valley, known for its art and craft centres. Continuing east, the road rejoins the MR3 at the industrial estate of Matsapha – also the location of the country's only operating airport – from where it is just a short hop to Manzini.

Manzini itself is quite different in character from Mbabane: older, livelier and less European in feel, it is shorter on tourist attractions but is nonetheless the gateway to the wilder lands of the lowveld. If that's the way you're headed, and wish to travel directly between Mbabane and Manzini, it is a simple 20–30-minute drive of some 35km along the MR3. That way you'd miss out everything in between. But you'd be missing out an awful lot.

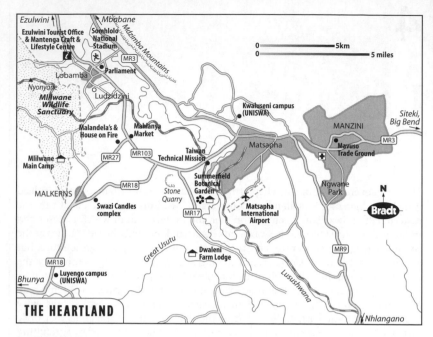

The following text labels appear on the map:

Ezulwini | Mbabane
Ezulwini Tourist Office & Mantenga Craft & Lifestyle Centre
Somhlolo National Stadium
MR3
Lobamba | Parliament
Nyonyane
Mlilwane Wildlife Sanctuary | Ludzidzini
Mdzimba Mountains
0 ——— 5km
0 ——————— 5 miles
Kwaluseni campus (UNISWA)
Siteki, Big Bend
MANZINI
Malandela's & House on Fire | Mahlanya Market
Matsapha
Mavuso Trade Ground
MR3
Mlilwane Main Camp | MR27 | MR103 | Taiwan Technical Mission
MALKERNS | MR18 | Stone Quarry | Summerfield Botanical Garden
Ngwane Park
N
Bradt
Swazi Candles complex | MR17 | Matsapha International Airport
Great Usutu | Dwaleni Farm Lodge | MR9
Lusushwana
MR18
Bhunya | Luyengo campus (UNISWA)
THE HEARTLAND | Nhlangano

LOBAMBA

Heading east out of the Ezulwini Valley, the MR103 crosses the Lusushwana River – a tributary of the Great Usutu – and rises up a gentle incline. At the top, a broad avenue on the left leads to the National Museum, Somhlolo Stadium and King Sobhuza II Memorial Park. On the right, beyond the ramshackle cluster of Lobamba village, is the royal kraal at Ludzidzini, ringed by the plains on which the nation gathers for the annual Incwala and Umhlanga. This whole area is known as Lobamba and has been playing host to Swaziland's royalty for over 200 years.

NATIONAL MUSEUM Swaziland's National Museum (⊕ *Mon–Fri 08.00–16.30, Sat–Sun 10.00–16.00; tourist entry fee SZL20*), known in siSwati as *Umsamo Wesive*, was built in 1972. It sits just behind parliament, some 500m off the main road, and can be identified by the reconstructed beehive village beside the car park. The museum is the headquarters of the Swaziland National Trust Commission (SNTC), custodians of the nation's heritage and cultural archives, and contains exhibits on Swaziland's culture, history and natural history. For many years it stood rather neglected, the main curiosity being the late King Sobhuza's fleet of huge, 1950s American cars that were rusting gently away in an otherwise empty showroom. After recent renovation, however, it is now a rather impressive museum. The SNTC arranges that every schoolchild in Swaziland makes at least one visit, to ensure that each successive generation grasps the importance of its heritage.

Natural history The natural history section is in a separate wing to the left of reception. Here you will find three large dioramas illustrating, respectively, Swaziland's highveld, middleveld and lowveld habitats, complete with mounted animals – including a pride of lions chasing down a zebra and circling vultures hanging from the ceiling. These are the work of American model-maker Paul

Rhymer from the Smithsonian Institute in Washington DC who, using meagre resources, knocked up some miraculous creations. Check out the lichen-encrusted highveld boulders (mostly chicken wire) and replica marula tree, perfect right down to the flaking bark and individual leaves. Volunteer artists, including this author, helped with the painted backdrops. Among other exhibits are a cross section of Swaziland's geology, nocturnal and aquatic dioramas, and a stuffed crocodile that was shot after it had attacked a local child, who managed – heroically – to fend it off using the old stick-between-the-jaws trick.

History and culture The museum's history and culture section, to the right of reception, was revamped in 2011 under the guidance of Bob Forrester, local historian, anthropologist and author (see page 302), who is also responsible for the museums at Bulembu, Mahamba and Ngwenya. It is an excellent introduction to the way in which people have lived in what is now Swaziland since prehistoric times. A chronological sequence of displays guides the visitor from the time of the earliest hunter-gatherers right through to independence. Individual cases, models and dioramas, complete with informative captions in both English and siSwati, explore the forces that have shaped Swazi culture. You will find exhibits on everything from beadwork, architecture and indigenous cereal crops to social structures, traditional belief systems and the impact of Christianity. Life-sized mannequins dressed in traditional regalia demonstrate the complex symbolism of costume. Among the more impressive artefacts on display is a 75,000–80,000-year-old stone spear, so fine that it could only have served for ceremonial purposes. There is also a wonderful frieze of archive photographs depicting the colonial era, and, to bring things up to the present, a good display of contemporary Swazi painting. Look out for the bus-rank canvases of Sunshine Nxumalo: a kind of Swazi LS Lowry in technicolour.

KING SOBHUZA II MEMORIAL PARK The memorial park (⊕ *Mon–Fri 08.00–16.30, Sat–Sun 10.00 16.00; entrance SZL80)*, immediately opposite the museum and parliament, is the landscaped expression of a personality cult. The late, revered King Sobhuza II (see page 57), father of today's King Mswati III, has assumed an almost deified status in contemporary Swaziland, his various celebrated utterances trotted out like the wisdom of Solomon. *'Anginasitsa'* ('I have no enemies') is the motto emblazoned on the large brass statue of the monarch that stands at the centre of this formal garden.

After the king died in 1982, this memorial park was built with Taiwanese money at the site where his body lay in state before being buried in sacred mountains in the south. Its formal hexagonal layout has various symbolic resonances, with the statue of Sobhuza facing east towards his father's burial site in the sacred Mdzimba Mountains. A glass mausoleum that preserves the very spot where the body lay is guarded day and night, with photographs strictly forbidden; a flame is lit here for important occasions. Sobhuza's long life is documented in a small museum display with archive photographs and some fascinating nuggets of information. He was, for instance, the first Swazi king to have had a formal education (sent away to Lovedale School in Cape Town). He was also very unhappy about flying: 'The British are trying to kill me,' he is once reputed to have said, while refusing to board a plane.

PARLIAMENT Swaziland's parliament, or Libandla, sits – literally – next to the National Museum. It was opened in 1969 by Princess Alexandra on behalf of Queen Elizabeth II, and was a post-independence gift from the departing British.

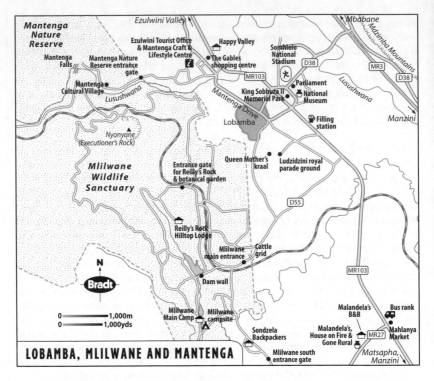

Beneath its hexagonal roof, topped with a brass dome, are the two houses: the Senate, or Upper Chamber, and the House of Assembly (see *Parliament and the prime minister*, page 63). If a guide is on hand you can have a brief tour of the premises: look out among the corridors for a large stuffed lion and hippo, both of which were shot in the lowveld and presented to Sobhuza. Visitors are free to visit parliament when the House of Assembly is sitting (08.30–12.30) and watch from the public gallery. Indeed, there is a refreshing accessibility to the whole place, compared with the security paranoia that tends to colour any such institutions in Europe or America: when I visited, my guide pulled up beside a parking spot labelled Minister of Finance. 'Let's hope we'll be in the money,' he said.

SOMHLOLO STADIUM The 20,000-capacity national stadium is named after Swaziland's King Sobhuza I, also known as Somhlolo. The founding father of the Swazi nation, he reigned from 1805 to 1839 and was the one who experienced those prophetic dreams that supposedly anticipated the arrival of Europeans (see *The Europeans reach Swaziland*, page 56). The stadium was built in 1968, for Swaziland's independence, and was used for the coronation of Mswati III on 25 April 1986. Over the years it has hosted various major musical and sporting events including, during the 1980s, performances by R'n'B greats Percy Sledge and Peter Tosh, and exhibition matches by English football clubs Tottenham Hotspur and Liverpool. This was at a time when sanctions against apartheid prevented such events from taking place in South Africa, so crowds poured over the border. Today the stadium is more important as a football ground for the national team and occasional national events – such as the 40/40 celebration of 6 September 2008, when, to a pageant of marching bands and traditional dancers and a cavalcade of African heads of states, Mswati celebrated both his own and his country's 40th birthdays. National uproar followed the discovery in 2009 that somebody had cut chunks of turf from the stadium's pitch – mostly around the goalposts and centre circle – in order to bury secret charms (see *Muti*, page 81) in a bid to influence results.

LUDZIDZINI Continue east along the MR103 past the museum – and beneath a road bridge emblazoned with Swaziland's national emblems – and you'll find the countryside opening out into expansive plains, its rolling sward cropped almost bald by wandering livestock. About 1km beyond the museum turn-off, just after a large Caltex filling station on the left (⊕ *06.00–20.00*), a long palm-lined avenue on the right leads to Ludzidzini. Here, among the clustered dwellings of the royal village, is the queen mother's royal kraal, the walls of which are symbolically reinforced with reeds during the annual Umhlanga (see pages 92 and 93). In front is a parade ground, with terraced seating for VIPs, where the concluding ceremonies of the Umhlanga take place. During the Umhlanga and Incwala, the surrounding plains swarm with crowds of people in traditional dress, either joining the festivities or commuting back and forth. With the Mdzimba Mountains behind, it makes for a truly spectacular sight. Parking for spectators is set up in a field to the right of the entrance road.

MLILWANE WILDLIFE SANCTUARY

Mlilwane is the country's best-known nature reserve. Meaning 'little fire', the name refers to the lightning strikes that sometimes set the hillsides ablaze, but could apply metaphorically to the flash of inspiration in which Swaziland's conservation movement was born. It was here in 1961 that Ted Reilly – whose father had settled the property in 1906 – first took action to save what remained of the kingdom's fast-vanishing wildlife. Reilly senior had been a farmer and tin-miner, who brought electricity to Swaziland and married the 'only white woman between Manzini and Mbabane'. Ted, who was born on the farm in 1938, converted the 460ha property into a wildlife sanctuary by planting trees, digging dams, securing the perimeters and rounding up any wildlife he could capture around the kingdom to bring back for safe keeping.

The reserve was opened to the public in 1964. Since those early days, Big Game Parks (BGP) – the independent conservation trust that Reilly subsequently founded (see page 52 and advert on the inside back cover) – has flourished, acquiring the larger and wilder lowveld reserves of Hlane and Mkhaya. But Mlilwane remains the spiritual home. Indeed, BGP has its headquarters here and the old family home at Reilly's Rock is now a luxury lodge for visitors. The property today is ten times bigger than the original farm, and its 4,560ha include the peak of Nyonyane, or Executioner's Rock, and much of the Mantenga Valley to the north.

Equally important to Mlilwane's popularity is its location: just a 15-minute hop from the heart of the Ezulwini Valley. Inevitably, this proximity to the bright lights compromises the reserve's sense of wilderness: from the higher ground you look down on the busy sprawl of Lobamba and Ezulwini. Inside, the reserve itself is far from pristine: there are substantial stands of alien gum trees, an abandoned railway line and ugly scars from the old tin mines. Nonetheless it represents an impressive natural oasis, so close to the hurly burly of the heartland.

Guests today have a wide choice of accommodation and plenty to keep them occupied, including hiking, game drives, mountain-biking and horseriding. Many, however, simply come for a family day out in the pleasant environs of Main Camp, where you can slap some meat on the braai, take a dip in the pool and commune with the wandering warthogs. And with a night gate allowing 24-hour access to the reserve, MIilwane also serves as a relaxed retreat from which to make sorties into Ezulwini and the other neighbouring attractions.

LANDSCAPE AND HABITATS Mlilwane effectively falls into two sectors. All the accommodation and activities, with the exception of the longer horse trails (see page 182), take place in the southern sector. This is dominated by Nyonyane Mountain, whose peak has become known as Executioner's Rock from the grisly fate that befell the condemned individuals once led to its summit and shoved off. Main Camp is located in the south of this sector, below a chain of dams, and a network of roads and hiking trails radiates out from here around the reserve. The northern sector is a wilderness area with no roads or trails other than ranger tracks, and bounded by the Lusushwana River, which divides Mlilwane from Mantenga Nature Reserve to the north (see page 171). It is a wild region, with pockets of indigenous forest in the gulleys and bare, granite slopes on top.

The reserve's natural habitat is mostly middleveld, with areas of highveld grassland at higher altitudes – largely towards the north. There are tracts of open savanna, with native woodland along the drainage lines and up the lower slopes of the mountains. Alien plants are a problem, however – not only the dense stands of gum trees, but also the lantana, guava and other non-native species that flourish on disturbed land – and Big Game Parks does constant battle with these invaders in an attempt to protect the indigenous ecosystems that they threaten to overwhelm.

WILDLIFE Mlilwane is home to numerous mammals, many of which have thrived since introduction. In open areas, you should see zebra, blesbok, impala and blue wildebeest, while greater kudu and nyala frequent the thickets, often along drainage lines. Nyala and impala often wander through camp, as do warthogs, which have become remarkably tame. Smaller antelope include grey duiker, red duiker and steenbok, although these are shy and seldom seen.

A number of less common antelope have been introduced to an enclosed area near Reilly's Rock (see page 180). These include grey rhebok, red hartebeest, oribi and roan, the last courtesy of a remarkable project that brought breeding stock all the way from Marwell Zoo in the UK. This area is accessible only on a guided drive; on my last visit we discovered the beguiling sight of a one-day-old roan fawn hidden in the long grass, betrayed only by a twitch of its tasseled ear. Reilly's Rock itself is home to some of the shyest of southern Africa's antelope species: suni patter around the small forest trails; blue duiker – hare-sized bambis – often tiptoe out to visit the bird table; and klipspringers frequent the rocky areas, including the garden's own large rockery.

Back in the '70s there were white rhinos in Mlilwane but the habitat proved unsuitable for these bulk grazers. A handful of giraffes that once roamed the plains have now also gone. Today, the only real heavyweights are the hippos, which tend to hang out in the main dam (check the small island near the southwestern corner) but also visit the waterhole at Main Camp, where you can see them from the Hippo Haunt restaurant. One famous hippo named Somersault, now sadly no more, lived here for years and would entertain visitors by scoffing his supplementary pile of grain right beside the low camp wall.

Predators in Mlilwane are elusive. There are very occasional sightings of leopards – or, at least, of their tracks – and wandering wild dogs have even put in a couple of appearances over the years. Smaller hunters include black-backed jackal, large-spotted genet and water mongoose, and servals have been recorded, but most of these animals are active only at night so you are unlikely to come across them. Three of Swaziland's four primates inhabit the reserve: vervet monkeys along the watercourses, baboons on the rocky slopes and greater bushbabies all over. The last of these offer wonderful sightings at Reilly's Rock, where they arrive after dark for a nibble of banana.

Mlilwane's patchwork of habitats is great for birds. A noisy waterbird colony at the back of the Hippo Haunt waterhole is home to egrets, ibis and herons, while other aquatic species, such as pied kingfisher and black crake, frequent the water's edge. Main Camp is a good spot to get to know your typical middleveld birds – paradise flycatcher, diederik cuckoo, black-headed oriole, scarlet-chested sunbird and purple-crested turaco were all flitting about when I last visited – and an amazing 81 species have been recorded from the veranda at Reilly's Rock, where a semi-tame flock of crested guinea fowl often visits the busy bird table. Away from camp, you should see grassland species such as widows and longclaws, plus white-fronted bee-eaters among the old mining gulleys. Keep your eyes peeled for birds of prey over the higher ground: Verreaux's eagle and crowned eagle breed here – I saw both these magnificent raptors during my last visit – and black sparrowhawks sometimes wheel over the gum plantations.

Among reptiles, the big hitters include crocodiles – a large one often basks at the Hippo Haunt waterhole – and pythons. According to Ted Reilly, the latter are responsible for the disappearance of several oribi inside the fenced rare antelope sector, and a number have been captured and removed. Look out for southern tree agamas around Main Camp, the breeding males scuttling up tree trunks to nod their bright blue heads. And keep your eyes peeled for even smaller stuff. I once saw a gripping battle at Reilly's Rock between a large wolf spider and its nemesis, a spider-hunting wasp. The latter prevailed and dragged its paralysed prey – over twice its own size – 10m to its nest under the roots of a jacaranda. Trumps a lion kill any day.

GETTING THERE AND AWAY Mlilwane lies to the west of the MR103 and is signed via a gravel road 800m south of the Ludzidzini turn. This road, the D55, continues through a small settlement and eventually over a cattle grid to the entrance, from where, after signing in and paying your SZL40 conservation (entrance) fee, a 2.5km drive leads via the large dam to Main Camp. Take it easy on the dirt roads: there are some steep drainage humps and hidden animals may dash out of the long grass. An alternative southern entrance gate off the MR27 Malkerns Road (see page 182) leads directly to Sondzela's Backpackers. An old gate in the north, across the Lusushwana River from Mantenga Drive (see page 171), is now closed to the public.

WHERE TO STAY AND EAT Main Camp, the park headquarters, is the base for most accommodation, visitor facilities and activities. Guests can also stay at Sondzela Backpackers, 2km to the south, or – if your budget allows – in the upmarket comfort of Reilly's Rock, the old family home, which sits on a hill north of the main dam. All bookings are through central reservations (\ 2528 3943; e reservations@ biggameparks.org; www.biggameparks.org/mlilwane).

Main Camp The first thing you'll notice at the entrance gate to Main Camp is a tangle of wire snares confiscated from around Swaziland: a salutary reminder of just why sanctuaries like this one are so important. After this rather sombre sight, however, you enter a spacious, shady campground, where smoke from camp fires

4

drifts between the buildings and birdsong trickles from the large indigenous trees. It's a delightfully mellow spot, and the animals – notably warthog, nyala and impala – seem oblivious to people as they stroll around. From Hippo Haunt restaurant and bar, where meals are served for breakfast, lunch and dinner, you can watch crocs, hippos and birds at the waterhole immediately below. Other facilities include braai stands, a shop with basic supplies, and a large swimming pool that is a favourite with school parties and day visitors. There is also a natural history 'interpretarium', with a fascinating if slightly dilapidated display. It includes the skulls of two sparring bull kudus that died on the reserve with their spiral horns fatally interlocked and are displayed just as they were found. Accommodation is as follows:

🏠 **Beehive villages** (43 units) 3 separate 'villages' (Roan, Nyala & Blesbok), each comprising a circle of 15 thatched beehive huts. Huts traditional in appearance but modified for comfort, with en-suite bathroom. Each beehive sleeps 2 in dbls or twins. Nyala village also has family units: 2 x 3-sleeper, all sgl beds; 2 x 1 dbl + 2 sgl beds. B&B rates available. **$$**

🏠 **Rest camp huts** (8 units) 4 dbl huts, 2 family huts (1 dbl, 2 sgls) & 2 twin beehive huts, all with en-suite bathroom. Located in central camp area near restaurant. B&B rates available. **$$**

🏠 **Rondavels** (3 units) 2 self-catering rondavals each with en-suite bathroom & kitchenette; 1 sleeps 2 & 2 sleep 3. Just west of main camp entrance, a short walk from central camp &

swimming pool, with private braai area & good views across a *vlei* below. **$$**

🏠 **Shonalonga cottage** (sleeps 6) Large self-catering cottage, with 1 dbl bedroom & 1 room with 4 sgl beds. Kitchen, living area & en-suite bathroom. Veranda at back overlooking private garden with indigenous trees (including euphorbia, fever tree & sycamore fig) & view of the vlei beyond. Braai area in garden & public pool next door. Good-value family option, its spacious stone & thatch design reminiscent of old Kruger Park lodges. **$$**

🏕 **Campsite** (20 level pitches) Set in mature eucalyptus forest at edge of camp, with good views over the vlei. Communal ablutions, power points, benches & braai/BBQ area. Short walk from central camp area & swimming pool. **$**

Other

🏠 **Reilly's Rock Hilltop Lodge** (sleeps 19) The old Reilly family home offers upmarket accommodation in an impressive colonial house, set among enormous jacarandas, with sweeping verandas, polished stone floors, tin roofs & a fine view east across the Ezulwini Valley. A separate cottage, Down Gran's Cottage, lies below the house beside an orchard. Wildlife is everywhere: blue duiker, suni & klipspringer forage around the grounds; bushbabies visit after dark for banana handouts; & there is a constant traffic of birds around the bird table on the lawn. Trails explore the hillside & botanical garden, which has numerous rare plants, including the endangered cycad *Encephalata woodii*. The lounge has become a museum to wildlife conservation in Swaziland, with such oddities as a rhino scratching post. Main house: 2 luxury dbl & 2 standard dbl en-suite

rooms in the house; 2 en-suite rooms (1 dbl, 1 twin) in garden cottage outside; home-cooked meals served on terrace; rates include dinner, B&B. Down Gran's Cottage 200m below main house: 1 en-suite dbl, 1 en-suite trpl & 1 en-suite twin; fully equipped for self-catering, but guests can choose to eat dinner at the house. **$$$$**

🏠 **Sondzela Backpackers** (sleeps 72) Popular backpacker hostel near park's southern boundary. Access from Malkerns Rd via southern entrance; free shuttle bus service from Malandela's (see page 185). Comprises campsite, dormitory, private dbl rooms & private twin rooms. Communal bathrooms. Also: swimming pool, large garden, safe parking, braai area, bar, laundry, DSTV & games room. Activities available at main camp, 15min walk away. Watch out for the ostriches. **$**

WHAT TO SEE AND DO Many local visitors to Mlilwane are content simply to hang out around Main Camp. They've come more for the atmosphere than the activities. And why bother chasing after the wildlife, when nyala and warthog wander past as you flip a burger on the braai or take a post-prandial dip in the pool? There is much to be said for this approach – especially after a hard-working week. Visitors on a tighter schedule, however, might want to make more of their time, and they have plenty to choose from. Activities can be booked through central reservations (see *Where to stay and eat* above) or from reception at Main Camp. The two longer horse trails must be booked in advance.

Walks With no dangerous game to worry about – except for crocs and hippos in the dams – you can walk pretty much wherever you want. Short trails lead from Main Camp, following drainage lines across the grasslands. For more serious hikes, head up to Nyonyane, where you can follow steep trails along the ridges and to the summit of Executioner's Rock. Guides are available, and birdwatchers can arrange a 2½-hour guided bird walk with a ranger (from SZL170).

Game drives You can drive for free on any public roads and spot wildlife by yourself. The going is rougher on the steeper roads towards the north, where a 4x4 vehicle makes life easier. Alternatively, book a guided game drive in an open Land

NIGHT ON THE CHUBEKA TRAIL

The storm finally broke, thunder rumbling over the mountain at our backs and lightning flashes illuminating the dark valley below. From the mouth of our cave sanctuary, munching on roasted pumpkin and grilled chicken kebabs straight from the fire, we watched the rain lash the forest outside. The flames cast dancing shadows on the granite walls, where faint daubings of rock art revealed that people had used this natural shelter for centuries. Mind you, I can't imagine that those who went before us had enjoyed anything quite as comfortable as the pillows and bedrolls laid out invitingly for us on the warm sand at the back of the cave.

We had reached our rocky refuge just as the light was fading, tying up our horses in a paddock below then scrambling up among boulders and tree ferns to the entrance, discreetly screened by a spreading waterberry. It had been a four-hour ride from Main Camp, first meandering down through the *vlei* then riding out across the open plains, our trusty steeds barely acknowledging the wildebeest and zebra that cantered beside us. In the undulating foothills of Nyonyane we had dismounted and scrambled to the summit of Executioner's Rock, looking out across the plains of Lobamba to the Mdzimba Mountains and back to the meandering Mantenga Valley. Peering over the precipice had brought shudders all round at the thought of those who once met their fate here. But a single Verreaux's eagle drifting overhead had returned our attention to the glowering skies, and our guide Maja Tzabedze had led us back to the horses to press on, over the ridge, towards our shelter.

The storm blew out as suddenly as it had started. By the time my daughter was toasting the promised marshmallows, the stars were back in the sky and all around we could hear the drip of the glistening greenery. Later, snug in my bedroll, I listened to a bushbaby shrieking from deep in the forest and heard the soft flutter of wings as a nightjar hawked insects around our embers. It felt wild – timeless, even – and hard to believe that we were just 2km from a casino, supermarket and multi-screen cinema. But that's Swaziland for you.

Rover. The two-hour sunset and sunrise drives (from SZL270) are best for wildlife and photography, and include drinks and snacks.

Mountain-biking Mlilwane's roads and trails are ideal for two-wheel exploration, offering both gentle rides over the plains or more strenuous excursions into the mountains. This is the location of the annual Nedbank Swaziland Imvelo Mountain-bike Race, contested by hundreds of participants every June (details of each year's race posted on the Big Game Parks website and local listings magazines). Cycling can get you surprisingly close to wildlife. Bikes are for hire at SZL120 per hour – or bring your own for free.

Horseriding Well-stocked stables beside Main Camp have horses for all-comers. You can book guided rides by the hour (from SZL150), ranging from 'kiddies' rides' around camp to a three-hour 'Rock of Execution Challenge' that takes more experienced riders to the reserve's highest point. Horseback is an excellent way to approach wildlife, with your horse's scent masking your own, and it is possible to ride almost among the zebra and wildebeest. Those of an equestrian bent can also try two longer rides. The 'Chubeka' overnight cave trail (from SZL1,355) takes riders up and around Nyonyane to a hidden cave, in which you spend the night – complete with cosy bed roll, fire and three-course dinner – before riding back to Main Camp after breakfast the following morning. The two-night 'Klipspringer' trail (from SZL2,750) is the longest, and represents your only chance to explore the northern sector. Camp is pitched beside the Lusushwana River, with two-person dome tents, long-drop toilets, canvas sinks and a hot shower (courtesy of a donkey boiler) in a natural rock cubicle. All meals are provided. This is Mlilwane's wildest activity and takes you to areas otherwise inaccessible to the public.

Umphakatsi cultural experience This two-hour tour (from SZL80) visits a chief's village just outside Mlilwane for a dose of Swazi culture. You will don traditional *emahiya* and remove your shoes before entering the homestead, where you will meet the family and join in traditional chores such as grinding maize and plaiting grass. You may even learn some Swazi song and dance.

MAHLANYA AND THE MALKERNS VALLEY

The Malkerns Valley provides an interesting diversion off the MR103, midway between Ezulwini and Manzini. It is essentially a large expanse of farmland that centres upon the small settlement of Malkerns, home to the Swazican fruit canning plant. Among the well-watered fields are some excellent craft markets and workshops, a riding stables and the Malandela's complex, one of Swaziland's premier tourist spots, which offers everything from restaurant and internet café to bed and breakfast cottages, weaving centre and a dazzling outdoor theatre.

GETTING THERE AND AWAY The turn-off to Malkerns lies at Mahlanya, 4.5km south of Lobamba, where a large fruit and vegetable market sits to the left of the road at the top of a small rise. Immediately over the rise, opposite the lower entrance to the market and over some mountainous speed humps, a right turn signs you west to Malkerns along the MR27. This road leads past extensive pineapple estates, identifiable by their spiky grey-green leaves. Look out during the February–May harvesting season for gangs of pickers, their limbs clad in protective plastic, tossing the hand-grenade-like fruit into the back of a tractor.

above The Ngwempisi Gorge is one of numerous locations around Swaziland where nature lovers can find both solitude and adventure amid genuine wilderness (MU) pages 241–3

right Phophonyane Falls, just north of Piggs Peak, forms the centrepiece of an enchanting nature reserve (L/S) pages 224–6

below The sacred Mdzimba Mountains are off-limits to the public, with secret royal burial caves hidden among the boulders (MU) page 170

above left Stone carver Anton Khoza displays his wares at the Peak Craft Centre near Piggs Peak (MU) page 228

above right A trader at Manzini Market demonstrates how to play the marimba. Traditional music is a central part of Swazi culture (MU) pages 90 & 198

left Ezulwini Craft Market comprises some 126 stalls, displaying crafts and curios from around the country and further afield (MU) page 167

below Workers at Mantenga Cultural Village construct a traditional homestead. Techniques centuries old are still in use around Swaziland today (MU) pages 171–2

above At the Swazi Candles Factory near Malkerns you can watch the candle-makers at work (MU) page 187

right Detail from *Real Life* by Sunshine Nxumalo, at the National Museum, Lobamba. Swaziland's museums and galleries display work from a new generation of artists (MU) pages 174–5

below Located at Malandela's, House on Fire is a unique performing arts venue that hosts the celebrated Bushfire Festival every May (MU) page 186

left   Giraffe (*Giraffa camelopardalis*) have been successfully introduced to several lowveld reserves, including here at Mbuluzi (MM) pages 16–17

below left   Breeding herds of elephant (*Loxodonta africana*), like this small group at Hlane, tend to stick close together (MU) pages 12–13

below   Nyala (*Tragelaphus angasii*) often enter reserve rest camps. Males (shown here) differ from females by virtue of their horns and shaggier coats (MU) page 18

bottom   An endangered black rhino (*Diceros bicornis*) browses in a thicket at Mkhaya, using its hooked lip to tear off thorny twigs (MU) pages 14–15

above left   The rock hyrax (*Procavia capensis*) lives in colonies among boulders. Despite appearances, it is closely related to the elephant (MU) page 28

above right   Burchell's zebra (*Equus quagga burchellii*) are indigenous to the lowveld and can also be seen at Malolotja and Mlilwane (MU) page 17

below   Vervet monkeys (*Chlorocebus pygerythrus*) are resourceful primates that won't think twice about plundering your picnic (MU) page 27

above left   A Narina trogon (*Apaloderma narina*) at Phophonyane Falls. This elusive species is widespread in Swaziland (RdV) page 34

above right   Hlane's breeding colony of white-backed vultures (*Gyps africanus*) is the largest in southern Africa (MU) pages 32–3

left   Crested guineafowl (*Guttera pucherani*) are common around Stone Camp at Mkhaya (MU) page 32

below   The southern yellow-billed hornbill (*Tokus leucomelus*) is a conspicuous lowveld resident (MU) pages 34–5

right Look out for Drakensberg crag lizards (*Pseudocordylus melanotus*) sunning themselves on boulders in Malolotja (MU) page 40

below left This emperor moth (Saturnidae family) is among numerous fascinating insect species found throughout Swaziland (MU) page 49

below right Snake expert Thea Litschka-Koen holds a black mamba (*Dendroaspis polylepis*) captured near a Lubombos homestead. The snake will be released far from harm's way (CK) pages 43 & 267

bottom The Nile crocodile (*Crocodylus niloticus*) is Africa's largest reptile and inhabits most lowveld rivers in Swaziland (MU) pages 39–40

Blesbok (*Damaliscus dorcas phillipsi*) troop across a hillside in Malolotja Nature Reserve. This rugged mountain wilderness offers some of the finest hiking in southern Africa (PP/FLPA) pages 20 & 207–16

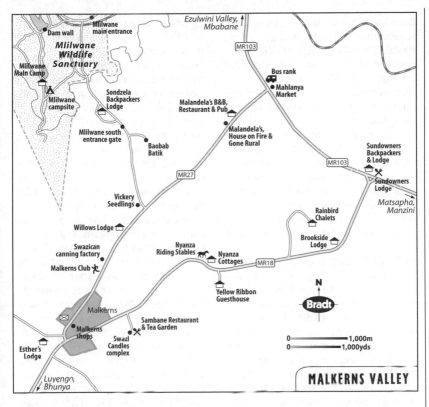

MALKERNS VALLEY

The Malandela's complex is 1km along this road on the right. After another 2km you will see Vickery Seedlings nursery, beside which a dirt track leads to the Baobab Batik workshop and Sondzela Backpackers Lodge (see page 180). Then, after passing the unprepossessing Swazican canning plant – also on the right – you will reach the ramshackle settlement of Malkerns. After the small cluster of shops and services the road arrives at a T-junction. A right turn here leads south, via Luyengo, taking you either towards Mankayane and the southwest or back to Mbabane via Mhlambanyatsi (see page 240). A left turn takes you back east along the southern side of the Malkerns Valley, passing the Swazi Candles complex on the right, before returning to the MR103 some 3km southeast of Mahlanya. Just before the main road is a small hill, sheltering the ePhondvo royal residence. This was once a game farm, and you may spot the odd blesbok in the nearby fields.

WHERE TO STAY

🏠 **Brookside Lodge** (17 units, sleeps 58) ✆ 2528 3765; m 7604 7798; e brookside-lodge@ realnet.co.sz. Large complex located 1km from MR103 on road to Swazi Candles (see page 187). Self-catering apts comprise 6 family units, each with 2 en-suite bedrooms; 11 dbl units, each with 1 dbl en-suite bedroom. All rooms with kitchen, lounge, AC & DSTV. Also: mini golf, swimming pool, BBQ, Wi-Fi, à la carte restaurant & bar, fishing dam

(bass & bream) & children's farm. Weddings, events & conference facilities for 45. Clean & good value, although extensive paving detracts a little from rustic surrounds. Rates for B&B & self-catering. **$$**
🏠 **Esther's Lodge** (sleeps 22) ✆ 2528 3552; m 7602 8997; estherslodge.com. Self-catering & B&B accommodation at western end of MR27; turn-off signed between Malkerns & T-junction. Dbl, sgl & family rooms, all with TV & Wi-Fi; family

chalets have kitchen. Utilitarian feel: aimed more at business travellers than tourists. **$$**

⌂ **Malandela's B&B** (sleeps 15) ☏ 2528 3448; e bookings@malandelas.com; www.malandelas. com. Highly original B&B accommodation in converted country farmhouse behind Malandela's complex (see opposite). 8 individually designed rooms, comprising sgls, dbls & 1 family room, all en-suite, with colour theming, original 'Afro-chic' décor & recycled materials. B/fast served on pool terrace. Private guest facilities include swimming pool, private grounds & botanical garden with display of indigenous flora. Other facilities shared with Malandela's complex, including restaurant, pub, internet café, craft shops & House on Fire performance venue. Charming, good-value retreat at the heart of a happening place. **$$**

⌂ **Rainbird Chalets** (4 chalets, sleeps 12) ☏ 2528 3452; m 7603 7273; e rainbird@swazi. net; www.rainbirdchalets.com. Quiet B&B & self-catering accommodation on working farm 1km off MR18 between MR103 & Swazi Candles. Comprises 2 sgl wooden chalets (2-person) & 2 dbl family chalets (4-person) in spacious grounds with dam. All rooms with en-suite bathroom, AC, DSTV, open-plan kitchen, lounge & dining room & braai area. B/fast served on patio at main house, with view of gardens, dam & mountains. Also: on-site bass fishing (catch & release; rods available), swimming pool & internet at main house. Restaurants nearby. Abundant birdlife. Transport to airport (15mins) available. Comfortable, secluded & good value. **$$**

⌂ **Willows Lodge** (14 chalets, sleeps 34) ☏ 2550 4552; m 7602 1284/7603 0670; e enquiries@swaziwillows.com; www. swaziwillows.com. Self-catering accommodation in secure grounds among trees, midway between Mahlanya Market & Malkerns on MR27. Comprises 14 fully furnished brick chalets (sgl, dbl, trpl & qdpl), including 9 self-catering, with fully-equipped open-plan kitchens. All chalets with DSTV. Internet access in office. Dinner (SZL70) available on request. Family-friendly restaurant/bar. Tranquil rural setting near road, with pineapple fields, small dam & birdlife. B&B rates available. **$$**

⌂ **Yellow Ribbon Guesthouse** (sleeps 10) ☏ 2518 7063; m 7602 2375; e bookings@ yellowribbonguesthouse.com; www. yellowribbonguesthouse.com. B&B in 2 twin bedrooms & 2 sgl rooms, sharing bathroom, plus 1 dbl bedroom & 1 garden cottage, both en-suite. Lounge, DSTV, gardens with swimming pool & mountain view. Boardroom for 12. Whole house available for rent. Crammed with interesting décor & handicrafts, all for sale. **$$**

⌂ **Nyanza Cottages** (sleeps 23) ☏ 2528 3090; e info@nyanza.co.sz; www.nyanza.co.sz. Family-run self-catering farm 2km east of Swazi Candles (see page 187), attached to stables & animal rescue centre. 2 spacious, fully equipped, en-suite cottages set in secluded gardens, each with 2 bedrooms, plus sleeper couches & space for extra beds if required; family/backpackers lodge, with 1 dbl en-suite room & small kitchenette, plus communal dorm with 6 bunk beds, 1 bathroom & small kitchen; fully furnished, 6-berth caravan with veranda, cooking facilities & separate ablution block; also space for camping. Mellow & friendly, with rustic farmyard feel. Spacious grounds, with birdlife, indigenous trees & farm animals (horses, donkeys, dogs, cats, chickens, peacocks, etc). Great for children. Riding available on farm & around local area (see page 188). **$–$$**

⌂ **Sundowners Backpackers and Lodge** (28 beds) ☏ 2528 3829; e swazilandbackpackers@realnet.co.sz. Mellow backpackers in converted Portuguese farm among orchards. Off MR103, opposite MR18 turn-off to Swazi Candles. 2 dorms (10-bed & 6-bed), & dbl, trpl or 4-bed rooms. Spacious campground: tents provided or bring your own. Also: lively pub with music & board games, pool table, large swimming pool, internet, shared bathrooms, large kitchen, laundry facilities & security. Friendly, helpful staff, clued-up on local activities. Meals on request. Attractive & well lit, with murals, chill-out areas & generally a young, laid-back vibe. Located 4km from nearest shops. Kombi stop outside. Sundowners Lodge bar & restaurant next door. **$–$$**

WHERE TO EAT Malkerns itself has no eating places of note, beyond a few local street cafés and take-aways, and a hot food counter at the Pick 'N' Pay supermarket. However, there are one or two good restaurants nearby.

✗ Malandela's Farmhouse Restaurant and Pub ✆2528 3115; ⏲ daily 11.00–15.00 & 18.00–late, closed Christmas & Boxing Day. Excellent restaurant that was the 1st building block of the Malandela's complex (see below). Original à la carte menu features farmhouse-style meals at mid-range prices, prepared with fresh local produce & home baking, including good vegetarian options. 3-course set menu available for large groups. Dining inside or on terrace. Rustic ambience, overlooking sugar-cane & pineapple fields, with botanical gardens & fine view. Popular pub next door has draught beer, DSTV & regular curry nights. Big blazes in huge outdoor fireplace on winter nights. Best to book.

✗ Sambane Restaurant and Tea Garden ✆7604 2035; ⏲ daily 08.00–17.00. Popular restaurant & coffee shop at heart of Swazi Candles complex (see page 187). Imaginative menu features inexpensive & original light meals, such as Hawaiian mozzarella wraps & Cajun calamari. Variety of coffees & excellent home baking, sumptuous cakes. Pleasant atmosphere enhanced by Swazi décor, hand-woven mats & original mosaics.

✗ Sundowners Lodge ✆2528 3059; m 7607 5363. Roadside pub & grill located just off MR103 beside Sundowners Backpackers (see opposite). Standard mid-range menu includes steaks, burgers, salads, platters & various 'combos' (seafood platter for 2: SZL240). Lively; popular with business travellers – expect the TV turned up loud. Accommodation available.

✗ Willows Lodge (see above) Family-friendly restaurant & bar in quiet rural location just off Malkerns Road. Serves a variety of inexpensive meals.

WHAT TO SEE AND DO

Mahlanya Market Mahlanya has come to mean 'madman'. The name is said to derive from an occasion on which King Sobhuza conversed with a deranged individual he encountered on this spot. I have never noticed any conspicuous insanity here, however, just vast quantities of fruit and vegetables piled up at what is Swaziland's most impressive fresh produce market. Drop in during the fruit season – best from December to April – and you will find avocados and mangoes of a size, quality and cheapness that would shame your local supermarket back home. Nowhere else have I tasted pineapples so sweet, and all year round the stalls are heaped with onions, tomatoes, pumpkins and other goodies fresh from the local fertile soils.

Hot snacks, including roasted mealies, grilled chicken and boiled groundnuts (usually in a twist of newspaper), are sold at the vendors' stalls around the parking area. A parade of local shops behind the market includes a small supermarket, general store, garage and filling station, and you will need to dodge an army of yellow-bibbed MTN airtime vendors. There is also a bus and kombi rank – Mahlanya is a transport hub, equidistant between Manzini, Ezulwini and Malkerns – so beware of traffic.

Malandela's (✆528 3423; e info@malandelas.com; www.malandelas.com) When I first visited this tourist hotspot during the mid-1990s it was simply a lovely restaurant that served the best food between Manzini and Ezulwini, with a lively pub next door, where locals went for a pint and a chance to berate their team on the sports television. Since then, however, it has added an internet café, a funky boutique, a gorgeous botanical garden and an extraordinary performing arts venue, House on Fire, that scarcely seems to belong in sleepy little Swaziland. It has also sprouted excellent bed and breakfast accommodation (see opposite), located discreetly away from the action but designed with the same flair as everything else, while the handicraft outlet next door, Gone Rural, has blossomed into a major industry, supporting hundreds of local families and exporting its products worldwide.

Malandela's started in 1974 as a market stall for the Thornes, a local farming family. First they added a pub and then a wine cellar. Earth from the excavations was used to build the restaurant and shops, moulded with the organic contours

4

The annual Bushfire festival (*www.bush-fire.com*) is an explosion of performing arts – including live music, theatre, poetry and dance, and DJs – the likes of which Swaziland had never seen before its inaugural year in 2006. Held on multiple stages within and around House on Fire, this festival is Swaziland's biggest annual entertainment experience and has become one of the top international festivals in Africa. Major artists from all over southern Africa – and some from further afield – come to perform, drawing up to 20,000 visitors over the three days of the festival. Bushfire has created not only a platform for the development of the arts in Swaziland, but also raises funds for one of the country's most pressing social causes, donating all profits to orphan sponsorship NGO Young Heroes (see page 143). You will also find film, workshops, craft and design, a Fair Trade market and a global food fair – in short, everything you'd expect from Swaziland's answer to Glastonbury.

and ochre hues of a traditional African settlement. Jiggs Thorne, the family's eldest son, returned from studying drama in South Africa with new creative influences, forming a local artists' collective and inspiring the flamboyant architecture of House on Fire. Happily, all this growth has not damaged the mellow vibe. While travellers hang out around the internet café and tour groups troop from restaurant to craft shop, the serenity of the sweeping lawns and sculpture gardens, with their blossom and birdsong, remains unruffled. It is worth popping in just to catch the atmosphere, even if you have no intention to buy, eat or watch anything at all.

House on Fire (*www.house-on-fire.com*) This unique outdoor performance arena and art gallery centres upon a sunken 'Afro-Shakespearian Globe Theatre'. Around its main stage are creative spaces on multiple levels for exhibitions, performances and whatever other forms of creative expression you might envisage. Constructed in an eclectic fantasy style with a healthy dose of humour – kind of Gaudi meets Terry Gilliam in an African village – it is embellished with mosaics, sculptures and inscriptions from numerous artists. Jiggs Thorne, who got the ball rolling, talks of 'cultural meeting points' that express 'harmony and contrast'. It all sounds a little chaotic in theory but is stunning in practice. Slipped discreetly into the nooks and crannies you will find sculpted thrones, benches and candle stands – all original work produced at an in-house studio by resident artists Shadrack Masuku, Phuzu Mthsali, Noah Mdluli and Thorne himself, and on sale to visitors and collectors. The stage hosts an ever-changing line-up of local and international artists, from reggae bands to performance poets, and every May is the venue for Bushfire, one of Africa's liveliest music festivals (see box above). Find out from the website and local listings what's on during your visit.

Gone Rural (*www.goneruralswazi.com*) Beside Malandela's are the showrooms and workshop of this award-winning weaving enterprise, which uses *lutinzi* grass – the material that is plaited into rope for beehive huts – to create place mats, baskets, table runners and other home products. From humble beginnings it has grown into an international company, with more than 1,000 outlets in 32 countries, and provides employment for over 730 rural women – most of whom work from home, so have no problems with childcare. A non-profit organisation, Gone Rural boMake, helps support the women's communities through health and education programmes. It's worth visiting the showroom just for the wonderful rustic aroma of all that woven grass. Take a look around the workshop, where you might catch some of the women finishing their work.

Zoggs (↘ *7605 5015;* e *zoggs@posix.co.sz*) Another string to Malandela's creative bow, this funky little boutique has a range of bold and quirky products in various colourful materials, from hand-painted watering cans to papier-mâché piggy banks. All are made by local women.

Internet café (↘ *7528 3423*) Malandela's internet café and information centre (aka Ziggy's) is a hotspot for any traveller in need of touching base, with Wi-Fi, phone, fax, scanning, picture downloading, CD burning and typing services. It also has a helpful tourist information service, with decent maps, and doubles as the bookings office for All Out Africa (see page 141).

Swazi Candles complex This is not a condition that requires a psychotherapist but rather a cluster of handicraft outlets around the showroom and workshop of Swazi Candles, a highly successful local enterprise. It is a popular tourist spot, so you may well meet a coach tour pulling up in the car park, but there's space for everyone beneath the huge jacarandas that shade the large courtyard and car park. You will also find a children's playground, and the excellent Sambane Café (see page 185), where you can recover from your retail exertions over coffee and cake – or something more substantial.

Swazi Candles (↘ *2528 3219/3263; www.swazicandles.com*) If you spot one Swazi item in an ethnic gift shop back home, there's a good chance it will be one of these little wax masterpieces. Inside the converted farmhouse workshop you can watch the candle makers shaping and colouring their exquisite creations. Plastic bowls of water fill steadily with bobbing piles of elephants, tortoises, eggs, pillars and other popular lines as individual hand finishing ensures that no two candles are the same. The colouring technique, known as *millefiori* ('thousand flowers') was developed centuries ago by Venetian glass blowers but has transferred seamlessly to wax. A hard veneer means that the candles melt only on the inside when lit, creating a translucent stained-glass window effect for the luminous colours.

The enterprise started in an old dairy cowshed in 1981, the brainchild of two South African art graduates, who soon built up a skilled Swazi team around them. By the mid-'90s the workshop employed over 200 local people and exported candles all over the world, working strictly to Fair Trade principles. Like all Swaziland handicrafts for export, Swazi Candles are not cheap (from SZL25 for the smallest candle), but you'll get better deals direct from the showroom here (which displays a seductive selection) than back home. Look out for damaged or flawed 'seconds', sold at a discount, which often have a charm of their own.

Other handicrafts Beside the candle factory you'll find studios and boutiques for several other handicraft enterprises: Rosecraft Weaving sells fine mohair garments, produced at its workshop in the Egebeni Hills (see page 243); Amarasti sells beaded hand-crafted bags in bold cloth designs, embroidered by rural women; and Umgololo Gallery has a broad selection of handicrafts and curios. There is also a bookshop and gift shop, and, in the main courtyard, some more informal craft stalls where you can sometimes watch the wood carvers at work.

Nyanza Riding Stables (m *7621 4181;* e *info@nyanza.co.sz; www.nyanza.co.sz*) The stables at Nyanza Farm (see page 184) are home to some 50 horses, many of them 'rescue' animals, rehabilitated after a life of neglect, and offer trails and rides for all levels. Owners Wandy Williams and Ann Davies are devoted to their animals, as you will see from the horse biographies on their website, and the charmingly ramshackle grounds are full of livestock of one kind or another. The horses range from thoroughbreds to Basuto ponies, and include ex-racehorses, advanced competition ponies and a number of Boerperds – a hardy South African breed that dates from the first Dutch settlers in 1652. Trails run straight from the property into the surrounding farmland. They vary from one-hour walks for beginners and young children, to whole-day rides for experienced riders, and include sundown trails and lunch packages with a break at Malandela's (see page 185). Horses are geared to each rider's age and ability. You can book lessons, and even organise a five-day course that includes accommodation (*rides and group lessons start from SZL190 per hour & must be booked 24hrs in advance*). The farm stalls at the entrance gate sell excellent homemade preserves.

Baobab Batik (ᐰ *2528 3242;* e *info@baobab-batik.com; www.baobab-batik.com*) This local enterprise produces a range of patterned fabrics using melted wax and dyes, including clothing, cushion covers, wall hangings and table linen. The business started in 1991, employing ten local women, but has since tripled its workforce and has outlets in several places around Swaziland. Visitors can take a peek around the workshop at Under African Skies, located beside the south entrance to Mlilwane Game Sanctuary at the end of the turn-off to Vickery Seedlings on the MR27, and watch the batiks being made. Live demonstrations are also sometimes held in the Baobab Batiks shop at Malandela's (see page 185).

Malkerns This small settlement gets its name from Malcolm Kerns Stuart, a turn-of-the-century trader who settled in these parts. Today it is dominated by the Swazican canning factory, about 1km north along the MR27, which accounts for most local employment. There's not much for visitors, beyond a small parade of shops on the south side of the MR27, with a supermarket, filling station, garage and bus rank. Opposite, on the north side, is a post office, telephone exchange and the Malkerns Club (ᐰ *2528 3018*), which offers private facilities – including a swimming pool, bar and squash courts – free to members. Non-members must pay an entrance fee of cSZL20. The club's cricket pitch was used for the cricketing scenes in *Wah-Wah* (see page 91), complete with a hastily assembled cast of local extras in pads and whites. Behind the shops is a high-density township, which makes a stark contrast to the expansive colonial bungalows that house most local commercial farmers.

MATSAPHA

Matsapha is Swaziland's industrial hub. As such, it is of limited interest to the average sightseer – other than for its airport, which at present provides the only aerial route in and out of Swaziland. The industrial estate grew up in the 1960s, starting with a cardboard box factory. Today its labyrinth of factories, warehouses and offices is home to such big hitters as Conco, the Coca-Cola concentrate plant, and Fashion International, a garment manufacturer that employs over 1,250 people. Other notable industries include Macmillan Swaziland, the country's leading publisher and supplier of school textbooks, and Swaziland Beverages, which produces local soft drinks and beers. A railway terminus at the heart of the

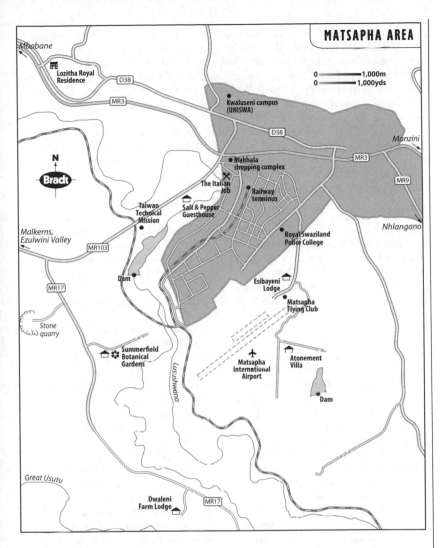

Mbabane

Lozitha Royal
Residence

D38

MR3

Kwaluseni campus
(UNISWA)

D38

Manzini

MR3

N

Bradt

Mahhala
shopping complex

MR9

The Italian
Job

Railway
terminus

Taiwan
Technical
Mission

Salt & Pepper
Guesthouse

Malkerns,
Ezulwini Valley

MR103

Nhlangano

Royal Swaziland
Police College

Dam

MR17

Esibayeni
Lodge

Stone
quarry

Matsapha
Flying Club

Summerfield
Botanical
Gardens

Lusushwana

Matsapha
International
Airport

Atonement
Villa

Dam

Great Usutu

Dwaleni
Farm Lodge

MR17

estate provides a southeast freight link on Swaziland Railways to the Maputo and
Durban/Richards Bay lines. Just to the west is the Taiwan Technical Mission, which
is of vital economic importance to Swaziland (see box on page 191).

The small Mahhala shopping complex has a number of places to eat – mostly of
the cheap, cheerful and take-away variety (catering for a large workforce on short
lunch breaks). There are also some high-density residential areas, including an
incongruous cluster of apartment blocks along the MR3 just to the east. Unless you
live here, however, there is no real need to stay the night – especially with Manzini
just 6km to the east, and Malkerns and Ezulwini a short drive back west. Most
hotels lie out of town or around the airport.

GETTING THERE AND AWAY Matsapha is effectively an industrial western suburb
of Manzini, its sprawl of development continuing unbroken to the larger town.
Arriving from the west along the MR103, you first pass a right turn south signed to

Summerfield Botanical Gardens (see opposite), just after a large quarry. Continuing, it is a further 4.5km along the MR103, past the Taiwan Technical Mission, to a large roundabout, where the road joins the MR3 Mbabane–Manzini highway. A turning leads into the industrial estate just before the roundabout. Arriving from the Manzini direction, you turn left into Matsapha at a junction some 300m before the roundabout. The northbound exit from this roundabout leads to the UNISWA campus at Kwaluseni (see page 192).

Matsapha International Airport lies 3km due south of the industrial complex. You can navigate there through Matsapha by following signs from the roundabout. It is easier, however, to turn south off the MR3 at a signed junction some 2.5km east of the roundabout. Follow this road (Police College Road) until you reach the airport turn-off after 1.5km on the right.

WHERE TO STAY
Upmarket
⌂ **Summerfield Botanical Gardens and Exclusive Resort** (25 rooms, sleeps 66) ☎2518 4693; e info@summerfieldresort.com; www.summerfieldresort.com. Upmarket resort located 6km west of Matsapha among lush botanical gardens. Accommodation in 13 executive suites (2 person), 13 luxury suites (2 person), 5 garden villa suites (2 person) & 1 Dove's Nest Private Lodge (2 bedrooms/4 person). All rooms are spacious & lavishly furnished. Facilities include AC, DSTV, Wi-Fi, bar/fridge, espresso machine, large en-suite bathroom, & large patio. The garden villa suites (the most exclusive) come with separate his/her dressing rooms, private garden & butler service on request. Fine dining at Red Feather Pool Bar (b/fast), Summer Terrace Bistro & Grand Palm Cascades Restaurant. Also: swimming pool, billiard lounge & 100ha of botanical gardens (see opposite). An extraordinary place, unlike anywhere else in Swaziland. Its opulent style, with extravagant architecture (sculpted animals, water features, towering thatched pavilions) & lavish décor (elaborate carved furniture, Hollywood prints) may be a little too much for some. But you can't help but admire the energy & ambition. Besides, the food is sumptuous, the service excellent, the grounds gorgeous & the beds *very* comfortable. **$$$$–$$$$$**

Mid-range and budget
⌂ **Atonement Villa** (6 rooms) ☎2550 2514; m 7602 1427; e atonementvilla@swazi.net; www.visitswazi.com/atonementvilla. Small lodge near airport. Comprises 5 bedrooms, each with en-suite bathroom, private balcony, AC & DSTV. Queen suite comes with gym, Wi-Fi, walk-in wardrobe & jacuzzi. 2 lounges. Meals in à la carte dining room & on verandas. Pedicures & other beauty treatments available. Secure parking. Located off Airport Rd on Tubungu Estate; turn off directly opposite Esibayeni Lodge, then follow signs after 1km. **$$–$$$**

⌂ **Esibayeni Lodge** (sleeps 300) ☎2518 4848; m 2605 1650; e esibayenilodge@swazi.net; www.esibayenilodge.com. Big hotel 500m from airport. Accommodation comprises 200 en-suite rooms with TV & AC (most twin, some dbls); 28 thatched 1- & 2-bedroom self-catering chalets with kitchen & private veranda; 2 backpackers dorms (40-bed; separate dorms for men & women) with in-house ablutions. Also: free Wi-Fi, 2 restaurants, 3 bars, 2 swimming pools, braai/BBQ area, children's playground, tropical gardens & extensive conference facilities (taking up to 2,000 people total). A very large establishment that is geared towards large groups, conferences, weddings & events. Good value but a little short on character. **$–$$$**

⌂ **Dwaleni Farm Lodge** (12 chalets, sleeps 37) ☎2550 4380; m 7690 3008; e dwalenifarmlodge@swazi.net. Farm property west of Matsapha on MR17, 5km south of Summerfield. B&B accommodation in 12 en-suite chalets, individually decorated, with twin beds & DSTV. Restaurant with open-air dining area. Swimming pool, farmyard animals (including ostrich, peacocks, guinea fowl) & walks to nearby Usutu River. Pleasant, rustic atmosphere. Good for children. **$$**

⌂ **Salt and Pepper Guesthouse** (8 rooms, sleeps 12) ☎2404 2106; m 7604 8591. Cheap & lively local hangout with restaurant, sports bar & pool table. **$–$$**

WHERE TO EAT Matsapha has various cafés and take-aways at the Mahhala shopping centre and scattered around the industrial estate. After office hours, however, the place largely closes down, and for a good meal you are best off heading further afield to Summerfield or beyond.

✕ **Summerfield** See below. Excellent dining for guests & non-guests alike. Palm Cascades Restaurant is an impressive dbl-storey African-style thatched pavilion, with ornate classical embellishments, surrounded by lakes, walkways & water features. A fine à la carte menu has probably the greatest international variety in Swaziland, from Portuguese seafood & tequila-flamed chicken to 'Tantalising tastes of Thailand' & 'Chinese wok wonders'. Good vegetarian options & superb desserts (especially the stuffed pancakes). Lavish b/fasts are served at the Red Feather Pool Bar, while the Summer Terrace Bistro offers lighter lunches & English cream teas. A place to see & be seen: high prices, but good food & excellent service – especially given how far the waiters have to walk.

✕ **The Italian Job** ✆2518 6063; e Radicalatin@ gmail.com; ⏲ Mon–Sat 08.30–17.30. Newish Italian restaurant on King Mswati Av at centre of industrial complex, with a good reputation for homemade pasta & pizzas. Karaoke on Wed.

SHOPPING AND OTHER PRACTICALITIES The Mahhala shopping complex comprises a parade of shops beside the roundabout at the main entrance to the industrial estate. There are supermarkets, newsagents, pharmacies, mobile phone and clothes stores, and several take-aways – among them, the inevitable KFC, which is a hangout for local youth. There is also a post office and banks. In front of the shops is a large car park and filling station, from where you can exit straight onto the roundabout. Matsapha police station is located at Sigodveni, on the road to the airport and, since the Royal Swaziland Police College is just a little further down this road, you should find no shortage of new recruits to help you out.

WHAT TO SEE AND DO
Summerfield Botanical Gardens Summerfield is well worth visiting, whether or not you can afford its lavish menus and luxury suites (see above). This unique

FRIENDS IN THE EAST

The oriental architecture and paddy fields of the Taiwan Technical Mission along the approach road to Matsapha may cause visiting motorists the odd double take. But Swaziland's close relationship with Taiwan – aka the Republic of China – is of great economic importance to the kingdom. It all started in 1968, when newly independent Swaziland set out on a diplomatic charm offensive around the world. Its overtures were welcomed by Taiwan, whose claim to sovereign status is not recognised by the UN and has long infuriated its huge neighbour, the *People's* Republic of China. Today, Swaziland is one of only 23 nations worldwide that recognise Taiwan's sovereignty, and the kingdom's loyalty has been rewarded by aid, investment and technical support. The Taiwanese have funded many of Swaziland's most important recent infrastructure and tourism projects, and have also poured money into agriculture and industry, notably several major textiles plants in Matsapha. State visits have reinforced diplomatic ties: King Mswati III to Taiwan in 2006 and Taiwanese premier Chen Shui-bian to Swaziland in 2007. Doubters fear that this love-in may not be entirely in Swaziland's interests, however, especially since China – the People's Republic – has lately become the dominant overseas player on the African stage.

attraction began as a botanical garden, its restaurants and accommodation an afterthought that arose from the suggestions of visitors. It is the brainchild of local businessman John Carmichael, former Minister for Public Works and Transport, who, upon retiring from politics, threw himself into his lifelong passion for horticulture. The 100ha property, located in the Nokwane Valley and prominently signed down the MR17 about 4.5km west of Matsapha, was a wasteland when Carmichael acquired it in 1984. A laborious landscaping process followed, with hundreds of tonnes of topsoil trucked in, dams excavated and precious trees all planted by hand. Droughts and bushfires brought early setbacks but today, from the moment you turn down the long jacaranda-lined entrance avenue, it is clear that a dream has been realised.

The gardens are now a designated national conservancy, with Swaziland's largest collection of plants. Wander the grounds and you'll find indigenous trees, cycads, palms, succulents and orchards all in separate collections. Despite the manicured feel, Carmichael has been guided by the ecological importance of preserving indigenous plants, and his success to this end is reflected in the wildlife around the grounds – a chorus of painted reed frogs and the mellifluous songs of white-browed robin-chats were especially prominent during my visit. The extravagant buildings, lakes and water features laid out among the greenery all bear the stamp of the owner's expansive imagination. Their in-your-face opulence and somewhat eclectic medley of styles may not be to all tastes. Yet behind the grand façade is a commitment both to the local environment and the local community: Carmichael employs over 90 people in the gardens alone and helps provide education to the workers' children. Talk to the charming owners and you can't help but share their excitement at what they have achieved.

Matsapha International Airport Swaziland's only airport is overdue for replacement by the spanking new Sikuphe Airport (see page 248). But until the latter is completed – which, at the time of writing, did not look imminent – then this facility 3km south of Matsapha remains the only means of flying in and out of the country. Don't be confused if you read about 'Manzini Airport' on airline schedules: it refers to the same place. Flights from here once served much of the region – including Maputo, Maseru, Harare and Lusaka. Since the demise of Royal Swazi Airways, however, the only scheduled destination is Johannesburg, to which daily flights depart by Airlink (see page 108) on a Jetstream 41.

'International' it may be, but this airport is no Heathrow. Founded in the 1960s, it has just a single tarred runway – which, at 2,600m, is not large enough for the biggest international jets – and one small terminal building with a snack shop, airline counter and the offices of Imperial and Avis car rentals. Wi-Fi hotspots have recently been installed but, given the imminence of the new airport, there are no plans for further development. Outside is a large car park, and a few hundred yards back down the road the Matsapha Flying Club, a relaxed watering hole where members – and, in my experience, pretty much anyone else – can grab a bite and a beer with a view of the runway.

Kwaluseni (University of Swaziland) The main campus of the University of Swaziland (UNISWA) is at Kwaluseni, 1km north of Matsapha (signed off the MR3/MR103 roundabout). This is the university's nerve centre, housing its central offices, five faculties, the Institute of Distance Education (IDE), the Institute of Post-Graduate Studies and the main library. Its other campuses are at the Faculty of Agriculture at Luyengo (see page 240) and the Faculty of Health Sciences in Mbabane.

UNISWA is a historical offshoot of the joint University of Botswana, Lesotho and Swaziland (UBLS), which was established in 1965 at the Roma campus near Maseru, Lesotho. Independence in 1968 prompted the three countries to review their inherited colonial education system and, in particular, the capacity of UBLS to provide the higher education required by a new generation of officials and professionals. Following a 1970 report, which recommended establishing separate campuses in each country and developing a unified higher education and vocational training policy, the three governments drew up plans for new campuses in Gaborone (Botswana) and at Kwaluseni. Donor funding came from, among others, the governments of the UK, US and Netherlands. In 1975 unrest on the Roma campus caused Lesotho to pull out of the UBLS plans, leaving the University of Botswana and Swaziland, which was established in 1976, with one college in each country. With student numbers rising, however, it soon became clear that each country required its own independent institution. In 1982 they agreed to go their own ways, and that year UNISWA was created in Swaziland by an act of parliament.

MANZINI

Mbabane and Manzini are chalk and cheese in temperament. Perhaps it's the weather. Mbabane, up in the cool highveld, is the seat of administration and diplomacy, and has a measured character to match; Manzini, down in the sweatier middleveld, is the commercial hub, and is more heated and feisty. Its general African hustle and bustle has none of the colonial reserve that Mbabane inherited from the Brits. And, being so preoccupied with its own affairs, Manzini has never worried much about outsiders. It has few tourist attractions, and most visitors – unless they have friends or business here – tend not to stick around much longer than it takes to do the shopping, change buses or top up the tank.

Manzini was known for decades as Bremersdorp after early concessionaire Arthur Bremer, who in 1886 bought up the first trading post here. In 1890, Bremer sold his properties to the British to use as their colonial headquarters, on condition that the new settlement bore his name. The town served this purpose until the outbreak of the second Anglo–Boer War (see page 57) when, in 1902, the departing Boers razed it to the ground. The British promptly shifted their administrative headquarters to Mbabane, where government remains to this day. Bremersdorp was quickly rebuilt and soon developed into the country's commercial, agricultural and transportation heart. In 1915, the Riverside Hotel – the first since the reconstruction – opened on the banks of the Mzimene River, which flows through town. (The historic hotel has since been replaced by a shopping mall; there is little sentimentality in Manzini.) In the 1920s the agricultural show came to town and, now recast as the Swaziland International Trade Fair, it has become the country's best-attended annual event. In 1960 Manzini got its Swazi name back (it was named after local chief Manzini Motha) and in 1994 the burgeoning town was declared a city. Today its population stands at around 100,000 making it marginally bigger than Mbabane.

The heart of Manzini is on two parallel one-way streets: Ngwane Street running east and Nkoselhusaza Street running west. These are the two lanes of the MR3 highway, which divides as it passes through town. Here you will find the main bus rank, the bustling Bhunu Mall, and numerous shops, services, filling stations, hotels and eateries. Nearby is Manzini Market – the liveliest in the country – the Catholic cathedral and Jubilee Park. You can bypass the town centre entirely, however, by following Central Distributor Road, which loops north off the MR3 as you enter

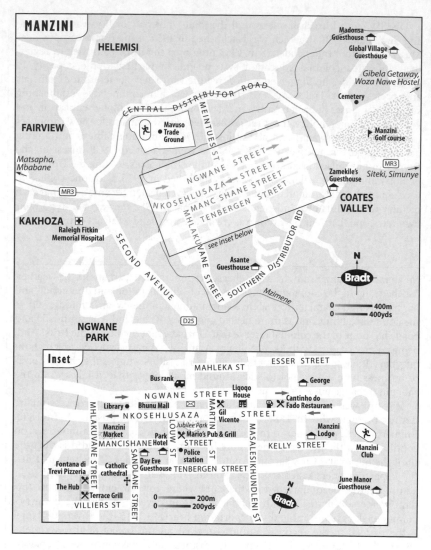

town from east or west. Near the western end of this loop is Mavuso Trade Ground, which has been developed as part of Swaziland's Millennium project and is home to the Swaziland International Trade Fair, plus various sporting events and facilities.

Manzini's residential areas encircle the centre. The ramshackle KaKhoza township sprawls alongside the MR3 to the west. More middle-class districts, such as Fairview and Helemisi estates, lie to the north – the former developed by the British in 1964 as Swaziland's first integrated residential neighbourhood. To the east is the upscale neighbourhood of Coates Valley and to the south, along Second Avenue, the large lower- and middle-class Ngwane Park township. Crammed among these neighbourhoods are pockets of informal settlement, where people live in poverty on marginal land with few amenities.

Today, residents of other parts of Swaziland – particularly expatriates in Mbabane – may tell you that Manzini is a dangerous place, best avoided. This generalisation is rather over the top. Like most of Swaziland, people here are usually helpful and friendly, and I personally have never experienced any kind of problem. Nonetheless, it remains true that tourists are a rarer sight than in Mbabane or Ezulwini, and conspicuous tourist behaviour – such as waving a camera around – will attract more attention, not all of it desirable. You are best advised not to wander around after dark unless you are with a trusted local friend.

GETTING THERE AND AWAY Manzini is at the centre of Swaziland's transport network. It lies on the main east–west MR3 highway, along which it is a mere 35km (30-minute) drive west to Mbabane. At a large junction 2km west out of town, a left turn leads south to Nhlangano on the MR9 (see *Chapter 6*). Another left turn 1km later leads to Matsapha International Airport, just 15 minutes' drive from town. In Matsapha itself, the MR3 passes over a roundabout, from where the MR103 leads to the Ezulwini Valley, offering a slower (but more interesting) alternative route to Mbabane.

Eastbound, Manzini is your gateway to the lowveld. Some 10km east of town is a large road junction at Hhelehhele, from where a right turn leads southeast along the MR8 to Big Bend (see *Chapter 8*) while the MR3 continues straight on towards Siteke (see *Chapter 7*). If taking the latter, you will reach a junction at Mafutseni, after 10km, from where a back road leads to Piggs Peak via Bhalekane. This is a pretty route, although not as quick as going via Mbabane.

All these routes are well serviced by bus or kombi. Downtown Manzini is very compact and you can walk from one end to the other in 15 minutes. Getting to the suburbs is trickier. Kombis visit some areas, but better-off neighbourhoods have little use for public transport so you may need to take a taxi. These use fixed prices, so ask the driver before getting your ride how much it will cost.

WHERE TO STAY Manzini has plenty of places to stay, although many are more the domain of the business traveller or contract worker than the tourist.

Mid-range

⌂ **Asante Guesthouse** (10 rooms, sleeps 30) Corner Southern Distributor & Lugagane roads; \2505 3556; m 7673 5718; e info@restaurantmarimba.com; www.asanteswazi.com. Rooms comprise 3 family suites, 4 sgls & 3 dbls, each with en-suite bathroom, AC, DSTV, Wi-Fi & tea/coffee. Rooms individually decorated with pan-African cultural themes. Marimba restaurant serves good range of African dishes. Located short walk south of town centre in an attractive Cape Dutch-style building. Meeting room, conference facilities, guest lounge & braai/BBQ facilities. Pool available next door. Tranquil vibe. **$$–$$$**

⌂ **Global Village Guesthouse** (25 rooms, sleeps 50) \2505 2226; e info@globalvillage.co.sz; www.globalvillage.co.sz. Clean, comfortable B&B accommodation in quiet Madonsa suburb, 2km northeast of city centre (north of golf course; follow signs from Central Distributor Rd). Rooms comprise dbls, sgls & king suites, all with DSTV,

AC, tea/coffee & room service. À la carte restaurant serves pizzas, international & African fusion dishes indoors or on pool terrace. Bar, swimming pool & conference facilities. Runs local tours & excursions. **$$–$$$**

⌂ **The George Hotel** (53 rooms, sleeps 75) Corner Ngwane & Du Toit sts; \2505 2260; e info@tgh.sz; www.tgh.sz. Rooms comprise 45 standard, 6 luxury & 1 exclusive suite, all with DSTV, AC, tea/coffee & safe. Good dining, with buffet & set menus in 3 restaurants, light meals in coffee shop, & drinks in Egg Yolk pub & sports bar. Sun terrace lunch popular with families. Also: pool & gardens, off-street parking, conference room, business centre (internet access slow) & spa with range of treatments. Formerly the Tums George Hotel, this is the most popular hotel in town. Clean & comfortable, with good food, & a popular hangout for locals, with entertainment (including bands & DJs) when fully booked. B&B rates. **$$–$$$**

Budget

🏠 **Park Hotel** (36 rooms, sleeps 50) 9 Mancishane St; ✆2505 7423/4/5; e expo@swazi. net; www.swaziplace.com/parkhotel. No-frills hotel on busy street in centre of town. Sgl & dbl rooms, all with DSTV, AC & en-suite. Restaurant for b/fast, lunch & dinner. Menu reflects Asian management (includes curries, tandoori chicken & halal dishes). Cheaper Sun rates. **$$$**

🏠 **Gibela Getaway** (6 cottages, sleeps 39) ✆2505 3024; e gibela@pureswazi.com; www. visitswazi.com/gibela. Rural self-catering out-of-town accommodation in 6 cottages, with sgls & dbls. All rooms/units have TV, bar/fridge, tea/ coffee, balcony, kitchen & en-suite bathroom. Also: swimming pool, TV, mountain view & small livestock. 20ha of bush on property offers hiking & birding. Located 10km east of Manzini: exit on Nkosehlusaza Rd (MR3); after 5km turn 1st left after Impilo Clinic; opposite Sunnyside supermarket turn right & follow signed dirt road for 5km. B&B rates available. **$–$$**

🏠 **Madonsa Guest House** (12 rooms, sleeps 22) ✆2505 5725; e info@madonsa.co.sz; www. madonsa.co.sz. Clean, comfortable B&B in quiet Madonsa suburb, 2km northeast of city centre (off Central Distributor Rd). All rooms with TV & en-suite bathroom. Swimming pool, bar, dining room & secure parking. Conference facilities for 40. Cooked meals on request (SZL75). Friendly atmosphere. **$–$$**

🏠 **Woza Nawe Hostel** ✆2505 8363; m 7604 4102 e wozanawe@realnet.co.sz. Friendly, rural backpackers lodge east of Manzini run by 'Myxo' (Mxolisi Mdluli; see page 105). Clean & simple accommodation in 2 dorms & 2 private rooms in old 2-storey farmhouse. About 6km east of Manzini on MR3, past Manzini clinic on left: after Sunnyside supermarket take signed left turn to Myxos Backpackers, then turn left at T-junction & continue to the last house at the bottom (1.5km on dirt road). **$**

WHERE TO EAT Manzini is crammed with fast-food outlets, including the usual American and South African chains, plus cheaper local cafés and take-aways. Classier food is available at hotels in town, such as the George. Otherwise, there are one or two independent restaurants where you are assured of a good meal.

✕ **Cantinho do Fado Restaurant** Nkoseluhlaza St, next to Galp filling station; ✆2505 2958; ⊕ Wed–Mon 09.00–23.00. Lively Portuguese restaurant that opened in Nov 2010 & quickly gained a good reputation. Fresh Mozambique seafood & good pizzas. Specials include *feijoada portuguesa*, traditional bean stew & shellfish platter for 2 (SZL342). Medium–high prices. Extensive wine list. Live music Fri & Sat night.

✕ **Fontana di Trevi Pizzeria** The Hub shopping centre, Mhlakuvane St; ⊕ Mon–Sat 08.30–21.00, Sun 10.00–18.30. Good pizzas & pasta at mid-range prices. Also serves take-aways.

✕ **Gil Vicente** Ilanga Centre, Martin St; Tue–Sun 08.00–24.00. Imaginative Portuguese menu, with variety of authentic dishes. Medium–high prices; good service.

✕ **The Mongolian** Villiers St. The best Chinese food in town. Wide variety of inexpensive dishes.

✕ **Terrace Grill** Tenbergen St; ⊕ Mon– Sat 8.00–24.00, Sun 10.00–24.00. Sports bar that serves good Spanish & Portuguese food at mid-range prices.

NIGHTLIFE Many will warn you that Manzini's nightlife can be a little too lively for the newcomer and that, given the city's poor reputation for street crime after hours, you'd better off having a quiet night in. This guide will not dispute that, except to say that the happening spots these days include Y2K, Tiger City, Tinkers and Mario's Pub and Grill. If you want to give them a try, take some local friends with you.

SHOPPING AND OTHER PRACTICALITIES Manzini's main shopping mall, stores and most services are concentrated in the busiest part of town, and the best way to find what you need is to park where you can then head out on foot. The streets are lively, with pavement vendors, car-wash touts, shoeshine boys and music blasting from street speakers. There is also more conspicuous poverty, with a scattered underclass of beggars and street kids – especially on Ngwane Street and around the bus rank – entreating your charity. Nowhere is very far from anywhere else (you can walk the main street in 15 minutes), and the US-style grid makes the streets easier to navigate than Mbabane's.

Town centre You can find most of what you need on Ngwane Street, which is where you enter town on the MR3 from the west. Bhunu Mall, the city's largest shopping centre – and boasting Swaziland's first escalator – looms after a couple of blocks on your right. Here you will find a large Shoprite supermarket, clothes and shoe stores, stationers, a pharmacy and internet café. Diagonally opposite Bhunu Mall, further up Ngwane Street, is Manzini's main bus rank, with its attendant fruit and veg stalls. Continuing towards the George Hotel at the end, you will pass the smaller Manzini Shopping Mall on your left and, on the right, the main post office. There are also branches of Nedbank and Standard Bank here.

Cutting south onto the parallel westbound Nkoseluhlaza Street, you will find the back entrance to Bhunu Mall, plus more branches of Standard Bank and Nedbank. You will also pass Jubilee Park – a hangout for slightly dubious characters and best avoided at night. There is a public lavatory here, although I can't vouch for its quality. One block south of Nkoseluhlaza Street is Mancishane Street (where the traffic flows both ways again), home to Park Hotel plus several lively bars and restaurants, including Mario's Pub and Grill. Manzini Market (see page 198), at the western end, is well worth a visit.

The Hub For slightly more relaxed shopping you could try The Hub complex on Mhlakuvane Street, just south of the town centre and reached by taking the first right off Ngwane Street after entering town from the west. Here you'll find ample parking and numerous shops, including a large Spar supermarket. There are also several cafés and restaurants, including the Fontana di Trevi Pizzeria, and public lavatories downstairs.

General services
Banks Nedbank, FNB and Standard Bank have branches on Ngwane Street, Nkoseluhlaza Street and at The Hub.

Bus rank The main bus and kombi rank is on Ngwane Street (corner of Meintues Street). There is also another kombi rank at the western end of Tenbergen Street.

Communications Main Manzini post office (⊕ *Mon–Fri 08.00–16.00, Sat 08.00–12.00*) on Ngwane Street, with internet café attached. Internet cafés also on Mancishane Street and in Bhunu Mall. George Hotel has free Wi-Fi in public areas.

Filling stations Large Galp filling station on Ngwane Street and Total station on Nkoseluhlaza Street. Other filling stations and garages located on the roads in and out of town.

Hospitals Raleigh Fitkin Memorial Hospital (✆ *2505 2211*); National TB Hospital (✆ *2505 5170*); Manzini Clinic Private Hospital (✆ *2505 7430/8*)

Police station Corner of Mancishane and Louw streets.

WHAT TO SEE AND DO

Manzini Market (⏰ *Mon–Fri 07.00–17.00*) Sprawled across the eastern end of Mancishane Street, near the junction with Mhlakuvane Street, this is Swaziland's largest and most interesting market. And it's a genuine working market – noisy, crowded and a little ripe at times – rather than a sanitised tourist version. Thursday is the day to go, when buyers and sellers arrive from all over the region. You can find pretty much anything here, from the usual arts and crafts, fruit and veg, clothing and household items to leather goods, traditional dress and some fascinating *inyanga* stalls, selling herbs and animal parts for *muti* (see box on page 81). Fabrics come from as far afield as Zimbabwe, Congo and Mozambique, and local tailors will knock you up a Swazi outfit. The prices are good, with excellent bargains if you nose around, and there is no hard sell to tourists.

Sports The Manzini Club (📞 *2505 2254*) has various facilities for members and their guests, including tennis courts, five-a-side football and a nine-hole golf course, which lies just beyond the roundabout at the eastern end of town. If you prefer watching sports, you could nip along to the Manzini Trade Fair Sports Ground, where the 5,000-seater stadium is the home venue for local football favourites Manzini Sundowns.

5

The Northwest

Swaziland's northwestern region is a stirring highveld landscape of airy, panoramic uplands. The muscular hills and dramatic river valleys form the eastern edge of South Africa's Drakensberg escarpment and are crowned by the nation's two highest peaks, Emlembe (1,862m) and Ngwenya (1,829m). Winter nights up here are chilly – temperatures occasionally falling below freezing – and mist often cloaks the higher ground. Indeed many visitors liken the climate and landscape of this part of Swaziland to Scotland. Especially Scottish ones.

The natural habitat of the highveld is Afromontane grassland (see page 8), with undulating hillsides, scattered rock outcrops and pockets of deep forest. In many places, however, this has given way to subsistence agriculture and, around Piggs Peak, some of the world's largest forestry plantations. Where the hills fall away – chiefly in the Nkomati river valley and in the far north – a band of middleveld brings a more subtropical climate and vegetation.

The region described in this chapter all falls within Hhohho province. It is sparsely populated, with Piggs Peak the only settlement of any size. The main attraction is Malolotja Nature Reserve, a genuine wilderness hailed by nature lovers as Swaziland's greatest natural asset. Others include Ngwenya, with its ancient mine and glass factory; Maguga Dam, a large lake created by the damming of the Nkomati River; Nsangwini, the site of Swaziland's best rock art; and Phophonyane Falls, an excellent little nature reserve. There is also horseriding, craft centres and – for those seeking relief from all that fresh air and exercise – the celebrated casino at Piggs Peak Hotel. And a special mention must go to Bulembu, on the mountainous South Africa border. This former asbestos-mining community has been reborn as a pioneering social-welfare project and visitor attraction, with its original mining infrastructure preserved as a living museum.

Northwest Swaziland is easily accessible from Mbabane, which lies at the very south of the region. Its attractions line up conveniently along the MR1 – or King Mswati II Highway – which starts 15km west of Mbabane and extends north to the South Africa border at Matsamo. You could also reach them from the South African side via one of three road borders, or on one of several roads from eastern Swaziland. Wherever you start from, it takes just around 1½ hours to drive the length of the MR1, so everywhere described in this chapter is within an easy day trip of Mbabane and the Ezulwini Valley. Spending a night or two is highly recommended, however, especially to do justice to the nature reserves.

NGWENYA

Ngwenya is the siSwati word for crocodile. The region that goes by this name is too high and cold to harbour any of these predatory reptiles, but it lies beneath

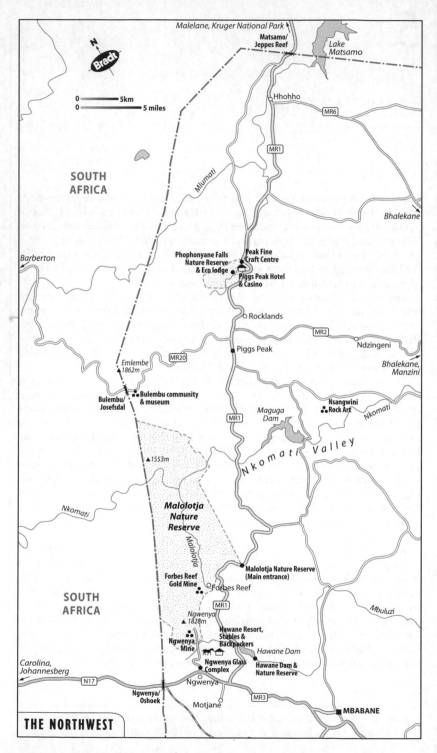

Malelane, Kruger National Park

Matsamo/
Jeppes Reef

Lake
Matsamo

N
Bradt

0 ————— 5km
0 ————— 5 miles

Hhohho

MR6

SOUTH
AFRICA

Mlumati

Bhalekane

Barberton

Phophonyane Falls
Nature Reserve
& Eco lodge

Peak Fine
Craft Centre

Piggs Peak Hotel
& Casino

○ Rocklands

MR2

Ndzingeni

Emlembe
▲1862m

MR20

■ Piggs Peak

*Bhalekane,
Manzini*

Bulembu/
Josefsdal

Bulembu community
& museum

Maguga
Dam

Nsangwini
Rock Art

Nkomati

MR1

Nkomati

▲1553m

N k o m a t i V a l l e y

*Malolotja
Nature
Reserve*

Malolotja

Malolotja Nature Reserve
(Main entrance)

Mbuluzi

SOUTH
AFRICA

Forbes Reef
Gold Mine

○ Forbes Reef

MR1

Ngwenya
▲1828m

*Carolina,
Johannesberg*

Ngwenya
Mine

Hawane Resort,
Stables &
Backpackers

Hawane Dam

N17

Ngwenya Glass
Complex

Hawane Dam &
Nature Reserve

Ngwenya/
Oshoek

○ Ngwenya

MR3

Motjane

■ **MBABANE**

THE NORTHWEST

Swaziland's second highest mountain, which is said to resemble a croc in profile. The mountain, which looms just to the north of the Ngwenya border post, is the southernmost and highest of the peaks along Swaziland's northwest boundary with South Africa and, like the others, lies within Malolotja Nature Reserve. Crocs or no crocs, Ngwenya today means three things to the visitor: the South Africa border, the ancient iron mine and the glass factory.

WHERE TO STAY AND EAT Ngwenya is a short drive from Mbabane and the Ezulwini Valley. It is also just a short distance south of Hawane Resort (see page 205), which has chalets, a backpackers hostel and restaurant. You could also try the following:

🏠 **Stan's Lodge** (9 rooms, sleeps 18) ☎2553 2041; m 7603 0505; e stanslodge@swazi.net; www.saharaonline.co.za. Located 5km south of Ngwenya along good gravel road & signed from junction of MR3 & MR1. Comfortable self-catering 1-bedroom chalets, each with fully equipped kitchen & fireplace (it gets cold here in winter). Open grounds in rural surroundings, with water

feature & braai area. Bar & swimming pool planned. B/fast available at SZL65. **$$$** 🍽 **Ngwenya Glass** ☎2442 4053/4142; www. ngwenyaglass.co.sz; ⏰ daily 08.00–16.00. This coffee shop on the terrace outside the glass factory has good coffee & savoury snacks, including excellent pancakes.

WHAT TO SEE AND DO
Ngwenya border The Ngwenya border is where most of Swaziland's overland visitors enter the country. It is open from 07.00–22.00 and lies 23km from Mbabane on the MR3. This is Swaziland's busiest road border, but entry formalities are generally painless provided you have the necessary documents for yourself and your vehicle (see *Red tape* on page 105). There is a cluster of services on the Swaziland side, including a filling station, phone boxes, vegetable stalls (I always find it helps to buy an onion or two as soon as I enter a country) and some fast-food take-aways. Perhaps most useful is the gaggle of yellow-bibbed MTN vendors, offering starter packs for local mobile phone network coverage (see page 137).

Ngwenya Glass Complex This popular tourist stop comprises the Ngwenya glass-blowing factory and showroom, plus a café and cluster of smaller handicraft outlets. It is laid out around well-tended lawns and walkways, with wheelchair ramps, a large-scale relief map of Swaziland, a children's play area and even wandering peacocks. As well as being an interesting diversion in its own right, it also makes a handy pit stop for visitors in search of gifts, curios and a decent coffee. The centre is well signed off the MR3 some 5–6km from the Ngwenya border on a road that continues to Ngwenya Mine.

Ngwenya Glass Factory (*www.ngwenyaglass.co.sz*; ⏰ *Mon–Fri 07.00–16.00*) Ngwenya Glass was originally a Swedish aid project established in 1979. Using EU funding, the Swedes built the factory, imported the machinery and trained local workers, sending a select few to study under the masters at the celebrated Kosta Boda glassworks in Sweden. In 1981, management of the factory – then known as Swazi Glass Craft – was transferred to the Swaziland Small Enterprise Development Corporation. Four years later production came to a halt. Fortunately the products had already acquired a devoted following of collectors – among them, the Prettejohn family from South Africa, who came to investigate what had happened to their beloved glass animals. By June 1987 they found themselves the proud new

5

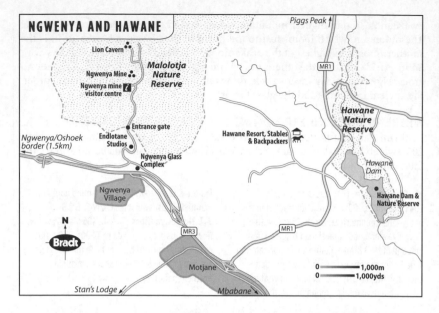

owners of Africa's only glass factory. In August, after renovating the machinery and tracking down staff, they resumed production. Today there are six of the original staff among the 70 workers, including master glass-blower Sibusiso Mhlanga, who has worked with some of the world's leading glass-blowers and now tutors new apprentices.

The factory's animal figurines, vases and tableware are exported worldwide, and its success has spawned a sister factory in Johannesburg. Perhaps the most impressive aspect of the whole enterprise, however, is that all these products are made from 100% recycled glass – primarily old soft-drinks bottles – collected from around Swaziland. Ngwenya Glass runs environmental awareness programmes with local schools, in which children join roadside clean-up campaigns in exchange for building materials and sponsorship of their soccer team. The company also donates a percentage of its profits to its conservation charity, the Ngwenya Rhino and Elephant Fund.

On weekdays, you can watch from a balcony over the factory floor as the glass-blowers breathe, spin and tease their miraculous creations into life straight from the glowing furnaces. The adjoining showroom has an impressive array of products, all displayed beneath the natural illumination of their own refracted light. Staff will wrap your fragile purchases securely and can make arrangements to ship any larger ones overseas. Keep an eye out for the discounted rejects, whose flaws – such as bubbles in the glass – often provide added charm. A small café outside sells good coffee and excellent pancakes.

Other craft shops Among the other handicraft outlets beside the glass factory are many of Swaziland's usual suspects, including Rosecraft, Tintsaba and Gone Rural (see *Arts and crafts*, page 86). Smaller local boutiques sell everything from ceramics and handmade chocolates to Swazi traditional dress – so no shortage of last-minute gift options, then, when rushing for the border.

Worth a look, in particular, is the Rocking Horse Company. Run by English carpenter/joiner Brian Roberts, the workshop showcases a selection of his original creations. Each horse comprises some 20 pieces, carved from local kiln-dried hardwoods and embellished with handmade tack. No two are the same, and a small cavity in the body allows personal items – photos, a lock of hair – to be sealed inside. If space allows, Brian also pops in a copy of the *Times of Swaziland* from the day on which the horse was finished. These may be a bit big for that border dash, but you can have them packaged for sea-freight.

Ngwenya Mine Continue up the road some 3km past Ngwenya Glass and you'll pass through the southern gate of Malolotja Nature Reserve (see page 207) to reach an archaeological site that is not only the most ancient in Swaziland but also has huge significance worldwide. Simply put, it is the oldest mine in the world, having been dated by archaeologists to at least 43,000 years ago. In the broader context of human prehistory, that's more than 10,000 years before Neanderthals disappeared from Britain and nearly 30,000 years before *Homo sapiens* first crossed from Asia into the Americas via the Bering Strait.

Today a ten-minute walk leads from the car park and visitor centre (see page 204) around the hillside and descends a metal walkway to what remains of the ancient mine – now a modest hole in the hillside known as Lion Cavern. The prehistoric mine is not to be confused with the much larger hole that you skirt in order to reach it. The latter, a huge flooded quarry, which dominates the site, was left by more modern industrial mining operations that finally ground to a halt in 1980.

Prehistoric mining The ancient mine was discovered in the 1960s by archaeologist Adrian Boshier, who was working for famous South African paleoanthropologist Raymond Dart, following reports of numerous Stone Age tools being found in the area. The tools were made of dolerite, foreign to the area, and turned out to be picks, choppers and other mining implements. They were found not only on the surface but also buried in deep depressions beneath thousands of tonnes of hacmatite (iron ore) left by mining during more recent times. Local people confirmed that it had been the custom to back-fill any such excavations in order to avoid offending ancestral spirits.

Below the ridge – the high points of which were named Lion and Castle after the two popular brands of South African lager – Boshier found shafts dug deep into the mountain. Their purpose was to extract another ore, called specularite, which does not occur at the surface. Specularite has a glittering sheen and was traditionally worn by chiefs and sacred diviners, who smeared it on their body and hair as a kind of glitter paint for ceremonial occasions. A pestle and mortar used to grind the specularite was also found.

Archaeologists already knew from the tools that there had been mining at Ngwenya as early as the Middle Stone Age. To establish a more precise date, they had charcoal nodules from some of the ancient workings radiocarbon-dated at Yale and Groningen, which confirmed a date of about 43,000–41,000BC. This made Ngwenya the oldest known mining operation in the world. It is thought the ores were mined until at least 23,000BC, with at least 1,200 tonnes of ore removed from Lion Cavern alone. The excavators also found the skeleton of a child buried at least 50,000 years ago, together with a shell pendant, which is arguably the first recorded evidence of personal adornment in our species.

Castle Cavern has long gone but Lion Cavern is now a national monument. A guide from the information centre will lead you on a short tour. There is no longer much to see but the guide's explanation of the history is fascinating and the views are superb. Don't expect to find any specularite – but rub a finger along the rock around the cave and you will soon discover the red ochre that made this area such a rich source of ceremonial cosmetics.

Iron and the modern mine Iron only began to figure in local technology and lifestyle once the first Bantu peoples reached Swaziland some 1,600 years ago and began smelting it. Huge quarries were dug into Ngwenya, from which thousands of tonnes of red haematite were removed. Before modern mining destroyed these quarries (see below), carbon dating placed their origins at around AD400. They continued to supply ore until the importing of cheap iron – probably sometime in the late 19th century – made it no longer worth the effort.

Modern commercial extraction began in 1946, when the Geological Mines and Survey department first started prospecting Ngwenya. By 1957 prospecting operations had identified reserves of high-grade (60–80%) ore of at least 30 million tonnes. The Anglo-American Corporation of South Africa, which held the concession, formed the Swaziland Iron Ore Development Corporation and started production in 1964. By 1977 some 20 million tonnes of high-grade hematite had been removed. This mining activity was highly destructive: as well as obliterating much archaeological evidence, it literally took the top off Ngwenya. Nonetheless, the SIODC deserves some credit for leaving untouched over one million tonnes of ore that lie directly beneath Lion Cavern.

Commercial mining brought with it many innovations, including a new road system, and a rail network that allowed export via the ports of Lourenço Marques (now Maputo) and Durban. The main overseas market was Japan. By 1977, however, war in Mozambique had put paid to the Maputo railway, and falling mine profits, caused by a decline in ore quality as the miners dug deeper, meant Durban had become too expensive an alternative. In 1980, Anglo-American closed down the mine and donated it to the Swaziland National Trust Commission (SNTC), which today manages it as a visitor attraction. Peer into the red-walled depths and you will see a 28m-deep lake at the bottom. This is filled from underground so does not vary in depth with the rains. It now provides a convenient location for training police divers.

Visitor centre (⏰ *daily: 08.00–16.00; entry SZL22*) The excellent Ngwenya visitor centre, opened in 2005, displays some fascinating exhibits, including samples of the various mineral deposits, archive photographs of early mining days, a life-size diorama of an Iron Age smelter at work, and a British-built steam engine that was shipped to Swaziland in 1913. A large relief map helps make sense of what you are about to see (or have just seen), and the information boards are provided in both English and siSwati so serve as well for local schoolchildren as for visiting tourists. Once you've paid your entry fee, the resident guide will also escort you to Lion Cavern. There is a picnic site, but to buy food or drink you'll need to return to the café at Ngwenya Glass, five minutes down the road.

Endlotane Studios On the short stretch of road between the mine and the glass factory you will find Endlotane Studios (✆ *2442 4196; www.swaziplace.com/ endlotane*). This German weaving enterprise employs around 40 Swazi women in creating high-quality mohair tapestries from merino wool, karakul and other specialist natural fibres. The designs feature animals and human figures inspired by San rock art, and make fine wall hangings. More contemporary Swazi motifs are derived from *emahiya* and other traditional clothing. The studios and workshop are open to visitors all week.

Hawane is the first stop of any note on the MR1 highway north to Piggs Peak. It consists of a resort that runs activities in and around Malolotja Nature Reserve (see page 207), and a small nearby nature reserve with a dam that is good for birdwatching and fishing. Hawane Resort is signed, along with Piggs Peak, at the turn-off from the MR3, some 8km from the Ngwenya border. Indeed, Hawane Resort's owners have a flair for publicity and you will find large signposts to it wherever you travel in Swaziland.

WHERE TO STAY AND EAT

🏠 **Hawane Resort** (23 chalets, sleeps 46) ☎2444 1744; m 7627 6714; e infohawane@ realnet.co.sz; www.hawane.co.sz. This Swazi village-style complex is arranged inside a large fenced boma. The 2-person en-suite thatched chalets (dbl & twin) resemble a cross between Swazi beehive hut & alpine ski chalet. They are well lit by glass-panelled front walls, with imaginative décor in earthy African tones, a bath/shower sculpted like a natural rock pool & huge beds. Family units each have 1 dbl bed & 2 sgls, & a bigger bathroom. All rooms have heaters (invaluable on a winter's night in the highveld). Though hardly remote – you can hear the road from your chalet – the place has a relaxed rural ambience, with hills & horses all around, & the landscaped grounds feature indigenous plants, water features & a swimming pool with a fine view. Also: restaurant (see below), stables, conference centre, internet at reception (but no Wi-Fi) & numerous local activities. Follow signs off the MR1, from where a good gravel road leads for 1km to the resort entrance. **$$$**

🏠 **Hawane Backpackers** (sleeps 50) Located behind the main resort, this converted barn comprises several dormitories partitioned into separate 'stables', each with 3–5 beds. It is an ingenious arrangement, although rather dark inside. Showers, toilets & communal kitchen. Guests may use the facilities at the resort. **$**

✗ **Taste of Africa Restaurant** The resort restaurant is open to guests & visitors alike. Described as 'African fusion cuisine,' the menu offers nothing especially exciting but has a decent choice of standard fare & a good selection of South African wines. There is a sports bar at the back. B/fast starts 07.00.

WHAT TO SEE AND DO

Hawane Resort Whether or not you are staying at Hawane Resort (see above), you can take advantage of the many activities that it offers, both on site and further afield. Most also come in a number of packages, lasting from two to seven nights.

Horseriding Hawane started life as stables and today has around 30 ponies of various breeds, suitable for all levels of horsemanship. Riding packages are tailored to the rider and, for the more experienced, include out-rides into the rugged southern section of Malolotja Nature Reserve, with a chance of encountering wild animals (*riding trails from SZL120 per hour*).

Other on-site activities There are plenty of self-guided walks around the resort, including into the southern section of Malolotja Nature Reserve and to either of the two nearby dams. Other outdoor activities include archery, volleyball, and fishing and kayaking on nearby Hawane Dam (see below), with kayaks and basic fishing tackle provided. In addition, there's an outdoor swimming pool (chilly in winter), sauna and bush spa. A games centre caters for children, with babysitters available for hire.

Into Malolotja Hawane Resort took over the running of visitor activities in Malolotja Nature Reserve (see page 207) from the SNTC in 2004, and you can now

The Northwest HAWANE

5

make bookings directly from the resort. Most popular is the Malolotja Canopy Tour – a zipline route down one of the reserve's deepest gorges (see page 215). There are also game drives (SZL200 per person), hikes of varying lengths, mountain-biking (bikes available for hire from SZL94 per hour), and quad-biking trails on the periphery (from SZL250 per hour).

Maguga Dam Houseboat Hawane Resort keeps its own houseboat, the *Fish Eagle*, at Maguga Dam, half an hour's drive to the north. This fully equipped, self-catering cruiser sleeps a family of four and is available for daily rentals or longer packages – with the services of a driver, if required (see page 217).

Hawane Dam and Nature Reserve
This small conservation area was established by the SNTC in 1978 to protect a locally important wetland along the upper Mbuluzi River. In 1983 the river was dammed to provide drinking water for Mbabane, and the reserve was extended northwards to ensure that its wider catchment remained unpolluted. Today the reserve is an important sanctuary for the endemic red-hot poker plant (*Kniphofia umbrina*), with its colourful spikes, and provides habitat for such wetland wildlife as Cape clawless otter, striped reed-frog and water monitor. It is especially good for birds, with a large roost of egrets and ibis at the northwest corner of the dam – a designated bird sanctuary – and various wildfowl, raptors and grassland species found throughout the area. I have seen both marsh owl and striped flufftail here, neither of which is an easy find.

Access is via a short unsigned gravel road immediately opposite the entrance to Hawane Resort. Entrance fees (cSZL25) can be paid at the Malolotja main entrance, although the dam receives few visitors and in practice people tend to wander in without paying. A birdwatching trail leads around the perimeter. Fishing can be arranged at Hawane Resort and the dam is well stocked with carp, bream, bass, barbel and trout. No motorised craft are permitted. In recent years there has been some concern that the dam level is falling, with possible implications for Mbabane's water supply.

Forbes Reef Gold Mine
Some 8–10km north of Hawane Dam, the MR1 passes through a small settlement, surrounded by exotic forests, known as Forbes Reef. There is little here to interest the visitor: just a few roadside vegetable stalls, a dusty bottle store and, in winter, neatly chopped stacks of firewood for sale on the verge. It was around here, however, that Swaziland's first gold rush occurred and some of the old mine workings can still be seen today.

To reach the mine you must head a little further up the road to Malolotja Nature Reserve (see opposite), where the staff at the gate will give you directions. A short walk from Forbes Reef Dam, near the reserve's environmental education centre, leads through a woodland of wattle and gum trees to the mines. Here you will find a large open pit with a number of smaller horizontal entrance tunnels – or adits – leading off it. Some mineshafts were reputedly sunk more than 115m into the hillside. You are welcome to explore, but there are no tourist facilities, so bring a torch and keep to the path. Look out for the colony of Geoffroy's horseshoe bats that sometimes roosts in the tunnels.

Forbes Main Reef was Swaziland's first gold mine, discovered in 1884 by Alex Forbes, a relative of the original concession holders. A dam was soon built, shafts sunk into the hillside and within a few years the mine was producing 2,000 ounces of gold per month. Without a railway, however, the costs of transporting the ore over the mountains by ox-wagon made it hard to turn a profit. At the end of the

Boer War, in October 1902, Forbes Reef Gold Mining Company became part of the Swaziland Corporation Ltd. Gold continued to be extracted, but production remained sporadic and profits elusive. In 1932 the Swaziland Corporation opened the area to public prospecting. This brought about a brief gold rush but by 1935 mining at Forbes Reef had ground to a halt. Nothing now remains of the old workshops, sawmill, fort and engineers' quarters that once stood here.

There has been other gold mining elsewhere in Swaziland, notably in the Piggs Peak area, and recent times have seen sporadic extraction on a smaller scale – including in the Red Reefs, just outside Malolotja, in 1976–77. Many prospects have been adjudged too small or too low-grade for exploitation, although the financial woes of the concession companies may also have been a factor.

MALOLOTJA NATURE RESERVE

Malolotja Nature Reserve is the big green blob that occupies most of the map between Ngwenya and Piggs Peak, to the west of the MR1. It is not only Swaziland's premier natural attraction but, to those in the know, one of the very best highland reserves in southern Africa. Its 18,000ha of grasslands, peaks and gorges may seem modest by African standards but the reserve offers a genuine wilderness in which hikers can lose themselves for days. Like Swaziland itself, its diminutive size on the map belies the great sense of space you experience once inside.

The reserve dates back to the 1970s, when it was one of the first areas identified by the Swaziland National Trust Commission (see page 52) as worthy of protection. A subsequent petition to the late King Sobhuza II got the royal thumbs-up once the king received assurances from local chiefs that the area had little agricultural potential. Once the reserve was declared, some 63 families living within its borders were re-settled on good farmland outside.

Seen from the MR1, Malolotja appears to be nothing but high rolling hills. But as you enter the reserve and crest the first ridge you will see the land fall away dramatically to the west, where a series of valleys have carved a toast-rack of mountain peaks that stretch away into South Africa. The reserve's altitudinal span, ranging from the peak of Ngwenya (1,829m) to the floor of the Nkomati Valley (640m), accounts for its variety of habitats, from short grassland on the tops to riverine scrub in the gorges, bushveld in the valleys and Afromontane forest in the deeper clefts.

Water is never far away in Malolotja – although you may find yourself gasping for it when toiling uphill in the midday heat. Among several perennial streams, the Malolotja River rises in the east and meanders through a large upland bog, or vlei, before tumbling down the precipitous Malolotja Falls, which at 95m is Swaziland's highest. It then carves a passage north, passing through a steep gorge and the extraordinary 'Pot-holes' at Mahulungwane Falls, where several deep circular pools tempt the swimmer (though, as with any wild swimming, great care must be taken), before meeting the Nkomati River. This larger waterway flows due east, cutting across northern Swaziland towards Mozambique and the Indian Ocean. Virtually the entire catchment areas for the Malolotja, Mgwayiza and Mhlangamphepha are contained within the reserve, which means these rivers remain largely free from pollution. The same cannot be said of the Nkomati, however, which rises on the South African side.

Malolotja's climate is more temperate than subtropical. Most rain falls during summer, when thick mists are also common, but rain and mists may also occur during winter. Conditions fluctuate considerably: it can be bitterly cold camping

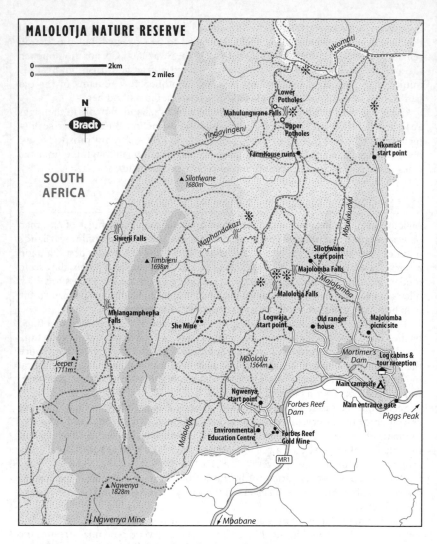

MALOLOTJA NATURE RESERVE

0 ——— 2km
0 ——— 2 miles

N

Bradt

SOUTH
AFRICA

Nkomati

Lower
Potholes
Mahulungwane Falls
Upper
Potholes

Yingayingeni

Farmhouse ruins

Nkomati
start point

Silotfwane
1680m

Maphandakazi

Mbulukudu

Siweni Falls

Silotfwane
start point

Timbileni
1698m

Majolomba Falls

Majolomba

Malolotja Falls

Mhlangamphepha
Falls

She Mine

Logwaja
start point

Old ranger
house

Majolomba
picnic site

Jeeper
1711m

Malolotja
1564m

Mortimer's
Dam

Log cabins &
tour reception

Main campsite

Ngwenya
start point

Forbes Reef
Dam

Main entrance gate

Piggs Peak

Malolotja

Environmental
Education Centre

Forbes Reef
Gold Mine

MR1

Ngwenya
1828m

Ngwenya Mine

Mbabane

at night in winter and baking hot climbing the slopes in summer. In short, and
as with mountains anywhere, the weather is unpredictable and hikers should
come prepared.

However timeless and untouchable Malolotja may appear, though, it should
never be taken for granted. Various proposals to exploit the reserve's resources
have reared their ugly heads from time to time. During the 1990s a Taiwanese
project secured permission from the king to mine green chert from the Nkomati
Valley. This operation – which some believe intended to pass off its product on
the international market as the more valuable jade – would have destroyed large
tracts of mist-belt forest and done irreparable ecological damage. Thankfully, and
despite vigorous support for the mining in some government quarters, a concerted
environmental campaign ensured that in 1991 the project was shelved. It also
proved that the king had been misled into believing that the mining site would
be outside the reserve boundaries. With luck, Malolotja's new-found status as an

integral part of the Lubombo Transfrontier Conservation and Resource Area (see page 50) should help to keep any future threats at bay.

WILDLIFE The Malolotja wildlife experience is more about quality than quantity. The reserve's species lists are not as long as those of Swaziland's lowveld reserves, where a more subtropical climate supports greater biodiversity. Furthermore, this is not a big game park; large mammals – which include zebra and various antelope – are not really the point. Instead, it offers a chance to find some of the more specialised creatures associated with montane grassland, mist-belt forest and other habitats for which the reserve is a conservation bastion. Our knowledge of Malolotja's wildlife has much to do with the efforts of individuals such as former warden Richard Boycott, who conducted extensive surveys, notably of the reptiles and amphibians.

Mammals A number of larger mammals have been reintroduced to Malolotja over the years in order to restore their original populations. The most conspicuous – especially near the entrance area – is the blesbok. This fleet-footed antelope crops the short grass in small herds and is readily identified by the white blaze on its long face. You should also encounter small groups of zebra, often with blue wildebeest and – if you're lucky – a few of the much rarer black wildebeest, the latter being a highveld speciality. Grey rhebok and mountain reedbuck graze the higher slopes, while common reedbuck hang out in marshy areas. Among smaller antelope, common duikers are widespread, red duikers frequent native forest patches, oribi are best seen grazing the newly burnt grasslands and klipspringers may be spotted perching on rocky ridges. Eland and red hartebeest are present but scarce, while a handful of impala, which don't fare well at this altitude, are all that remain of a misguided reintroduction programme many years ago.

As for predators, a few shy leopard roam the hills and gorges. You are highly unlikely to see one, although spend a day on the trail and it's a safe bet that one will have seen you. A smaller spotted cat, the serval, is reasonably common, judging by its abundant scats, and you may glimpse one hunting the grasslands by dawn or dusk. Another predator worth looking for at the end of the day – especially in winter, when it becomes active earlier – is the aardwolf: Malolotja is as good a place as any to spot this elusive ant-eating hyena, with the area between Logwaja and Ngwenya viewpoints

WANDERING JUMBOS

In 1992, hikers rounding a bend in Malolotja's Nakomati Valley were surprised – and not a little alarmed – to find large steaming mounds of dung splattered across the trail. Stopping in their tracks, they soon heard the unmistakable crunch of feeding pachyderms from the forest ahead. They were not imagining it: two young bull elephants had entered the park from the contiguous Songimvelo Game Reserve on the South African side. These visitors found the lush riverine thickets along the Nkomati and lower Malolotja valleys so much to their liking that they took up residence, remaining in the area for at least ten years. Although they had an inevitable impact on the vegetation, they never showed any sign of aggression to people – and indeed generally showed little of themselves beyond tracks and droppings. The wandering duo have not been seen since 2008, and it is presumed they packed their trunks and returned to Songimvelo.

especially productive. Other carnivores include black-backed jackal, water mongoose and Cape clawless otter, the last of these leaving its distinctive crab-filled droppings on riverside rocks but seldom revealing itself to the visitor.

Tramp the grasslands and you can't fail to notice the diggings of aardvarks. These curious animals are impossible to see unless you wander the hills in the small hours (neither recommended nor permitted), but fresh red earth around a ransacked termite mounds betrays any recent activity. Many other animals make use of aardvark burrows, including warthogs (which are common here) and porcupines, whose sharp quills and clusters of fibrous droppings litter hiking trails. Other mammals among Malolotja's 63 recorded species include baboons, which you will often detect by their alarm barks; vervet monkeys, in the riverine woodland; and rock hyraxes, a large colony of which inhabits the boulders around the campsite. At the other end of the scale is the occasional hippopotamus that makes its way into the reserve along the Nkomati River. Amazingly, two elephants once followed the same route and ended up staying in the Nkomati Valley for over a decade (see box *Wandering jumbos*, page 209).

Birds Birders in Malolotja may not manage to tick off as many species in a day as they would expect in the lowveld but their list will include specialities that are hard to find elsewhere. Indeed, BirdLife International has designated the reserve as one of Africa's Important Bird Areas (IBAs), as it supports a significant number of species that are Globally Threatened (9) or Near Threatened (14), and many others that are restricted by range or ecological zone.

Among Malolotja's 280 recorded species, special mention must first go to the blue swallow, a rare inter-African summer migrant – and major draw-card for birders – that breeds in only a handful of sites across southern Africa. Look out for these elegant birds from September to March in the high grasslands, especially around the campsite. They are entirely navy blue, with extremely long tail streamers, and tend to fly low along the watercourses hawking for insects. Be careful not to confuse them with other swallow species, such as the all black, shorter tailed eastern saw-wing.

Each of Malolotja's habitats supports a different avian community. In the grasslands, songbirds such as red-collared widow, Cape longclaw and wing-snapping cisticola display above the grasses, while nectar-feeders such as malachite sunbird and Gurney's sugarbird visit flowering aloes and proteas. Rock outcrops are the haunt of buff-streaked chats, Cape rock thrushes and ground woodpeckers, while jackal buzzards, white-necked ravens and – if you're lucky – Verreaux's eagles, soar overhead. Other grassland species of note include the southern bald ibis, which has one of its two Swaziland breeding colonies on the cliffs above Malolotja Falls, and Denham's bustard, a tall bird that is most conspicuous in summer when males strut around with their white breeding plumage puffed up. The stately secretary bird is a regular visitor.

Any water can be productive: the dams, rivers and streams host various wildfowl, kingfishers – including the uncommon half-collared kingfisher – and other aquatic birds. You will find more middleveld species deeper into the valleys, including green pigeon, purple-crested turaco and little bee-eater. In forest patches listen out for the braying of trumpeter hornbills, the growling of Kynsna turacos and the '*Willie!*' call of the ubiquitous sombre greenbul. And keep an eye on the sky for the formidable crowned eagle, which sometimes soars above the canopy. In larger patches of mist-belt forest – especially north of the Nkomati – such skulking forest denizens as chorister robin-chat, bush blackcap and the rare orange ground thrush forage through the understorey.

Reptiles and amphibians Among Malolotja's 66 recorded species of reptile are the endemic Swazi thick-tailed rock gecko and near-endemic Barberton girdled lizard (*Cordylus warreni barbertonensis*). This is also the only place in the region where all three of southern Africa's legless grass lizards (*Chamaesaura* species) have been recorded. More conspicuous lizards include the Transvaal crag lizard, males flaunting their bold breeding colours from atop boulders, and you might disturb a big water monitor among riverside vegetation in the lower valleys.

Snakes of the high grasslands include the puff adder, boomslang and rinkhals. Of particular interest is the Swazi rock snake (*Lamprophis swazicus*), a non-venomous species endemic to northwest Swaziland and adjoining areas of South Africa. Malolotja is also the only place where I have ever seen the scarce berg adder (*Bitis atropos*), a small viper of rocky slopes. Lower down, the river valleys are home to middleveld species such as black mamba, Mozambique spitting cobra and even Southern African rock python.

Malolotja has just one tortoise, the serrated hinged terrapin (*Pelusios sinuatus*), found along the Nkomati River. It has 25 recorded species of frog, however, including several rare highveld species found nowhere else in Swaziland. These include the Natal ghost frog (*Heleophryne natalensis*), the striped stream frog (*Strongylopus fasciatus*) and the long-toed running frog (*Semnodactylus wealii*). From October to February listen out for the incessant calling of the Mozambique rain frog (*Breviceps mossambicus*), a tiny, short-snouted species that emerges from the ground with the rains.

Flora Malolotja is justly celebrated for its flora. Several threatened species that are largely restricted to the Barberton greenstone belt occur in the reserve, and wild flowers provide an impressive display throughout the year – notably during the spring months of October and November, when lilies, orchids and amaryllids thrive among the grasslands and boggy upland vleis.

Among the highveld blooms identifiable by even the non-botanist (such as this author) are such showy species as the agapanthus, candelabra flower, red-hot poker and Natal watsonia (*Watsonia densiflora*). Trees are in short supply on the higher grasslands, where typical plants include the monkey's tail (*Xerophyta retinervis*), which grows in grass-like clumps on granite slopes, its thick fibrous stems blackened by the fires it has evolved to withstand. The clumpy crowns of cabbage trees protrude from around rocky outcrops, where various aloes, including the mountain aloe (*Aloe marlothii*), bring a blaze of orange from May to September, and stands of silver sugar bush (*Protea roupelliae*) point to Malolotja's prehistoric affinity with the *fynbos* flora of South Africa's Cape. Palm-like grassland tree ferns (*Cyathea dregei*) mark the route of watercourses, which sprout a denser riverine growth lower down, with trees such as waterberry (*Syzygium cordatum*) and glossy bottlebrush (*Greyia sutherlandii*), the latter's showy scarlet flowers visible from afar in season. The middleveld habitat of the valley floors supports more trees, and impressive species such as the white stinkwood (*Celtis Africana*) and forest fever tree (*Anthocleista grandiflora*) flourish in deeper forests. The forest floor is also home to two threatened species of cycad, the Barberton and Kaapsehoop cycads (*Encephalartos paucidentatus* and *E. laevifolius*).

GETTING THERE AND AWAY Malolotja is easily reached along the MR1. The main entrance is some 20km north of the junction with the MR3, just a 30–40-minute drive from either Mbabane or Piggs Peak, and there is a bus stop a few hundred yards south of the reserve entrance. The entrance gate (⊕ *06.00–18.00 winter, 06.00–18.30*

5

ROCKS OF AGES

Malolotja's rocks are truly ancient. They form part of what is known as the 'archaean basement', which laid the very foundations of the African continent. The high ground near the main road and entrance is mostly granite, an igneous rock cooled in the earth's crust and subsequently exposed by erosion. Known as Lochiel granite, it has a rough, speckled appearance and has been dated to just over three billion years old – almost three-quarters of the way back to the formation of our planet. Amazingly, though, this is not the oldest rock in Malolotja. The rest of the reserve, including Ngwenya, the Malolotja Valley and the high western ground, comprises rocks of the Swaziland Supergroup, which are among the oldest metamorphic rocks in the world. Laid down as ocean sediment some 3.5 million years ago, their strata were subsequently drawn into the earth's crust where, under extreme heat and pressure, they metamorphosed into quartzites, shales, talc schists and other highly resistant forms. Folding, faulting and tilting have since returned them to the surface in a series of almost vertical bands, in which exposed fossils of blue-green algae represent some of the earth's very oldest life forms.

The Swaziland Supergroup comprises three subgroups. The oldest is the Onverwacht Group. This includes soft schists, known as soapstone from their soapy appearance and texture, and used by local stone carvers (see page 87). It also includes the more fibrous serpentinite, which contains the chrysotile asbestos once mined at Havelock (see page 229), and small quantities of gold, which was mined at Forbes Reef (see page 206). The second is the Fig Tree Group, found mostly in the far south and northwest. This includes shales, ironstones and highly resistant quartzites. Folding has contorted these strata into a vertical position and, in the south, has enriched the haematite ironstones to produce the iron ore once mined at Ngwenya. The third and youngest subgroup is the Moodies Group, which comprises a quartzite conglomerate metamorphosed from the eroded debris of other rocks. It is blue-black and gravelly in appearance.

---

summer) is set just off the main road. You pay your entrance fee (SZL28) at the office, where you will find some interesting – though slightly dilapidated – displays, plus trail maps and checklists of fauna and flora. If you are planning overnight hikes (see page 215) you should inform the rangers here of your intended route so they know where to look if you don't return.

Some 6km south of the main entrance gate along the MR1 is a signed turning to the Malolotja Environmental Education Centre. This provides an alternative entry point to the park and is the quickest route to the Forbes Reef Mine and Dam (see page 206), but you must first check in at the main entrance.

WHERE TO STAY Accommodation inside the reserve comes down to campsite or log cabins. Both are within 1km of the entrance: at the fork just inside the gate head right for the cabins and left for the campsite. There are also 17 rough campsites deep inside the park for intrepid backpackers (see page 129). The huts and campsite are booked at Hawane Resort (see page 205). You can also try directly at the gate office, where the staff may be able to help. There are numerous places to stay within just 30–40 minutes' drive of the reserve, including Piggs Peak, Maguga Dam and back in Mbabane.

⌂ **Log cabins** (13 cabins, 60 beds) Basic but comfortable self-catering wooden cabins (5 with 4 beds, 8 with 5 beds). Larger cabins have mezzanine level with extra bed, reached via steep wooden ladder. Bedding supplied. Kitchen has all essentials. Hot showers & wood-burning stove (firewood provided). Raised porch & sheltered braai area, with metal braai stand. Cabins arranged in 2 lines looking north into the reserve; 1–7 enjoy the best views. **$$**

⋏ **Campsite** (15 pitches) Each pitch has braai stand & water tap. Some take caravans. Communal braai area for larger groups. Ablution block is large & clean, with hot showers. A small, basic, A-frame hut below the campsite sleeps 2. An excellent & beautifully situated campsite. **$**

Those staying in cabins or campsite will find the surrounding area very productive for some of Malolotja's more interesting fauna and flora – notably blue swallows, which in summer can be seen flying up and down the drainage lines between the campsite and Mortimer's Dam. The boulders near the A-frame hut are home to a large colony of rock hyraxes (37 when I last counted), which bask in the first sunshine of the morning, and rocky outcrops between the pitches are great for malachite sunbirds when the aloes are in bloom. A stroll down to Mortimer's Dam is good for flowers and waterbirds, while one up to the cabins may reveal grazing blesbok, and perhaps a buff-streaked chat, Cape rock thrush or Transvaal crag lizard among the boulders. Listen out for red-winged francolins calling noisily at first light.

WHERE TO EAT Accommodation at Malolotja is self-catering. Just below the log cabins, however, is the reception for Malolotja Canopy Tours (see page 215), where you will find a restaurant and bar. At present it is open 08.00–16.00 daily, which is fine for breakfast but not so good for dinner. There is also a small souvenir shop and a good supply of maps, brochures and checklists. A small store just inside the entrance gate, the Malolotja Trading Post (⊕ *daily 08.00–16.00*) sells basic provisions. Don't count on anything fresh or refrigerated, though; rather, stock up in Mbabane or Piggs Peak before you arrive.

WHAT TO SEE AND DO

On wheels Malolotja is not primarily a reserve for game drives. The limited network of roads, each of which comprises two strips of cobbles either side of a grass ridge, serves mainly to reach the viewpoints from where hikers set out on foot. Although designed as suitable for a normal car, these roads are poorly maintained, with stretches that are heavily eroded and really require a higher-clearance or 4x4 vehicle. Take advice from parks staff before setting out. In such terrain, two wheels are often better than four, and the reserve is perfect mountain-biking country. You can hire bikes at the entrance gate (SZL95). Again, be careful, stick to the main tracks and take it slow: experienced cyclists have come a serious cropper here on the rough terrain.

On foot Malolotja's 200km of trails offer some of the finest hiking in southern Africa – not only because of the scenery and wildlife but also because, by contrast with better-known destinations such as the Drakensberg, you usually have the trail virtually to yourself. The excellent SNTC website (*www.sntc.org.sz/tourism/hikingmalolotja*) has good maps and descriptions of most trails. These vary from gentle morning walks to wilderness hikes of up to eight days. Main routes are marked with cairns and footprint signs. Trails that descend into the valleys can be very steep and stony. Never underestimate any trail; always wear sturdy footwear, take a hat and carry plenty of water.

Short walks The following walks can be completed within a morning and are all clearly marked on the SNTC trails map. They are listed in order of rough length, with the shortest first.

Forbes Reef Dam A short, easy walk through reedbeds and grasslands that is good for birds. Starting from the parking area, follow the perimeter of the dam until you reach the point where the Malolotja River (just a stream) enters it. Follow the river a little further downstream and return along the track, via a small bird hide. Look out for common reedbuck below the dam wall.

Malolotja Vlei This large, boggy area between Mortimer's Dam and Forbes Reef Dam is rich in wild flowers and grassland birds. Start from Ngwenya or Logwaja start points, or Forbes Reef Dam. There is no marked path. Keep to the edge of the vlei so as not to damage the flora or get stuck in the wet bog.

Malolotja Falls From Logwaja start point follow a steep path, with superb views down the Malolotja Valley, to the top of Malolotja Falls. This walk is closed August–October to prevent disturbing the southern bald ibis nesting colony. An alternative way to see the falls at that season is on a longer day walk (see opposite), which descends north of the falls, also providing views of the Majolomba Falls.

Majolomba Gorge The Majolomba Gorge plunges into the Malolotja Valley between the Silotfwane and Logwaja start points. From either of these you can reach the top of the gorge, where there is a small pool and a steep waterfall. Or extend this walk into a longer loop via the Malolotja Valley.

Upper Majolomba Park at Majolomba picnic site (braai stand, long-drop toilets) and follow the marked trail down through a marshy vlei. This is a good area for flowers, grassland birds and common reedbuck. Cross the road and continue towards the Majolomba Gorge, with views of Silotfwane Mountain beyond. Look out for game such as zebra, blesbok and warthog. Cross over the Majolomba River and return south over the high ground to the picnic site.

Nkomati Viewpoint Park at Nkomati start point, from where trails to the north and west lead you to impressive views of the Nkomati Valley. Look out for mountain reedbuck, grey rhebok, klipspringer and Verreaux's eagles around the rocky slopes and rock outcrops. I have seen leopard tracks on this trail.

Day trails The following longer trails require the best part of a day and are graded here from A (easy) to E (very strenuous), with the easiest listed first. D and E are not suitable for young children. Go well prepared and take plenty of water.

Upper Malolotja Falls Trail (8km; 5–7 hours; B) A long but gentle trail. Good for wildlife on the slopes of the upper Malolotja Valley, plus grassland flora.

Silotfwane Viewpoint Trail (6km; 3–4 hours; C) A steep, strenuous trail into the Malolotja Valley. Mountain scenery and plentiful wildlife, with a chance of black-backed jackal, warthog, baboon, otter and oribi.

Upper Mahulungwane Falls Trail (7km; 4–5 hours; C) A fairly easy trail that leads to the Mahulungwane Falls and Upper Pot-holes; swimming is possible in these circular natural pools, but they are deep and surrounded by steep rocks so take care. Good for middleveld birds and flora.

Mbulukudvu Trail (10.5km; 5–7 hours; C) An impressive and varied trail into the Malolotja Valley, with a relatively gentle descent to the Malolotja River but a steeper return. Interesting geological features.

Nkomati River Trail (8km; 4–5 hours; D) A strenuous trail, with some steep sections. Allows a chance to see the Nkomati River, with its broad-leaved riverine forest and middleveld birdlife.

Lower Mahulungwane Falls Trail (9km; 5–6 hours; D) A strenuous trail, with fine views and varied scenery. Take care around the waterfalls and Lower Pot-holes. Look for otters along the river and, from June to October, bald ibis on the cliffs.

Malolotja Falls Trail (11.5km; 5–8 hours; D) A steep, rocky descent to the river, with impressive views of Malolotja and Majolomba falls, and Silotfwane Mountain. Look out for large Barberton cycads in the forest at the bottom.

Maphandakazi Trail (13.5km; 7–10 hours; D) A long day's hike on a mostly gentle trail that crosses the Malolotja River. Look out for red duiker in the woodlands and otters along the river.

Silotfwane Mountain Trail (17km; 7–10 hours; D) A long, steep trail only for fit, experienced walkers. Offers superb views right back across Swaziland and into Mozambique. Look out for larger game on the higher slopes. Varied flora includes species of riverine forest and protea woodland.

Overnight trails These are for experienced backpackers prepared to carry all their gear and make do with minimal facilities. The 17 rough campsites scattered across the reserve are little more than small clearings at points beside the trail, and nothing like the main campsite back at the park entrance. The SNTC website publishes a list of recommended trails that make use of these campsites, together with a trails map – available at the main gate – that indicates pretty accurately the average hiking time between each point. The trails vary from two days (one night) to eight days (seven nights). This is serious mountain hiking, not to be undertaken lightly. Choose a trail you are confident of completing and always inform the rangers at the gate where you are going and how long you will be gone. The weather is unpredictable, so take a waterproof tent and always carry clothes and sleeping gear suitable for the cold. The reward for all this effort is a memorable wilderness experience.

Malolotja Canopy Tour For a more rapid view of Malolotja's dramatic scenery, without having to slog for hours up and down stony hillsides, try the Malolotja Canopy Tour. Launched in 2010, this private enterprise is located in the Majolomba Gorge, where a 50m suspension bridge and 11 wooden platforms have been ingeniously affixed to the steep sides. Participants descend the gorge by ziplining down on a steel cable from platform to platform high above the forest canopy and Majolomba River. Some lines are more than 300m long. This operation follows a model developed in Costa Rica and subsequently introduced to South Africa. It has been smuggled reasonably discreetly into Malolotja's scenery, causing little visual or environmental impact.

5

The tour lasts around 2½ hours and costs SZL450 per person, including all equipment, guides, transport, refreshments and lunch afterwards. It starts out from the Malolotja Canopy Tours reception (⊕ *daily 07.00–16.00 summer, 08.00–15.00 winter*), just below the log cabins, where you pick up your harnesses, helmets and full safety briefing. You are then driven to Silotfwane viewpoint, learning a little about the reserve's flora and fauna en route, from where a ten-minute trail leads to the first platform. From the last platform, a shorter, steeper trail leads out of the gorge to where your vehicle awaits.

The excellent guides will instruct you thoroughly, including how to balance and brake when on the line. In truth, there's little to it and the braking happens via an automatic mechanism, whether or not you do your bit. While on the platforms you are harnessed to a safety line at all times, and nervous first-timers should take comfort in the fact that children aged five have completed the tour. In theory, it offers a unique perspective on an otherwise inaccessible location and a chance to spot elusive wildlife. In practice, however, you may be too busy clinging on for dear life. During my trip, I heard Kynsna turacos in the trees and saw baboons on the ridge. But that was from platform one, before the first line. The rest, I'm afraid, was a white-knuckle blur.

Tours leave every 45 minutes and run in most weathers. Groups normally comprise eight or fewer but larger groups are taken on request. You will need closed footwear and comfortable clothing (shorts are OK but not skirts). Secure your camera and sunglasses to prevent them from plunging down into the gorge (where they'll join any flipflops you might inadvisedly have worn). You can book tours in advance (m 7613 3990/7697 5704; *www.malolotjacanopytour.com*). Alternatively, book directly at trails reception, at Hawane Resort (see page 205) or through Swazi Trails (see page 104).

Malolotja stone carvers Outside the entrance gate, a few hundred metres back towards Mbabane, is a cluster of stalls where local stone carvers display their wares. These are among the best of their kind in Swaziland. The carvers – including individuals such as Philip Shongwe and Christian Mangwe, who have been at it since the early 1990s – produce some excellent work, and their products are often cheaper here than you may find at more commercial outlets elsewhere. Most carvings are made of soapstone, an easily workable local rock (see page 87) with a natural grey-green colour that may be enhanced by oiling or varnishing, or darkened with shoe polish. They include a standard selection of small animal curios, such as tortoises and hippos, but also many more original one-offs – including, when I last looked, skeletal chameleons and busts with removable hats. Some are enormous and would require sea-freighting home. Stop for a chat; not only might you strike a bargain, but also learn more about the work and perhaps discover some unusual pieces that are not on display.

THE NKOMATI VALLEY

The Nkomati (sometimes spelt simply Komati) is Swaziland's second largest river. It enters from South Africa in the west and cuts across the northwest corner of the country, passing through Malolotja Nature Reserve and Maguga Dam before taking a left near the town of Bhalekane and exiting at Mananga in the north. The first half of the river's course is a dramatic valley, deeply incised through the hills of the highveld. It then descends to the middleveld and, after Bhalekane, meanders more sedately across the flat lowveld.

The Nkomati effectively splits northwest Swaziland in two, dividing Mbabane from Piggs Peak. For years the only way to cross it was on the MR1. The road begins its long descent shortly after the entrance to Malolotja, winding down to the bridge over the Nkomati before taking an equally long time to wind back up the other side, eventually reaching Piggs Peak at the top. It is a highly scenic journey but slow-going when stuck behind a logging truck. Don't rush it. Instead, pull over at the bottom to take in the view; you'll be amazed how much hotter it is down here than in the hills. There are numerous roadside curio stalls – some advertised by children, who dress up in leaves and perform impromptu *sibhaca* dances for prospective customers, but should probably be at school.

Since 2001, a parallel, equally scenic and slightly quicker route has opened over the Nkomati. This – the Maguga Dam Road, leads to Maguga Dam, where it crosses the Nkomati at the dam wall, then rejoins the MR1 just south of Piggs Peak. Along the way it passes Nsangwini Rock Art (see page 219). The turn-off is well signed in both directions: heading north, on the right, 6km after the Malolotja entrance gate; heading south, on the left, 2km out of Piggs Peak.

WHERE TO STAY

⌂ **Houseboat** (sleeps 4) ↖ 2444 1744; m 7627 6714; e infohawane@realnet.co.sz; www.hawane.co.sz. The *Fish Eagle* is an upmarket cruiser owned by Hawane Resort (see page 205). Sleeps 4 in en-suite cabins. Kitchen fully equipped for self-catering. Facilities include BBQ, fish-finder & depth-gauge. Packed meals, daily rentals & gillie services available, plus boat driver if required. $$$$–$$$$$

⌂ **Maguga Lodge** (35 rooms, sleeps 90) ↖ 2437 3975/6; e info@magugalodge.com; www.magugalodge.com. The only accommodation option on the shore of the dam, with stunning views over the lake & surrounding hills. 35 'luxury' en-suite rondavels; each has DSTV, AC, African-themed décor & semi-private patio. Other options include a 2-storey family suite, with main bedroom upstairs & 2 sgl beds downstairs; a self-catering fisherman's cottage set in secluded bay, with en-suite bathrooms, kitchen, lounge & sleeper couch; small, secluded campsite, with 4 pitches, water, power outlets & ablutions. Large terrace restaurant, bar, swimming pool & braai area all overlook lake. Large conference centre. Wi-Fi available. Activities include boat cruises (see page 219), fishing, mountain-biking & hikes to local rock art. $$$–$$$$

⌂ **Sobantu Guest Farm** (sleeps 29) m 7605 3954; e sobantu@swaziplace.com; www.swaziplace.com/sobantu. New eco-friendly

family tourist venture 7km north of Maguga Dam in scenic, rural location. Accommodation in dbl rooms, backpacker hostel & campsite. DTSV lounge with fireplace, self-catering kitchen & popular bar with local music vibe & coal/wood stove in winter. Basic groceries & frozen food sold on site, with healthy b/fasts & Swazi meals available on request. Local activities include birdwatching, nature walks, mountain-biking, home-stays with rural families & canoe hire on Maguga or Hawane dams (3-seaters SZL250 half-day, SZL485 full day). Day trips arranged to local attractions. Regular shuttles to Piggs Peak & Mbabane. $

⌂ **Mtunzi's Paradise Village** (2 4-person huts, camping) m 7608 0469; e swazivillage@mailfly.com; www.swaziplace.com/mthunzi. Budget accommodation & traditional Swazi hospitality in rural village just south of Maguga Dam. Activities include hikes to bushmen rock paintings & waterfalls, fishing on Nkomati River & nights around the fire with singing, dancing & traditional beer. Guests can even have a run-out with the local 'Rock City' football team. Reach the village on the Mbabane/Piggs Peak bus by dropping off at Nkomanzi Station & asking directions. Or ask at Phezukwemkhono grocery shop, where they can radio the village to arrange a pick-up. One-day package includes accommodation, meals & activities. Additional nights & camping available. $–$$

WHERE TO EAT

✗ **Lapa Restaurant** Maguga Lodge (see above); ⊕ 07.00–22.30 daily. Superbly situated terrace restaurant overlooking the dam. Tastefully furnished with African art & décor. Extensive à la carte menu & wine list. Popular buffet lunch on Sun.

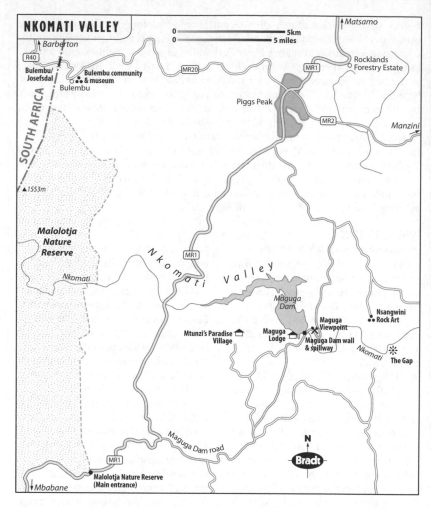

NKOMATI VALLEY

↑ *Matsamo*

↑ *Barberton*

0 ⸻ 5km
0 ⸻ 5 miles

R40

Bulembu/
Josefsdal
Bulembu community
& museum
Bulembu

MR20

MR1

Rocklands
Forestry Estate

Piggs Peak

MR2

Manzini

▲1553m

*Malolotja
Nature
Reserve*

N k o m a t i

MR1

V a l l e y

Nkomati

*Maguga
Dam*

Nsangwini
Rock Art

Mtunzi's Paradise
Village

Maguga
Lodge

Maguga
Viewpoint

Maguga Dam wall
& spillway

Nkomati

The Gap

Maguga Dam road

MR1

N

Bradt

Malolotja Nature Reserve
(Main entrance)

↓*Mbabane*

✖ **Maguga Viewpoint Restaurant** ☎2668
6637. Friendly, community-run restaurant
overlooking dam spillway, with good-value menu,
including spare ribs, paninis, chocolate brownies
& pancakes. Licensed bar & fresh coffee on tap.

All-day b/fasts available, with novelties such as
'aphrodisiac flap jack stack'. Also craft stalls &
information centre with excellent diorama of the
valley.

WHAT TO SEE AND DO

Maguga Dam Maguga Dam lies 11km south of Piggs Peak and, heading north
from Mbabane, 13km off the MR1. Swaziland's largest reservoir, with 332,000,000m³
of water (give or take a bucket or two), its blue expanse is an impressive and somewhat
unexpected sight as you round the last bend. The dam wall, which the road crosses,
is equally impressive: it stands 115m high, measures 870m along the top and 400m
along the base, and comprises some 800,000m³ of clay, 2,800,000m³ of granite and
43,000m³ of filter material. There are only three larger dams in southern Africa: the
Katse Dam in Lesotho, and the Kariba and Cabora Bassa dams on the Zambezi. The
dam wall was built to withstand flooding along the Nkomati, but the raising of the

water level behind meant that the original low-level road bridge across the MR1 had to be replaced by a new higher-level bridge – a major engineering project in itself.

The dam was built under the auspices of the joint South Africa/Swaziland Komati Basin Water Authority (KOBWA), and today produces hydro-electric power and supplies irrigation to farmers across a wide area. When completed in 2001, it received the South Africa Institute of Civil Engineering award for 'most outstanding achievement' in the international category. Not everybody was thrilled, however. The flooding of the valley affected more than 150 homesteads, with over one-third obliged to relocate completely. New homes and grazing had to be found for the displaced families and many lost their ancestral burial grounds to the flood. Compensation payments were made but disputes remain ongoing. The lake has also proved a mixed blessing for wildlife: on the one hand, the rising waters have destroyed important habitat for many species, including the endemic Swazi thick-tailed rock gecko; on the other, it has created a new habitat for waterbirds, including the African fish eagle and elusive African finfoot. Hippos have occasionally made their way into the dam along the Nkomati and while crocodiles are rare, the numerous warning signs around the shore should be taken seriously.

Activities at Maguga Dam

Around the dam For many visitors Maguga Dam is just a scenic pit stop between Mbabane and the Kruger Park. In this respect, the Maguga Lodge restaurant and Maguga Viewpoint Restaurant (see *Where to eat*, page 217) are both beautifully located. The former sits on the southern shore, its terrace overlooking the glittering waters, while the latter looks down on the dam wall spillway, with fine views east down the deep Nkomati Valley. With more time, you can enjoy hikes to local bushman paintings and waterfalls, birdwatching and mountain-biking, all organised through the various places to stay (see page 217). The whole area is still developing, so who knows what else you might find?

On the water The main activities on the dam (the reservoir, not its wall) are boating and fishing. With little boat traffic, the experience is generally a tranquil one – provided you go easy at the onboard bar. Maguga Lodge (see page 217) offers both, including sundowner cruises on its 15-seater cruiser (SZL100 pp) and fishing packages for anglers lured by the abundant carp, yellowtail, bream and tilapia. There is an annual 'monster bass' competition, with the current record standing at 5.4kg. Boat owners can make use of the lodge facilities to launch their own craft (*gates ⊕ daily 06.00–18.00; boat with trailer SZL35, boat locker SZL50/night & SZL300/ month*). Houseboats available for hire include the fully equipped self-catering *Fish Eagle* (see page 217). For boating on a more modest scale, hire a canoe through Sobantu Guest Farm (see page 217) or other local operators. Whatever your vessel of choice, a boat trip is an excellent way to enjoy the birdlife and soak up the sunsets.

Nsangwini Rock Art Nsangwini preserves Swaziland's best bushman paintings and is one of the country's most impressive cultural attractions. The site (**m** 7637 3767; ⊕ *daily 09.00–16.00*) is a community project and reached from the Maguga Dam Road via a signposted turn-off 7km north of Maguga Dam. From the turn-off, follow a well-maintained dirt road 7.5km to reception, passing along the northern rim of the Nkomati Valley. Opposite the small, secure car park is an information hut with some leaflets, a few snacks and drinks for sale, and a comment book for visitors. This is where you pay your entrance fee (SZL20) and collect your guide. If no guide is in evidence, ring the bell and he or she will quickly appear from a nearby homestead.

The site is reached via a 15–20-minute walk down a steep, rocky trail, with stirring views of the Nkomati Valley below. It lies beneath a large rock overhang and is screened by a wooden fence. Once inside the fence, it is not immediately easy to understand what all the fuss is about. But as your eyes adjust to the shadows, and your guide indicates the forms and figures etched on the rough granite, the magic of the place begins to take hold.

The caves were discovered in 1955. Dating the paintings has, however, proved trickier: they could be anything from 400 to 4,000 years old, and were probably created over hundreds of years. Whatever their age, this was the work of the San (see page 54) and pre-dates colonial times. On the rock you will see various animals clearly delineated, including elephant, lion and the only rock-art wildebeest south of the Zambezi. More intriguing are the human figures. Some are clearly hunters, walking in line bearing spears. Others are more bizarre, apparently floating on raised legs and embellished with feathers and, in one case, the head of a mantis. To the right of a vertical fissure in the rock the figures are supernaturally tall.

Archaeologists now believe that these paintings were completed in a shamanic trance and that many carry symbolic meaning. The elephant, for example, represents rainmaking – the cave probably hosted sacred rain ceremonies – while the fissure represents the division between the material and the spirit or 'power' world, with the hunters undergoing a transformation as they pass over into the latter (hence their towering stature). Blacker figures higher on the wall depict the first Bantu pastoralists to arrive in Swaziland. The work has been executed with amazing delicacy and precision using red ochre and animal blood. Given the ravages of time, it seems little short of miraculous that it has survived at all, let alone with such colour and clarity.

The excellent young student guides at Nsangwini are trained at the National Museum (see page 174). Visitor revenue benefits the local community and helps preserve the site, so this project deserves support. Please take the trouble to complete the visitor book, as your feedback is always welcome and will help to improve this wonderful place for generations to come.

The Gap In a wild gorge some 3.5km downstream of Maguga Dam the entire Nkomati River disappears down a narrow fault line in the rock, some 15m deep, then re-emerges around 75m later. This impressive feature, known as 'The Gap', is not marked on any map. Some lodges in the area organise visits; ask at Maguga Dam. Alternatively, if you fancy an adventure, you can reach the site via a left (east) turning off Maguga Dam road some 6km south of the dam. Follow this winding dirt road for 11km then take another road to the left. Continue for around 4km north to the end and park at the Shongwe homestead. From here it is a 20-minute walk to The Gap. If in doubt, ask. Take water and be prepared for some scrambling.

PIGGS PEAK

Piggs Peak has no pretensions to greatness. Even the council's own website refers to the town as just 'a small service centre'. Nonetheless, this is the only settlement of any size in northwest Swaziland. Located midway between Mbabane and the Kruger, it makes a convenient pit stop, with shops, banks and filling stations, and a good base from which to explore the northwest.

The town's name is often Africanised in local parlance to 'Spiggy-Speegy'. Whatever its pronunciation, it derives (despite the absence of any possessive apostrophe) from the French prospector William Pigg, whose son, ironically, went on to marry a girl with the surname Hogg. Pigg made his fortune not in bacon but gold, after discovering a reef in the nearby hills in 1884. His 'peak' was the nearby summit of Emlembe, Swaziland's highest mountain. As mining developed in the region – first gold and then asbestos – so the intersection of the Bulembu supply road with the Mbabane–Matsamo corridor became a local hub, offering services to settlers. This was the origin of today's town.

The Piggs Peak gold mine was once the most important source of gold in Swaziland, employing up to 400 people and sinking shafts down to 250m. By the time it was exhausted in 1954 it had already been surpassed by the more profitable Havelock asbestos mine at nearby Bulembu (see page 229). When this mine closed in 2001, however, forestry had long since eclipsed mining as the most important local industry, and to reach Piggs Peak today you must pass through miles of pine and eucalyptus plantations. These belong primarily to two timber companies, Peak Timbers Ltd and Swaziland Plantations, each with its own sawmill.

Today's visitor to Piggs Peak will find a quiet settlement of some 5,700 residents that still has something of a frontier feel. Its high altitude – at around 1,050m it is just a little lower than Mbabane – brings a crispness to the air that contrasts with the surrounding lowlands. Most amenities cluster along the MR1, which runs straight through town. Of more interest to the average visitor, however, are the attractions just a few kilometres beyond, including the Piggs Peak Casino, the old mining town of Bulembu, and Phophonyane Falls Nature Reserve.

GETTING THERE AND AWAY Piggs Peak is 65km north of Mbabane by road and 40km south of the South Africa border at Matsamo, from either of which it is an easy drive on the MR1 (one hour from Mbabane, 30 minutes from Matsamo). An alternative route from South Africa is via the border at Bulembu, 20km due west of town along the R40/MR20. This gravel road is in poor repair, however, and in a normal vehicle may take almost as long as the drive to Mbabane. Once over the border the descent to Barberton is steep, spectacular and, thankfully, tarred.

To reach Manzini from Piggs Peak without passing through Mbabane, take the MR2 due east out town. This scenic back road winds along the Nkomati Valley, passing through some of Swaziland's most rural landscapes. At the small settlement of Bhalekane, which has little except a prison, it meets the MR5 at a T-junction. Turn right here for Manzini via Mafutseni, or left for Mananga, Tshaneni and the northeast.

WHERE TO STAY
Upmarket
⌂ **Phophonyane Falls Eco Lodge** (sleeps 28) ☏ 2431 3429; m 7604 2802; e lungile@ phophonyane.co.sz; www.phophonyane.co.sz. This exquisite retreat located in a private nature reserve is one of the very best places to stay in Swaziland, with imaginative accommodation & a beguiling natural ambience. Located via a signed turn-off 10km north of Piggs Peak (just south of the Piggs Peak Hotel), from where a steep dirt track descends for about 2km to the entrance. Guests can choose from 3 kinds of accommodation. There are 3 rustic cottages, set among shaded trees in private gardens, with patio & braai. Each is individually decorated with African hangings & artwork, & has a large fireplace, fine wooden furniture, modern bathroom & fully equipped kitchen. Cottages 1 & 2 are dbl-storey, with views from upstairs into the forest canopy; each sleeps up to 5 people. Cottage 3 is sgl-storey & sleeps 2. Below the cottages, upstream from the falls, 5 safari tents sit on wooden decks in riverine forest, looking directly onto a series of pools & mini-cascades. All have comfortable beds, furniture, carpeting & electricity. Tents 1 & 2 form a 'tented camp', with a shared kitchen between them that has a balcony overhanging the river. Tents 3 & 4 are a short distance downstream & do not have a kitchen. Each tent has its own individual bathroom linked by a short walkway (lit by lanterns at night). Tent 5 is the 'luxury' safari tent, with en-suite bathroom. Downstream from the lodge, 2 beehive huts offer

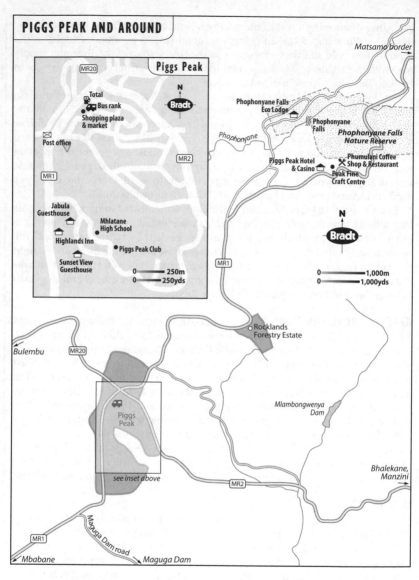

Piggs Peak

Matsamo border

MR20

Total
Bus rank
Shopping plaza
& market

Post office

MR1

MR2

Jabula
Guesthouse

Mhlatane
High School

Highlands Inn

Piggs Peak Club

Sunset View
Guesthouse

0 ———— 250m
0 ———— 250yds

Phophonyane Falls
Eco Lodge

Phophonyane

Phophonyane
Falls

Phophonyane Falls
Nature Reserve

Piggs Peak Hotel
& Casino

Phumulani Coffee
Shop & Restaurant

Peak Fine
Craft Centre

MR1

0 ———— 1,000m
0 ———— 1,000yds

Rocklands
Forestry Estate

Bulembu

MR20

Piggs
Peak

Mlambongwenya
Dam

see inset above

MR2

Bhalekane,
Manzini

MR1

Maguga Dam road

Mbabane

Maguga Dam

a luxurious take on Swazi accommodation, with a view over the falls & down the valley. Beneath their traditional thatched dome are windows, en-suite bathrooms, & original artwork & ceramics. Beehive 1 sleeps 2; Beehive 2, which has the superior view, sleeps 3. Meals are either self-catering (though not for guests in the beehives or tents 3–5) or at the Driftwood Restaurant up at the lodge, which overlooks the main pool & the valley panorama. The broad à la carte menu includes some traditional Swazi dishes, & the b/fast buffet

– with good coffee & homemade muffins – is excellent. Guests can relax around the gardens, decks, pool, lounge & library, hike the reserve's trails or take organised local excursions. Internet is available at reception. **$$$$**

🏠 **Piggs Peak Hotel & Casino** (104 rooms, sleeps 225) ☏ 2431 3104/5; e reservations@ piggspeak.com; www.piggspeakhotel.com. Upmarket, 4-storey hotel located 12km north of Piggs Peak on the MR1, & best known for its casino (see page 226). Caters largely to business

& conference guests & tour groups. There are 89 standard, 7 corner rooms (with adjoining doors, suitable for families) & 8 suites. All rooms are en suite, with DSTV & balcony with a superb mountain view. There are 2 restaurants, offering à la carte & buffet menus, & a separate lounge bar. The extensive grounds have a badminton court, tennis courts, pool with terrace & braai area, volleyball, crazy golf & bowling green. Indoor facilities include squash courts, a 'kids' zone' (with cinema) & a gym/sauna/beauty parlour that offers aerobics, massage, pedicure & other treatments. The huge lobby area has the upmarket Tekwane curio shop. Other services include free Wi-Fi in public areas, a large conference centre & scheduled airport shuttle. Recently refurbished, the hotel offers comfortable accommodation, good food & numerous activities & excursions. Some may find the layout a little characterless & the planners missed a trick by screening the fabulous view behind the hotel from its restaurant & pool, but the staff are helpful & you're assured of a comfortable stay. Interesting touches include a huge chess set hidden away on the ground-floor stairwell & local art hung on the walls. **$$$$**

Mid-range

⌂ **Highlands Inn Hotel** (18 rooms, sleeps 30) ☎2437 1144. This sleepy establishment located on the MR1 about 1km south of town is an old converted colonial house converted into a hotel with a separate room block. All rooms have AC, TV, shower & heater but are rather cramped. There is a large, timber-floored dining room, plus private bar with TV. Service is slow – don't expect to find anyone at reception, let alone such mod cons as Wi-Fi – but the garden terrace, with its scented frangipanis, is a pleasant place from which to watch the world go by. Reputedly the oldest hotel in Swaziland (though not the only one to make that claim), it doubles as the Mbabane Clinic in Richard E Grant's film *Wah-Wah* (see page 91). **$$**

⌂ **Sunset View Guesthouse** (4 units, sleeps 10) ☎2437 1534; m 7642 8770; e sunsetviewguesthouse.sz@gmail.com; www. sunsetviewguesthouse.net. Small, friendly property in residential area 5mins from town centre: follow signs at the first 3-way stop on the MR1 as you enter Piggs Peak from the south (also signed to Mhlatane High School). Accommodation comprises 4 guest units, 2 of which can be linked for families via adjoining doors. Each has its own entrance, outdoor area, bathroom & DSTV. Self-catering facilities, tea & coffee provided. B/fast basket available on request. Owners Ian & Julie Blair from New Zealand have developed the property in an eco-friendly way, using permaculture, solar heating & rainwater irrigation. Chickens roam the orchard & ponds are being built to attract local birdlife (40 bird species recorded to date). Secure parking. **$$**

WHERE TO EAT Piggs Peak is well provided with street cafés and fast-food outlets. These cheerful establishments are mostly clustered around the shopping plaza and bus rank. I recommend the Kula Kwemvelo restaurant (beside Saverite supermarket), with a lively atmosphere, interesting murals, and a hefty portion of chicken curry and rice at the bargain price of SZL20. Alternatively you can find a more tourist-priced meal at any of the following outlets.

✗ **Driftwood Restaurant** Phophonyane Falls Eco Lodge (see page 221). The restaurant at this attractive nature reserve has a varied menu & wonderful view. Order your meal when you arrive then enjoy the reserve while the food is being prepared. The natural ambience of running water & birdsong comes with opportunist vervet monkeys, so keep an eye on your plate. A bar & light meals are also available.

✗ **Highlands Inn** (see above) Serves hot meals, light snacks & drinks in the large colonial dining room or outside on the front terrace. Bring a good book, as service is not exactly zippy (I waited 40mins for a toasted sandwich), but the food is good value & the laid-back atmosphere makes this a good spot to kick back for a while.

✗ **Orion Piggs Peak Hotel and Casino** (see opposite) Piggs Peak's swankiest dining place is this large out-of-town hotel, with a large buffet restaurant & separate à la carte restaurant. Drinks & light meals are available at the Esangweni Bar & pool bar.

✗ **Peak Fine Craft Centre** (see page 227) Large handicraft centre 500m from the Orion Hotel where you can enjoy wholesome meals, local baking & good coffee over a panoramic view from

5

the terrace of the Phumulani Coffee Shop (\2437 3059; ⊕ daily 08.30–17.00). Alternatively, you can get cold drinks & cheaper but less interesting food at the viewless Imbevane Restaurant, beside the car park (⊕ 08.30–17.00 daily).

SHOPPING AND OTHER PRACTICALITIES Piggs Peak has most things you might need from a town. These include:

Banks Branches of all major banks, with ATMs, along the high street.

Bus/taxi rank Behind the Total garage and beside the Boxer shopping complex at the north end of the high street.

Communications World Connect Internet café (m 7621 4649) on the first floor of Mambo House, on the east of the high street at the south of town. Public payphones located outside Ellerines furniture store on the high street.

Filling stations Large Total garage at the north end of the high street, plus an Excel garage opposite. Both have toilets and shops. These are the last reliable filling stations en route north to the Kruger National Park.

Library Next to the town council offices.

Post office On the high street next to the Ministry of Agriculture offices.

Shops The plaza at the north end of the high street has a car park and large Boxer supermarket (one of four in Swaziland), plus furniture, clothing and general stores. A large local market beside the bus rank has numerous stalls with clothes, vegetables and other commodities. Shops line the high street.

WHAT TO SEE AND DO
Phophonyane Falls Nature Reserve
Phophonyane is one of those destinations that inevitably attracts the travel cliché 'best-kept secret'. On the surface it may seem nothing extraordinary: a modest 500ha of forested middleveld hillside, relieved by some rocky outcrops and the meandering Phophonyane River, which tumbles over the 80m-high Phophonyane Falls. It is beautiful but not mind-blowing; wild but not wilderness. Such observations, however, belie the subtle combination of Phophonyane's charms. This place has a magic all its own.

Owner Rod De Vletter acquired the property via his family in 1975 and with his wife Lungile has since converted it from an abandoned farm to the haven that visitors find today. De Vletter is a tourism and environment consultant who has worked on a number of major conservation projects, including both the Lubombo and the Kruger/Mozambique Transfrontier Conservation Areas (see page 50). It's reassuring, then, that he has been able to do such a good job in his own backyard, using real imagination to open up this precious little pocket of bush to visitors.

Access is straightforward. Take the signed turn-off about 10km north of Piggs Peak and follow the steep dirt track – fine for a normal vehicle if you take it slowly – for about 2km down to the reserve entrance. Once inside, you're soon seduced by the place. The cluster of buildings, all painted in African ochres and adorned with hangings and frescoes, nestles discreetly into the lush subtropical vegetation, with natural streams ingeniously diverted through the grounds and carvings lurking among the greenery. Just enough bush has been cleared to create an apron of lawn around the main lodge, and to allow impressive views down the valley beyond. Otherwise nature runs rampant, with birdsong blending into the ubiquitous trickle of running water.

Phophonyane makes a great stop for day visitors, who can eat in the restaurant, hike the trails, enjoy the birdlife and swim in a subtly landscaped natural rockpool above the falls. (Don't stray from the marked areas here: there has been at least one serious accident on the slippery rocks, despite the large warning signs.) It's well worth treating yourself to a night or two, however, if you want to make the most of the place.

Wildlife Phophonyane is not a big-game reserve. The largest mammal you might encounter here is a bushbuck and, even then, you're more likely to see droppings than the animal itself. Walk quietly on the trails, however, and you may spot a timid red duiker, while vervet monkeys often hang around the lodge and troops of banded mongoose forage in clearings. Night brings out genets and bushbabies, and Cape clawless otters forage along the river.

With no expectations of big game, you can concentrate on the smaller stuff, and birders find Phophonyane particularly rewarding. Among some 240 recorded species, pride of place goes to the dazzling Narina trogon, an elusive bird that is the reserve logo and regularly nests around the lodge. A quiet walk along the trails may produce such skulking bush dwellers as eastern nicator, gorgeous bush-shrike and terrestrial brownbul, while paradise flycatcher, purple-crested turaco and crowned hornbill are all common. My best sightings have included an elusive red-breasted sparrowhawk dashing across the river, wood owls outside my tent at night and a crowned eagle soaring over the canopy with a vervet monkey clutched in its talons.

If it doesn't fly, it slithers or scuttles. Abundant reptile life at Phophonyane ranges from pretty (and harmless) spotted bush snakes camouflaged in the undergrowth to rainbow skinks dashing across rocky outcrops. De Vletter has stories of big black mambas and pythons, although snakes – as everywhere – keep themselves to themselves. Among the more conspicuous mini-beasts are a profusion of millipedes, and kite spiders that string their webs across forest trails.

Trails Many visitors to Phophonyane simply hang out around the lodge or pools and commune with nature in a sedentary way. The more energetic, however, can explore walking trails of varying lengths. All involve steep climbs at some point – the terrain falls away sharply with the Phophonyane River – but there are steps cut into the hillsides and a number of viewpoints where you can catch your breath. Trail maps are available at reception.

Trail one Stays west of the Phophonyane River and descends to the 'otter pool' at the bottom (where otter sightings are not guaranteed, although droppings prove they're around). It passes close to the property boundary, from where the sounds of rural village life drift up pleasantly from the valley below.

Trail two The longest, taking two to three hours, depending on your pace and what you see. It is also the most rewarding, as it cuts through most of the reserve's habitats, including the 'python cliffs', riverine forest along the Mbevane stream at the bottom, and a wonderful grove of lowveld chestnuts on the upper slopes, whose large, spiky seed cases litter the ground below.

Trail three Branches off trail two and descends steeply to the Phophonyane River, with great views of the falls. Take a close look at the stream-sculpted rock slabs

Among the tamer wildlife you might encounter at Phophonyane is Rod and Lungile's cat, Iggy. That is, if his luck has held since I last visited. Life may seem pretty good for Iggy, as he sprawls on the sunlit patio of the family residence. But this is Africa. Lungile recounts one hair-raising incident when she was home alone and heard a mighty crash from downstairs, followed by a terrified Iggy rocketing past her. Venturing down to look, she found an adult crowned eagle spreadeagled, literally, on the dining room table. This huge raptor, a bird that frequently captures monkeys in its skull-crushing talons, had swooped at Iggy on the patio but missed its target, followed through into the house and knocked itself senseless against the back wall. As Lungile wondered what to do next the eagle came back to life and, with one flap of its 2m wings, launched itself back out of the French windows and into the forest. Big birds are not the only hazard: just before my last visit, Rod had helped a neighbour remove a large python from an adjoining property – with his cat still inside it. Iggy was duly warned.

as you cross the river below the cascade: glinting golden and charcoal, as though permanently illuminated by the late evening sun, they are part of the 3.5-billion-year-old Barberton greenstone belt (see page 211) and among the oldest rocks on the planet. Then take a deep breath before scaling the steep flight of steps back to the lodge.

Other activities The lodge organises guided walks into the community, where you can visit the primary school, and hikes along the nearby Gobolondo mountain ridge, with panoramic views north over the Makhonjwa mountains and east towards the Lubombo escarpment. An easier though less deserving way to enjoy the views from Gobolondo is on a guided drive in one of the lodge's 4x4 vehicles (SZL95 for adults, SZL55 for children), complete with picnic lunch at the top. Excursions to other local attractions such as Nsangwini can also be arranged.

Piggs Peak Hotel and Casino (see page 222) This large hotel – and especially its casino – has long been synonymous with Piggs Peak, and is splendidly situated on the crest of a ridge, 10km north of town, with fine views across Phophonyane to the hills beyond. Its fluctuating ownership over the years has brought it various names, including Piggs Peak Protea and Orion Piggs Peak. Whatever it's called, however, this grand four-star establishment offers comfortable accommodation and can arrange for its guests pretty much anything they might want to do in the region, from tours of the Kruger National Park to clay-pigeon shooting.

Much the most important of the hotel's activities is the casino (⊕ 10.00–24.00 Sun–Thu; 10.00–04.00 Fri–Sat), to which non-guests are very much welcome. Like other casinos in Swaziland, this one dates back to a time when gambling did not pass muster with the strict moral custodians of neighbouring South Africa, many of whose residents would thus sneak over the border for a flutter. Today South Africa is awash with casinos and Swaziland has lost its niche status. Nonetheless, this one continues to pull optimistic punters; the happy hour on Wednesday is especially popular with locals. There are automated table games, a flashing/bleeping wall of slot machines and, I believe, anything else you might want from a casino. Non-gamblers might also find the ATM useful.

Peak Fine Craft Centre (✆ 2437 3059; *www.swaziplace.com/peakfinecraft*;
⊕ *daily 08.00–17.00*). Of all Swaziland's many handicraft centres, this one –
located 500m north of the Piggs Peak Hotel, beside the MR1 – has indisputably
the best view. Among the line-up of handicraft boutiques are some highly
professional businesses that export their hand-crafted, high-quality textiles
around the world. You can thus expect high prices – although it is still cheaper
buying here than overseas, and there are bargains to be had. Irrespective of price,
this is an opportunity to see the work displayed in front of the landscape that
inspired it, to meet its creators and perhaps see some of them in action. Have a
browse; the products are gorgeous, and afterwards have a drink – or a bite – at
the Phumulani restaurant, whose terrace looks all the way down the valley to the
Makhonjwa mountains.

Coral Stephens Hand-Weaving (✆ 2437 3059; e *coralstephens@mweb.co.sz*;
www.coralstephens.com) This impressive enterprise, which comprises a workshop
and boutique, is the focal point of the craft centre and a real local success story.
Coral Stephens founded the company in 1949 after arriving in Piggs Peak from
Pretoria with her husband, who established Swaziland's first forestry plantations.
She brought with her Sylvia Mantanga, with whom she had learned traditional
hand-weaving back in South Africa. The two women import mohair from South
Africa and taught their skills to local Swazi women, who helped inspire new
designs. Their curtains caught the eye of visitors and the hobby became a business,
taking orders from Johannesburg and beyond. Soon Coral was employing spinners
to supply the weavers and local mechanics to build the wheels.

Coral passed away some time ago and Sylvia, who worked until her final
day, died in 2010 at the age of 84. Today, Murrae Stephens married to Coral's
grandson, Tommy – runs the operation, which employs 38 staff and exports its
products around the world. The workshop was formerly located at the nearby
Stephens's family home, Boshimela, which featured as the main residence in the
Richard E Grant film *Wah-Wah* (see page 91), but moved to the craft centre after
the house burned down in the forest fires of 2007. This was a tragedy for the family
(although, mercifully, the only fatality was a turkey) but proved better news for
visitors, who can now watch the weavers in action. Visits are by prior appointment
(✆ 2437 1140) and the process, which involves traditional looms and wood-fired
dyeing pots, is fascinating. Products now include curtains, carpets, upholstery,
blankets and cushion covers, and the workshop has diversified from mohair into
silk, raffia and other materials.

Also in the Coral Stephens shop, look out for tiles, tableware and other ceramics
by local potter Monique Wilson, who has her own kiln beside the weaving
workshop. Monique's bold, adventurous designs feature among the extraordinary
architecture of House on Fire too (see page 186).

Tintsaba Crafts (✆ 2431 3380/3260; e *admin@tintsaba.com*; *www.tintsaba.com*)
This weaving enterprise was created in 1985 by Sheila Freemantle and has since
mushroomed from a cottage industry to a major business that has trained around
900 local women to produce everything from baskets to jewellery. The material
used is fine-spun sisal, an exotic fibrous plant – originally from Latin America –
that grows wild around Swaziland. Tintsaba places great emphasis on supporting
women in the community, including with health and literacy. It also has outlets
at the Piggs Peak Hotel (see page 222), Ngwenya Glass (see page 201) and Happy
Valley Hotel (see page 163).

The Northwest PIGGS PEAK

5

Likhweti Kraft A branch of Tintsaba (see above), Likhweti Kraft produces locally crafted silver jewellery, including rings, earrings, bangles, necklaces and other items, many using designs and motifs drawn from traditional Swazi culture and folklore. Look out for the highly original 'framed sisal jewellery' range, which integrates silver with sisal disks in earrings, necklaces and pendants.

Ethnic Bound Next door to Coral Stephens Hand-Weaving. Sells artefacts and crafts from all over southern and west Africa. It also has an African-themed range of clothing for men, women and children.

Carvings Before leaving the craft centre, take a look at the curio stalls beside the car park. Here Anton Khoza is among several local carvers displaying some excellent work in both wood and stone. Anton uses invasive tree species for his wooden pieces and, if you are in the area for a while, will happily take commissions.

MATSAMO

From the Piggs Peak Hotel it is a 25km, 20-minute drive along the MR1 to Matsamo, Swaziland's border with South Africa. The road winds down steeply through dense middleveld bush, twice crossing over the Phophonyane River. It then continues more gently through the picturesque landscape of northern Hhohho, with the Makhonjwa Mountains lining the western horizon. This is a lovely drive, but don't let the scenery distract you from wandering cattle.

Some 10km before the border you will pass the neat rows of orange, lemon and grapefruit trees marking the Ngonini citrus estates. Near the entrance is a filling station, with supermarket, toilets and payphones. A few kilometres further on you will pass a right turn signed east to Madlamgempisi on the MR6, with a cluster of curio stalls. This road – a good tar one – takes you east to Tshaneni and the northeastern lowveld (see page 247). Watch out for the speed bumps if you head this way, especially after about 19km where the road passes the Ebuhleni royal residence.

Four kilometres later the road crosses the Mlumati River (or Lomati River, depending on your map). Another 3km takes you to the border. Here you will find a Total garage with toilets, plus the usual cluster of fruit and veg stalls, and 'La Boutique' take-away. The border is open from 08.00 to 20.00 and is seldom busy. Look out for a small baobab tree growing in the car park outside South African immigration – the southernmost I have ever seen. The South Africa side of the border is known as Jeppes Reef. From here it is just 46km to the Kruger Park entrance gate at Malelane. The first 15km or so, as you pass through the settlements of Jeppes Reef and Schoemansdal, can be chaotic, with people and cattle all over the road, so rein in your excitement and take it slowly.

BULEMBU

Bulembu is an extraordinary place: part community, part charity and part museum. It lies on the South Africa border due west of Piggs Peak, among some of Swaziland's most impressive scenery, including the 1,862m summit of Emlembe, the kingdom's highest mountain. Built in the late 1930s to serve the Havelock asbestos mine, this was once a thriving community of some 10,000 people (nearly twice as many as Piggs Peak today) and the mine, with its celebrated cableway to Barberton, the mainstay of Swaziland's economy. As asbestos mining declined, however, so

Bulembu declined with it. In 2001 the company that had operated the mine for more than 60 years pulled out and the town was soon abandoned.

Amazingly, this historic location has received a new lease of life, courtesy of Bulembu Ministries Swaziland (see page 141). This pioneering charity project has restored the community through a combination of social welfare – notably the rehousing of vulnerable children in old miners' accommodation – and cottage industry. Volunteers come from around the world to help, while tourists can visit the museum in which the old mine machinery is preserved, stay at the resurrected Bulembu Country Lodge and hike high into the hills.

To quell any concerns, the latest external studies – completed in May 2012 – concluded that neither visitors nor residents in Bulembu face any health risks associated with the former mine. Air-quality samples showed that asbestos fibre concentrations did not exceed the international recommended standard.

GETTING THERE AND AWAY Bulembu is a mere 18km from Piggs Peak on the MR20. Just turn west at the main crossroads in the centre of town (also signed to Barberton) and keep going. Be warned, though: the gravel road is a rough one, with a pot-holed surface and numerous lumbering logging trucks. Allow plenty of time, especially if in a normal car, and don't travel during heavy rains.

The road up from Barberton, on the South African side, used to be even worse, disappearing constantly into an unsigned maze of logging tracks. But it has since been tarred and, although the 42km of steep hairpins have their white-knuckle moments, this is now a perfectly straightforward drive – with superb panoramas over Songimvelo Game Reserve to the west. Coming up from Barberton, follow the signs to Josefsdal (the border) and Piggs Peak. The road deteriorates as soon as you cross the border, from where it is a pot-holed 2km to Bulembu, with the lodge signed after 500m on your right and the old mine workings set back from the road a little further on.

WHERE TO STAY

🏠 **Bulembu Country Lodge** (sleeps up to 178) m 7602 1593; e reservations@bulembu.org; www.bulembu.com. This mid-range property is Bulembu's only lodge. Accommodation comprises: 12 en-suite rooms (29 people); 5 fully-equipped self-catering houses, on FB or self-catering basis (up to 51 people, 9+ per house); & a hostel comprising twin rooms & communal bathrooms (up to 98 people sharing). All structures restored from original mine buildings, including the old general manager's house & former directors' cottages. Not upmarket, but clean & comfortable; old-fashioned baths, huge windows, polished wooden floors & cosy log fires re-create the colonial charm of the community's 1930s heyday. The restaurant seats 45 & wholesome meals are served from a set menu, with braais on request. Also: snooker room, outdoor swimming pool, TV lounge & conference facilities. Internet available at reception on request. All profits go to the Bulembu Project (see page 230). **$–$$**

HISTORY Prospectors first started exploring Bulembu in 1886, when they established a mineral concession over the area called the Havelock Swaziland Protection Syndicate (named after the then British governor of Natal, who had supported Boer annexation of Swaziland). It wasn't until 1923, though, that asbestos fibres were discovered along the banks of a local stream. Mining companies were initially wary, due to the challenges of operating in such a remote region. In 1930, however, the British–Canadian mining house Turner-Newell invested in a large-scale operation. They bypassed the difficulties of road building by constructing a huge cableway to Barberton. This immense engineering project was 20km long and at one stage the largest of its kind outside Europe. Its 224 cupolas moved down a 25mm-thick steel cable that was suspended from 54 pylons and, in places, hung 190m above the ground. Production began in 1939 and the town of Bulembu, set a little distance from the noxious mine workings, was built to house workers.

Asbestos, with its extreme malleability and heat resistance, was in high demand during the mid 20th century. Havelock mine became one of the five largest in the world, producing at its peak a steady 30,000–40,000 tonnes a year and remaining Swaziland's biggest earner of foreign currency until it was overtaken by sugar in 1962. Meanwhile Bulembu flourished in its glorious isolation. Not only did the inhabitants enjoy the essentials of housing, schools, hospital and jail, they also had a cricket pitch, cinema, swimming pool and even a polo field. And all, of course, with a fabulous view.

But the good times couldn't last. Problems started as soon as scientists worldwide, alerted by workers' health problems, found that the very fibres that made asbestos such a wonder mineral also caused the insidious lung disease asbestosis. By the 1980s several countries had already banned asbestos and, with a declining yield and shrinking market, production at Havelock began to slow. By 2000, when it had fallen to just 12,690 tonnes, the mine was no longer viable. The following year Turner-Newell packed up and left. Bulembu, almost overnight, became a ghost town. Only about 150 residents remained.

THE BULEMBU PROJECT When the mine shut down and Bulembu's lights went out – literally and figuratively – few could have anticipated that the place would return to life within just three years. In 2003, however, the Bulembu Development Corporation bought the entire property and in 2006 transferred it to the trust of Bulembu Ministries Swaziland. This Christian charity set about restoring the place though the complementary strategies of community care and community enterprise.

The community care programme aims to tackle Swaziland's mounting problem of children left orphaned or vulnerable by the HIV/AIDS epidemic. Children from all over the country have been rehoused in the old miners' accommodation, modified for their needs, and provided with family structures, schooling, health services and round-the-clock care. The project's ambition is to create an environment and infrastructure for 2,000 such children.

The community enterprise scheme aims to create employment, foster vocational and leadership skills, and make the community self-reliant once again. It has established a number of small-scale local businesses, including honey, dairy, forestry, mineral water, crafts, lodge and a bakery. Already there is a new sawmill and over 800 beehives in the forest, and the herd of more than 70 Jerseys is supplying butter for national consumption. The project is ambitious, and so far seems to be working: unemployment among the growing population of some 1,500 is almost zero. You can find out more – and perhaps make a contribution – at www.bulembu.org.

WHAT TO SEE AND DO One achievement of Bulembu's rebirth has been the preservation of its original 1930s structures. Today you can visit the old mine buildings or wander down Winston Churchill Street to explore the abandoned entertainment complex, with its cinema, bar and stage. A new museum housed in the cableway station preserves much of the old machinery that once made the country's fortune. This museum was under development at the time of writing, with new displays going up, and there is even a plan to resurrect the cableway to allow short journeys for visitors. I can only hope that this includes a rescue plan: during the 1980s a would-be border jumper who tried to steal a free ride to South Africa found himself hanging halfway along when it shut down for the evening. Stuck there all night, he froze to death.

For those who want to explore the stirring scenery there are numerous hiking trails. These range from a 300m walk to a nearby waterfall viewpoint to a five-hour hike up the summit of Emlembe. Trails are well signed, and guides are available at the lodge. The excellent local birdlife includes montane grassland and mist-belt forest species, such as malachite sunbird and Knysna turaco.

BULEMBU BORDER The Bulembu border is called Josefsdal on the South Africa side. It is one of the smallest and sleepiest of Swaziland's road borders and, all being well, should take you no more than 15 minutes to cross. (Consider yourself extremely unlucky if you meet a coach party up here.) The gates are open from 08.00 to 16.00, so make sure that you have allowed adequate time before setting out on the arduous drive from Piggs Peak or Barberton.

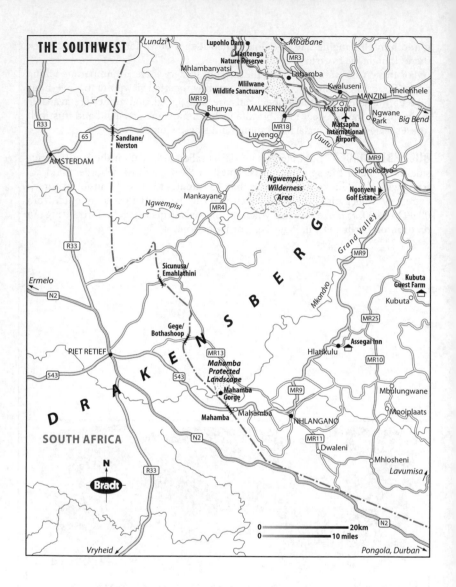

THE SOUTHWEST

Lundzi • Lupohlo Dam • • *Mbabane*
Mantenga
Nature Reserve
Mhlambanyatsi
MR3
Lobamba
Mlilwane
Wildlife Sanctuary
Kwaluseni
MANZINI
Hhelehhele
MR19
Bhunya
MALKERNS
Matsapha
Ngwane
Park
Big Bend
R33
65
Sandlane/
Nerston
MR18
Luyengo
Matsapha
International
Airport
Usutu
AMSTERDAM
MR9
Sidvokodvo
Ngwempisi
Wilderness
Area
Ngonyeni
Golf Estate
Ngwempisi
Mankayane
MR4
R33
Grand Valley
MR9
Ermelo
Sicunusa/
Emahlathini
Mkondvo
Kubuta
Guest Farm
Kubuta
N2
MR25
Gege/
Bothashoop
MR13
Assegai Inn
Hlatikulu
MR10
PIET RETIEF
Mahamba
Protected
Landscape
543
543
Mahamba
Gorge
MR9
Mbulungwane
Mooiplaats
Mahamba
Mahamba
NHLANGANO
SOUTH AFRICA
N2
MR11
Dwaleni
Mhlosheni
N
Lavumisa
R33
Bradt
0   20km
0   10 miles
N2
Vryheid
Pongola, Durban

6

The Southwest

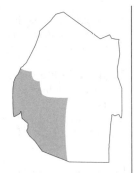

This chapter describes the bottom left quarter of Swaziland, roughly that region that lies south of the Great Usutu River and west of the MR9. It does not include the Mhlambanyatsi area, which you can reach easily from Mbabane and is thus described in *Chapter 3* (see page 147).

Much of southwest Swaziland is highveld, its rolling uplands extending west over the border into South Africa. The Great Usutu, Swaziland's largest river, enters from this direction and flows east. It acquires two tributaries from the south: the Ngwempisi, which slices a wild gorge through the Ngwempisi Wilderness Area; and the Mkondvo, which does a similar thing at Mahamba, then continues north through the Grand Valley, forming a picturesque corridor between Nhlangano and Manzini. Dense middleveld bush carpets these valleys, but otherwise the landscape is largely montane grassland, with extensive forestry plantations around Nhlangano in the south and Bhunya in the north.

Southwest Swaziland cuts across two administrative regions: Shiselweni to the south and Manzini to the north. The largest town is Nhlangano, capital of Shiselweni, which is located in the far south. Smaller centres include Sidvokodvo, Hlatikulu and Mankayane, none of them of great interest to the tourist. Beyond these towns, the population is dispersed across small, rural subsistence communities.

Today this is perhaps the least visited region in Swaziland, much of its traffic being in transit. This belies its historical importance, however. Ngwane III, founder of the Swazi nation, established his first ceremonial capital near Nhlangano. And it was via this route that many of the country's early settlers arrived, over the hills from nearby Piet Retief in South Africa. These included the Wesleyan Missionaries who established Swaziland's first mission – and, subsequently, church – at Mahamba. Hlatikulu once served as a regional headquarters for the British, and it was in Nhlangano in 1947 that George VI met Sobhuza II during the only ever visit to Swaziland by a British monarch.

If history is not your thing, southwest Swaziland also offers magnificent scenery with some great hiking – notably at Ngwempisi and Mahamba – plus a golf estate, a weaving centre and, if you're feeling lucky, a casino.

SOUTH TO NHLANGANO

The MR9 to Nhlangano is one of Swaziland's great drives. You pick up the road at a large junction on the MR3 some 3km west of Manzini and head south. The first stretch passes through open farmland, with wild hills beyond. Then, after crossing the Usutu, the road enters the impressive Grand Valley. Here it winds through thick bush and scattered homesteads alongside the Mkondvo River before climbing dramatically up an escarpment onto the exposed plateau of the highveld, where

Nhlangano sits amid its apron of forestry plantations. This 90km drive should take you about an hour and a quarter, travelling directly, but there are a few diversions along the way.

TO SIDVOKODVO The first stretch of the MR9 passes through Manzini's outlying suburbs, including Ngwane Park to the east, through which a left turn after 4km offers a short cut into town. The road then descends gently into the Usutu Valley through heavily grazed Swazi Nation Land. Just before crossing the Great Usutu, 20km south of the MR3, a left turn leads to Sidvokodvo. This small town has little to detain the visitor but there are one or two nearby attractions.

Where to stay and eat

🏠 **Nkonyeni Golf Estate** (sleeps 78) ☎7602 4880; e enquiries@nkonyeni.com; www.nkonyeni. com. Plush resort just south of the Usutu River, built around a luxury retirement village with an 18-hole golf course (1 of only 2 in Swaziland), plus game reserve, restaurants & resort facilities. Visitor accommodation comes in 3 kinds of unit: 7 riverfront chalets each sleep 2, with en-suite bathroom & veranda overlooking the river; 7 pool villas each sleep up to 8, in 4 bedrooms, but can be rented by the bedroom – they are nestled in the bush, with private pool, veranda & huge kitchen, DSTV & AC. Inside the game reserve are 4 mountain chalets; each sleeps 2 & comes with a butler; meals are self-catering or at the restaurant. **$$$$**

🏠 **Tum's Waterworld** (sleeps 54) ☎2540 0050/0055; m 7694 9342; e tumswaterworld@ realnet.co.sz; tumswaterworld.com. 500m off the MR3, 1km north of the Usutu Bridge (see map, page 242). Comprises 21 bedrooms (10 dbls & 11 twins) & a campsite. Pleasant restaurant & bar serves reasonably priced food, including Swazi specials, with a view of the Usutu & Grand Valley. Landscaped grounds, with huge sculpted animals & 2 small dams. Also: swimming pool, children's playground, conference centre & bird hide. Activities include fishing, paddleboats & canoeing. Popular local venue for weddings & functions. **$$$–$$$$**

🏠 **The Vineyard Bed and Breakfast** (sleeps 14) m 7695 0020; e stocksian@gmail.com. Small family-run B&B on Etibusisweni Farm, Swaziland's only wine-producing estate. East of Sidvokodvo: pass through town, continue 3km from the tar road then turn right towards the Great Usutu on a smaller farm road, which leads to the entrance after 3.9km (see map, page 242). Rooms in the main house & garden rondavels. Facilities include a swimming pool, games room (with pool table) & private bar. Activities include tours of the estate, mountain-bike trails & walks to the river (with a private frontage & picnic spots). Commanding location, overlooking the river & sugar-cane fields. The estate has been bottling wine since 2007 & has a Shiraz under the Vindziwo label, meaning 'wine from the traditional clay pot'. **$$**

🏠 **The Cowshed** (sleeps 24) m 7615 2604. Backpackers hostel in converted dairy just south of the Usutu (see map, page 242). Part of the Nkonyeni Golf Estate but reached via separate turn-off to the north. Ingenious design includes old cowshed transformed into 4 dbl rooms & dormitory for 16 people, plus milking parlour recast as the Pickled Pig bar & swimming pool. Fully equipped kitchen & outside ablutions. Fine views of the river & mountains. Pleasant & welcoming but was struggling when I visited in 2011 so check in advance that it is still open. **$**

What to see and do

Nkonyeni Golf Estate This impressive resort is one of a kind in Swaziland. It sits close to the confluence of the Ngwempisi and Usutu rivers and is well signed along a gravel road off the MR9 just south of the Usutu. The road continues west to the MR4 near Mankayane (see page 240), but you reach the imposing thatched entrance to Nkonyeni after just 2km on the right.

Nkonyeni's mosaic of cottages, paved roads, sports facilities and pristine fairways, all artfully landscaped into tracts of indigenous bush, is a somewhat unexpected sight amid the surrounding wild country. The estate is essentially a luxury retirement village, comprising more than 250 individual plots. Residents get a swimming pool, health spa, tennis courts, two five-star restaurants and a top-notch golf course for their money, the last of these featuring a shot across the Usutu to the 18th. In short, all the facilities you'd expect from a top-notch resort. The well-tended grounds teem with birdlife (rare ground hornbills were recently recorded), and the fenced 500ha reserve is home to zebra, impala, kudu, waterbuck and other game.

Unless you are a golf fanatic or approaching imminent retirement, you might think that Nkonyeni is not for you. Certainly, from a visitor's perspective, this manicured retreat seems to have little to do with the Swaziland beyond its boundaries. Nonetheless, visitors can enjoy an excellent meal with a lovely view at the restaurant, attached to the clubhouse. And if you splash out on a night or two, you can make use of all the facilities, which include game drives, clay-pigeon shooting, quad-biking, mountain-biking and, of course, golf. All-inclusive weekend packages, including the full 18 holes, are available (*two nights from SZL1,750 pp*).

Rider's Ranch This place is signed on the west of the road just north of Tum's Waterworld (see opposite). It is, as you will gather from the motorbike mounted on its gates, a bikers' haunt. The Swaziland Rally takes place here every August and there are – so rumour has it – plans to develop a biker's getaway, with rooms and a restaurant. Beyond that, information is hard to find; I suspect that you'd need to be a member of the biking community to find out more. The owner, apparently, is the BMW dealer in Manzini, so you could try asking there.

GRAND VALLEY

The MR9 crosses the Mkondvo, another tributary of the Great Usutu, 5km south of Nkonyeni. For the next 20km or so road and river meander alongside one another down the eastern flank of the Grand Valley. This is a glorious drive, with dense bush on either side and colourful vignettes of village life along the riverbank: children swimming and playing; women washing clothes; herdsmen leading their cattle across the shallows.

Just south of a pedestrian suspension bridge across the river – the legacy of a US aid project in the 1980s – the Mkondvo and MR9 diverge. The road winds steeply east, tight against the flank of the escarpment. At its steepest point the two lanes divide to form a dual carriageway – the northbound (downward) lanes set lower than the southbound (upward) lanes – which certainly makes it easier to get round the heavy trucks that crawl up this arduous stretch. The views are stupendous in both directions, the unbroken bush offering some reassurance that not all Swaziland's wilderness is confined to reserves.

At the top of the hill the road levels out and deposits you back in the highveld. Over the steep escarpment walls, the tangled scrub gives way abruptly to undulating grasslands and stands of gum trees, with forestry plantations lining the horizon ahead. It's a different world. Get out of the vehicle and you'll find it's a cooler one too.

HLATIKULU Hlatikulu, which means 'big trees' or 'thick bush', was an important centre during the British colonial era, with an administrative function for the whole of southern Swaziland. It was also the name of Swaziland's first nature reserve (see *Conservation in Swaziland*, page 51), which stretched across much of the south. Today, however, it has been rather left behind. Google 'Hlatikulu' and you are more likely to be directed to the bush lodge of this name in South Africa.

There is not much here: one or two shops, a church, a post office, a Standard Bank, Styles restaurant and bar, and a single hotel, the faded Assegai Inn. There is also a market, and – to the left of the crossroads at the end of town – a bus and taxi rank.

Getting there and away Hlatikulu lies on the MR26, which loops off the MR9 around 70km south of Manzini. Follow the road round and you will enter town after 7km. From the end of the high street, past the police station, a dirt road continues south, ultimately to Hluti. The loop returns you to the MR9 after another 3km, from where you turn left for Nhlangano.

Where to stay

⌂ **Assegai Inn** (sleeps 30) ☏ 2217 6421; assegai@swazi.net. This old hotel on the high street is the only place to stay in town & has something of a roadhouse feel. Comprises 7 dbl rooms, 1 'family cottage' & 14 backpacker rooms. Tea/coffee & DSTV. Also: secure parking, children's playground, conference hall, campsite, restaurant, 2 bars (both with billiard tables) & adjoining bottle store. No pool &, when I last visited, no internet access. Restaurant offers basic inexpensive menu, with BBQs on Fri & Sat nights. No credit cards. **$$**

⌂ **Kubuta Guest Farm** (16 beds) ☏ 2344 1626; e kubuta@swazi.net; www.visitswazi.com/ kubuta. Located in a remote valley just east of the region covered in this chapter but best reached via Hlatikulu. Self-catering accommodation in 2 rondavels with separate kitchen & bathroom, 1

family suite with en-suite bathroom, 1 en-suite guest room & a 6-person cottage with 3 bedrooms & 2 bathrooms. Kitchens fully equipped. No shops nearby so bring all food. Activities include local walks, fishing & hiking to the top of Lokolwane, the highest local peak. Within 1hr's drive of Nkonyeni Golf Estate (see page 234) & Mkhaya Game Reserve (see page 277). To reach Kubuta, take the MR26 north from Hlatikulu & turn right at a T-junction 2km before the MR9. Around 2.5km after this road becomes gravel, take the left fork signed to Kubuta. After 23.4km you reach Kubuta Banana Farm: continue past an old red engine on the right & a farm stall on the left. Take the first right, past an island planted with palms, & enter the gate. The road condition varies with the rains but is OK for a normal vehicle. **$$**

NHLANGANO

Nhlangano is the capital and largest town of Shiselweni, with a population of some 10,000. At 1,051m, it sits at roughly the same altitude as Piggs Peak and its highveld climate makes it reputedly the coldest town in Swaziland in winter. Like Piggs Peak, it is surrounded by forestry plantations.

The town was founded in 1921 as a local farm supply centre. The Boer farmers named it Goedgegun, which means 'well-favoured' in Afrikaans, but in 1947 it was renamed Nhlangano, which means 'meeting place', when King George VI met King Sobhuza II here. The British king had come to thank his Swazi counterpart for the kingdom's help during World War II, and he brought with him his wife and the young princesses Elizabeth and Margaret. This occasion remains the only ever visit by a British monarch to Swaziland, even though the country was a protectorate for more than 60 years. Today the town's main visitor attraction is its casino.

The centre of town has all the basic civic amenities, including shops, post office, pharmacy, filling stations and banks. On the south side of the high street is a large, pot-holed car park that serves a small shopping mall, with supermarkets, banks, eateries and clothes stores. Further along is the taxi rank. On a parallel street to the south you will find the old Phoenix Hotel (no longer a going concern) and police station. Continue out of town, past Evelyn Bering High School on the right ('sponsored by Kentucky Fried Chicken'), and you will reach a T-junction with the MR11, where a right turn leads to the casino.

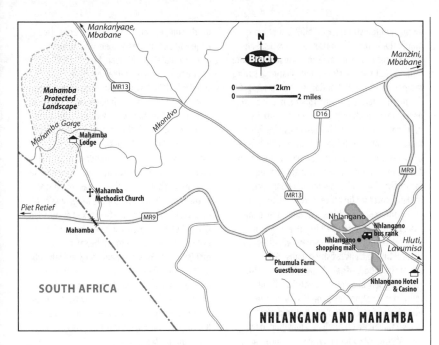

NHLANGANO AND MAHAMBA

GETTING THERE AND AWAY Nhlangano lies some 20km south of Hlatikulu along the MR9. After passing a sign saying 'Welcome to Nhlangano: Jesus loves you' (resolving at a stroke any doubts about both your location and spiritual well-being), you will first see a left turn signed to Nhlangano Casino. This leads to the hotel and casino (see page 239) 3km down the road and then onward east to Lavumisa. To enter town take either the first right off this road, after 1km, or continue along the MR9 and turn left where signed.

WHERE TO STAY

⌂ **Nhlangano Hotel and Casino** (sleeps 94) ☎ 2207 8211; e hotel@nhlanganoroyale.com; www.nhlanganocasino.com. Nhlangano's main attraction is also known as Nhlangano Casino Royale – perhaps to satisfy punters with James Bond delusions. The 47 chalets comprise dbls, family rooms & garden suites, all with Africa-themed décor, telephone & DSTV. Makhosini View restaurant offers à la carte menu & buffets, with specials including lamb cutlets & baby chicken, & an extensive South African wine list. The Two Kings lounge is adorned with posters detailing local history. Light meals can be taken by the pool & picnic baskets packed on request. The casino is behind the restaurant. Non-gamblers will also find a swimming pool, children's playground, tennis & volleyball courts, curio shop, putting & bowling greens, & cinema. Other offerings include a conference centre, which often hosts delegations

from across the border, an airport shuttle service & trips to local attractions, including Mahamba Gorge. Local activities include hiking, fishing, canoeing & quad-biking, & regular braai nights. This is one of Swaziland's better hotels, with an airy lobby, good & attractive gardens. Its crescent of wooden chalets set around the pool offer panoramic views southwest into the Makosini Valley. Built in 1978, it has changed hands several times over the years but was fully renovated by its current South American owners, who took over in 2008. The King Mswati III Dinner is held once a year after the Umhlanga to commemorate the historic meeting of the two kings in 1947. **$$$$**

⌂ **Phumula Farm Guesthouse** (29 rooms, sleeps 50) ☎ 2207 9099; e phumulaguesthouse@ swazi.net; www.phumulaguesthouse.co.za. B&B guesthouse set in attractive gardens among deep gum forests south of Nhlangano. Located along 1km forestry track off MR9, 9km before Mahamba border. Comprises 20 dbl & 9 sgl en-suite rooms beside main farmhouse in 4 separate units: 1 unit has 5 sgl/dbl rooms sharing a sitting room, small kitchen & patio; another has 2 sgl/dbl rooms sharing a sitting room & patio; a 3rd has 2 rooms, each with patio; 2 larger luxury units each have small kitchen & private patio. All rooms come with fridge, heater, ceiling fan, DSTV & tea/coffee. B/fast served in dining room beside main house. Dinner available on request (order by 15.00). Also: swimming pool, secure parking, internet (in office) & covered braai area with conference facilities. A friendly, personal vibe. Lush flora & rich birdlife are a haven amid the dark plantations. The owners will direct you to local hiking trails & fishing dams. **$$**

⌂ **Mahamba Lodge** (12 beds) `2237 0100; m 7617 9880; bookings through Swaziland tourist information (see page 101) or via the numbers above. Community tourism project (see below) built with EU funding & maintained by local Methodist community. In scenic location overlooking entrance to Mahamba Gorge (see page 238). Comprises 6 stone-walled, self-catering chalets for 2. Clean, functional wooden interiors, with comfortable bed, flush toilet, shower & kitchen with most basics except fridge. Solar electricity erratic but gas heats a 2-ring stove & provides hot water, while candles light your way after dark. Wooden deck in front offers fine views of gorge. Braai stand out back kept supplied with firewood. Community caretaker unlocks entrance gate & safeguards your vehicle. Information hut beside chalets has communal kitchen, but during my stay the fridge was out of gas & the catering facilities locked away. Food & supplies are allegedly sometimes sold & b/fast served here, but it might be safer to stock up first (supermarkets in Nhlangano & at Mahamba border). Like many community projects, this one does not always function as efficiently as commercial establishments, but what it may lack in facilities it more than makes up for in location & ambience. During my last stay I was the only occupant. **$–$$**

WHAT TO SEE AND DO

Mahamba The historic Mahamba area lies at the very south of the MR9 and has both Swaziland's first church and an impressive river gorge. It is also the location of Swaziland's main southwest road border with South Africa, from where it is a short drive to Piet Retief. Both church and gorge are reached by a dirt road that turns north from the MR9 just short of the border.

Mahamba Methodist Church The first Christian missionaries that came to Swaziland in 1844 were Wesleyans, who quickly founded a mission school and managed to gather a small congregation. Unfortunately they became embroiled in a local dispute between the king and some of his enemies and, when bloodshed erupted in the mission grounds, they fled the country in terror. 'Mahamba' means, appropriately, 'those who have run away'.

It wasn't until 1912 that a church was built on this spot. This was the first place of Christian worship in Swaziland and today still stands at the heart of a local Methodist community. Located on the left of the road to Mahamba Gorge, among a small community of homesteads, it is a striking sandstone structure in Gothic style that in 2005–06 was carefully restored with EU funding. Displays inside, complete with archive photographs, document the history of the mission and the restoration of the church. A plaque commemorates the foundation stone, 'laid by Rev Amos Burnet 31 July 1912', and a stroll around the graveyard reveals colonial names on the crumbling headstones. Worshippers today use the new Methodist church next door.

Mahamba Gorge Another 3km past the church will take you to the end of the road, where Mahamba Gorge swings into view as a deep cleft in the rocky, aloe-studded ridge ahead. This marks the spot where the Mkondvo River – which you will already have passed if you travelled down the Grand Valley (see page 235) –

carves its passage through the mountainous border with South Africa. Pass through the gate to the picnic area and information centre. Day trippers will find this a good spot for a picnic or braai. With more time, you can overnight in the chalets (see page 237), which accommodate up to 12 people. Either way, there is a modest entrance fee of SZL12, which you pay at the gate, open normal working hours.

Trails lead in different directions from the picnic site. One winds to the left around the southern cliffs of the gorge. Another winds to the right, through a patch of forest and down to the river – which you can ford on a shallow bend – before continuing up the steep northern side, with views of a waterfall. You can explore by yourself or get a community guide to lead you. Either way, take care: these trails can be treacherous underfoot, with loose scree, and the cairns and painted signs are easily overlooked. Inside the gorge, with just the sound of the river and birdsong echoing off the cliffs, you leave the outside world behind. Continue, and you will see through to South Africa beyond, its farmland appearing rather tame by comparison with the wild ravine in which you are standing. Trails continue up over the ridges, for hikers who want to get more miles under their boots.

The cliffs protect one of Swaziland's only two colonies of southern bald ibis, their nest sites betrayed by the splash of white droppings. Look out for these rare birds at dusk and dawn as they commute between their colonies and the surrounding fields – but don't confuse them with hadeda ibis, which often feed near the river and can be distinguished by their raucous calls in flight. Red-winged starlings hop around the rocks, their mournful whistles drifting down the gorge, while jackal buzzards, white-necked ravens and rare Verreaux's eagles drift overhead. Rock hyraxes – fodder for the eagles – live among the boulders; watch out for these furry mammals basking in the early morning sun. Other wildlife I've encountered here includes a black-breasted snake eagle (rare in Swaziland), a spotted eagle owl hooting outside my chalet at night and, more alarming, a Mozambique spitting cobra foraging through my firewood. Klipspringers may possibly inhabit the more inaccessible cliffs, although the only ungulates I've ever spotted turned out to be feral goats.

Mahamba border post The Mahamba road border has the same name on both sides. It is open from 07.00 to 22.00 and often fairly busy, being the main southwest route into Swaziland and offering easy access from the South African town of Piet Retief just 35km away. On the Swazi side you will find most services but no ATM. A large Galp service station has fuel, clean toilets and a store with cold drinks and newspapers. The Welcome Swazi restaurant and supermarket sells cold drinks, bread and hot take-aways, but no fresh meat (worth knowing, if shopping for a braai). There is also a cluster of vegetable stalls and a few cafés and take-aways.

Nhlangano Casino Royale The casino has been part of the Nhlangano Hotel (see page 237) since it opened in 1978. Indeed, the hotel was once a rather less family-orientated establishment that catered largely to South Africans in search of weekend pleasures. Today the casino sits behind the restaurant and does not impinge on the life of the hotel. It has slot machines of various types, plus tables offering poker, blackjack and American roulette. There are also free poker lessons (which I think is what's known as 'growing the market') and regular bingo nights.

Nhlangano to Lavumisa on the MR11 You can reach Lavumisa and the southern lowveld (see page 286) from Nhlangano by continuing due east past the casino on the MR11. This good tar road takes you from highveld to lowveld in just 90km, thus perfectly illustrating Swaziland's compact topography. There are few

settlements except the small centre of Hluti, halfway along. You may be able to find fuel here but you'd be better off topping up before setting out: there is a large Total station at the junction of the MR11 and MR9.

From the casino the road soon descends into the middleveld. It crosses a sequence of rivers: the Mahosha (after 11km), the Mlongwane (after 22km) and the Mantambo (after 34km). After 43km you can see the long blue ridge of the Lubombo Mountains on the horizon ahead. A few kilometres later you will reach Hluti, from where a back road leads north to Hlatikulu. Here you will find bottle store, garage, butchery, vegetable vendors, bus stop and police station. Another 41km of hot, dry lowveld takes you to Lavumisa, and onward to Durban or Big Bend. As ever, watch out for cows on the road.

NHLANGANO TO LUYENGO, VIA MANKAYANE AND BHUNYA

From Nhlangano you can return to Mbabane and Manzini along a quieter western route via the small hill town of Mankayane. It involves an initial stretch of gravel road, takes in two border posts, climbs north through some wild country and eventually emerges at Luyengo, where the University of Swaziland has its agriculture campus.

GEGE AND SICUNUSA BORDERS Some 2km outside Nhlangano on the road to Mahamba, a right turn is signed to Gege on the MR13. This is a gravel road that continues for 38km to Sicunusa. It passes first through open Swazi Nation Land then, after crossing the Mkondvo River, a large tract of forestry plantations. Emerging from the forests, you will reach the small settlement of Gege, from where a gravel road leads 5km west to the Gege border. This border – a very quiet one – is open 08.00–16.00. It is called Bothashoop on the South Africa side, from where it is less than 20km to Piet Retief.

From Gege the MR13 continues due north for another 15km, passing between the South Africa border to the west and wild, bare hills to the east, until it reaches the tarred MR4 at a T-junction among forests. A left turn takes you some 4.5km to the Sicunusa border, known on the South Africa side as Houdkop. This border is open 8.00–18.00 (so two hours later than Gege). The right turn is signed to Mbabane and continues to Mankayane (see below).

MANKAYANE TO LUYENGO From the Sicunusa T-junction (see above) the MR4 leads northeast, back towards Manzini and Mbabane, past wild mountainous country to the east. After 16km it crosses the Ngwempisi River and after another 20km rises to the small town of Mankayane, to the east of the road. This is one of Swaziland's oldest towns and dotted with quaint colonial buildings. Today it has little for the visitor, and nowhere to stay, but serves as a useful pit stop, with a bank, supermarket, post office, bus rank and filling station.

North of Mankayane the MR4 continues through deep plantations and after 5km takes a sharp turn to the right. Continue straight here and you will cross the Usutu and emerge on the MR18, from where you can turn left to Bhunya (15km) or right to Luyengo (7km). Take the right turn and you will follow the MR4 along a longer, windier route to Luyengo that passes the turn-offs to Ngwempisi Wilderness Area (see opposite). This way takes you across the Great Usutu and onto the MR18 further east. Luyengo is the home of the University of Swaziland's Faculty of Agriculture (see page 72). From here you can head north via Malkerns to Manzini (30 minutes) or Mbabane (40 minutes).

BHUNYA Follow the MR18 west along the north bank of the Great Usutu, and you will soon see the massive contours of the abandoned Usutu Pulp Mill looming over a bend of the river like a fallen giant too big to bury. In the mill's heyday – when it produced some 190,000 tonnes of wood pulp per year – you could smell this place before you saw it, the rotten-fish stench of processed wood chips fouling the air for miles around. In 2010, however, the mill closed. Its owners, South African giant Sappi (South African Pulp and Paper Industries Ltd), blamed the 'accumulative severe impact' of the recent forest fires that had devastated their plantations – 40% of the timber crop having been lost in August 2008 alone. With the mill went around 600 jobs, dealing a heavy blow to the community. The closure was, though, a double-edged sword: on the one hand, plunging hundreds of families into economic hardship; on the other, ending the environmental problems associated with the mill, which for years had been blighting people's health and polluting the river downstream.

Who knows what will happen to Bhunya? While rumours circulate, a small local timber industry is producing planks and other products, and Sappi continues to maintain the forests. For now, the best view of the mill is probably in your rear-view mirror. So continue to a roundabout where the MR18 meets the MR19. Here you have a choice: a right turn leads north through miles of plantations to Mhlambanyatsi (see page 159) and Mbabane; a left turn crosses the river, passing the old workers' cottages (now rented out) on the left, then continues west to the South Africa border at Sandlane.

SANDLANE BORDER The Sandlane border, Nerston on the South Africa side, is open 08.00–18.00. It is reached via a straightforward 25km drive from Bhunya. This is a convenient route into Swaziland for South Africans coming from the Ermelo direction and used by many weekenders at the Foresters Arms Hotel (see page 152). From the border it is about one hour's drive to Mbabane.

NGWEMPISI WILDERNESS AREA

This wild corner of Swaziland offers challenging hiking and remote accommodation to those prepared to rough it. Its rugged landscape centres upon the densely wooded walls of a steep 20km gorge, formed where the Ngwempisi River carves east through the sandstone and shale of the Ntfungulu Hills. The gorge drops from 800m on top to just 50m at the bottom, creating a spectrum of habitats that spans grassland, thick bush and lush riverine forest. The views, needless to say, are impressive.

Access comes via two community tourism projects: Ngwempisi Hiking Trails, to the north, offers huts on the north side of the gorge and a 33km network of trails around its rugged slopes; Khelekhele Trails, upstream and to the south, has a camp built on a sweeping riverside sandbank, with trails downriver. A high-clearance 4x4 vehicle is recommended for the former and indispensible for the latter.

Sounds perfect? Unfortunately these camps no longer measure up to the glossy brochure, which promises facilities that 'rival those of South Africa's premier hiking trail, the Otter Trail'. At the time of my last visit, in 2011, Kopho Lodge was the only camp in use, and itself in a state of some neglect, with no water to power the 'flush toilets' and 'hot showers' mentioned in the literature. Would-be visitors to this beautiful place must find out from a clued-up source such as Swazi Trails (see page 104) precisely what to expect. That said, for self-reliant travellers it is still potentially one of Swaziland's most exciting experiences. Bookings can be made through Swaziland tourist information (see page 101) or directly by telephone (\ 7625 6004/7624 9146).

The Southwest NGWEMPISI WILDERNESS AREA

6

241

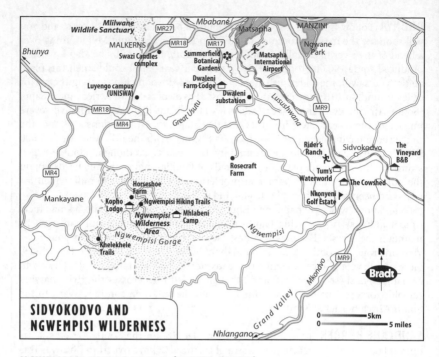

SIDVOKODVO AND
NGWEMPISI WILDERNESS

NGWEMPISI HIKING TRAILS (KOPHO LODGE) This is not the easiest place in Swaziland to find. The turning lies off the MR4, 7km east of the turn to Mankayane. Take the left-hand of two gravel roads that lead south. After 6–7km, turn right on a road signed to Horseshoe Farm, passing an abandoned hiking hut on the left. After 1km you pass the driveway to the farm, a superbly located private residence on the very lip of the gorge. Continue left and after another 2km you will reach Etjebovu School at a T-junction. Turn right here and, after 500m, right again. After another 500m down a steep, deteriorating track you reach a small homestead. Beyond is wild bush. This is where the trail starts.

The homestead belongs to the Tsela family. One hut serves as reception, with leaflets and curios for sale. With luck, Make (Mrs) Tsela will be there. She can kit you out with blankets and paraffin lamps, and advise you on the state of play at the lodge (eg: water or no water). This is also where you pay when you leave. Kopho Lodge is some 800m directly below you. Practised off-roadsters can brave the perilously steep and rutted track – much of it bare rock – in a 4x4 vehicle. Alternatively you can leave your wheels safely at the homestead and lug your gear down on foot. It is a 20-minute stroll, affording your first glimpses of the wonderland that you are about to enter. A sign on the left directs you to Horseshoe Estate, but just keep going straight. I have heard from two sources that a large black mamba inhabits this area and sometimes suns itself on the track. Just saying.

Kopho Lodge is an ingenious structure. Wedged among massive granite boulders, and split over five levels, with interconnecting passages and walkways, it brilliantly complements the natural rock formation. The view down to the gleaming Ngwempisi is stunning – and even better if you climb a rickety ladder onto the huge boulder that overhangs the lodge. This is not a place for health and safety zealots: the open-plan interior is riddled with holes, the wooden structures creaking and crumbling, and you have to watch your footing on the shiny floors (don't walk in socks) and your head on the rock ceilings. But it is nonetheless a thing of beauty, with wild aloes and succulents providing the interior décor, and a view from the balcony that trumps the best hotel in the land. As for facilities, I found 16 bunk beds on the top floor, with grubby though serviceable mattresses; the kitchen was big on tea towels but short on crockery; and the two-ring gas stove worked only erratically. Water dribbled from one of the two sinks, but from neither of the two toilets or showers (though the outside toilet and shower on the lower level are worth visiting just for the view). There are two braai areas – one above and one below, each with a braai stand and wood provided.

I am told that things have since improved, with fittings repaired and water supplies restored. Find out before setting out and, if in any doubt, bring your own bedding, food, water, loo roll and candles. Whatever the facilities, a night at Kopho Lodge is a memorable one. And you'll be sharing it with the local wildlife: colourful flat lizards dash around the walls, mice nibble at unguarded supplies and, during my stay, a pair of mocking cliff-chats fluttered in and out of their nest in the ceiling. At night, you'll look out across the vast unlit wilderness beneath a canopy of stars, with no sound but the rush of the river, the shriek of bushbabies and the tremulous whistle of fiery-necked nightjars.

Hikes from the lodge head either straight down to the river, which takes you to a good swimming point, or east along a higher trail that eventually descends to the river. A day's hike on the latter rises to Mhlabeni Camp, another trail hut, but I am told this is in a state of near collapse. All trails are marked by signs and cairns, but also feature unsigned forks and unmapped turnings. The going is rough underfoot and very steep in places. Clearings and granite outcrops make wonderful viewpoints. You can swim in shallow pools at the bottom and there are sandy beaches on slower stretches, but be careful of the current when the river is in spate. Purple-crested turaco and black-headed oriole are both conspicuous among the rich birdlife. Look out for reptiles among the rocks and perhaps a shy duiker or even a bushbuck in the riverine thickets.

KHELEKHELE Khelekhele is even harder to reach than Kopho Lodge. Take the right-hand of the two gravel roads off the MR4 and continue south for 8km until a good sign directs you left to the lodge. Unfortunately, this is the last good sign. The remaining 4km or so down to the river takes you through a maze of tracks and it is easy to choose the wrong one. If lost, stop and ask, but bear in mind that older people in this rural area may speak little English.

The lodge stands on a natural sand beach deposited by the river and comprises three separate chalets, built of river rock and connected by wooden walkways. In theory, it offers the same basic facilities as Kopho. In practice, however, it was not operating when I last investigated – indeed you had to chase out the goats. Lodge or no lodge, there are still trails to be enjoyed along the river and into the gorge. The horseriding promised by the brochures has never got going but an exciting alternative is river tubing, organised by All Out Africa (see page 141). Guests float downstream in large adapted inner tubes, kitted out with safety helmets. The route passes for about 5km through the rapids of Ngwempisi Gorge and ends below Kopho Lodge, where you deflate the tubes and hike up to the top. It sounds like a wonderful option, but its continued operation may depend on the facilities at both ends.

ROSECRAFT FARM

This secluded rural retreat combines a local weaving enterprise with a variety of visitor accommodation. It lies between the Usutu and Ngwempisi valleys, northwest of the Ngwempisi Wilderness Area, on the lower slopes of Makungutsha Mountain. The farm has a glorious view down to the rural community below and up to the wild, forested hillside above, and various hiking trails on which you can explore for yourself.

The easiest route to Rosecraft is via the MR17, off the Mbabane–Matsapha road. Follow this road past the turn-off to Summerfield until, 4km after it becomes gravel, you reach the Dwaleni electricity substation. Turn right here onto another gravel road, signed to Rosecraft 12km. Continue over a low-level bridge across the Usutu to a T-junction. Follow the signs from here for another 3.5km until you reach the farmhouse, workshop and tented camp at the top of a hill beneath some shady trees.

This whole enterprise is the brainchild of Rose Roques, whose daughter Molly Lanir runs the workshop and is also the trained cordon bleu chef behind the Sambane Tea Garden at Swazi Candles (see page 185). It is built around the family home, a grand stone-and-thatch farmhouse set among attractive gardens full of birdlife. The grounds feature a natural rock swimming pool and a memorial garden for Rose's late husband, in which a chapel-like contemplation shrine is decorated with beautiful stained glass and mosaics. The whole place has both a quirky character and a tranquil ambience.

WHERE TO STAY AND EAT

⌂ **Wide Horizons** (sleeps 9) ☎ 2505 3915; m 7604 1373; e roseroques@googlemail.com; www.visitswazi.com/widehorizons. The accommodation side of Rosecraft is known as Wide Horizons. A self-sufficient tented camp downhill from the main house sleeps 2 in honeymooner privacy, with a large dbl bed, sunken bath, open-air kitchen, outdoor shower, solar lights & balcony with sunset views down the valley. The old stables sleep 2–3 in an en-suite dbl bedroom & small sgl bedroom, with kitchen & braai. A separate wing of the main farmhouse is given over to B&B, with 2 en-suite dbl bedrooms, each imaginatively decorated & with its own veranda. Dinner cooked on request by the family, who live upstairs. **$$–$$$**

WHAT TO DO Rosecraft Farm is tailor-made for taking it easy. But the more energetic will find plenty of walking options, from guided tours of the local community to serious hikes over Makungutsha Mountain. The weaving workshop and sculpture trail (see below) should not to be missed, while other activities include tennis, swimming, 4x4 trails and fishing at the local dam.

Weaving The weaving workshop (*www.rosecraft.net*) sits beside the farmhouse, its charm enhanced by a small stream that runs between the buildings. It is open 08.00–16.00 on weekdays (call to arrange a tour, if you are not staying overnight). One of the workers will show you around the looms, where you can watch the women weaving and finishing the products. Large cooking pots are used for the dyeing, which produce Rosecraft's signature colours. Spinning, knitting and crocheting are done back at the homesteads. All the materials are local, and include mohair, organic cotton, bamboo, wool and silk. The enterprise is Fair Trade-accredited and employs some 40 people from neighbouring homesteads. Check out the products at Ngwenya Glass (see page 201), Mantenga Craft Centre (see page 167) and Swazi Candles (see page 187), or take a peek online.

Sculpture trail This delightful 1km trail follows a stream through rich native vegetation above the farm. It offers a chance both to enjoy nature and appreciate the work of local artists and sculptors along the path, some of it smuggled ingeniously into the undergrowth. Children can have fun tracking down the sculptures, and use a leaflet to identify trees and learn about their medicinal properties. There are shady picnic spots and cascades along the way.

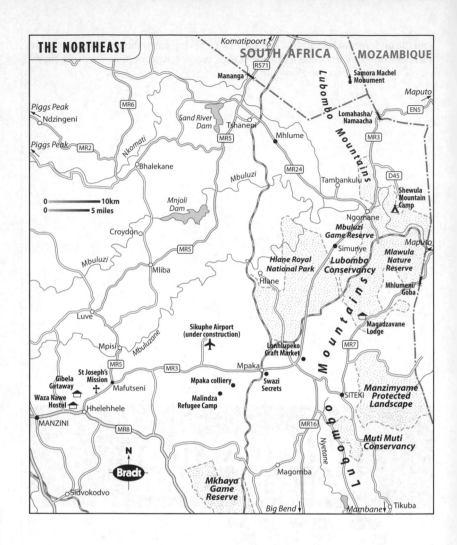

THE NORTHEAST

Komatipoort

SOUTH AFRICA   MOZAMBIQUE

R571

Mananga

Lubombo Mountains

Samora Machel
Monument

Maputo

ENS

MR6

Piggs Peak
Ndzingeni

*Sand River
Dam*

Tshaneni

Lomahasha/
Namaacha

MR3

Piggs Peak   MR2

Mhlume

Nkomati

Mbuluzi

MR24

Bhalekane

Tambankulu

D45

Shewula
Mountain
Camp

10km

5 miles

*Mnjoli
Dam*

Ngomane

*Mbuluzi
Game Reserve*

Maputo

Croydon

MR5

Simunye

*Lubombo
Conservancy*

*Mlawula
Nature
Reserve*

Mbuluzi

Mliba

*Hlane
Royal
National Park*

Hlane

*Mhlumeni/
Goba*

Luve

Magadzavane
Lodge

Mpisi

Mbuluzane

Sikuphe Airport
(under construction)

MR7

Lonhlupeko
Craft Market

Gibela
Getaway

St Joseph's
Mission

MR5

MR3

Mpaka

Swazi
Secrets

*Manzimyame
Protected
Landscape*

Waza Nawe
Hostel

Mafutseni

Mpaka colliery

SITEKI

Lubombo Mountains

MANZINI

Hhelehhele

Malindza
Refugee Camp

MR8

MR16

*Muti Muti
Conservancy*

N

Nyetane

Bradt

Magomba

Sidvokodvo

*Mkhaya
Game
Reserve*

Big Bend

Mambane   Tikuba

246

7

The Northeast

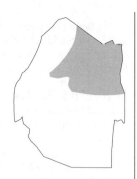

Northeast Swaziland is the wildest region of the country: a great expanse of flat bushveld that rises steeply in the east to the long rhyolite ridge of the Lubombos. In bygone days it was a place of drought, malaria and marauding lions – altogether too challenging for the colonial settlers, who largely stayed away. 'A place for fools and impala,' they called it.

The Lubombos, however, provided a conduit to Mozambique and the Indian Ocean. And it was at the top of a rough mountain road, known as the 'gin route' and reputedly plagued by highwaymen, that Siteki came into being. Spared by hilltop breezes from the heat of the lowveld, this sleepy town enjoyed a period of colonial plenty during the early 20th century. Today the good times are long gone but Siteki nonetheless serves as the capital of what is now Lubombo – Swaziland's largest but least populous province, and the one into which most of this chapter falls.

The advent of the sugar estates – first at Mhlume in the late 1950s and then Simunye in the late 1970s – had a major impact. Their headquarters soon became, if not exactly towns, then local centres, bringing employment, services and amenities hitherto unknown in the region. With sugar came irrigation and roads, and with irrigation and roads came other means of making a living. For those not working on the estates, however, life remains hard. The lions may be gone and malaria, happily, seems to be following, but drought remains a perennial problem for the rural farmer. The remote communities of this region, especially in the Lubombos, are perhaps more cut off from modern life than is anywhere else in Swaziland.

Visitors have the luxury of a more relaxed perspective, and many top tourist attractions are in this corner of the country. Most involve wildlife in some form, notably the reserves of Hlane, Mlawula and Mbuluzi, which make up the Lubombo Conservancy. Although the free-roaming herds that once made this area the hunting ground for Swazi royalty are no more, enough good habitat has remained to provide a basis for a successful conservation and restocking programme. And the region's general biodiversity is prolific.

The Lubombos themselves are wild and beautiful – home to some exciting hikes, excellent community projects and rare fauna and flora. On a good day, you can see from the top clear down to Maputo and the Indian Ocean. And if these views tempt you into further explorations, there are two good road borders, Lomahasha and Mhlumeni, from where it is just an hour's drive to the sea. The last I heard, highwaymen were no longer a problem.

MANZINI TO SITEKI

The main route to northeast Swaziland from the country's heartland starts at Hhelehhele, 10km east of Manzini on the MR3, where a right turn takes you south to Big Bend (see page 279). Ignore this turn and continue straight along the MR3, signed for Siteki. The road winds down through picturesque middleveld hills into the flat bush of the lowveld, the temperature rising all the way. There are no major tourist destinations along this stretch but a few sites of interest.

ST JOSEPH'S MISSION Some 4km east of Hhelehhele, at a right-hand bend, you will see a colourful archway on the left bearing the inscription '*Umphakatsi losebentela sive*' ('Work for the nation'). This marks the entrance to St Joseph's Mission, founded in 1914 by Austrian priest Franz Meyer. Today the mission is a school that provides education and boarding to more than 2,000 students, including many who suffer from severe learning and physical disabilities. The grounds enclose a small 80ha nature reserve, with a nursery for indigenous trees and a variety of wildlife, including more than 200 species of bird recorded. To arrange a visit contact Nozizwe Ginindza (\ *7618 0047;* e *noziag@gmail.com*). Donations are always welcome.

MAFUTSENI TO MNJOLI DAM Mafutseni is little more than a road junction and police station 10km along the MR3 from Hhelehhele. It is at this junction that you will emerge – with luck – when driving south to Manzini via the back route from Tshaneni or Piggs Peak (see page 221). A large Caltex filling station on the corner has shop, public toilets and an FNB ATM. The Mafutseni Trading Store (closed on Sundays) sells basic supplies.

From Mafutseni, the MR5 leads north to the border at Mananga (see page 272), around 95km away on a good tar road through rural country. It descends from middleveld to lowveld, passing through the settlements of Luve (after 16km) and Mliba (after 31km). At the latter the road bends left, passing the small settlement of Croydon – its road sign quite a surprise to any visitors from south London – and crossing the Mbuluzi River, before reaching Bhalekane, (after 45km). Here there is a T-junction: turn right on the MR5 for Mananga and the Lubombo Conservancy (see pages 268 and 255); turn left on the MR2 for Piggs Peak and the northwest highveld (see pages 220 and 199).

Just after crossing the Mbuluzi, before Bhalekane, a right turn leads east to Mnjoli Dam, a large reservoir formed by the damming of the river. This was the site of Dvokolwako diamond mine, which closed in 1996. The reservoir is not developed for tourism, although there is some private fishing and boating. It is a haven for waterbirds, however. And not only birds: on one stroll around the shoreline I was alarmed – to put it mildly – when a 3m crocodile crashed out of the bush and into the water at my feet. Binoculars revealed several other large crocs basking on an island in the middle. The moral is – as with any water body in the lowveld – keep back from the edge.

SIKUPHE AIRPORT You may be reading this having just exited Sikhupe's swanky new terminal, fresh from your arrival on a gleaming Boeing 747. If so, I can only apologise for my outdated account. At the time of writing, however, Swaziland's long-promised 'new' international airport remains a work in progress.

The airport lies about 10km north of the MR3, reached via a turning 38km east of Manzini. Construction began in 2003 as part of King Mswati III's US$1 billion millennium project. The idea was to create an international airport to supplant Matsapha's (see page 192), with the capacity to raise passenger figures from their current level of 70,000–80,000 to some 300,000 by means of a 3.6km-long runway that can handle Boeing 777, 747 or Airbus-size aircraft. Completion was originally due in March 2010. But funding problems, exacerbated by the general global downturn, have caused delays and as of November 2012 the airport remains unfinished. Costs, meanwhile, have gone through the roof (if indeed, a roof has yet been constructed), with the original figure of US$150 million now projected to have risen beyond US$1 billion by completion.

MPAKA This small community lies on the MR3 some 7km before the right turn to Siteki. It comprises a cluster of roadside buildings, including a take-away, general store and vegetable market, and a railway line that passes beneath the road. Mpaka railway depot, just down the tracks to the south, is an important stop for Swaziland Railways. It was once also ideally situated for the transport of coal from the Mpaka colliery, which lies just to the southwest but ceased production in 1992. There are

MY STORY: KHELINA MAGAGULA, MARULA KERNEL PRODUCER

I am 49 years old and live in the Hlane area. I got divorced nine years ago and have seven children. I started working with Swazi Indigenous Products in 2005 as a supplier of marula kernels. I am now a supplier of organic marula kernels, and I am very happy because I can use the income to buy maize-meal, laundry soap, sugar, salt and to pay school fees for my grandchildren. It also helps me to buy flour for baking cakes to sell outside the marula season.

Before selling marula kernels, I used to make and sell mats. This was time-consuming, as I had to collect reeds far from my village and would spend a week in that area, leaving my children alone. Now, because I crack the kernels from home, I can spend more time with my family. I also grow maize for subsistence, but this season there have been poor rains and I am not going to get any maize from my field. Because of the drought I plan to use most of my income from marula kernels to buy food.

I was the first woman in my village to sell marula kernels. But after I showed the others my money many have also become involved. I am happy with the price I get: I normally sell 20kg of kernels per month but today I sold 25kg of organic kernels. SIP has provided me with training courses and workshops in organic kernel production. This has helped me to identify the right areas to collect marula fruits, such as in the bush where no chemicals have been used, or from fields that have lain fallow or have used only organic manure during the last five years. After cracking the kernels, I dry them on clean grass where there is no possibility of contamination, and store the dried kernels in properly covered containers labelled 'organic kernels' – not in a room that has been sprayed for malaria control in recent years. I also learned how to grade the kernels, ie: separating grade A from grade B kernels.

Although I am divorced, I have noticed that the income from kernels has also empowered married women, who can now make their own decisions about money. Before, these women depended entirely on their husbands. You can now see more happiness in their homes, as they need no longer ask their husbands for money to buy salt, soap and sugar. With money from other economic activities like cropping, it is men who decide how to use it. But women who crack kernels can decide what to do with their own money – which is good, as men like drinking a lot.

Reproduced with kind permission from Swazi Secrets.

still considerable anthracite reserves in the ground and the government has been trying to attract investors to a new coal-fired power station project.

SWAZI SECRETS After crossing the Mpaka railway line on the MR5 a right turn leads to the railway depot. This turn is also signposted to Swazi Secrets (*www. swazisecrets.com*), just off the road on your left. By now, you will no doubt have seen their numerous roadside billboards, showing radiant models above captions such as 'Marula oils help prevent stretch marks', and 'Good for your soul; great for your skin.' Swazi Secrets makes natural cosmetic products – including body lotion, lip balm, soap and exfoliator – from marula oil, derived from the kernel of the marula tree (see page 9). The product is reputedly excellent: its golden-yellow, nutty oil is quickly absorbed by the skin and naturally rich in vitamin E, which acts as an additive-free preservative. The industry is also environmentally sustainable: the oil is cold-pressed from wild-harvested nuts; the trees grow on subsistence land, where few artificial fertilisers are used; and it is estimated that only 1% of marula seeds in the region are harvested, leaving the rest to return to the natural cycle.

Swazi Secrets has been a shot in the arm for the community: a not-for-profit enterprise that empowers impoverished rural women by generating an income from the natural products around them (see *My story*, page 249). In 2012, it was one of 25 shortlisted winners of the Equator Prize, an initiative launched by the UN and other international organisations to recognise sustainable development initiatives worldwide. You will find the products in many Swaziland hotels and can buy them direct from the factory in Mpaka. They are also marketed worldwide under the brand Swazi Indigenous Products (SIP).

MALINDZA REFUGEE CAMP The region southwest of Mpaka is known as Malindza. During the 1980s and '90s this was the site of a refugee camp for Mozambicans displaced during their brutal civil war. The Malindza Reception Centre, established by the United Nations High Commission for Refugees (UNHCR), once housed over 8,000 Mozambicans, among a peak of 20,000 refugees of Mozambican and South African origin during the mid-1980s. After the end of apartheid and the Mozambican war the UNHCR helped Swaziland repatriate 16,000 of these people. Malindza remains open for any refugee influxes that may occur in future.

SITEKI

Siteki, capital of the Lubombo region, perches on top of the Lubombo Plateau. To get there, take the MR16 towards Big Bend, 7km east of Mpaka, then after 4km a left turn east to Siteki on the MR7. This road passes through a veterinary cordon barrier, which was built during a foot-and-mouth outbreak in the east some years ago but today is generally open and unmanned. The road then climbs steadily uphill, with magnificent views back to the distant mountains in the west. The town lies at the top, heralded by a succession of substantial, unmarked speed bumps. Continue to a large junction, with a Galp garage on your left and the Siteki Hotel opposite. From here a left turn takes you to the Mozambique border at Mhlumeni and a right turn leads into town.

Siteki was once called 'Stegi', and many people still pronounce it that way today. Either way, the name means 'marrying place' and derives from a proclamation of Mbandzeni – king of Swaziland from 1875 to 1889 (see page 57) – who allowed his troops to get hitched while stationed here. By the early 1900s, the town had

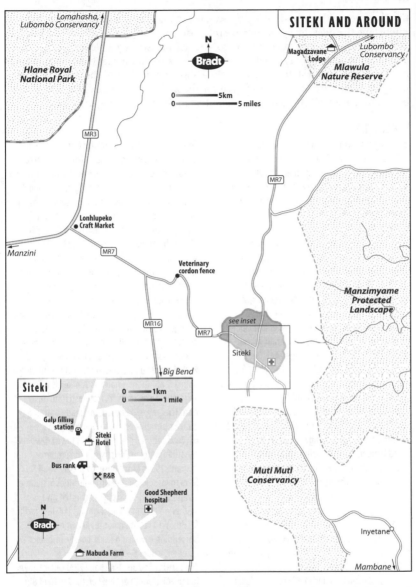

Lomahasha,
Lubombo Conservancy

Bradt

N

Magadzavane
Lodge

Lubombo
Conservancy

**Mlawula
Nature Reserve**

**Hlane Royal
National Park**

0 ———— 5km
0 ———— 5 miles

MR3

MR7

**Lonhlupeko
Craft Market**

Manzini

MR7

**Veterinary
cordon fence**

MR16

MR7

see inset

**Manzimyame
Protected
Landscape**

Siteki

↓*Big Bend*

Siteki

0 ——— 1km
0 ——— 1 mile

Galp filling
station

Siteki
Hotel

Bus rank

✕ R&B

**Good Shepherd
hospital**

N

Bradt

**Mutl Mutl
Conservancy**

Inyetane

⌂ Mabuda Farm

Mambane↓

become one of Swaziland's earliest colonial settlements, pre-dating Mbabane and
Manzini, with the country's first hotel and golf course. Settlers flocked to enjoy the
cooling breezes, and to take advantage of trade along the 'gin road' to Maputo (then
Lourenço Marques). With the money came a lively social scene, including colourful
characters such as Charles Dupont, who effectively ran the town for years, before
his misdeeds – which reputedly included murder – caught up with him, and he was
chased over the border by an angry mob.

The good times came to an end when a border post opened in Lomahasha
(see page 268) to the north, offering an easier route to the coast. Business dried
up and settlers moved away, leaving Siteki marooned. Today, it is hard to imagine

the glory years: the town is, even by Swaziland standards, hardly buzzing. Its local importance resides in its border patrol post and the Good Shepherd Hospital. You will, however, find a couple of good places to stay (see below), while useful amenities include banks, supermarkets, a bus rank, filling stations, shops, a local market and a police station – all within a short stroll around the two streets that make up the centre of town. And even for those just passing through, Siteki's laid-back ambience and fabulous views definitely make it worth lingering awhile.

WHERE TO STAY

🏠 **Magadzavane Lodge** (20 chalets, sleeps 40) 📞2415 0178/29, 2383 8885/8453; e mlawulares@ sntc.org.sz. Handsome lodge that officially opened in 2012. Located inside Mlawula Nature Reserve (see page 261), but more easily reached from Siteki – 17km away down the MR7 – than from the reserve entrance, hence most guests are from Siteki or overnighting en route to Mozambique, rather than visitors to the reserve. Comprises 20 en-suite chalets for 2, each with shower, kitchen facilities, TV & wooden balcony with (except for chalets 16–19) a superb view. Main boma has large swimming pool, restaurant, bar & conference centre. Activities in Mlawula include game-viewing, hiking trails, mountain-biking, birdwatching & fishing (see page 263), but at present the lodge has little connection with the wider reserve, offering no information or activities. This seems a missed opportunity. The location – high above Mlawula's pristine bush at the southern boundary – is glorious, with wildlife all around. I watched zebras on the ridge opposite my chalet, heard baboons barking behind the lodge & found birds mobbing a black mamba in the car park. The water supply has been erratic here so ask before you book in. Rates include B&B & self-catering. **$$–$$$**

🏠 **Siteki Hotel** (36 rooms, sleeps 64) 📞2343 6573/4/5; m 7602 3718; e sitekihotel@swazi. net; www.sitekihotel.com. 1930s hotel, renovated in 2005, located at north end of high street. Offers 27 twin/sgl rooms, 2 standard dbl rooms, 6 luxury dbl rooms & 1 executive suite, all en-suite with

DSTV, telephone, AC, tea/coffee & fridge. Internet available. Revamped interior is large, clean & cool. Sitegi Restaurant & Terrace serves à la carte & buffet meals. Cocktails served at the Wigman Lounge & Africa Bar, & bottle store outside. Also: swimming pool, pool bar, sauna, gym, internet café & fully equipped conference room for 120. **$$–$$$**

🏠 **Mabuda Farm** (39 beds) 📞2343 4124; e helen@mabuda.com; www.mabuda.com. Tranquil retreat 1km south of town, with superb views east across a wild gorge of the Lubombos. Well signed from town centre: look out for hornbill logo. Accommodation in spacious grounds comprises 3 thatched rondavels; 4 en-suite chalets; 1 large family self-catering rondavel; budget backpackers, comprising 6 rooms, each with double bunk; terraced campsite, with plug points & ablutions. Chalets & rondavels come as self-catering or B&B – b/fast fresh from dairy farm (creamy milk, fruit, homemade butter, etc). Emphasis is on peace & quiet: no TVs, bar or restaurant (all are available in town). Owners Jonathan & Helen Pons live on the property in grand 1930s farmhouse. Charcoal, wood & farm meat sold on site. Other facilities include swimming pool & old barn converted into 'gathering place' for larger groups (kitchen facilities for 30). Wi-Fi at main house. Activities include horseriding & walking trails. Lovely ambience & excellent value. **$–$$**

🏠 **Lituba Lodge** (see page 281) Out-of-town lodge 26km south of Siteki on the MR16 to Big Bend.

WHERE TO EAT

✕ **R&B restaurant** 📞2343 6248. Cheap & cheerful restaurant/bar on Ngwenya St in town centre, with local vibe & shady terrace that offers refuge from the Lubombos sun. Simple meals include burgers, pizzas, prawns & chicken.

✕ **Siteki Hotel** (see above) The Stegi Restaurant & Terrace serves both à la carte & buffet for b/fast,

lunch & dinner. An extensive menu includes an excellent seafood curry, Portuguese-style steaks & enormous pizzas at mid-range to high prices. Service is not speedy but take-aways are available & light meals are served at the pool bar. If you're just after a drink then you can choose either the Wigman Lounge or Africa Bar.

WHAT TO SEE AND DO

Lubombo Conservancy This large protected region of northeast Swaziland comprises several of the country's most important nature reserves (see page 7). All lie within a 30–40-minute drive of Siteki: just return to the MR3 and head north. You can also reach Mlawula Nature Reserve from the MR7, 16km north of Siteki, via its southern entrance at Magadzavane Lodge (see opposite).

Mabuda Farm This historic farm, located at the top of a steep hillside 1km south of town, offers a variety of accommodation (see opposite) and wholesome outdoor activities. Its welcoming owners, Jonathan and Helen Pons, live in a grand 1930s farmhouse – its walls crowded with game trophies – that overlooks extensive lawns and an impressive view. All around is a busy working farm, with the oldest dairy in Swaziland, which helps feed the local community. Guests can stroll among the hay bales, paddocks, hedgerows and Jersey cows, which lend a Constable-esque pastoral air to the landscape, or follow a series of trails down the hillside, where the dense bush immediately becomes more African in feel. Birdlife is impressive: I saw both crowned and trumpeter hornbills around the property, and a quiet walk on longer trails might turn up such Lubombo specials as Rudd's apalis and pink-throated twinspot. A simple trails map is available at reception. Other activities include pony rides, both for beginners and the more experienced. You can swim at the large pool by the house, retreat for quiet reflection to 'Grandpa's garden' or picnic beside the dam.

Good Shepherd Hospital When not farming, Jonathan Pons of Mabuda Farm (see above) is an eye surgeon at this hospital, which is just a short walk away, and can arrange visits for those interested in learning more. Located along the Maphungwane Road, this facility was established by the Catholic Church in 1949 and serves as the Lubombo Region referral hospital. Its bed capacity of 225 is frequently overstretched, due especially to the local prevalence of TB and HIV/AIDS. The hospital includes a nursing school, from which more than 60 students graduate each year.

Inyanga and _Sangoma_ School This government institution for the training of traditional healers and diviners (see page 80) is the only one of its kind in Swaziland. It is located on the premises of the now-defunct Bamboo Inn, on the road to Mhlumeni. Herbs and medicinal plants are collected from the surrounding bush – notably at Muti Muti Conservancy (see below), a traditional site for this purpose. You can arrange visits and consultations through tourist information in Mbabane (see page 149).

Muti Muti Conservancy The main entrance to this private nature reserve is 4km south of Siteki, to the right of the Maphungwane Road out of town, but access is easiest via Mabuda Farm (see opposite). It belongs to Rod and Lungile de Vletter, owners of Phophonyane Falls Nature Reserve (see page 224), and protects a large tract of indigenous Lubombo forest on the western slopes of the plateau. The pristine habitat supports specialised Lubombo fauna and flora, including birds such as African broadbill and white-eared barbet. It is the only place in Swaziland where I have heard samango monkeys, their alarm barks carrying up the gorge from the canopy below, and no doubt the wild terrain harbours other wildlife surprises. Practitioners at the _inyanga_ school in Siteki (see above) collect medicinal herbs here. The reserve is not developed for visitors and access is at the owners' discretion. If you're interested in taking a look, contact Rod and Lungile (see page 253) or ask at Mabuda Farm.

Mambane Continue south of Siteki on the Maphungwane Road and you enter one of the most undeveloped regions in Swaziland. The dirt road winds along the plateau, passing through scattered rural communities, with stupendous views into the Lubombo gorges on either side. It then gradually descends south until, after 25km, you reach a cattle gate into Mambane. Here you stand at the meeting point of three countries: look south, and you are looking across the Usutu Gorge into South Africa; east, and you are looking over the Lubombos into Mozambique.

From Mambane the road descends to the old and now defunct border with South Africa. From here on it deteriorates and only experienced 4x4 drivers should think of continuing. If you are one of those, and in search of adventure, then follow the steep track down, carefully, towards the Usutu. At the bottom you will find a small homestead with a few ramshackle huts and dusty mealie plots. Here you can wander down to the riverbank, just east of where it exits the 16km-long gorge. This is a wild place: I heard the distant grunts of hippos downriver and the son of the headman told me that a local child had recently been taken by a crocodile. He also told me, when I asked how often he made it up to Siteki, that most of his family's supplies come from a store across the river in Mozambique. So if you are heading this way, do bring a few basics – bread, soap, sugar, tinned fish – to help out the family.

Halfway down this final descent, I also found a group of labourers at work on a construction site, with timber and roofing materials piled nearby. This, apparently, was to be a new 'coffee shop', catering to investors visiting the Mambane area to investigate a new community ecotourism venture. At the end of such a bone-jarring, dead-end bush road, it all seemed rather improbable. But there may be a cunning plan. Were the border ever to reopen, then this road – given a bit of upgrading – would offer a vital cross-border transport route through the proposed Usuthu–Tembe–Futi TFCA (see box on page 50), which links conservation areas in Mozambique, South Africa and Swaziland. It would thus sit at the very heart of one of Africa's most exciting new conservation projects. For now, though, you may have to put that skinny latté on hold.

Lonhlupeko Craft Market This community tourism project (see page 88) is prominently signed on the MR3, just north of the MR16 turn-off to Big Bend and Siteki. Numerous stalls display handicrafts made by local community members, who used to sell their wares from the roadside. Among the various products are soapstone, batiks, beadwork, embroidery, candles, basketware, glassware and jewellery. It is a pleasant place to wander around, whether or not you have a shopping agenda, and a good opportunity to chat to local people, who can explain the cultural significance of the items on sale. There are also clean working toilets.

MHLUMENI BORDER

Mhlumeni is 28km northeast of Siteki along the MR7 (the Mbandzeni Highway). Since the improvement of this border, and the road either side, it has become the quickest and most popular route to Mozambique for those travelling from Mbabane – or, for that matter, from Durban. The border, which is known as Goba on the Mozambique side, is open 24 hours. Remember that you will need a Mozambique visa and all relevant vehicle documents (see page 105). On the other side, the road leads north, crossing the Mbuluzi River before joining the EN5, from where it is

50km east to Maputo. On the Swaziland side you will find a few services, including the Yebo Cash and Carry, the Goodwill Butchery and the Way Bottle Store. There is no filling station, though, so make sure you have topped up in Siteki.

THE LUBOMBO CONSERVANCY

The far northeast of Swaziland is the country's big-game hotspot. This is where the largest herds and the most large mammals are to be found and, with the exception of Mkhaya (see page 277), the only place where safari-goers have a realistic prospect of meeting any of the Big Five. The low, flat bushveld terrain, rising to the rugged Lubombos, is just like that of the southeast Kruger Park a little to the north. Indeed, before roads, borders, sugar estates and other impediments, this region was just as wild and teeming with big game as the Kruger is now.

You have a choice of reserves in which to experience this wild Swaziland of yesteryear. Hlane Royal National Park (see page 259) is managed by Big Game Parks (see page 102 and advert on the inside back cover) and home to abundant wildlife, much of it reintroduced; Mlawula Nature Reserve (see page 261) is an SNTC property, with pristine bush that reaches to the top of the Lubombos, but is more challenging in terms of both game-viewing and accommodation; Mbuluzi Game Reserve (see page 264) is effectively a small slice of Mlawula but, under private management, has easier game-viewing and better facilities; Shewula Mountain Camp (see page 265) is a community project high in the Lubombos, where visitors can combine wild nature with local culture.

Each reserve operates as a separate entity but all are bound up in a larger project called the Lubombo Conservancy, which was established – with help from Peace Parks Africa and Conservation International – in April 1999. This ambitious cross-border project also includes the Nkhalashane Siza Ranch and the Inyoni Yami Swaziland Irrigation Scheme (known as the IYSIS) to the north, Muti Muti Conservancy to the south and, on the Mozambique side, the Goba communal land. The 600km² conservancy, whose operations are directed by a board made up of members from each property, aims to protect the precious ecosystems of northeastern Swaziland while helping improve life for local people through a more sustainable use of natural resources. The idea, ultimately, is to establish a single unfenced reserve in which animals can roam freely. Ecotourism is critical to the whole venture – and the conservancy is perfectly placed to catch plenty of tourist traffic, being on the eastern route between the Kruger National Park and KwaZulu-Natal, and providing an ideal stop en route to the Mozambique coast.

The Lubombo Conservancy is, in turn, a vital component in the Lubombo Transfrontier Conservation Area (see page 50), a trilateral agreement between Swaziland, Mozambique and South Africa. This global biodiversity hotspot includes the Maputaland Centre of Endemism and five Ramsar sites (wetlands recognised as being of international conservation importance under the 1971 convention signed in Ramsar, Iran), and extends from the Lubombos in the west and Indian Ocean in the east to St Lucia, Africa's largest estuary, in the south. Its success would – among other things – reunite the last naturally occurring elephant populations of KwaZulu-Natal and southern Mozambique, creating the first major elephant stronghold along Africa's eastern coastline.

The Lubombo Conservancy is doing its bit for the grand plan. Getting nine landowners to agree on managing their land together has not been plain sailing. At present, for example, Mlawula simply does not have the security systems in place to guarantee the protection of rhinos and other rare species and, without

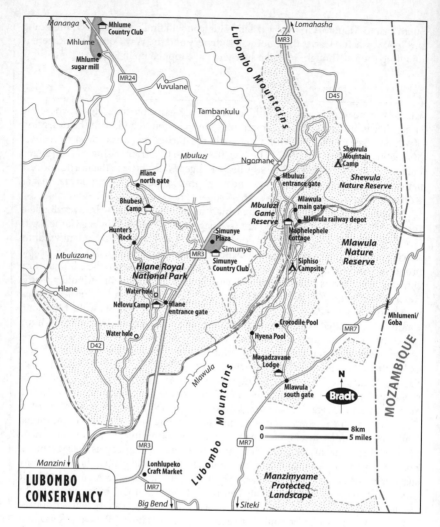

Mananga
Mhlume Country Club
Mhlume
Mhlume sugar mill
MR24
Vuvulane
Tambankulu
Lomahasha
MR3
Lubombo Mountains
D45
Shewula Mountain Camp
Mbuluzi
Ngomane
Mbuluzi entrance gate
Shewula Nature Reserve
Hlane north gate
Bhubesi Camp
Mlawula main gate
Mbuluzi Game Reserve
Mlawula railway depot
Maphelephele Cottage
Hunter's Rock
Simunye Plaza
Simunye
Mbuluzane
MR3
Hlane Royal National Park
Simunye Country Club
Siphiso Campsite
Mlawula Nature Reserve
Hlane
Water hole
Ndlovu Camp
Hlane entrance gate
Mhlumeni/ Goba
Crocodile Pool
MR7
Water hole
D42
Hyena Pool
MOZAMBIQUE
Magadzavane Lodge
N
Mlawula south gate
Bradt
MR3
Manzini
MR7
Lonhlupeko Craft Market
MR7
Big Bend
Mlawula
Lubombo Mountains
Siteki
Manzimyame Protected Landscape
0   8km
0   5 miles

LUBOMBO CONSERVANCY

these, BGP are not prepared to lift the fences that divide Mlawula from Hlane. Nonetheless, there have already been notable achievements, including a successful malaria-control programme, the improvement of the Mhlumeni border and Siteki-Mhlumeni Road, the new Magadzavane Lodge at Mlawula (see page 252), and the flourishing of Shewula Camp (see page 265) as a community-based conservation and development project. At the time of writing, the conservancy had just been awarded funding from the Critical Ecosystem Partnership Fund, which should allow further expansion as far south as Mambane on the Usuthu River, and a new headquarters.

Getting there and away To reach the reserves of the Lubombo Conservancy simply continue along the MR3 past the right turn to Big Bend and Siteki on the MR16. The road bends north at this point and after 9km passes a large sign that, reassuringly, reads: 'You are now entering Lubombo Conservancy'. Shortly afterwards, another sign announces that you are entering Hlane Royal National

Park. Here you cross a cattle grid and are immediately inside Hlane, where the overgrazed Swazi Nation Land gives way to wild bush.

The road through Hlane is a public one but you may well spot wildlife along the verge; impala are common, and I have also seen giraffe, kudu, blue wildebeest and – after dark – black-backed jackals. Hyenas are sometimes also seen at night. Drive carefully, as these animals – especially impala – sometimes dash out in front of vehicles. Another sign warns: 'Cyclists and pedestrians beware of lions and elephants'. Don't worry, you can safely get out and answer a call of nature: these more formidable beasts are confined to fenced areas inside the reserve and, barring breakouts, you won't meet them on the road. Look over the fence to the west, though, and the numerous dead, ring-barked knobthorn trees are stark proof of the presence of elephants.

Some 6km after the cattle grid you reach the turning to Hlane's Ndlovu Camp (see below). After a further 6km you will exit Hlane over another cattle grid. A turning immediately on your left leads you to Bhubesi Camp (see page 258). Next on your right are the neat lawns and bungalows of Simunye Village, the headquarters of Simunye Sugar Estates. Here you will find Simunye Country Club (see page 266) and Simunye Plaza. The latter has shops and services, including a Boxer supermarket, Caltex filling station, bottle store, pharmacy and various eateries. Behind the plaza is the bus rank, with some helpful garages (where I have had several punctures fixed) and an indoor market. This is where to stock up and sort yourself out before heading into the bush.

Continue from Simunye and you enter a landscape of sugar, with cane fields stretching away on either side. To the east, however, the wild ridges of the Lubombos draw closer to the road and after 7.5km a right turn leads to Mbuluzi Game Reserve (on the left) and Mlawula Nature Reserve (on your right). This road ends at the Lubombo railway depot, an important stop on the Swaziland Railways goods line, which continues across the border to Maputo.

Shortly after the turn to Mlawula/Mbuluzi, the MR3 crosses the Mbuluzi River. After the bridge, the MR24 leads off left to Mhlume and Mananga (see page 268). Continue straight on the MR3 another 20km to the Mozambique border at Lomahasha (see page 268). About halfway along you will pass the D45 on the right, from where a winding gravel road of some 16km leads up to Shewula Mountain Camp (see page 265).

A transverse agreement aims to allow visitors access to any part of Lubombo Conservancy via an entrance ticket bought at any of its individual properties. However, this is not yet fully operational. At present, an Mbuluzi entrance ticket gets you in anywhere; a Hlane ticket gets you into Hlane and Mbuluzi; and a Mlawula ticket gets you into Mlawula, Mbuluzi and Shewula.

Where to stay and eat Accommodation in the Lubombo Conservancy ranges from thatched rest camps and campsites to community lodges and a country club.

🏠 **Hlane Royal National Park** ☎2528 3943/4; e reservations@biggameparks.org; www. biggameparks.org/hlane. Hlane has 2 rest camps: Ndlovu (meaning 'elephant') & Bhubesi ('lion'):
🏠 **NDLOVU CAMP** (sleeps 56), the main camp, is just off the MR3. Accommodation comprises 14 twin en-suite thatched rondavels ('Wisteria Village'); 2 self-catering dbl cottages (dbl bed,

veranda & large braai area); 2 self-catering group cottages (2 twin rooms & 2 dbls); 1 self-catering family cottage (2 dbls rooms & 4 sgls) known as 'The Big Hut'; self-catering kitchens equipped with gas stove & fridge. No electricity at Ndlovu Camp but candles & paraffin lanterns provided, & firewood for braais & communal camp areas. (Ndlovu has the biggest solar-power system in

Swaziland to service the kitchen, restaurant, shops & offices.) All cottages overlook the waterhole, where game – including elephant, hippo & white rhino – can be seen & photographed at close quarters. (An electric fence keeps large animals at bay but smaller creatures roam the camp.) Spacious campsite has communal kitchen, laundry area & ablution block. Large restaurant serves full b/fast, light meals & dinner. Often quite busy, but always retains pleasant, laid-back bush ambience.

🏠 **BHUBESI CAMP** (6 cottages, sleeps 18) is much more secluded & lies 14km away in the northwest of the park. Reached on game-viewing roads through the park (OK for a normal vehicle but watch out for steep drainage humps) or via a left turning off the MR3 immediately after the cattle grid that marks the exit from Hlane – follow this road round to re-enter park via the north gate. Comprises 6 self-contained, self-catering stone cottages, each with 2 twin rooms, braai area, kitchenette & electricity. Situated in secluded spot, beneath towering riverine trees & overlooking dry riverbed of Umbuluzane. Park's main big-game attractions (rhino, elephant & lion areas) are back near Ndlovu Camp but there is plenty of smaller wildlife. (On my last visit I saw bushbuck & baboons around the cottages by day & bushbabies by night.) The terrain is rockier than at Ndlovu; Hunter's Rock, a short stroll away along the riverbed, is where Sobhuza reputedly saw his last lion. Basic camping is also available in the park's eastern Lusoti sector by arrangement at Ndlovu Camp; these sites are used by the Ehlatsini Trails (see page 261). **$–$$**

🏠 **Mbuluzi Game Reserve** (sleeps 27, plus camping) ☏ 2383 8861; e mbuluzi@swazi.net; www.mbuluzigamereserve.co.sz. Mbuluzi shares the same habitat as neighbouring Mlawula but offers quite different accommodation, with luxury private lodges & a campsite. The 4 large self-contained lodges are situated in the southern section on the Mlawula River, some distance apart. Each has a unique design & comes with fully equipped kitchen, large, comfortable living area, spacious veranda & deck, braai area with firewood, fridge/freezer & all cutlery/crockery. 2 have private swimming pools. Individual lodges as follows:

🏠 **MBULUZI TENTED LODGE** (6 people) has a comfortable thatched kitchen & lounge area, large veranda & swimming pool, 3 luxury canvas rooms with en-suite bathrooms & outdoor showers; overlooks steep cliffs across river.

🏠 **SINGWE LODGE** (8 people) has 4 dbl rooms with en-suite bathrooms, including 2 with outdoor shower & private deck overlooking Mlawula River; swimming pool adjoining large veranda, overlooking confluence of 2 streams

🏠 **MPHANGELE LODGE** (5 people) has 2 en-suite dbl rooms & 1 sgl room, wooden deck overlooking Mlawula River & hillside opposite, & is shaded by large riverine trees.

🏠 **NKHANKANKA LODGE** (8 people) has 4 dbl rooms with wooden deck overlooking natural pool on Mlawula River, with a main building of 2 bedrooms & bathrooms, kitchen & living area, & a satellite building with 2 en-suite rooms.

🏠 **THE CAMPSITE** is located in the northern section of the reserve among riverine trees close to the Mbuluzi: clean toilets & showers heated by wood-fired donkey boiler; reed bomas with braai/BBQ grid; water tap; no electricity. 2 private campsites are located a short distance away overlooking the river. Crocodiles occur in all rivers, so swimming is best confined to swimming pools. Most roads are navigable by standard vehicle, although high-clearance is preferable. **$** (camping); **$$$**

🏠 **Mlawula Nature Reserve** ☏ 2383 8885; e mlawula@sntc.org.sz; www.sntc.org.sz. Accommodation at Mlawula is a mixed bag. Not all the advertised options are always available – or, at least, not as described in the brochures – so a night here is best enjoyed with a dose of initiative:

🏠 **MAPHELEPHELE COTTAGE** (sleeps 8) sits on a rise 1,800m south of the main entrance gate (turn right at junction 1). This self-catering cottage has 2 upper sleeping porches & 2 inside rooms, plus bath, sitting room, braai area, hot water, gas stove & fridge, fully equipped kitchen, bedding & towels. Nearby, Sara Bush Camp was located at a stunning cliff-top site overlooking the Mlawula River 200m further down this track but has recently been dismantled for renovation; check availability at the booking office. There is no electricity & the water supply is erratic.

🏠 **SIPHISO CAMPSITE** (tents & caravans) is on the valley floor 2km southeast of Maphelephele Cottage, between junctions 7 & 9. It has wide lawns, taps, braai facilities, shady trees & 2 thatched summerhouses. A thatched ablution block offers showers, baths, washbasins & toilets – but bring your own water in case of problems with the supply. This is a lovely, often deserted campsite with good walking trails nearby.

🏠 **MAGADZAVANE LODGE** (sleeps 40) is reached via a 40min drive south through the park (turn left at junctions 12 & 14). However, most people visit this smart 40-bed facility from Siteki (see page 256). Although visitors to Mlawula usually do their own thing, activities available from reception include fishing & guided walks. There are several picnic sites. The main entrance has trail maps, a payphone & a tired information display. The park's gravel roads are regularly graded & manageable in a normal vehicle, although high-clearance is preferable & everything is trickier after rains. The closest place for supplies is Simunye Plaza (see page 257). All reservations via SNTC head office; enquire about conditions. **$–$$**

🏠 **Shewula Mountain Camp** (sleeps 31, plus camping): ☎7605 1160/7603 1931; e info@ shewulacamp.com; www.shewulacamp.com. A community project (see page 265) set high on the Lubombo Plateau across the Mbuluzi River from Mlawula & Mbuluzi, offering traditional hospitality in a rural community. Comprises 7 comfortable stone-&-thatch rondavels: 4 with 4 beds (2 bunks & 1 dbl) & communal ablutions; 3 with 3 beds, en suite, with hot outdoor shower. Campsite takes up to 30. Huts are clean & simple, with comfortable bed, basic furnishings & gas combi boiler – though, sadly, no window onto view. No electricity, but paraffin lamps provided after dark. Fully equipped kitchen & communal dining area at reception boma. Self-catering, or meals prepared by camp staff – menu either Swazi- or Tuscan-style (the latter reflecting the Italian aid behind this project). Shared gas fridge. Camp located 16km off MR3 to Lomahasha (see page 257) & accessible on good dirt roads by normal vehicle: 6km after turn-off, turn right at a fork; after another 3km turn left to Shewula Nazarene Clinic; after another 2km, beside Majambeni Primary School, pass sign to Shewula Community Resource Centre; after another 4km reach the gates (past football pitch on left). Signs reasonably clear but stop & ask if unsure. Access also possible by local bus from Manzini, Simunye or Lomahasha. **$–$$**

🏠 **Simunye Country Club** (sleeps 90, plus camping) ☎2313 4758; e tlitschka@rssc.co.sz; www.simunyeclub.com. Friendly, colonial-style establishment set in spacious grounds on Simunye Sugar Estate, with plentiful accommodation & excellent food. Accommodation comprises 6 self-catering cottages for 4 people, 5 sgl en-suite rooms & 8 en-suite family cottages for 3, all with fridge, TV, AC & tea/coffee. Also: 2 executive suites for 2, each with kitchen, lounge, TV, tea/coffee, private veranda & covered parking; 4 en-suite wooden cabins for 2, more basic than cottages, but with all necessities; 3 fully-equipped 6-person houses; 1 executive house for 8 (500m down road from country club), with 4 luxurious en-suite bedrooms, 10-seater dining room, large lounge, fully equipped kitchen & lush private gardens with pool – booked by special arrangement. Restaurant, one of the best in Swaziland, offers buffet, carvery & à la carte, with many local specials – including Nozipho's Paella – from a chef who has been there since 1980s. Popular Fri braai night & Sun carvery. Caters for many events & private functions (including, for the last 10 years, the king's birthday party). Large licensed bar is popular with locals, with pool table, dartboard & large-screen TV. Fenced swimming pool. Activities (see page 268) include 9-hole golf course (free to overnight guests), squash courts, gymnasium, tennis courts & children's playground. In general, a relaxed, welcoming feel, with a family atmosphere. Lush, semi-tropical grounds are festooned with indigenous flora, including some impressive sycamore figs, & teem with birds – notably brown-headed parrots. **$$–$$$**

WHAT TO SEE AND DO

Hlane Royal National Park Hlane, which means 'wilderness', is Swaziland's largest protected area and home to the country's biggest game herds. Its 22,000ha of bushveld extend either side of the MR3. Most activities take place in the western sector, which is where the two camps are located (see page 261), although rough camping and guided bush trails also take place in the eastern Lusoti sector.

This area traditionally hosted the annual *Butimba*, or royal hunt. Over time, however, wildlife became so heavily depleted that the hunters began returning empty-handed. Realising that what remained must be preserved, the late King Sobhuza asked conservationist Ted Reilly to get to work, and in 1966 the area was set aside as a reserve. Today Big Game Parks (see page 102 and inside back cover) manages Hlane on behalf of the king, who holds it in trust for the nation. The *Butimba* is held every year in a dispersal area to the west, where the overflow of game from the park is hunted under the rules of the king and the security of the BGP ranger force.

Preserving Hlane was never, however, just a matter of setting the land aside. Securing the reserve from the rampant poaching that had ravaged its wildlife took time. Once this was achieved, animals were gradually reintroduced – some from MIilwane (see page 178), which had effectively served as a holding pen for game temporarily removed from Hlane – but also larger species such as giraffe and white rhino from South Africa. The first elephants, two orphaned bulls from the Kruger Park, were reintroduced in 1986, followed the next year by 18 more. Lions were introduced in 1994 to an enclosed area. A number of leopards have also been introduced over the years.

There have been challenges: Hlane lost many white rhinos during the brutal 'rhino wars' of the late 1980s (see box on page 14), and elephants have since caused such serious habitat damage – witness the dead knobthorn trees visible from the main road – that contraception is now employed to check their numbers. Nonetheless, the reserve teems with wildlife of all shapes and sizes. Its flat bushveld is reminiscent of the Kruger Park, with dense thickets, open grasslands, and stands of hardwoods such as knobthorn, leadwood and tamboti. Sandy riverbeds wind through the reserve, flanked with tall riverine forest, and shallow pans draw drinkers during the dry season. All in all, this feels like – and is – real big-game country.

Wildlife The major attraction for most visitors is the Big Five. Of these, elephant, white rhino, lion and leopard all occur, the one absentee being buffalo. Both the rhino and elephant are found in the fenced 'big game' area around Ndlovu Camp, where they often visit the waterhole in front of the chalets. The elephants, which tend to stick together, generally come to drink in the early evening. The lions live in a separate 3,000ha fenced area, where you can see them on a guided game drive (see opposite). You will often hear their roaring from Ndlovu Camp at night or early in the morning. Don't expect to see a leopard, though: this elusive cat leaves little sign of its presence other than tracks. The same goes for the growing population of spotted hyenas, whose whooping calls you may well also hear at night.

Other large mammals include giraffe, found throughout the reserve, and hippos, which move between the waterhole in front of Ndlovu Camp and Mahlindza Dam deeper in the park, though have only been at the former in recent years. The most abundant antelope species is impala, found in larger herds here than anywhere else in Swaziland. Nyala, greater kudu, blue wildebeest, waterbuck and zebra are also common, with bushbuck and common duiker found in riverine areas. Other mammals you might come across include warthog, vervet monkey, dwarf mongoose and, after dark, greater bushbaby and large-spotted genet.

Among more than 300 species of bird recorded from the area are numerous raptors, including martial, tawny and bateleur eagle, and a large breeding colony of white-backed vultures that is thought to represent the highest density of tree-nesting vultures in the world. White-headed, lappet-faced and even the occasional Cape vulture also occur, often in the company of marabou storks, whose breeding colony on the reserve is the southernmost in Africa. Among other avian highlights are huge colonies of red-billed queleas, and purple-crested turacos, which are common in fruiting trees. Birdbaths at Ndlovu Camp are a good place to spot waxbills, whydahs, weavers and other smaller species that visit by day, and you should listen out at night for the '*prrp*' of the resident African scops owls. Other wildlife includes a good selection of reptiles, with crocodiles in some pans and leopard tortoises common on the roads after the first rains.

Activities You are free at Hlane either to do your own thing (day visitors SZL40) or book guided activities from Ndlovu Camp, depending on what you want to see. The wide network of self-guided game-viewing roads is generally suitable for a normal vehicle – though be careful not to get bogged down after rains and watch out for the large drainage humps. These roads lead beyond the secured big-game area into the wider reserve beyond, but you cannot visit the lion enclosure on a self-drive. A map is available in reception and the roads are well signposted. Keep your eyes peeled and you should come across plenty of wildlife. Various picnic sites offer a chance to stretch your legs and, during the dry season, the game-viewing hide at Mahlindza Dam is a great spot to watch animals come down to drink. Morning, from around 7.00 to 10.00, usually sees the most traffic: zebra, wildebeest, impala and nyala all appeared when I was last there, with crocodiles and numerous waterbirds around the shoreline.

To see the big game up close – and to see the lions at all – you'll need to book one of the reserve's guided game drives. These last 2½ hours and are conducted in an open vehicle through the secured big-game areas. Your guide will point out fauna and flora along the way and tell you about the reserve and its habitat. Sunrise or sundown drives, which include drinks and snacks, are for those overnighting at the camp; midday game drives are fine for day visitors, who will still see most of the animals. A dedicated rhino drive aims to get as close as possible to these horned giants and, safety permitting (which generally means no elephants nearby), allows you to disembark with your ranger and approach the rhinos on foot. You'll learn plenty about rhino behaviour and ecology (over 13s only).

Other activities, conducted outside the big-game area, include a guided birding walk and a guided mountain-bike trail (bikes provided). Both are good opportunities to explore the park outside the cocoon of a vehicle. Real bush aficionados can book the one- or two-night Ehlatsini bush trails, which allow a guided group of up to eight to explore on foot the wild Lusoti section of the park, east of the main road. Facilities are basic, with ground mats, bedrolls, long-drop toilet and cold tree shower, but all food is provided. You will need to bring your own water bottle and sleeping bag, and to wear natural-coloured clothes (nothing white or bright).

If you want a break from the wildlife, there is also the Umphakatsi Cultural Experience, in which you visit the homestead of a local chief and get a taste of rural Swazi culture – visiting a kraal, entering a hut, learning to grind maize and so on. Alternatively, you need not do anything at all, as Hlane is a top spot simply to kick back in the bush. At Ndlovu Camp you can watch the rhinos come to drink and tick off the birdlife without moving from your chalet. At night, by the flickering paraffin lanterns, you can enjoy a *sibhaca* dancing display around the campfire while lions roar from the darkness beyond. And Bhubesi Camp is the essence of peace and quiet: nothing but the sounds of bushbabies, nightjars and treefrogs to disturb the night.

Mlawula Nature Reserve

Mlawula lies to the east of the MR3. It is slightly smaller than Hlane, covering some 16,500ha, but more varied in terrain, extending high into the Lubombos. The area has a long history of protection but was not proclaimed as a reserve until 1980, following the Niven family's donation of the Blue Jay Ranch and the government purchase of Ndzindza and other adjoining estates. It is now a state-subsidised reserve, under the auspices of the SNTC, and is contiguous (divided only by game fences) with Mbuluzi and Shewula to the north, and Hlane to the west. The reserve straddles a transition zone between two bio-geographic regions: the dry thorn savannas of the west and the moister coastal thickets of the east. It comprises three main habitat types: the low-lying bushveld of Siphiso Valley; the broad-leafed woodland of the Lubombo slopes; and the open grasslands of the Ndzindza Plateau. The Lubombo Mountains run down the eastern flank of the reserve, forming the border with Mozambique. A chain of lower rhyolite ridges also rises to the west of the Siphiso Valley. The perennial Mbuluzi River flows along the northern boundary and exits via a gorge in the northeast. Its tributary, the smaller and more seasonal Mlawula, winds across the northwest. Seasonal rainwater pans sometimes form on the plateau.

This ecological diversity means that Mlawula is even richer in wildlife than Hlane, and indeed its habitat is in better condition, having suffered less over the years from ranching and other disturbance. However, you will not see more animals – at least, not the big stuff. Mlawula has never enjoyed the security of Hlane, and poaching remains commonplace. White rhino, which were once found here, were poached out entirely during the 1980s. Zebra, antelope and other large herbivores occur in much smaller numbers and are noticeably more skittish.

For the visitor, then, Mlawula's shaky infrastructure and elusive game make it a more challenging destination than Hlane. You should not go with the expectation of ticking off one animal after another on a comfortable game drive then returning to camp for a hot shower and ice-cold beer. But if you abandon the idea of a big-game safari and instead see the place as simply a wild and very beautiful tract of bush to explore on your own terms – including on foot – then Mlawula is fantastic. The gates open at 06.00 and close at 18.00, but these times are not strictly enforced and latecomers are usually welcome. Day visitors pay an entry fee of SZL28.

Fauna and flora Some 60 species of mammal have been recorded from Mlawula, including rarities such as pangolin. The most productive area for larger game is the Siphiso Valley, where impala are especially numerous. Zebra, blue wildebeest, nyala and greater kudu are widespread throughout the park. Waterbuck frequent the river valleys, while bushbuck and common duiker stick to the riverine thickets. Among the more unusual antelope, oribi have been recorded on the Ndzindza Plateau and klipspringer may be seen on rock outcrops, notably along the steep final stretch of the road to Magadzavane (see page 252). Warthogs and bush pigs are both widespread, but only the former commonly seen.

Large predators comprise the occasional shy leopard and a small population of spotted hyenas, which den in the park and are frequently heard at night. I have often seen hyena tracks and droppings in the vicinity of Siphiso Campsite. This is a good reserve for baboons, which roost on cliffs in the Lubombos and forage across the valley floor by day; listen out for their telltale warning barks. Night drives (see opposite) offer a chance to spot nocturnal creatures, such as large-spotted genet, black-backed jackal or possibly even an aardvark.

Mlawula's 350 recorded species of bird represent around 70% of Swaziland's total. Among these are numerous raptors, including martial eagle, secretary bird, and white-backed, white-headed and lappet-faced vultures. Owls are also well represented, with African barred owlet and giant eagle owl being local specialities. Look out for African finfoot, half-collared kingfisher and white-backed night-heron along the river – the last of these at night near the entrance gate bridge. Birders will also hope to tick some of the eastern coastal forest specials, such as African broadbill, purple-banded sunbird and bearded scrub robin. I have recorded more than 100 species in a day here during the rainy season, including several, such as Retz's helmetshrike and scaly-throated honeyguide, that I have seen nowhere else in Swaziland. A bird hide has recently been built at the south end of Siphiso Campsite and there are plans to develop a vulture restaurant that can be viewed from here.

Reptiles include Nile crocodile, Natal hinged tortoise, rock monitor and Lubombo flat lizard. I have heard stories of a 2.5m black mamba crossing the trail and of a huge python basking on a rock shelf, complete with warthog inside, but the only snakes I have encountered here personally have been the harmless spotted bush snake and marbled tree snake. Frogs produce a major racket after the first rains, bubbling kassinas and brown-backed treefrogs competing with the African scops owls around Siphiso Campsite. More than 40 species of fish frequent the rivers, and giant African land snails are conspicuous among innumerable invertebrates.

Mlawula is of great interest to botanists, with some 1,035 species recorded. These include large stands of Lubombo ironwood in the rocky ravines, plus an endemic cycad, *Encephalartos umbuluziensis*, an endemic aloe, *Aloe keithii*, and a number of unusual succulents and climbers.

Activities Mlawula's network of gravel game-viewing roads is generally manageable in a normal vehicle, though you should take care after rain and on the stone-strewn hillier routes. A map is available at the main gate, and directions follow numbered junctions 1–16. There are several marked picnic spots and with no dangerous game you can get out wherever you like. Two small pools in the south, Hyena Pool and Python Pool, are both reached via turn-offs from junction 14. A road due north from near the entrance gate leads to Mbuluzi Gorge, where you'll find excellent fishing opportunities – and crocodiles.

Night drives are permitted at Mlawula, offering a chance to spot nocturnal wildlife. It is best to confine your drive to the main roads around Siphiso Campsite – and do inform staff at the gate so that they won't be surprised by a light moving around the reserve after dark. When spotlighting, swing the beam slowly back and forth, looking for eye shine. Avoid directing it into the eyes of larger animals as this can disorientate them. And don't forget to bring binoculars, which work perfectly well down the beam.

The best way to explore Mlawula is undoubtedly on foot. In fact, this reserve offers a rare opportunity to wander unguided in pristine African bushveld and to explore for yourself the compelling world of tracks, signs and mysterious rustles. The ten walking trails vary in length from 1.5km to a full day's hike. All are clearly marked on the map and, in theory, by signs and cairns along the trails – although some are overgrown and their markers hard to find. The Ndzindza, Leopard and Siphiso trails lead from the Siphiso Campsite around the Siphiso Valley and are excellent for birding. The Liwula and Ironwood trails climb onto the plateau, with fine views down to the Mozambique coast; look out for baboons on the way up. On top, a number of poorly marked tracks criss-cross the Ndzindza Plateau, including one down to the Mbuluzi Gorge that passes through an impressive ironwood forest – a good spot for African broadbill and African barred owlet, plus other forest-edge bird species.

In the south of the park, the trails to Khabane Cave and Waterfall Cave both involve steep climbs and are a chance to see rarer flora, such as the endemic Swazi euphorbia, plus rock-loving wildlife such as klipspringer and mocking cliff-chats. Mahlabashane Gorge can be reached via a hike over the Ndzindza Plateau from the Mbuluzi Valley road and is home to rare plants, endemic ironwood forests and uncommon birds. Look out here for red duiker and, possibly, samango monkey.

If in doubt about any trail ask at the office first. You may be able to arrange a guide. If alone, however, bear in mind that this is wild country and you're unlikely to meet anyone else out there. It can get very hot – especially during summer, when the heat radiates off the rocks – and you'll have to carry all your water. Mlawula is notorious for ticks, especially on the plateau, so wear long trousers, spray around your legs and feet with insect repellent, and check yourself carefully afterwards. Any pool, however small, may have crocodiles.

Other activities include fishing on the Mbuluzi and Mlawula rivers (rangers will direct you to the good spots) and mountain-biking – if you bring your own bike. Supplies are available in Simunye (see page 266), a 15-minute drive away, where a shopping centre has everything you might need, including fuel.

Mbuluzi Game Reserve
Mbuluzi abuts Mlawula to the northwest. At 3,000ha, it is less than one-fifth the size, but its privately managed bushveld is in tip-top condition and supports a secure population of wildlife that is notably easier to see. The reserve falls into two sections, divided by the road. The southern section has the four private lodges (see *Where to stay*, page 258), each beside a private stretch of the Mlawula River. The northern section has the campsite, which is close to the banks of the Mbuluzi. Game-viewing roads and hiking trails extend across both sections, and a mountain-bike trail that winds through the bush and crosses the Mlawula River in several places offers plenty of single-track excitement. Day visitors are also welcome.

The reserve was established as a conservation area in 1980 and set up as a company in 1993. Each lodge is built on an individual shareblock and has its own distinct character. The terrain is extremely beautiful, undulating from 150m to 450m in altitude, with the Mbuluzi River and steep Lubombo escarpment forming an impressive backdrop to the north and east. Manager Matt McGinn's enlightened approach to conservation and habitat management has achieved minor miracles, especially in the control and eradication of alien species, ensuring that this relatively small area has a fantastic diversity of habitat. This includes dense riverine forests with towering sycamore figs and wild date palms, rocky cliffs, knobthorn savanna, acacia bushveld and open grassland.

With good habitat comes good wildlife. Large mammals include giraffe, greater kudu, blue wildebeest, waterbuck, zebra, impala, bushbuck, nyala, common duiker and warthog. A small population of hippos moves in and out of the reserve along the Mbuluzi River, and their resonant grunting can be heard over the reserve. The spotted hyena is the only large predator commonly encountered, although a recent sighting of a leopard by a guest – it was sauntering over the hillside opposite the lodge in broad daylight – suggests that these big cats are more frequent visitors than is commonly thought. Smaller predators recorded include African civet, large-spotted genet, serval, black-backed jackal and honey badger – although you will see these only at night.

Unsurprisingly, this is another top birding spot, with many of the same species as found at Mlawula. Over 300 have been recorded, including rarities such as dwarf bittern, Narina trogon and African finfoot. Reptiles are similarly abundant, with this stretch of the Mbuluzi having perhaps Swaziland's highest population of crocodiles. The McGinn family, who live in the ranger's house on the banks of the Mbuluzi, know this all too well: they lost their dog to a croc.

Activities Activities at Mbuluzi are strictly do-it-yourself. The roads are best suited to high-clearance vehicles, although with a little care you can go most places in a standard family car. They pass viewpoints, picnic spots and, at one spot, a bird-

In March 2011, Matt McGinn, manager of Mbuluzi Game Reserve, faced an unusual dilemma. Local fisherman Nkhosinathi Nkwanyane had discovered a hippo trapped inside a natural rock pot-hole in the bed of the Mbuluzi River. The weakened animal, which had been there for a while, was unable to climb out over the steep sides. McGinn and his game guards sprang to the rescue, but finding a solution proved tricky. Their first strategy was to divert the river's flow into the pot-hole in order to float the hippo out, but the animal could not get enough of a grip on the slippery rim to haul itself free. Next, Mick Reilly and George Mbatha arrived from Hlane with a team of rangers and helpers. They decided to fill the pot-hole with tyres, giving the animal a platform on which to climb to safety. Despite using more than 30 tyres, however, this strategy also failed. The work was extremely hazardous, according to McGinn, as the distressed hippo – one of Africa's most dangerous animals – lunged out of the water 'like a torpedo' at anybody who approached too close. As the beast became increasingly exhausted, however, the rangers managed to slip a noose around its neck. A great cheer went up as they hauled the animal out and towards the safety of the bank. After taking ten minutes to recover, it then wandered back to the safety of the river. The whole operation lasted over ten hours. Had the hippo not been spotted and rescued, it would have starved to death. Nkwanyane worked with the rescuers throughout and was strongly commended by Big Game Parks for his actions.

viewing hide over a small pool. In the southern section the road fords the Mlawula River at a low-level bridge. In the north, it completes a circuit inside a tight meander loop of the Mbuluzi, with impressive views from a narrow saddle down to the river on both sides. From here you can see up to Shewula Mountain Camp (see below) on the Lubombo escarpment and scan along the river for crocs – and possibly an African finfoot. At night, you can drive these roads with a spotlight in search of their nocturnal residents.

A more intimate wildlife experience comes by walking the many trails that lead around the reserve. These take in key viewpoints and picnic spots and all are interlinked, so you can complete individual walks or set out on one long circuit. Other activities include mountain-biking on the roads and dedicated bike trails (bring your own bike), and fishing, for overnight guests, in the Mlawula and the Mbuluzi. Both these perennial rivers support a healthy population of large-scale yellowfish, barbel and bream. A catch-and-release policy is encouraged.

You can reach Mbuluzi via a right turn off the MR3, 7.5km north of Simunye. Reception and the entrance to the northern section is 750km down the road on your left. There are maps here, plus cool drinks and a selection of handicrafts from Shewula for sale. The entrance to the southern section is opposite. Day visitors pay an entry fee of SZL35.

Shewula Mountain Camp This community ecotourism project, built in 2000, was the first of its kind in Swaziland and has become one of the most successful in southern Africa. It is the fruit of co-operation between the Shewula community, who set aside 2,650ha of land for conservation, and the adjacent reserves of Mlawula and Mbuluzi. The community own and manage the project, and put all profits towards local development.

Funding from Japan, the EU and COSPE, an Italian NGO active in this area, helped build the camp and the other community projects. These projects include an orphans care programme, an indigenous plant nursery, a soil programme that restores degraded land and encourages sustainable agriculture, a wind-power programme that generates electricity for community income, and a clean-water programme, in which water from local springs is filtered through sand into an underground cistern and piped to community taps.

The camp itself perches in a spectacular position on top of the Lubombo Plateau, looking across the Mbuluzi River far below. On a clear day you can see down to the Indian Ocean in the east and to the mountains of Malolotja in the west. It is well signed off the MR3, along 16km of dirt roads to the end of the D45. Once you arrive, you are unlikely to want to rush off again: the place has that end-of-the-world feel that suggests you need to slow down for a while.

Shewula has had a major impact on its community, which was among the poorest in Swaziland. It is a model of the kind of enterprise envisaged throughout the Lubombo TFCA (see page 50), in which ecotourism helps a community to prosper in a sustainable way at the heart of a conservation area. Project manager Nomsa Mabila studied tourism in Italy, courtesy of the project sponsors, and her drive has played a major part in the project's success. She'll be happy to chat to you about how this remarkable place came about and explain just what is happening in the community.

Activities While staying at the camp, which consists of stone-and-thatch chalets around a communal living area (see page 259), there is plenty to do. A guided nature walk will take you down to the Mbuluzi Gorge below camp in search of birds, crocodiles and other wildlife. Alternatively, a cultural village walk will take you around the community up top: a chance to meet local people, visit a school and perhaps share some stories over a local beer. These walks do not feel contrived; the village simply gets on with life while you join in as much or as little as you like. Your hosts can also arrange visits to the local *sangoma*.

To explore further afield, try a mountain-bike trip around the plateau. The guided, mostly flat route will take you via the nearby Shewula Community Resource Centre, which has handicrafts and traditional products for sale, plus schools and various scenic spots. Bikes can be hired at the camp. Or go by donkey cart, which should also be booked in advance.

Of course you needn't leave camp at all. The sunsets are spectacular and the laid-back vibe makes it highly tempting simply to stay put. You can join the communal Swazi meals at the large dining area and watch – and even join in – *sibhaca* song and dance displays by community youngsters.

Simunye Country Club
The wide lawns, swimming pool and large car park of this establishment, bang in the middle of Simunye Sugar Estates, seem a far cry from the wild bush of the surrounding reserves. But the place offers a convenient watering hole at the very centre of the Lubombo Conservancy. It also has a pleasant, relaxed feel, excellent food and numerous activities.

The club belongs to the Royal Swaziland Sugar Corporation (see box on page 270). Simply follow the signs of the MR3 through Simunye Sugar Estate. Day visitors can use the swimming pool and other facilities provided they buy a meal. The lush grounds are well worth a stroll, with their native trees and teeming birdlife. On my last visit I watched red-billed buffalo weavers, green wood-hoopoes, yellow-billed hornbills, purple-crested turacos and – a local special – brown-hooded parrots, all from my breakfast table.

Among regular local events are Friday night barbecues, popular with all-comers. And the biggest day in the local calendar is the club's annual fair. Held over a weekend in October, this has attracted an amazing 30,000 people, many from South Africa. And it is more than just a few tombola stalls: there are fairground rides,

SNAKE WOMAN

'I love that smell,' says Thea. She touches a crumbling smear on the wall, sniffs her finger, and shines her torch up into the narrow roof cavity. Black mamba droppings, apparently, smell like curry.

It's a moonless evening and I'm out 'on call' with Thea Litschka-Koen, manager of the Simunye Hotel. We're crouched in the abandoned outhouse of a diplomatic residence in Siteki. Somewhere above us, we're assured by the terrified gathering outside the door, is a 2m black mamba. The watchman saw it disappear into the hole just an hour ago and called Thea immediately. It hasn't emerged yet.

We poke around in the outhouse with grab sticks and head-torches for another half-hour or so. It's nerve-racking work. Clifton Koen, Thea's husband, is up on the roof outside, removing tiles. But the mamba doesn't show. I'm not sure whether I'm disappointed or relieved. 'Call me in the morning if you see it again,' she tells the foreman. 'And don't take your eyes off it.' With that, we jump in the car and drive back to Simunye, pausing only for Thea to jump out halfway down the hill, remove a large, hissing puff adder from the road and stuff it in a sack, ready for her next demonstration.

Thea had no interest in snakes until she helped out her son with a school project. Her research soon became an obsession. She learned to identify the snakes she'd grown up with in the bush and took a course in how to handle them. She also learned that snakes are fascinating and important animals, and that the dangerous ones – including black mambas, Mozambique spitting cobras and puff adders – become much less dangerous once you know more about them. Word got around, and soon Thea was being called out to identify and remove snakes from people's property, the terrified phone calls coming at all times of day and night. This developed into a more formal role, running courses and educating the community, and soon herpetologists elsewhere were calling on Thea's expertise – especially her experience with black mambas, from which she has obtained vital DNA samples for research.

From rescuing snakes Thea soon turned to rescuing people. Her work convinced her that snakebite in Swaziland's rural communities is more of a problem than is commonly imagined (she has more than once witnessed the death of a child). Antivenoms are seldom available – certainly not for people in impoverished rural circumstances. Thea carries her own supply, with which she can help those victims with whom she comes into contact. Just as important, however, are her snake education courses that explain simple measures for reducing the risk of snakebite and sensible steps to take if bitten. Rural people, perhaps unsurprisingly, see her skills and courage as something supernatural. Indeed, a 2009 BBC TV documentary made about Thea was entitled *Black Mamba, White Witch*. Thea's ambition is to build a local snakebite clinic. However, she still receives no funding. Visit her website (*www.antivenomswazi. org*) to find out more, or even make a much-needed donation.

The Northeast   THE LUBOMBO CONSERVANCY

7

a stage for bands and DJs, and such bizarre events as the 'Ascot goat races'. I'm told you should beware the vodka slush puppies. Check the club's website (*www. simunyeclub.com*) for precise dates and other details.

Activities The club will keep you active with a swimming pool, nine-hole golf course, squash court, gym, tennis court and children's play area. There is also fishing on the local dams, where you will spot waterbirds and even the odd crocodile. Local excursions arranged for guests include sunset cruises on Sand River Dam, 40km away (see page 271), and tubing on the Mbuluzi River. You can also take a guided tour of the sugar mill. Club manager Thea Litschka-Koen runs snake-handling and identification courses, which offer a unique opportunity to learn – at very close quarters – all about the serpent life of Swaziland (see *Snake woman*, page 267). Contact the club in advance.

LOMAHASHA BORDER

Lomahasha is 28km northeast of Simunye at the end of the MR3. The road crosses the Mbuluzi River before winding up onto the escarpment. The border, known as Namaacha on the Mozambique side, is open from 07.00 to 22.00. Services on the Swaziland side include two filling stations (Galp and Total) and a Yebo supermarket, plus hardware, stationery and bottle stores, vegetable vendors and fast-food joints. The Mozambique side is more developed. From the border, the road leads east on the EN5 down to Maputo, 70km away. Remember that you will need a Mozambique visa and all relevant vehicle documents (see page 105). And have your Portuguese phrase book handy.

MANANGA AND THE TOP END

Swaziland doesn't have an official 'Top End' like Australia's. In the absence of anything better, however, I have used this term to describe that far northern region that lies midway between Simunye in the northeast and Piggs Peak in the northwest. The area is equally accessible from either town but, with much of its hot, lowveld landscape managed by the Royal Swaziland Sugar Corporation estates, it would seem to belong most logically within this chapter.

To reach the Top End from the Lubombo Conservancy take the MR24 west, just after crossing the Mbuluzi River. This road continues straight past miles of cane fields. It passes three separate estate villages, each with a country club: the first is Tambankulu, on your right after 6km; the next is Mhlume, 25km further on and also on your right (3km after the Mhlume sugar mill on the left); and the third is Tshaneni (sometimes spelt Tjaneni), 7km further up the road on the left. Tshaneni also has the Inyoni Plaza shopping complex, with a Standard bank, Caltex filling station, Boxer superstore and post office.

Shortly after the Tshaneni turn you will reach a large roundabout. From here, a right turn takes you north to the Mananga border (see page 272), a left turn takes you south to Manzini or Piggs Peak via Bhalekane (see page 216), and the road straight on leads to Sand River Dam (see page 271).

WHERE TO STAY AND EAT The country clubs of the sugar estates are something of a blast from the past, both in décor and clientele. They were built mainly for the recreational needs of the expats who work on the sugar estates, and come with the golf courses, sports bars and other facilities you might expect. But they are by

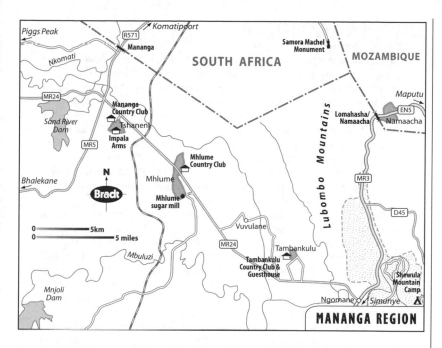

MANANGA REGION

no means stuffy or exclusive, and offer a pleasant place to eat or spend the night – generally in large and attractive grounds.

🏠 **Mhlume Country Club** (22 rooms, sleeps 40) ☎ 2313 4350; e dorrieL@rssc.co.sz; www. mhlumcclub.com. Recently refurbished club, with good restaurant, attractive grounds & impressive sporting facilities, owned by RSSC & managed by same team as Simunye Country Club (see page 266). Located in Mhlume sugar estate village, where it is well signed. Accommodation in 11 en-suite B&B units that sleep 2 & can take 1 extra bed, each with TV, bar, fridge, AC, tea/coffee & private veranda; separate guesthouse in 2 blocks, each with 3 en-suite units & all facilities; large, luxury 'Executive Directors' guesthouse available by special request, with 2 en-suite bedrooms, lounge, dining room, fully fitted kitchen & large patio. Club facilities available to guests include large sports field (handles soccer & cricket tournaments), squash & floodlit tennis courts, competition-sized swimming pool, modern gym, sauna & wellness centre (daily aerobics classes at 06.00 & 18.00), & children's playground. Popular Ligwalagwala restaurant serves à la carte, buffet & take-aways. New management has set out to restore some of the club's old colonial charm, while updating facilities & services. **$$–$$$**

🏠 **Tambankulu Country Club and Guesthouse** (14 rooms, sleeps 30) ☎ 2373 7111; e tambguest@swazi.net; www.tambankulu. co.za. Popular watering hole at end of gravel road 3km off MR24. Guesthouse has 14 en-suite bedrooms, with choice of standard, executive & honeymoon suite, all with TV, AC & telephone. Set in lush gardens, with 2 swimming pools. Guests can use club facilities, including golf course, tennis, squash, bowls & swimming. B/fast served either in b/fast room or on patio. Home-cooked lunches & à la carte candlelit dinners served on request; extensive menu includes fresh seafood. Grass runway for small aircraft (in case you need to park your Cessna). **$$**

🏠 **Mananga Country Club** (sleeps 36) ☎ 2323 2404; e mananga@swazilive.com; www. swazilive.com/wheretostay/mananga_club.htm. Located on the west of the Tshaneni estate, inside private 21ha game reserve, where wild game – including warthog, impala & giraffe – wanders right across 9-hole golf course. Accommodation in 2 large, fully-equipped guesthouses offering 9 rooms between them & sleeping 22 guests; b/fast provided or self-catering available if entire

7

Sugar came to northeast Swaziland at Mhlume in 1955, following trials undertaken by the Commonwealth Development Corporation (CDC). Mhlume (Swaziland) Sugar Company Limited was registered as a sugar factory and cane estate in a joint venture between Sir J L Hulett & Sons and the CDC. In 1957, the Komati River Barrage, with its 88km gravity canal, was built to provide irrigation. The mill was commissioned in 1960, with a production capacity of 90 tonnes of cane per hour. In 1966, CDC bought out Hulett & Sons to acquire sole ownership. Then in 1977 the king acquired 50% of the company in trust for the Swazi nation. In 1994 Mhlume took over 3,800ha of neighbouring cane fields, making it Swaziland's second largest cane producer, on an area of over 9,000ha.

Simunye ('We are one') Sugar Estate was developed by the Royal Swaziland Sugar Corporation (RSSC), in conjunction with the Swazi government and royal investment company Tibiyo TakaNgwane. The late King Sobhuza II opened the estate in October 1978. Some 10,000ha of bush were cleared to provide over 9,000ha of irrigated cane fields, with roads, water storage, canal systems, offices, stores and workshops. In 1980 the Simunye sugar mill was commissioned, initially capable of producing 120,000 tonnes of sugar per annum. In 2002 the RSSC merged with the neighbouring Mhlume Sugar Company to launch the new enlarged RSSC. Listed on the Swaziland Stock Exchange, it is the largest company in Swaziland, employing over 3,500 staff and producing two-thirds of the country's sugar. It owns and manages over 15,607ha of irrigated sugar cane on land leased from the Swazi nation and manages a further 5,018ha for third parties, delivering some 2.3 million tonnes of cane per season to its two mills. RSSC also operates a sugar refinery at Mhlume that produces 170,000 tonnes of refined sugar per season, and a 32-million-litre capacity ethanol plant, adjacent to Simunye mill. In 2005 Mananga Sugar Packers was established at Mhlume mill to pack and sell sugar within the region. In 1995 RSSC built a distillery beside Simunye mill to produce industrial-grade ethanol and spirit from molasses. This now utilises all the molasses from both Mhlume and Simunye to produce over 32 million litres per year, most of it exported to the EU and west Africa.

guesthouse booked; en-suite bedrooms, with communal sitting room, kitchen, braai area, shaded patio & large dining-room; guesthouses overlook golf course, with waterhole in front where game comes to drink. Also separate 4-bed bush camp, with campsite for another 6. Fully equipped houseboat on nearby Sand River Dam (see opposite) sleeps 4, with additional guests by arrangement; comes with motorboat for transport to & from shore. Clubhouse facilities include Nguni à la carte restaurant & bar (open to non-residents); menu features local beef & seafood fresh from Maputo. Conference centre & children's play area. Activities include swimming (pools at guesthouses & clubhouse), squash, tennis & golf. Cycling & walking trails around the property promise close encounters with relaxed wildlife & excellent birding. (Mbabane Natural History Society clocked up 106 bird species over a w/end.) Off-site activities centre on nearby Sand River Dam, with fishing & boating. The club offers sunset cruises on its 25-seater boat, with full bar & catering as required (SZL500 per trip). A spacious, relaxed property, with wildlife all around. (When I last visited, an orphaned zebra foal had struck up a friendship with the club's Jack Russell.) Just 5.5km from Mananga border & 40km from Lomahasha, it is a popular stopover for South Africans en route to the Kruger Park & Maputo. **$–$$**

🏠 **Impala Arms Hotel** (34 rooms, sleeps 63) 📞 2323 2431. This cheap & rather run-down establishment, opposite Inyoni Plaza in Tshaneni Estates, is a far cry from the country clubs. When I dropped by, the receptionists did not look up from their card game & the swimming pool had clearly been empty a long time. Caters mainly to contract workers at Mhlume. Perhaps it grows on you if you stay the night. **$**

WHAT TO DO The country clubs at Tambankulu, Mhlume and Mananga offer various activities and facilities, from tennis and squash to golf and fishing. Many are reserved for overnight guests and/or club members but some can be booked by day visitors, sometimes via temporary membership. Contact individual clubs (see above for details).

Sand River Dam Aside from the country clubs, this large reservoir built for the irrigation of the local citrus and cane plantations is the area's main attraction. It is full of fish, including bream and barbel, which makes it popular with anglers. It also has a sizeable population of crocodiles and is set in a small game reserve where wildlife can be seen around the shore. Activities include boating of various kinds, from yachts to houseboats, and fishing – either from boats or the shore, where jetties keep you out of the reach of crocs. Access to the dam is restricted to members and their guests, but fishing and boat cruises can be arranged from all the country clubs, including Simunye (see page 266).

FATAL FLIGHT

On 19 October 1986, President Samora Machel of Mozambique was returning from Lusaka, Zambia, when his Tupolev Tu-134 presidential jet crashed in the Lubombo Mountains, near Mbuzini, South Africa (close to the borders of both Mozambique and Swaziland). Machel was among 35 officials who died. Ten survived. The Margo Commission, set up by the South African government, concluded that the accident was caused by pilot error. This was accepted by the International Civil Aviation Authority but rejected by both the Mozambican and Soviet governments. The latter claimed that the South Africans had lured the plane off course using a decoy radio navigation beacon. Speculation has continued to the present day, particularly in Mozambique. Leading Portuguese journalist José Milhazes, who has lived in Moscow since 1977, contends that the crash was due to simple errors by the Russian pilot and crew, but that both the Soviet and the Mozambican authorities had an interest in spreading the theory of South African sabotage as the Soviets wanted to preserve their reputation and the Mozambicans wanted to create a hero. In his 2007 memoirs, however, Jacinto Veloso, one of Machel's most loyal supporters, suggested there had been a conspiracy between the South African and Soviet secret services, both of which wanted to get rid of Machel. According to Veloso, the Soviet ambassador had recently asked for an audience with Machel to convey the USSR's concern about Mozambique's perceived shift towards the West, to which the president had supposedly replied, '*Vai à merda!*' ('Eat shit!'). Convinced that Machel was now beyond their control, the Soviets allegedly did not hesitate to sacrifice their own plane, together with its pilot and crew.

MANANGA BORDER Mananga border lies at the end of the MR5, 5km north of its intersection with the MR24, where the Nkomati River flows out of Swaziland into South Africa. The border, also known as Mananga on the South Africa side, is open from 08.00 to 18.00. From here, it is 75km north on the R571 to the Kruger Park's Crocodile Bridge gate, via the town of Komatipoort. A left turn 200m before the border crosses the Nkomati and heads west to join the MR6, from where you may continue to Piggs Peak or the Matsamo border (see page 228).

There is one attraction just over the border that you might want to check out while in the area. Some 15km into South Africa, a right turn signs you to the Samora Machel Monument. This marks the spot where the plane carrying the then president of Mozambique crashed in 1986 (see *Fatal flight*, page 271). It incorporates some of the wreckage and features 35 steel tubes that wail in the wind. The monument was inaugurated by Joaquim Chissano and Nelson Mandela in 1999 and declared a South African National Heritage Site in 2006. Nelson Mandela married Machel's widow, Graça, in 1998.

8

The Southeast

The area covered in this chapter is, roughly speaking, the bottom-right quarter of the country. It extends either side of the MR8, which links Manzini to the South Africa border at Lavumisa and is the region's only major transport route. Over the border, this road becomes the route to Durban, along which visitors from KwaZulu-Natal generally enter Swaziland.

The Swaziland that greets anyone arriving from this direction is quintessential rural Africa: hot and dusty, with skinny cattle, flat-topped acacias and scattered mud-and-thatch villages. Its unforgiving terrain seems a world away from the cool, undulating hills of the west. Lining the eastern horizon are the Lubombo Mountains, which form the border with first South Africa and then Mozambique, and continue north into the Kruger Park. This long ridge is broken only by the Great Usutu, Swaziland's largest river, which meanders southeast across the region before exiting sharp left through a steep gorge into Mozambique.

The aptly named Big Bend, built beside this kink in the river, is the region's largest settlement. It is dominated by a towering sugar mill and surrounded by miles of lush green irrigated cane fields. Beyond Big Bend the MR8 curves northwest, tracing the river's course through wild lowveld bush – into which Mhkaya Game Reserve is smuggled – to the small centre of Siphofaneni. It then rises towards the middleveld, through scenic hills and tumbling rock formations, to end at Hhelehhele, 8km east of Manzini.

This region bridges two provinces: the southern part of Lubombo and the eastern part of Shiselweni. Relatively large, it is poorly developed and suffers from drought, with water scarce except in the Usutu River and the various dams and irrigation channels it supplies. Away from the sugar estates, which are pivotal to Swaziland's economy, there is little to sustain people. The scattered population scrapes a meagre living from the harsh, dry land.

The southeastern lowveld once teemed with game. Today, wildlife remains the main attraction for the visitor – notably at Mkhaya, Swaziland's most exclusive safari destination, but also at the smaller reserves of Nisela and Mhlosinga. Thrill-seekers can enjoy whitewater rafting on the Great Usutu in the northwest of the region. Accommodation options are limited to the private nature reserves and a handful of places around Big Bend.

MANZINI TO SIPHOFANENI

The main route into southeast Swaziland from the country's heartland is east from Manzini on the MR3. After 8km, at Hhelehhele, a right turn signs you south to Big Bend on the MR8. A large Galp filling station at this junction, with shop and toilets, is your last convenient pit stop until Siphofaneni, 36km down the road.

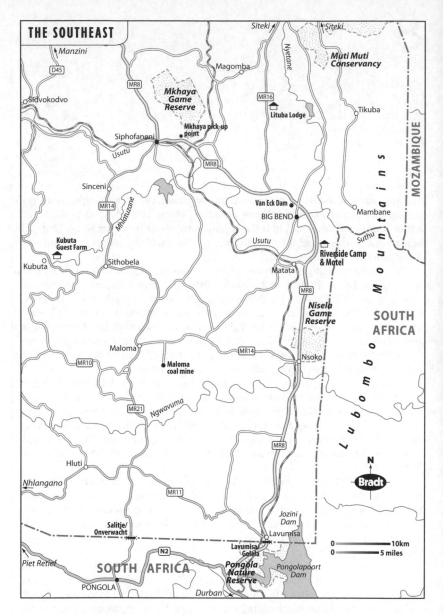

THE SOUTHEAST

Manzini
D45
Sidvokodvo
MR8
Mkhaya
Game
Reserve
Siphofaneni
Usutu
Mkhaya pick-up
point
Sinceni
MR14
MR8
Mhlatuzane
Kubuta
Guest Farm
Kubuta
Sithobela
Maloma
MR10
Maloma
coal mine
MR21
Ngwavuma
Hluti
Nhlangano
MR11
Salitje/
Onverwacht
N2
Piet Retief
SOUTH AFRICA
PONGOLA

Siteki
Siteki
Nyetane
Magomba
Muti Muti
Conservancy
MR16
Lituba Lodge
Tikuba
Van Eck Dam
BIG BEND
Mambane
Usutu
Suthu
Riverside Camp
& Motel
Matata
MR8
Nisela
Game
Reserve
SOUTH
AFRICA
MR14
Nsoko
MR8
Jozini
Dam
Lavumisa
Lavumisa/
Golela
Pongola
Nature
Reserve
Durban
Pongolapoort
Dam

MOZAMBIQUE

Lubombo Mountains

N
Bradt

0 _____ 10km
0 _____ 5 miles

From Hhelehhele the road descends into the lowveld. This next stretch is one of the country's most picturesque, with small homesteads nestled into dense bush and impressive wind-sculpted rock formations piled up as though by a giant hand. Larger, wilder hills stretch away to the south. Take it slowly: not only will you have more time to enjoy the view, but there are often speed traps along this stretch and some severe speed bumps, especially – and quite rightly – in the vicinity of the several primary schools.

After 4km you will meet a right turn to Sidvokodvo on the D45, which cuts through to the MR9 and on to Nhlangano and the southwest (see *Chapter 6*). After

22km you pass a left turn on the D44, which cuts back north to the MR3 and on to Siteki and the northeast (see *Chapter 7*). And after 36km, with the Great Usutu gleaming ahead, you reach Siphofaneni.

SIPHOFANENI Siphofaneni provides a centre for a wide rural community, with its market, bus station and railway line (for goods trains). It does not really cater to tourists, however, and there is nowhere to stay. Useful services include the Wayside pharmacy, branches of FNB and Standard banks, a supermarket and the Nokuphila shopping complex, with various cafés and take-aways. There is also a Galp filling station with shop and toilets. A large junction in the centre of town is signed to the right along the MR14 to Hlatikulu (see page 235). Beyond this on the left is the police station.

Siphofaneni feels like the gateway to the lowveld. Heading east out of town you see the first cane fields, the blue line of the Lubombo Mountains on the horizon and, after some 6km, the entrance to Mkhaya Game Reserve.

WHAT TO SEE AND DO
Rafting the Usutu Whitewater rafting arrived on the Usutu in 1991, the brainchild of South African adventure sports aficionado Darron Raw. Under his company Swazi Trails (see page 104), it now takes pride of place among an impressive portfolio of activities around the kingdom. Trips are run on the Bulungapoort section of the Usutu River, between Sidvokodvo and Siphofaneni. They start from the Swazi Trails office in Ezulwini (see page 170), from where the 45–60-minute drive takes you via Sidvokodvo to a launch site on the southern bank.

This is a remote and inspiring stretch of river. Its brown waters thunder through clefts and gorges, alternating with calmer stretches of bush and grazing land. You can expect fine views of rural Swaziland, with imposing rock formations, riverbank community life and a fair amount of wildlife from waterbirds such as hamerkops and pied kingfishers to terrapins, water monitors and even the odd small crocodile. You can also expect to get drenched.

For most of the year this is generally a Grade III (medium difficulty) rafting river. In peak flow, however, it rises to Grade IV, and even has Grade V and VI sections, which the rafting trips avoid. As the trips use two-person inflatable rafts, with no guide on board, there is more to do than when simply floating downstream on a ten-man raft, where you need only hold on. That said, it is perfectly suited to first-timers, especially during the May–October low-water season.

THE GREAT USUTU

The Great Usutu, known in siSwati as the Lusutfu, is the largest river in Swaziland and drains approximately half the country. It rises in the South African highveld near Ermelo and enters Swaziland just north of the Sandlane border. In Swaziland it has three major tributaries: the Lusushwana (Little Usutu), Ngwempisi and Mkondvo. After leaving the country through the Lubombo Mountains east of Big Bend, flowing through the 16km-long Usutu Gorge, it joins the Pongola River for its final journey to the Indian Ocean in the Bay of Maputo, Mozambique. For this last stretch it is known as the Rio Maputo. The Usutu has plenty of wildlife, with hippos, crocodiles and tiger fish among the more impressive residents of its lower stretches. It is also a key source of water for Swaziland's sugar estates, many of which line its banks.

After a thorough safety briefing, you don PDF (life jacket) and helmet, and launch your raft, with one paddle per person. An initial gentle stretch is good for practising paddling and building up confidence. Things then become more vigorous, continuing through a series of rapids, with names such as 'Monica Lewinsky' (don't ask) and the 'Initiator'. Trickier rapids are negotiated one boat at a time, with the guides first pulling the group over for instructions. (When about to hit rocks, apparently, you should throw your weight *towards* rather than *away from* them.) At the fiercest rapids, you may have to disembark and carry your raft to the next navigable stretch.

After two–three hours paddling, depending on conditions, and some 7km of river, lunch is at the impressive Holomi Falls. This is where those on the combo trip (see below) do their abseiling, and any thrill-seekers who don't yet feel wet enough can leap 10m from the cliff into a plunge pool below. The falls mark the end of the half-day trip and the vehicles are waiting here to take you back after lunch. The full-day trip continues from here for another 7km, culminating in an impressive rapid called 'Zambezi'. See below for information on booking and prices.

No worries Safety is the first priority for any reputable rafting operation and that includes this one. Trained guides accompany all trips and Swazi Trails is aligned to South Africa's stringent code of guide training and safety through the African Paddling Association (APA). You do not need previous experience or any special level of fitness. Neither do you have to be a good swimmer: should you capsize (and you probably will), the PFD will keep you afloat. Nervous non-swimmers might feel safest during the low-water season, however, when the river is generally shallow enough to stand up in. The recommended age for rafters is 12–65 years; older or younger participants may be taken on request, but not if the river is in flood. Young children can travel with the guides, who are unlikely to capsize. Crocodiles do inhabit slower-flowing stretches – I saw three on my last trip – but are generally small, shy and not considered a problem. Bilharzia (see page 116) may be present in parts of the Usutu but has never been recorded among the rafting guides, who grew up here. Darron's position on risk is straightforward. 'If you're brave enough to try it,' he says, 'you'll find us brave enough to take you.'

Rafting packages Swazi Trails (⚓ 2416 2180; e *info@swazi.travel*; *www. swazitrails.co.sz*) is Swaziland's sole rafting operator and runs daily trips throughout the year, as follows:

Half-day rafting (⏲ 08.30–14.00; SZL820 pp) Covers 7km of river, including the most popular rapids; ends with picnic lunch at Holomi Falls.

Full-day rafting (⏲ 08.30–17.00 Nov–May only; SZL950 pp) Starts with half-day stretch and continues after lunch for another 7km (14km total).

Full-day rafting, abseiling/tubing combo (⏲ 08.30–17.00 Jun–Oct only; SZL950 pp) After the half-day rafting (see above), participants choose either abseiling or tubing in the afternoon; abseiling is on a cliff at Holomi Falls lunch spot; tubing involves returning upstream to re-run sections of the first stretch in one-person inflatable tubes.

All trips begin and end at the Swazi Trails office in Ezulwini (see page 170), although pick-ups and drop-offs can be arranged elsewhere. They include transport, equipment, river guides, first aid, drinking water, picnic lunch, refreshments and free photos (when available) via online Flickr site.

Mkhaya Game Reserve This private reserve is the crowning glory of Big Game Parks (see page 102 and advert on inside back cover) and Swaziland's most exclusive safari retreat. Here you will be escorted around the bush by expert guides in search of big game, then return to your private camp to dine beneath the stars, before drifting off to sleep in your chalet to the noises of the night. The ambience is pure bush, the wildlife in-your-face and your creature comforts fully taken care of.

The reserve comprises around 10,000ha of undulating bush to the north of the Umzimphofu River. Its habitats are chiefly acacia thornveld in the south – *mkhaya* being the siSwati name for the knobthorn tree (*Acacia nigrescens*), which flourishes on these lowveld soils – and broadleaved woodland in the north, with magnificent stands of riverine forest along the watercourses, notably in the vicinity of Stone Camp. Big Game Parks acquired the reserve in 1979. The idea then was to protect Swaziland's last herd of indigenous Nguni cattle (see page 68) but as the reserve expanded so did its ambitions. Today Mkhaya is a sanctuary for endangered species such as black rhino and sable antelope, and home to other large mammals that once roamed Swaziland freely. Most were translocated from elsewhere in Swaziland or South Africa, and have since established self-supporting breeding populations. Security was a priority from the outset and by the late 1980s, when an onslaught of poaching swept Swaziland (see *Rhino wars*, page 14), the heavily fortified Mkhaya became the last refuge for many of these animals, notably rhinos.

Today you can expect to see most safari A-listers you might hope for in, say, the Kruger Park, with the exception of big cats. By comparison with such huge parks elsewhere there is no hiding the fact that Mkhaya is small, and its security fences, which enclose breeding camps for endangered species around the ranger base, can detract a little from the sense of wilderness. But the habitat is authentic, the animals wild and a night here definitely feels like a night in deepest, darkest Africa.

Getting there and away Mkhaya is signposted off the MR8, 6km east of Siphofaneni. A short dirt track takes you to the pick-up point, behind Vokuzibonele Grocery, where a guide will be waiting for you at the appointed time (10.00 or 16.00). He will then drive you into the reserve or, if you have your own vehicle, will ask you to follow behind him. Either way, you first cross the Umzimphofu River – which is generally dry – then enter the reserve, passing through a succession of high-security game fences until you reach the old farmhouse that now serves as reception. Here you leave your vehicle, check in, sign the waiver forms (the usual 'If anything eats, gores or tramples me it's my own stupid fault,' or words to that effect), and your adventure begins. If the river is flowing and impossible to ford, you can leave your vehicle at the pick-up point under the gaze of a permanent security guard.

Where to stay and eat

⌂ **Stone Camp** (12 units, 33 beds) ✆2528 3943; e reservations@biggameparks.org; www.biggameparks.org/mkhaya. This rustic but comfortable safari camp is Mkhaya's only accommodation & gets its name from the dolerite rocks of which its 12 thatched cottages are constructed. These comprise 4 twin cottages, 4 dbl cottages, 1 trpl cottage & 3 family cottages (Nkonjane: 2 rooms, 2 dbls & 1 sgl with bath & shower; Sinkankanka: 1 room, 1 dbl & 4 sgls with shower; Narina: 1 room, 4 sgls & shower). All have steepling thatched roofs & are open-sided, with bedroom & bathroom looking onto the bush. Beds are large & comfortable, with tea/coffee & spacious en-suite bathroom open to the bush. Cottages are linked by sandy paths but screened from one another by dense vegetation. The camp is delightfully situated in shady riverine forest along a dry riverbed, beneath towering sycamore figs, leadwoods & sausage trees. There is no electricity, but paraffin lamps light pathways & cottages after dark. Wildlife such as nyala wanders through at will (though elephants & other larger species are fenced out) & birdlife is prolific. The whole set-up strikes an excellent balance between bush & comfort. Hearty al fresco meals include impala stew, with wildlife wandering past as you tuck in. Ice-cold drinks are always available & a warm homemade muffin before your morning game drive hits the spot. Rates include all meals & activities, with various packages available, depending on your cottage & length of stay. **$$$$$**

What to see and do
Wildlife and game drives Mkhaya's main attraction is, of course, its big game and the easiest way to find this is on a game drive in an open Land Rover, your guide often traversing fearsome terrain in the process. For overnight guests, game drives take place in the early morning (06.00–08.00) and late afternoon (16.00–18.00), which are when animals are most active and the light is best for photography. Drives for day visitors are conducted in the middle of the day, but sightings are still good, as distances are small and the rangers know where to find the wildlife.

White rhinos are numerous, sometimes gathering in groups of up to a dozen, and will allow you to approach very close. Black rhinos are shyer and stick to thick bush, but rangers can often find them at favoured haunts. The reserve's elephants comprise a single herd, whose breeding has now been arrested via contraception to prevent them from completely ransacking their habitat. They tend to stick together, often in the open woodland, and must be approached with more caution. Other must-sees include a decent herd of buffalo, plentiful zebra and giraffe, and a pod of hippos at the reserve's main dam.

Roan, sable and tsessebe are the stars among various antelope species, the first two of these found in separate fenced areas where their welfare can be better monitored. Otherwise, blue wildebeest, greater kudu and nyala are common, the last especially around Stone Camp, and impala abundant. Scarcer antelope include bushbuck, red duiker and suni – the last of these also often around camp – and warthog are everywhere. The few leopard that frequent Mkhaya are seldom seen, but you may come across spotted hyena, or at least hear their whooping calls at night. Among various other nocturnal species are black-backed jackal, large-spotted genet, thick-tailed bushbaby, porcupine and scrub hare.

Birdlife includes numerous raptors, such as martial, brown snake, African hawk and crowned eagles, plus waterbirds at the dams and usual bushveld suspects like yellow-billed hornbill and lilac-breasted roller. Among the more unusual avian highlights of my last visit were violet-tipped courser and lizard buzzard. Birding is especially good around Stone Camp (see *Wildlife in camp*, opposite). A few sizeable crocodiles can usually be seen lounging around the main waterhole, while pythons are reputedly common, and rock monitor and leopard tortoise were among other reptiles I encountered.

Game walks An exciting alternative is to ditch the wheels and head out on foot. For close encounters with rhinos, Mkhaya's guided bush walks compete with anywhere in Africa. They are led by expert guides and take place in designated areas – well away from the elephants, which are unpredictable and best avoided.

White rhinos are generally approachable, and the guides know individual animals well enough to get you extremely close. All you need do is stay quiet, move slowly and obey instructions. Few things concentrate the mind more than having one of these two-tonne behemoths look up from its grazing and eyeball you at just

10m – although in reality the threat is minimal. Black rhinos are a very different proposition, however, being more nervous and aggressive, and also frequenting such dense bush that finding them is difficult and potentially hazardous. Luckily you are with experienced, armed rangers. The morning I spent tracking a female black rhino and calf through Mkhaya's dense thickets – checking the wind, pausing as they paused and hardly daring breathe as the click of my camera shutter had the female's radar ears rotating wildly – ranks among my more thrilling safari moments. Tracking black rhinos is for small groups only and arranged on request.

Guided walks are not just about big game: they are a full immersion in the sights, sounds and textures of the bush that, by comparison, makes watching wildlife from a vehicle seem like watching it on television. Your guide's expert eyes will reveal the secrets of your surroundings – from the air-conditioning of a termite mound to the architecture of a spider's web. He will divine from a few scrapes in the sand which animals passed by last night, in which direction they were heading, and why. Highlights of my last walk at Mkhaya included finding the dragline of a recent python, distinguishing the droppings of a bush pig from those of the much more common warthog and – most exciting – listening to the growls of young hyenas deep in their den below our feet.

Wildlife in camp If you'd rather simply relax in camp there's plenty to see there too, especially for birders. Feathered specials include Narina trogons, which have nested near reception, pink-throated twinspots, which creep around the trails (often among parties of firefinches), and a semi-tame flock of crested guineafowl that scratch away in the leaf litter. The birdbath beside the dining area is usually busy with bulbuls, mousebirds, waxbills, robins and, if you're lucky, purple-crested turacos. A new bird hide allows you to sit back during the quiet hours and spy discreetly on the avian comings and goings. Meanwhile nyala browse around the cottages and a quiet stroll may reward you with a shy suni tripping through the undergrowth. After dinner the night noises take over: listen for the quavering whistle of fiery-necked nightjars, the unearthly shriek of greater bushbabies and the whoop of spotted hyenas. On my last visit, a large-spotted genet slunk along the wall right beside our fire.

BIG BEND

Big Bend lies 25km southeast of Siphofaneni on the MR8. More community than town, this place was built to serve the sugar industry but has grown into a regional centre for southeast Swaziland. Emerald-green cane fields have supplanted the dusty bush, the spray from their sprinklers glittering in the sun, and the huge, smoke-belching sugar mill is visible from afar. Visitors here will find shops, services and a handful of places to stay and eat.

The main settlement is just south of the MR8 on the banks of the Usutu, where the river describes the tight meander loop that gives the place its name. Arriving from Manzini, you pass the Van Eck Dam (see page 282) on the right followed by a left turn to the mill and finally the right turn that leads into town. This road passes a bus rank on the right then Ubombo village (the residential home of the sugar estate) on the left, identified by its massive ornamental mill wheel and neat rows of staff housing. Opposite the village is a small shopping complex, with banks and a supermarket, among other facilities. The road then continues south for 8km as a gravel track, crossing a low causeway over the river, to the Matata shopping complex (see page 284).

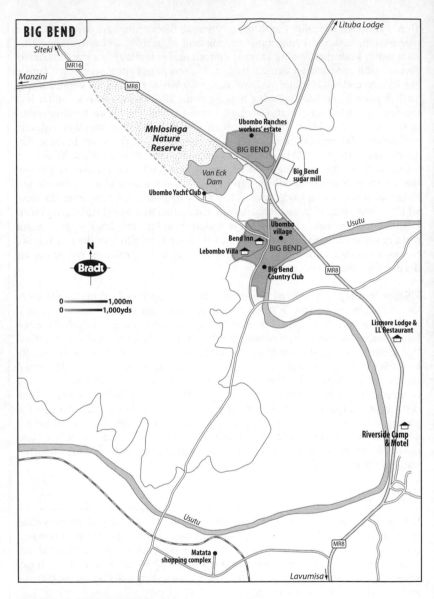

↑ Lituba Lodge

BIG BEND

Siteki

MR16

Manzini

Mhlosinga Nature Reserve

Ubombo Ranches workers' estate

BIG BEND

Van Eck Dam

Big Bend sugar mill

Ubombo Yacht Club

Ubombo village

Usutu

Bend Inn

BIG BEND

Lebombo Villa

Big Bend Country Club

MR8

N

Bradt

0 — 1,000m
0 — 1,000yds

Lismore Lodge & LL Restaurant

Riverside Camp & Motel

Usutu

Matata shopping complex

MR8

Lavumisa

WHERE TO STAY AND EAT Big Bend is not really set up as a tourist town. Its few hotels and guesthouses cater more to business travellers, contract workers and locals in search of happy hour. But most offer comfortable accommodation, a good meal and a chance to relax over sundowners after a hot day in the lowveld. As well as the properties listed below, you will find out-of-town safari accommodation at Mkhaya Game Reserve (see page 277) or Nisela Game Reserve (see page 284).

🏠 **Bend Inn** (28 rooms) ☎ 2363 6725; e bendinn@swazi.net. This laid-back establishment, the oldest in the area, is set on an aloe-studded hillside overlooking a sweep of river & cane fields, with a panoramic view from the terrace. Rooms come with AC, DSTV, telephone

& minibar. Restaurant serves a decent range of inexpensive meals. Other facilities include pool, terrace, conference room & internet access. The general dusty somnolence, punctuated by reputed bar-room revelry come Fri night, creates a distinct Wild West ambience – something no doubt enhanced by stories of the infamous car park shoot-out. **$$**

⌂ **Lebombo Villa** (10 rooms) ☎7603 6585; e thevilla@swazi.net. Secluded guesthouse offering B&B accommodation in quiet residential area, well signed off main street. Mediterranean-style exterior set in pleasant tropical garden with inviting pool. Rooms in main house on 2 storeys: upstairs, 8 en-suite dbls, including 1 with adjoining en-suite sgl; downstairs, 4 twin rooms & 1 king-size bedroom with patio. All rooms have AC & DSTV. Also: bar, snooker table, widescreen TV

& conference facilities. Secure parking for trailers & boats (security boosted by some very large but extremely friendly dogs). Home-cooked meals served in dining room. **$$**

⌂ **Lituba Lodge** (9 rondavels, sleeps 45) ☎2550 9016; m 7628 8110; e info@litubalodge.com; www.litubalodge.com. Newish (2008) out-of-town lodge, 21km north of Big Bend on MR16 to Siteki. Sits in fenced compound, surrounded by wild bush & game farm, with impressive Lubombos backdrop. Accommodation in en-suite rondavels, some twin & some dbls, all with AC & TV (DVDs). Family rooms have 2 twin beds & 1 bunk bed with dbl below & sgl above. Large thatched bar & restaurant. Menu specials include fresh, good-value Mozambique seafood (crab curry SZL55, queen prawns SZL99), traditional Swazi food & various standard dishes. Local activities

ONE LUMP OR TWO?

The success of sugar in southeast Swaziland would have surprised Swaziland's early colonists, who generally shunned the lowveld in favour of the country's cooler western regions. An exception to this trend was Allister Miller (see page 148), who believed that Swaziland's good soils had the potential to make it 'the California of South Africa', and in 1912 Miller bought a huge 380km^2 cattle ranch just north of the Usutu River. This ranch had its ups and downs – the latter including malaria, drought and crocodiles – but at one stage housed over 18,000 head of cattle.

By 1927, following a crash in world beef prices, the cattle were sold off and the land abandoned. In 1942, various investors moved in to buy up the land and form Ubombo Ranches, turning from livestock to crop cultivation. Sugar arrived in the 1950s, and in 1954 productivity picked up with the construction of a new irrigation canal. In 1958 the first sugar mill was transported on trucks from South Africa. By 1960 this had been replaced by a larger mill and Big Bend was established to service the estate. Irrigation continued to improve, with the construction in 1970 of the Van Eck Dam, and yields to increase.

In 1996 Todd's Big Bend Sugar Company and Ubombo Ranches, the two principal sugar companies, merged to create Ubombo Sugar Estates. The following year this was bought by the South African Illovo Sugar Group – in which Tibiyo Taka Ngwane (Swaziland's royal investment fund) has 40% shareholding. Today Ubombo Sugar has 1,193ha of land under cultivation, yielding an average 101 tonnes per hectare, and its factory produces over 200,000 tonnes of sugar per year, 40% of it refined.

Ubombo Sugar dominates the Big Bend community today. It has over 3,000 employees, many housed in the Ubombo Village, where they receive education, medical care, a school and other services. The company helps boost the community by supporting small local farmers on Swazi Nation Land, and in Mhlosinga Reserve (see page 282) it has made some recompense for all the natural habitat lost to sugar.

can be arranged, including fishing, quad-biking & clay-pigeon shooting. W/end entertainment nights feature local musicians & DJs. $$

🏠 **Lismore Lodge & LL Restaurant**
(22 rooms) 📞 2363 6019/6080; e riverside@ realnet.co.sz. Sister hotel to Riverside Motel (see below), located 2km to the north off MR8. Accommodation includes 1 family room. Also: pool table & bar with large-screen TV. LL Restaurant was known as the Lubombo Lobster under previous management, when it was reputedly the best place in Swaziland for fresh Mozambique seafood, including a legendary crab curry. It still has the same chef & the menu, featuring LM prawns (see

page 129) & seafood curry, is good value. Light meals also available. Rates as for Riverside Motel (see below). $$

🏠 **Riverside Restaurant and Motel**
(23 rooms) 📞 2363 6910/6012; e riverside@ realnet.co.za. Basic roadside hotel at the Riverside Complex, 9km south of Big Bend on MR8, which serves generally as travellers' stopover. Rooms comprise dbls, sgls & en-suites, all with AC & TV. Also conference facilities. Under same ownership as nearby Lismore Lodge & LL Restaurant (see above), & enjoys similar good reputation for fresh seafood. $$

WHAT TO SEE AND DO

Van Eck Dam and Mhlosinga Nature Reserve   Van Eck Dam (pronounced Van *Ike*, like 'bike') sits beside the MR8 2km north of Big Bend and was created in 1970 as an irrigation reservoir for the sugar estates. The northern shores lie within Mhlosinga Nature Reserve, a private conservation project managed by Ubombo Sugar that extends for a further 4km north alongside the highway, from where wildlife is often visible. Mhlosinga is the siSwati name for the fever tree (*Acacia xanthophloea*), whose green-yellow trunks are a prominent feature of lowveld watercourses.

Ubombo Ranches developed the reserve in 1986, with the aim of restoring some of the area's once rich biodiversity. An electrified game fence was erected around 300ha of ranch land – an area that has since been extended by a further 700ha. Animals once indigenous were reintroduced, including zebra, warthog, impala, greater kudu, nyala, waterbuck, blue wildebeest, red duiker and common reedbuck. Giraffe were also brought in, and hippos have occasionally turned up from the nearby Usutu. Side-striped jackal and serval are among smaller predators that roam the acacia savanna.

An impressive number of birds have been recorded for such a small area, including raptors such as African fish eagle. Passing birdwatchers could do worse than pull over (safely) on the MR8, where the road passes the dam, and scan the waters and shoreline. There is usually a variety of herons, egrets and wildfowl to be seen, as well as other waterbirds such as African jacana, blacksmith lapwing and pied kingfisher. Crocodiles and pythons are among the reserve's more impressive reptiles. The dam's abundant tigerfish, barbel and bream make it popular with anglers – and the aforementioned crocodiles.

Both the dam and nature reserve are privately managed. Access is generally restricted to Ubombo Sugar employees and members of the Mhlosinga Wildlife Society. The Lubombo Yacht Club on the western shore has a boat ramp that enables members and guests to use the dam for watersports such as sailing and waterskiing, and there is also a small campsite nearby. Access for visitors is at weekends by permit only (📞 2343 6533; m 7624 9042; e Dducasse@illovo.co.za). You can reach the reserve via Big Bend: take a right turn 800m into town and continue for 2km to the entrance.

Big Bend Country Club and Golf Course   The Big Bend Country Club (📞 2363 6288) is attached to the Ubombo Sugar village. It offers a nine-hole golf course, tennis courts and various other facilities, plus access to Mhlosinga Nature Reserve and Van Eck Dam (see opposite). Unfortunately for visitors, the club is reserved for employees of Ubombo Sugar. If you want to attempt talking your way in, try the number above.

North to Siteki About 7km west of Big Bend, a turn-off to the north is signposted to Siteki. This road, the MR16, offers a short cut to Swaziland's northeastern lowveld (see *Chapter 7*) and is also the quickest route through Swaziland for those travelling between Durban and the Kruger Park. From Big Bend it is a drive of 47km to Siteki and 75km to the Mozambique border at Mhlumeni. There is little for the visitor along this road, other than Lituba Lodge (see page 281), but there are lovely views of the Lubombos along the eastern horizon and often plenty of birdlife by the wayside. When I last drove this way the tar surface was badly pot-holed in places.

SOUTH OF BIG BEND

After Big Bend the MR8 continues south past further miles of sugar plantation. Mangled sticks of cane, shed from the overloaded trucks, litter the asphalt, and children by the wayside are usually munching sweet, fibrous mouthfuls of the stuff. After about 1.5km, the road crosses a bridge over the Usutu. Pull over for a look: to the east you'll see the entrance to the Lubombo Gorge, where the river carves its passage towards the Indian Ocean, and you might spot a crocodile or two lazing on the sandbanks downstream. After the bridge, the MR8 bends due south. For the rest of the journey towards the Lavumisa border it runs parallel with the Lubombos, close enough to appreciate the rugged splendour of the wild, aloe-studded cliffs.

RIVERSIDE CAMP Some 7km after the bridge over the Usutu, a low ridge of the Lubombos runs close alongside the road to the east. On the left you pass the Lismore Lodge, whose LL Restaurant is popular for its seafood (see opposite). Around 2km further on, the Riverside Camp is a small complex comprising the Riverside Restaurant and Motel (see opposite), together with a filling station, bottle store and – that lifeline for locals – a braai and biltong shop.

The Southeast SOUTH OF BIG BEND

8

MATATA South of Riverside Camp the road runs close alongside the Usutu to the west. This is the southernmost curve of the river's 'big bend' and your final glimpse of its waters. After 5km look out for a right turn signed to Matata Spar, 'Swaziland's biggest supermarket'. Follow this for about 3km, crossing a railway bridge, and you will find on your right the Matata complex, which – as if the retail giant wasn't excitement enough – also boasts banks, an Engen filling station, a taxi rank and the usual vegetable stalls.

NISELA GAME RESERVE This private 4,000ha reserve lies roughly halfway between Big Bend and Lavumisa, and extends between the MR8 and the Lubombo Mountains to the east. It is just one component of a large estate, which includes extensive sugar and banana plantations among various other enterprises, and employs several hundred people. The reserve once housed an excellent reptile park, run by local snake expert Thea Litschka (see box on page 267), and was also home to several captive animals, including a huge male lion called Lucky who would charge his flimsy-looking fence with such ferocity that I feared someone's 'luck' might one day run out. Back then, the restaurant was more roadhouse bar, with loud music and televised sport somewhat undermining the place's safari ambience. It has since been upgraded, however, and the reserve now has a more organised, tourist-friendly vibe, plus plentiful accommodation and activities.

Where to stay and eat

⌂ **Nisela Safaris** (sleeps 70, plus camping) ☎ 2303 0318; e reservations@niselasafaris.co.sz; www.niselasafaris.com. Nisela offers various ways to spend the night. A self-catering lodge deep inside the reserve has 7 rondavels for 4 & a honeymoon suite. The rondavels are 2-storey, open-plan & en-suite, each with a private deck; the suite has 2 dbl rooms, 1 with wheelchair access. Lodge facilities include a pool & squash court. Giraffe, ostrich & other wildlife wanders through the lodge & the place teems with birds. A Swazi village-style boma near reception encloses 12 beehive huts (10 x 2-person; 1 x 3-person; 1 x 1-person), which are simple but comfortable, with male & female ablution blocks outside. Nearby, a caravan park & campsite has 10 pitches, with ablutions, electricity & braai facilities. The Nisela Guesthouse is 5mins drive to the south. This big colonial bungalow has elegant Portuguese furniture, shaded lawns & spreading jacarandas. It offers 2 family, 1 sgl & 7 dbl en-suite rooms, with AC & tea/coffee; catering is either B&B, with meals at the restaurant, or self-catering with a cook to prepare your meals. Facilities include bar, DSTV & private swimming pool. **$–$$**

What to see and do

Restaurant/reception The restaurant is behind reception and overlooks a small waterhole where impala and other game come to drink. It makes a pleasant and convenient lunch stop for long-distance travellers. A prominent 'Beware of crocodiles' sign has been somewhat redundant since the reptile in question – a big brute called Barry – wandered off to a larger dam at the back of the property. Still, you never know. The à la carte restaurant serves standard fare in big portions, including pizzas and an excellent oxtail. There is a buffet for breakfast or lunch, and light meals are available. Other facilities near reception include a children's playground, conference centre, campsite, braai area and Zogg's curio shop, which sells original local products, including appealing hand-painted watering cans.

The reserve The game reserve consists of picturesque acacia savanna beneath an imposing Lubombos backdrop. Its graded dirt roads are fine for small vehicles and, with no dangerous game, you can explore the trails on foot. Wildlife includes plentiful giraffe, plus zebra, blue wildebeest, greater kudu, nyala, impala, common reedbuck, common duiker and warthog. This is also one of the few places in Swaziland where you might see a shy steenbok. Among a rich reptile fauna are some large pythons, and there are crocodiles (including Barry) in the large dam to the south. Guided game walks and drives can be booked at reception.

Birders will delight in the more than 300 species recorded around here. Raptors are especially impressive: highlights from my last brief visit included white-backed vulture, secretary bird, gabar goshawk, lesser spotted eagle, African harrier-hawk and peregrine falcon. I also saw goliath heron and African spoonbill among numerous waterbirds on the dam and black-bellied bustard on the savanna. The reintroduction of game has also promoted the return of the red-billed oxpecker.

Trigger happy Perhaps less appealing to many visitors – although not incompatible with conservation – are Nisela's hunting safaris (*www.niselasafaris. com/hunting*). Clients accompany professional hunter/guides to a separate part of the reserve where they can bag game such as warthog and impala. There are strict quotas and size specifications. Bow hunting is popular, and there is an on-site skinning service and abattoir for processing meat and biltong. Hunting packages start from 1 April and last a minimum of three days. Fishing safaris (for bass) can also be arranged on the dam (from SZL1,050 pp per day for 2 people, excluding hire of forearms or equipment.

SOUTH TO LAVUMISA

Just south of Nisela the MR8 reaches Nsoko, where a cluster of amenities includes a bottle store and Exel filling station, the latter open until 21.00. To the east of the

BIG SIX OR WHITE ELEPHANT?

Along the MR8 between Big Bend and Lavumisa you will notice large signs to the 'Jozini Big Six'. But don't get too excited, because this project doesn't exist – at least, not yet. The idea was to set aside a chunk of bush between the road and the Lubombos, incorporating the northern arm of Jozini Dam, as a fenced game park. The Big Five – that's lion, leopard, buffalo, elephant and rhino – would all be introduced, with the 'sixth' being the tiger fish that already occurs in the dam. The reserve would then be developed – courtesy of a private investment consortium – into an upmarket resort, with lodges, golf course, casino, the works. What's more, it would link up with the Pongola Nature reserve as one part of the Greater Lubombo Transfrontier Park (see page 50). Unfortunately the South African developers were a little hasty, pressing ahead with insufficient regard for the Swazi authorities. Feathers were ruffled – including royal ones – and the upshot was, in the words of the *Swazi Observer* (4 November 2010): 'Jozini Big Six kicked out'. The government was unhappy with the cavalier way in which developers had proceeded and were not convinced the project was in the interests of the Swazi people. 'It was gathered that the land will revert back to the country,' continued the *Observer*, 'and be used for other development purposes that will benefit the nation and uplift the plight of the people in the drought-stricken and poverty-beaten community.' Sounds fair enough. What happens next is anyone's guess, but you'd do well to check the latest news before you follow the road signs into the back of beyond.

road is the Nisela Guesthouse (see page 284). A turn-off to the west is the MR14 to Maloma, some 25km away. Road signs in this area warn of game crossing the road, and I have indeed seen greater kudu – the very animal depicted on the signs – doing just that.

Maloma is the site of Swaziland's only productive mine. Operated by South African company Xstrata, it has three shafts, employs over 500 people and produces some 650,000 tonnes of anthracite a year, most of it exported to South Africa. The colliery was closed from 2005 to 2007 after three fatalities forced a revamp of its safety systems. It is now a successful operation, with plans to build a coal-burning power plant that would reduce Swaziland's dependency on South Africa for electricity. From Maloma the MR14 heads north to Siphofaneni, while a left turn on the MR21 leads south to join the MR11, which links Nhlangano and Lavumisa (see below).

South of Nsoko the MR8 crosses first the Ngwavuma River, which flows east through the Lubombos into South Africa, and then the railway line. Soon the cane fields and other commercial agriculture give way to Swazi Nation Land, with the scattered homesteads and mealie fields typical of small-scale subsistence farming. You will cross the dry beds of two more rivers, the Mhlofunga and Msuzuma, before you arrive at Lavumisa.

LAVUMISA Lavumisa is Swaziland's southernmost border with South Africa, whose own border, on the other side, is called Golela. From here it is a short hop to the N2, which leads south through KwaZulu-Natal all the way to Durban. The border can be crowded with long-distance trucks, often on their way to or from Maputo. It is also an important stop on the north–south rail link between Komatipoort and Richards Bay. At present the border is open from 07.00 to 22.00, although there are plans to extend these hours.

Lavumisa has a long history. Some of the battles that defined the first Swazi nation were fought in these parts, and soldiers returning from World War 1 were settled here. In 1927 the arrival of the Natal Railway in the town, then called Gollele, brought a burst of development, including the farming of tobacco and cotton. Today's visitor will find little except the border itself, together with its retinue of stores and services. On the Swazi side is a large Galp filling station (⊕ *06.00–22.00*), complete with shop and toilets. Other establishments include cafés and take-aways, plus a post office, police station and Standard Bank (with ATM). On my last visit the border post was under renovation so, with luck, you should now find it all shiny and new. Entry and exit formalities have always been straightforward.

Immediately after crossing the border, heading south, you will see on your left the blue waters of Jozini Dam, which extends up into Swaziland just east of Lavumisa. This lake, created by damming the Pongola River from KwaZulu-Natal, is surrounded by the Pongola Nature Reserve, through which the road continues for the next few kilometres (watch out for reedbuck). It would form, in theory, the centrepiece of the much larger 'Jozini Big Six' project (see page 285), were this dream ever to become reality.

Lavumisa to Hluti A roundabout marks the entrance to Lavumisa from the north. A left turn leads to the train station and a right turn takes you onto the MR11, which leads due west for 90km to Nhlangano (see page 236). This is a straightforward drive on a good road, crossing a series of rivers and the small settlement of Matsangeni. After 41km you will reach the town of Hluti, with its

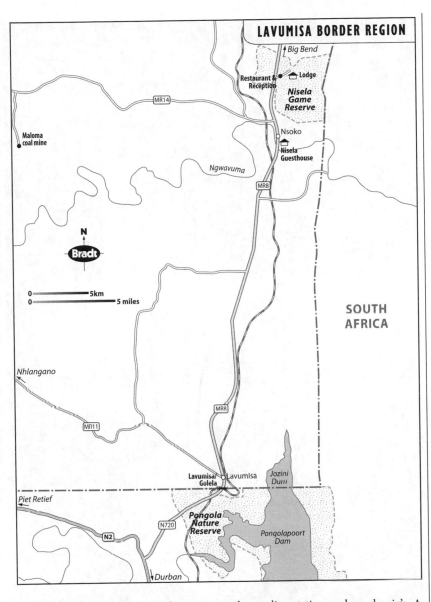

bottle store, garage, butchery, bus stop, market, police station and mechanic's. A right turn here leads north on a minor road to Hlatikulu. The MR11 continues for another 49km straight on to Nhlangano.

9

Over the Border

This book is not a guide to Swaziland's neighbours, which receive plenty of coverage elsewhere. It would be remiss, nonetheless, not to acknowledge that some world-famous attractions – including the Kruger National Park, Zululand and the Mozambique coast – lie just over its borders. Indeed, statistics confirm that the majority of Swaziland's visitors arrive en route to or from these attractions. And while the kingdom's 'transit destination' status may be irksome to its own tourist authorities, whose job is to champion Swaziland as a destination in its own right, there is no denying that having A-list tourist hotspots next door has helped pull in the passing punters.

The following section, then, is a brief round-up of places easily reached within an hour or two's drive from Swaziland and so suitable for a long weekend or a few days away. It does not provide full descriptions and details – you'll need a dedicated travel guide to South Africa and/or Mozambique for that – but aims simply to whet the appetite and point you roughly in the right direction. All are indisputably seductive destinations. My plea, however, would be not to let them turn your head so far that you lose sight of Swaziland. The kingdom's unique attractions fully justify making it the focal point of your trip to the region, with these excursions being excellent optional extras if time allows.

NORTH: THE KRUGER PARK AND DRAKENSBERG ESCARPMENT

KRUGER NATIONAL PARK A drive of less than one hour from either of Swaziland's northern borders gets you to the Kruger. At $22,000km^2$, this immense reserve – South Africa's conservation flagship – is substantially bigger than Swaziland and one of the world's greatest wildlife destinations. Here you will find more elephants than in Kenya, buffalo herds a thousand strong, rivers heaving with hippos, rhinos thundering through the thickets, and legions of zebra, giraffe and antelope browsing and grazing their way over the leafy terrain. Hot on the hooves of the herbivores come the full complement of predators, including leopard, cheetah, wild dog, spotted hyena and Africa's second-largest population of lions. This is safari on the grandest stage – and with a supporting cast that includes over 500 species of bird, 117 species of reptile and more colourful creepy-crawlies than you can shake a stick insect at, the park is a treat for wildlife lovers of all persuasions.

The explanation for this wildlife bonanza lies in a landscape that is varied, unspoilt and protected. Habitats range from the knobthorn-marula bushveld and granite hills of the southern sections (a landscape very similar to northern Swaziland's, so hinting at what the kingdom must once have been like) to the open savanna of the central regions and, further north, dense tracts of mopane woodland. However, the park's great size – 360km from north to south – and the slow pace at which you will

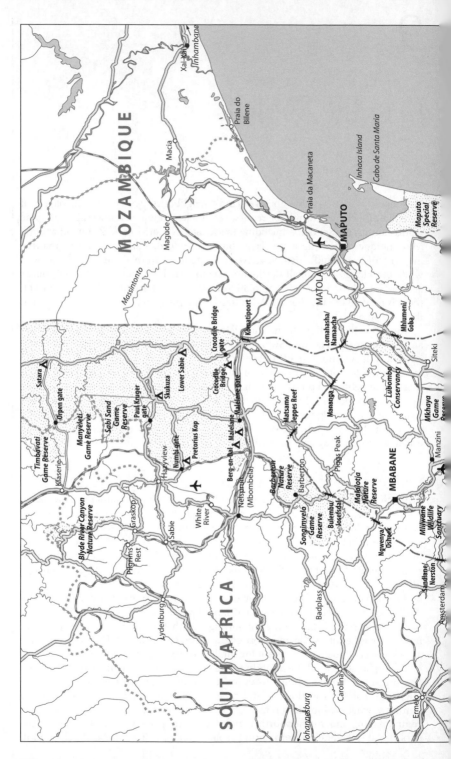

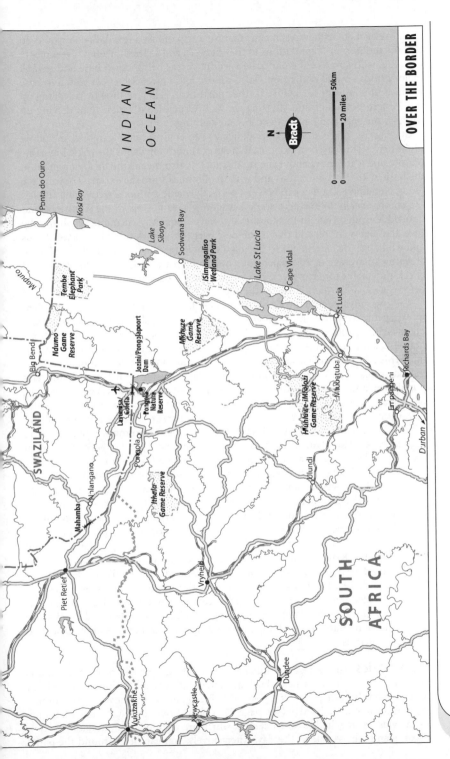

INDIAN OCEAN

Ponta do Ouro

Kosi Bay

Lake Sibaya

Sodwana Bay

iSimangaliso Wetland Park

Lake St Lucia

Cape Vidal

St Lucia

Richards Bay

Maputo

Big Bend

Tembe Elephant Park

Ndumo Game Reserve

Mkhuze Game Reserve

Jozini/Pongolapoort Dam

Lavumisa/Golela

Pongola Nature Reserve

Pongola

Hluhluwe-iMfolozi Game Reserve

Mtubatuba

Empangeni

Durban

SWAZILAND

Mahamba

Nhlangano

Ithala Game Reserve

Ulundi

Piet Retief

Vryheid

SOUTH AFRICA

Dundee

Vukuzakhe

Newcastle

N

Bradt

0   50km
0   20 miles

need to negotiate its byways, means that for a trip of just a few days you would do best to confine your explorations to the southern third. This still allows you plenty of scope, with some of the park's best wildlife areas being down here and several major camps – notably Berg-en Dal, Skukuza and Lower Sabie – at which to base yourself. If you want to explore further north, you can save time by travelling up the western boundary and entering through Orpen Gate, rather than driving up through the park and having to rush your sightings.

Staying overnight at any camp allows you to enjoy guided activities, including night drives (in search of nocturnal creatures) and day walks (to track big game on foot and learn more about the small stuff). It also means the thrill of a night in the bush, with the roar of lions and whoop of hyenas from the darkness beyond the fence. Nonetheless, a day trip is still a perfectly viable option. On day-long trips to the south, usually following a route between Malelane Gate in the southwest and Crocodile Bridge Gate in the southeast, I have frequently encountered all the Big Five and plenty more, and this is the best part of the park in which to see rhinos and wild dogs. Be careful not to bite off a route longer than you can chew: plan on covering an average of 20km per hour inside the park, adding time for stops, and check timetables to ensure you can get out of the park and back into Swaziland before gates and borders close for the night.

The great advantage of the Kruger over other famous African parks is its excellent infrastructure. Public camps, good roads, well-stocked shops, filling stations and other facilities make it perfect for the first-time, self-drive safari-goer. You don't need a 4x4 or a guide: just drive in, follow the map (and rules) and see what you can find. This DIY approach also keeps prices well below those of top national parks in the likes of Zambia, Tanzania and Botswana. The downside of such accessibility and popularity, argue purists, is that the Kruger has lost its wilderness edge. Certainly, with an annual quota of over 900,000 visitors, you can expect plenty of vehicles and busy camps. But Kruger's camps come in many different sizes, including small and secluded, and the place is so vast that it is easy to escape the crowds along the more remote back roads. For an authentic bush experience, the Kruger's three-night walking wilderness trails are up there with anything on the continent.

Of course, being both popular and cheap, the Kruger is perpetually full. Camps book up well in advance, most activities are oversubscribed and, with vehicle numbers strictly controlled, even day visitors may be turned away at the gate. So make sure you book well in advance. Camping (available at most main camps) increases your options when all other accommodation is taken. For a more exclusive safari you could try any of the numerous private lodges that are found both inside the Kruger and on several private concession areas along the park's western border (including Timbavati, Manyeleti and Sabi Sand). These offer all-inclusive packages, including game viewing with top-notch guides, at prices that range from steep to astronomical. Bargains can be found, but nothing as cheap as national parks accommodation. Some lodges, such as Mala Mala and Singita, are the last word in safari chic, with Big Five sightings as guaranteed as the canapés and designer toiletries.

Practicalities The easiest and quickest route into the Kruger from Swaziland is via either of the southern gates: Malelane in the southwest is a 30-minute drive from Matsamo border (see page 228); Crocodile Bridge in the southeast is a 45-minute drive from Mananga border (see page 272) or just over an hour from Matsamo. Both gates are attached to small camps, which are a good accommodation option if you plan to arrive late in the day. Alternatively, you can head around the park's western boundary and enter via Numbi, Paul Kruger or Orpen gates. This longer drive gets you more speedily to the central and northern sections of the park. From Johannesburg it is a direct drive of five hours to Malelane or Numbi gates, heading east along the N4 via Nelspruit.

The late dry season, July–October, is traditionally peak game-viewing time in the Kruger. But the rainy season offers more birds and reptiles, plus mammals with their young. In truth, with all-weather roads and varied habitats, there is no wrong time to visit. The South Africa National Parks website (*www.sanparks.org/parks/ kruger*) has all you need to organise and book a DIY trip. Book well in advance, especially for wilderness trails. Most tour operators that cover Swaziland (see page 102) also arrange Kruger safaris at a variety of budgets. Among Swaziland-based operators, All Out Africa (see page 104) offers a five-day budget Kruger Park camping safari. Malaria is present throughout the Kruger and more prevalent during the rainy season.

THE DRAKENSBERG ESCARPMENT West of the Kruger Park, in South Africa's Mpumalanga province, the land rises vertiginously up the escarpment of the northern Drakensberg Mountains onto a high plateau. This is a world of mists, ravines and forestry plantations, its abrupt transition from the hot bush of the Kruger mirroring the climb from lowveld to highveld in Swaziland itself. There is plenty for the visitor: protected pockets of highveld grassland and indigenous forest harbour rare flora and fauna, while local history resonates with the 19th-century gold rush. The more active will find hiking, whitewater rafting and canopy walkways, and some wonderful lodges are tucked into the forests and hillsides. Top spots include:

Barberton Gold-rush town one hour south of the Kruger on the Swaziland border, with ancient rock formations and a notable cycad forest nearby.

Blyde River Canyon Spectacular, 600m-deep canyon surmounted by imposing rock formations, with rugged hiking trails and abundant wildlife.

God's Window Dramatic escarpment viewpoint, with forest hiking trails and views – on a good day – clear across the Kruger to Mozambique.

Long Tom Pass Scenic drive between Sabie and Lydenberg, named after the 'Long Tom' canons that lined the route during the Anglo-Boer War.

Mac Mac Falls One of many impressive escarpment waterfalls; divides into two cascades that plunge in parallel for over 60m.

Pilgrim's Rest Gold-rush frontier town preserved from the 1870s, when prospector William Patterson carted his belongings around by wheelbarrow.

Sudwala Caves Oldest known caves in the world, with fine flowstone formations and a dolomite amphitheatre used for concerts; near Nelspruit (Mbombela).

Practicalities All the attractions of the escarpment lie within close range of the Kruger Park's southwestern gates and one or two hours from Swaziland's northwest borders at Matsamo or Bulembu. There is plentiful accommodation in and around the various towns, including White River, Lydenburg, Graskop and Sabie, and a proliferation of rural lodges and guesthouses. Details and bookings via the Mpumalanga tourist board (*www.mpumalanga.com*).

SOUTH: KWAZULU-NATAL

KwaZulu-Natal (or KZN for convenience) may be South Africa's smallest province but it is nonetheless more than five times larger than Swaziland, immediately to the north, and contains an impressive variety of landscapes, from the towering Drakensberg Mountains to the rugged bushveld of Zululand and the dune forests of the Indian Ocean coast. There is an overwhelming variety of attractions here for the visitor, from mountain hikes and wilderness trails to battlefield tours, cultural villages and scuba diving. To do all this justice, you really need a fortnight to explore the entire province. From Swaziland, however, the northern section, comprising the Maputaland nature reserves and coast, makes for an easy long weekend. And a further push south, ideally with an extra day or two, takes you into the heart of Zululand and its famous battlefields.

MAPUTALAND Maputaland, now dubbed the 'elephant coast' by KZN tourism, is one of southern Africa's ecotourism hotspots. Several excellent small reserves – small, that is, by Kruger Park standards – are clustered either side of the N2 highway that leads south from Swaziland to Durban, all within 100km of the Swazi border. Those to the west comprise mostly thick, hilly bush, incised by meandering rivers; those to the east lie on the coastal floodplain and include some impressive marine attractions. Between them are numerous private reserves and game farms, offering the same habitats, similar wildlife and plentiful accommodation. Key destinations include the following:

Hluhluwe/iMfolozi Game Reserve This combined conservation area west of the N2 was Africa's very first game reserve and is the undisputed rhino capital of the continent. The last refuge of the southern white rhino after near extermination in the 1930s, it is now an equally important retreat for the even more threatened black rhino and harbours numerous other large mammals, including the rest of the Big Five and most major herbivores. The terrain graduates from grassy hillsides and steep wooded valleys in the eastern Hluhluwe section to dry rolling thornveld in the western iMfolozi section, and can be explored by road and on foot. The wilderness trails concept was born here, and today the park's three–five-night on-foot excursions into the bush remain among the best of their kind in Africa.

iSimangaliso Wetland Park This UNESCO World Heritage Site (formerly the Great St Lucia Wetland Park) is Africa's largest estuary and one of the continent's most important wetlands. Its cornucopia of habitats supports an amazing biodiversity, from hippos and crocs in the freshwater lakes and rivers, to big game on the surrounding savannas and rare fauna in the coastal dune forests. Offshore, an unbroken coral reef teems with reef fish, corals and invertebrates, while dolphins surf the breakers and, in early spring, humpback whales pass close inshore en route to their Antarctic feeding grounds. The main part of the park is reached via St Lucia town, east of the N2, and offers lodges, boat trips, walking trails and seasonal whale watching. The park extends north along the coast, taking in several distinct conservation areas, including the popular fishing and dive resort of Sodwana Bay and the wetland complex of Lake Sibaya. Just short of the Mozambique border – and best reached by 4x4 – lies the unique four-lake ecosystem of Kosi Bay, where the local Tonga community still corral fish into traditional stick traps, sharing the waters with hippos and bull sharks, while turtles nest on the beaches.

Ithala Game Reserve Ithala lies a little northwest of Maputaland's other reserves and is reached via Pongola, west of Lavumisa. Its dramatic terrain is dominated by the gorges and cliffs of the Ngotshe Mountains, which rise to a highveld plateau and plunge to dense bushveld along the Pongola River. Wildlife includes elephant and both rhino species, plentiful giraffe, and an unusual cross-section of birds, including specials such as Verreaux's eagle and southern bald ibis.

Mkhuze Game Reserve This picturesque gem of a reserve, in the shadow of the Lubombos, now forms part of iSimangaliso Wetland Park. Its lush savannas, cathedral-like fig forests, dense sandveld and swampy pans support over 400 bird species – indeed this is one of South Africa's top birding spots – while large mammals include elephant, black and white rhino, hippo, spotted hyena, leopard and a dense population of nyala, Maputaland's signature antelope. Activities include night drives and day walks – with the main entrance less than 50km south of Lavumisa, this is an easy diversion from Swaziland.

Ndumo Game Reserve and Tembe Elephant Park These adjacent reserves lie along the Mozambique border just 'around the corner' from Swaziland, due east of Big Bend, and are reached from Lavumisa by rounding Pongolapoort Dam and heading northeast. Both form part of the proposed Greater Lubombo TFCA (see page 50). Ndumo harbours rhinos, crocodiles, hippos and a bird list as impressive as Mkhuze's. Tembe's thick bush supports a shy, irascible population of elephants – refugees from the former war in Mozambique – that conservationists hope will soon once again form part of a cross-border herd.

Pongola Nature Reserve This small reserve lines the shores of the Jozini/Pongolapoort Dam beside the Swaziland border at Lavimusa. There are hippos in the dam and plains game in the surrounding bush and savanna, all of which you can spy from boat trips and game drives. I met the largest wild python I've ever seen while tramping a lakeside trail here.

ZULULAND AND BATTLEFIELDS South of Maputaland and further inland you enter the heart of what is still known as the Zulu Kingdom. This picturesque rural region of hills and forests is renowned for its bloody history and rich autonomous culture, and its landscapes, people and general pace of life closely recall those of Swaziland. Extending roughly from the old Boer town of Vryheid, via the traditional Zulu centres of Eshowe and Ulundi, to the industrial port of Richard's Bay on the coast, the region's visitor attractions include Zulu cultural villages, museums, thermal spas, forest nature reserves and even tea estates. There are numerous places to stay, and a deluge of curios and handicrafts to buy.

Inland and further south lies the Battlefields region, where the main attractions are the sites, museums and memorials commemorating the bloody conflicts of the 19th century (see page 53), including Rorke's Drift, Isandlwana, Spionkop and Blood River. Dundee in the west – at the outer limit of long-weekend territory – is the tourist centre, offering plentiful accommodation and battlefield tours with expert guides, who will unpick the legends and elucidate the military strategies. The terrain is wild and beautiful, and other nearby attractions include impressive whitewater rafting on the Tugela River.

Over the Border **SOUTH: KWAZULU-NATAL**

9

PRACTICALITIES Maputaland's parks are easily reached by exiting Swaziland at Lavumisa (see page 286) and heading south on the N2. An alternative route to the Battlefields area is via Piet Retief, reached from Mahamba (see page 238), from where you can head south to Vryheid and Dundee on the R33. The attractions are year-round, although the coast can become too humid for some tastes during the summer months and wilderness trails at Hluhluwe-iMfolozi close over Christmas. Virtually everywhere in the region is accessible by normal vehicle, with the exception of some sandy routes around Kosi Bay and in Ndumo and Tembe. You can find out more and make bookings through the KwaZulu-Natal Parks Board (*www.kznwildlife.com*) and the provincial tourist board (*www.zulu.org.za*). Numerous private operators, including many of those listed in *Chapter 2* (see page 102), organise tours.

EAST: MOZAMBIQUE

When I first arrived in Swaziland in 1993, the brutal 15-year civil war in neighbouring Mozambique – which since 1977 had claimed the lives of over one million people and displaced an estimated 1.7 million more – had been over for less than a year. The short journey to Maputo was possible only by 4x4, preferably two in convoy, while wreckage from the conflict lined the potholed road, unmarked minefields lay on either side and the small wayside communities were shattered by years of atrocity and deprivation. Maputo itself was a city of burnt-out buildings, UN vehicles and amputees.

The transformation that took place over the ensuing years was remarkable, and by the time I left Swaziland five years later Mozambique was well on the way to becoming the fabulous beach and safari destination into which it has blossomed today, and which had made it the playground of the Portuguese a generation earlier. As roads were repaired, communities rebuilt and enterprise began to flourish, so tourism operators – especially from South Africa – moved in to stake their claims and conservationists began to investigate ways of rehabilitating the country's once legendary national parks.

Of course, this phoenix-from-the-ashes scenario belies a more complex reality. Mozambique remains a poor and deeply scarred country, and the initially unregulated scramble for tourism – mostly along the coast – has not always benefitted the rural communities and fragile natural ecosystems as well as it might have done. Nonetheless, that such an exciting and welcoming destination should exist at all, given the horrors of the recent past, seems little short of miraculous.

Mozambique is vast: some 1,800km as the pied crow flies between the northern border with Tanzania and the southern one with South Africa. It is thus really only the southern section – perhaps a fifth of the way up the coast – that is realistically manageable on a short trip from Swaziland. The good news, however, is that Swaziland has two excellent road borders that lie no more than 75km from Maputo and the great coast road north, offering up a coastline of exceptional marine life, fabulous beaches and lagoons, historic islands and a revitalised local culture. The following options are all for a five-day trip or shorter.

MAPUTO The Mozambique capital, home to 1.8 million people, emerged from the war damaged and dilapidated but with its heart still beating. Today it is a colourful and often bizarre mix of faded colonial grandeur and vibrant African culture. There are teeming markets, broad jacaranda-lined avenues, lively pavement cafés and hawkers selling everything from cashews to curios. Attractions include the

Jardim Tunduru Botanical Gardens, Central Market, Catholic cathedral, National Museum of the Revolution, Old Fort and Iron House. The last of these – its walls, ceiling and everything else fashioned entirely of iron – was designed by Gustave Eiffel during the late 19th century for the then governor but proved, unsurprisingly, too hot to live in. Down on the seafront are seafood restaurants that specialise in the local LM prawns and offer dreamy views of dhows across the Indian Ocean. Well-known places to stay include the grand – and pricey – Polana Hotel, and the characterful, if rather run-down, Costa Do Sol, which remained a happening jazz joint right through the bad years. Daily boat trips from Maputo visit **Inhaca and the Portuguese Islands**, just beyond the harbour, where you can explore the marine biology centre and ancient lighthouse, snorkel off the coral reefs and enjoy the local bird life and culture.

UP THE COAST The EN1 highway follows the coastline north from Maputo up the length of Mozambique, veering inland at points to skirt the coastal wetlands. This is a seemingly endless strip of beaches, lagoons and small fishing villages, with dive lodges, nesting turtles, some excellent fishing and snorkelling, and the opportunity for dhow trips. How far you go depends upon how much time you have. The popular surfing beach of **Praia da Macaneta** lies just one hour north of Maputo, reached by an old chain ferry across the Nkomati estuary. Further north you come to **Praia do Bilene**, with its fishing village and lagoons, and then the colourful regional centre of **Xai-Xai** (pronounced 'shy shy'). A long day's drive from Maputo will get you to **Inhambane**, where Tofo Beach offers some of the world's best viewing of whale sharks and manta rays.

DOWN THE COAST The small coastal strip of Mozambique that lies south of Maputo is exceptionally beautiful and – given its proximity to the capital – surprisingly inaccessible. With a decent 4x4 to tackle the deep sand tracks, however, you can make your way down to **Ponta do Ouro**, near the South Africa border, where bottlenose dolphins accompany surfers in the breakers and there is superb snorkelling straight off the beach. This stretch of coast is a key location for nesting leatherback and loggerhead turtles from October to December, while ragged-tooth sharks are among the marine species that divers may encounter off the reef. Inland, **Maputo Special Reserve** (formerly Maputo Elephant Reserve) has an elusive population of elephants among the forests and marshes, together with hippos, crocs, a few antelope and large flocks of flamingos on the lagoons. This reserve should benefit from its incorporation within the Greater Lubombo TFCA (see page 50) but at present facilities are few so you'll need to be resourceful and self-sufficient.

PRACTICALITIES Independent travel in Mozambique is a rather different prospect from in either Swaziland or South Africa. First up, you'll need a visa. This can be organised within a day from the Mozambique embassy in Mbabane (see page 107) or in advance from the Mozambique embassy wherever you live. Second, driving can be tricky. Many sandy, coastal roads are hard-going – especially south of Maputo where you'll get nowhere without a 4x4 – and on main tar roads you'll need to keep an eye out for over-zealous traffic police, who are prone to pulling over vehicles with foreign licence plates on a somewhat whimsical pretext. Your best route into the country is via Swaziland's eastern borders at Lomahasha (see page 268) or Mhlumeni (see page 254), from either of which it is just an hour's drive on good roads to Maputo; allow an hour for crossing the border. Alternatively you can make your way up the coast from KwaZulu-Natal via the border at Kosi Bay, though you'll need a good 4x4. Many of the beach 'resorts' are fairly basic by Indian Ocean standards – this is not the Maldives – but all the more charming for it.

A number of tour companies offer trips to southern Mozambique, taking in the capital and the most popular beaches and dive sites. Find out more and book accommodation and activities at www.mozambique-direct.com or from the official tourism website at www.visitmozambique.net/uk. A few Swaziland operators offer tours, including All Out Africa (see page 104), which runs whale-shark-watching and diving trips to Tofo Beach and dolphin conservation projects at Ponta do Ouro. The travel situation in Mozambique is very dynamic, and budget travellers should ask around at backpacker lodges and other tourism hangouts in Swaziland to find out the latest opportunities – or even cadge a lift.

Appendix 1

LANGUAGE

Unless you are already familiar with other African languages, you will probably find siSwati rather tricky. Both its structure and pronunciation lie well outside the comfort zone of Indo-European languages, involving clicks and other sounds that do not trip so easily off the European tongue (see page 75). Nonetheless, it is not hard to pick up a few simple everyday phrases, and your use of any siSwati at all – however inept – will make a hugely positive impact on any social situation in which you find yourself. The following phrases and vocabulary are just a few of those that might come in useful. Plural forms (eg: 'we' or plural 'you', rather than 'I') are given in brackets, where relevant; these may also be used to indicate respect or formality.

SOME HINTS ON PRONUNCIATION The most common of three click sounds (see page 75) is a dental click, produced by making a 'tutting' sound with your tongue against your front teeth. This is written as a 'c'. If followed by an 'h' it is aspirated (breathy).

- A 'k' is generally pronounced as a hard 'g', unless followed by an 'h', in which case it is aspirated.
- An 'hl' is pronounced with the tongue against the palate, a little like the Welsh 'll' in Llanlelli.
- The 'Ngi-' prefix at the start of a word denotes the first person singular ('I') and is pronounced like the last two letters of 'sing'. For the first person plural ('we') this changes to 'Si'.
- All vowels are long or longish (more 'sheep' than 'ship').
- There is no silent 'e'; *Babe* (father) is pronounced 'Barbay'

GREETINGS Greetings follow a ritual sequence of questions and responses, which you should try to complete if you get started.

Person 1: Hello/Good day (greeting)	*Sawubona (Sanibonani)*
Person 2: Yes, good day (response)	*Yebo!*
Person 1: How are you?	*Unjani? (Ninjani?)*
Person 2: I'm (we're) well	*Ngikhona (Sikhona)*
Person 2: I'm (we're) well (alternative)	*Ngiyaphila (Siyaphila)*
Person 2: And how are *you*?	*Unjani wena? (Ninjani nine?)*
Person 1: I am (we are) also well	*Nami ngikhona (Natsi sikhona)*

CIVILITIES

Yes	*Yebo*
No	*Cha*

Please (Please may I have …)	Ngiyacela (Ngiyacela …)
Thank you	Ngiyabonga (Siyabonga)
Thank you very much	Ngiyabonga (Siyabonga) kakhulu
Goodbye (literally 'stay well')	Sala (Salani) kahle
Goodbye response (literally 'go well')	Hamba (Hambani) kahle
Excuse me	Lucolo
It's OK	Kulungile
I'm sorry	Ngiyacolisa
What a shame!	Ncesi
I'm (we're) pleased/happy	Ngijabulile (Sijabulile)
It's nice/delicious!	Kumnandzi!
Good luck	Inhlanhla lenhle
Come in	Ngena

OTHER USEFUL EXPRESSIONS

I want …	Ngifuna…
I don't want …	Angifuni…
What do you want?	Ufunani?
Go!	Hamba
Let's go	Asambe
I'm (we're) going	Sengiyahamba (Sesiyahamba)
I'm hungry	Sengilambile
I didn't hear/understand	Angikuva kahle
I don't know	Angati
It's hot	Kuyashisa
It's cold	Kumakhata

PEOPLE

Father	Babe
Mother	Make
Husband	Indvodza (Emadvodza)
Wife	Umfati (Bafati)
Brother	Bhuti (Bobhuti)
Sister	Sisi (Bosisi)
Granny	Gogo
Old man	Mkhulu
Sir (general term of respect)	Nkhosi
Child (children)	Umtwana (Bantwana)

SOME USEFUL WORDS

Money	Imali	Meat	Inyama
Email	I-imeyili	Here	Lapha
Internet café	Likhefi le-inthanethi	Today	Nomuhla
Food	Ukudla	Tomorrow	Kusasa
Water	Emanti	Yesterday	Itolo
Bread	Sinkhwa		

EMERGENCIES

Help	Sita (Sitani)
Danger	Ingoti
Look out!	Caphela

SOME QUESTIONS (AND ANSWERS)

Where do you come from?	*Uphumaphi?*
(I come from Johannesburg)	*Ngiphuma eJozi*
I live in Manzini	*Ngihlala kaManzini*
What is your name?	*Ungubani libito lakho?*
(My name is Mike)	*Libito lami nguMike*
How much is this?	*Kungumalini loku?* (or simply *Malini?*)
What did you say?	*Utsiteni?*
What are you doing?	*Wentani?/Nentani?*
What is the time?	*Ngicela sikhatsi?*
Where are you going?	*Uya kuphi?* (or simply *Uyaphi?*)
I am (we are) going to Mbabane	*Ngiya (Siya) eMbabane*
What is this?	*Yini loku?*
Where is he/she?	*Uphi?* (*Baphi?*)
Where is the lavatory?	*Iphi indlu lencane?*

NUMBERS

One	*Kunye*	Eight	*Kusiphohlongo*
Two	*Kubili*	Nine	*Kuyimfica*
Three	*Kutsatfu*	Ten	*Kulishumi*
Four	*Kune*	Twenty	*Emashumi lamabili*
Five	*Kusihlanu*	Fifty	*Emashumi lasihlanu*
Six	*Kusitfupha*	Hundred	*Likhulu*
Seven	*Kusikhombisa*	Thousand	*Inkhulungwane*

DAYS OF THE WEEK

Sunday	*LiSontfo*	Thursday	*Lesine*
Monday	*uMsombuluko*	Friday	*Lesihlanu*
Tuesday	*Lesibili*	Saturday	*uMgcibelo*
Wednesday	*Lesitsatfu*		

IF YOU GET LUCKY

I love you	*Ngiyakutsandza*

IF YOU GET UNLUCKY

I've been accidentally shot	*Ngidubuleke ngengoti*

Appendix 2

FURTHER INFORMATION

In the impressive library of literature on southern Africa, Swaziland occupies one of the barest shelves. The few books that *have* been published, however, are generally worth reading, and guides to the history and natural history of the broader region generally include Swaziland in their remit. A greater breadth of information is available online, with an ever-expanding range of websites, some of them excellent. The following selection reflects what has proved most valuable to me – both while exploring the country and while researching and writing this book.

BOOKS
Guidebooks

Swaziland: Southbound Travel Guide by David Fleminger (Southbound Travel Guides, Johannesburg, 2009). Reasonably up-to-date and highly readable guidebook. Detailed history section occupies half the book and reflects the author's main passion.

A Traveller's Guide to Swaziland by Bob Forrester (Kamhlaba Publications, Mbabane, 2009). A comprehensive, entertaining and unflinching guide. The author, a local historian and archaeologist, has played a pivotal role in making Swaziland's ancient history and its archives accessible to a broader public. Information arranged in alphabetical order. Selective listings.

Mozambique: The Bradt Travel Guide, 5th edition, by Philip Briggs (Bradt Travel Guides, UK, 2011). Excellent, up-to-date guide with essential information on where to go and what to do if you visit Mozambique from Swaziland.

South Africa Highlights by Philip Briggs (Bradt Travel Guides, UK, 2011). Compact, readable and practical guide that focuses on the country's 'must-see' sights, including the Kruger Park, Zululand and other key destinations easily accessible from Swaziland.

Guide to Southern African Game and Nature Reserves, 4th edition, by Chris and Tilde Stuart (Struik, Cape Town, 1997). Comprehensive overview of all nature reserves in the region, including Swaziland, though now a little outdated.

Field guides
Mammals

Field Guide to Mammals of Southern Africa by Chris and Tilde Stuart (Struik, Cape Town, 2007). Revised edition of popular photographic guidebook. Includes key information on identification, range and behaviour, plus guide to tracks and signs.

Kingdon Field Guide to African Mammals by Jonathan Kingdon (A&C Black, London, 2003). Definitive field guide to the complete mammal fauna of Africa by a renowned authority, with his own excellent illustrations.

Birds

Kenneth Newman's Birds of Southern Africa, 10th edition, by Kenneth Newman (Struik Nature, Cape Town, 2010). Latest version of best-selling guide.

Roberts' Birds of Southern Africa, 7th edition, by Hockey, Dean and Ryan (John Voelcker Bird Book Fund, South Africa, 2005). Latest edition of the southern African birder's bible, completely rewritten. An infallible resource, though a little bulky for use in the field.

SASOL Birds of Southern Africa by Sinclair, Hockey, Tarboton and Ryan (Struik Nature, revised edition 2011). Handy and most comprehensively illustrated bird guide of the region.

Other wildlife

Field Guide to Snakes and Other Reptiles of Southern Africa, 3rd edition, by Bill Branch (Struik, Cape Town, 1998). Excellent photographic guide.

Field Guide to Trees of Southern Africa by B and P Van Wyk (Struik, Cape Town, 1997). Comprehensive photographic guide.

Southern African Insects and their World by Alan Weaving (Struik, Cape Town, 2000). Lightweight, colourful and fascinating introduction to the region's invertebrate fauna.

Southern African Wildlife, 2nd edition, by Mike Unwin (Bradt Travel Guides, UK, 2011). Covers all faunal groups, from mammals to invertebrates, and includes overviews of habitats, tracks and signs, key conservation areas and wildlife-watching tips. Fully illustrated.

Tracks and Tracking in Southern Africa by Louis Liebenberg (Struik, Cape Town, 2000). Handy photographic pocket guide to tracks, droppings and other wildlife clues in the bush.

Wild Swaziland by R Boycott, B Forrester, L Loffler and A Monadjem (P&J Perry Books, Mbabane, 2007). An excellent little wildlife guide and the only one devoted exclusively to Swaziland, covering both fauna and flora. Lightweight and fully illustrated. Available at bookshops in Swaziland or through the Natural History Society of Swaziland (see page 133).

General reading

Adventures in Swaziland: The Story of a South African Boer by Owen Rowe O'Neil (Forgotten Books, July 2012). Modern reprint of an old colonial classic.

In the Tracks of the Swazi Past by Michael Westcott and Carolyn Hamilton (Macmillan Boleswa, Manzini, 1992). Short and highly readable account of pre-colonial Swaziland developed from the Swaziland Oral History Project.

Love and Death in the Kingdom of Swaziland by Glenn Alan Cheney (New London Librarium, 2012). Contemporary story based on the work of a clinic and orphanage dealing with the scourge of HIV/AIDS.

The Wah-Wah Diaries: The Making of a Film by Richard E Grant (Picador, London, 2006). Fascinating and often hilarious account of how the actor returned to the country of his birth to direct a film about his childhood.

WEBSITES
Tourism

www.swazibusiness.com/discovery Online version of Swaziland Tourism Authority's 'Swaziland Discovery' guide. Comprehensive, though outdated.

www.swazimagic.com Up-to-the-minute travel resource with plenty of local information; bills itself as 'Swaziland's number 1 tourism publication online'.

www.swaziplace.com/whatshappening Online publication from the *Times of Swaziland*, with local listings and events.

www.swazi.travel/country_guide Useful resource for the traveller, with practical data and information.

www.swazitravelguide.com Online resource for the traveller, with reviews, articles, accommodation and events listings.

www.swaziwhatson.com Ads and listings on where to stay and eat.

www.thekingdomofswaziland.com Official Swaziland tourist office for UK and Europe. Provides direct links to lodges, hotels and tour and transport companies.

www.tourismswaziland.com Website of the Hotels and Tourism Association of Swaziland.

Environment

www.naturalhistorysociety.org.sz Website of the Natural History Society of Swaziland, with details of forthcoming indoor and outdoor events.

www.sntc.org.sz The official website of Swaziland National Trust Commission. Excellent detail on walks, wildlife, history and culture, though outdated on accommodation.

Media

www.observer.org.sz Website of the *Swazi Observer*, with local information, stories and listings.

www.times.co.sz Website of the *Times of Swaziland*, with a similar but broader range of information compared to that of the *Swazi Observer* (see above).

Index

Page numbers in **bold** indicate major entries; those in *italics* indicate maps